Brian Friel's (Post)Colonial Drama

Irish Studies   Sanford Sternlicht, Series Editor

Brian Friel. Photograph by Bobbie Hanvey. Courtesy the agency, London.

Brian Friel's (Post)Colonial Drama
Language, Illusion, and Politics

F. C. McGrath

Syracuse University Press

Excerpts from the poetry of W. B. Yeats reprinted with the permission
of Scribner, a Division of Simon and Schuster, from *The Collected Works
of W. B. Yeats, Vol. 1: The Poems,* revised and edited by Richard J. Finneran.
Copyright © 1924 by Macmillan Publishing Company, renewed 1952 by
Bertha Georgie Yeats.

The paper used in this publication meets the minimum requirements
of American National Standard for Information Sciences — Permanence
of Paper for Printed Library Materials, ANSI Z39.48-1984.∞™

Library of Congress Cataloging-in-Publication Data

McGrath F. C. (Francis Charles)

Brian Friel's (post)colonial drama : language, illusion, and politics /
F. C. McGrath. — 1st ed.

   p.   cm.   (irish studies)

Includes bibliographical references and index.

ISBN 0-8156-2813-7 (alk, Paper)

   1. Friel, Brian — Criticism and interpretation. 2. Political plays, English — Irish
authors — History and criticism. 3. Politics and literature — Northern Ireland.
4. Politics and literature — Ireland. 5. Northern Ireland — In literature.
6. Decolonization in literature. 7. Postcolonialism — Ireland. 8. Friel, Brian —
Language. 9. Ireland — In literature. 10. Illusion in literature. I. Title.
II. Irish studies (Syracuse, N.Y.)

PR6056.R5 Z825 1999

822'.914 — dc21   99-047935

Manufactured in the United States of America

For
Florence C. McGrath,
and
in memory of
Francis C. McGrath, Jr. (1911–1995)

F. C. McGrath is a professor and chair of the English Department at the University of Southern Maine, where he teaches Irish literature and culture, nineteenth- and twentieth-century literature, and literary criticism and theory. He has published widely on nineteenth- and twentieth-century writers, including a previous book *The Sensible Spirit: Walter Pater and the Modernist Paradigm.*

Contents

Acknowledgments

IN THE PRODUCTION OF THIS BOOK I owe a considerable debt of gratitude to a number of people and organizations. For taking the time to discuss many issues related to this book I wish to thank Brian Friel, Seamus Deane, Declan Kiberd, Terence Brown, Edna Longley, Hubert McDermott and Brian Donnelly. Past and present members of the staff of the Field Day Theatre Group have been extremely helpful and cordial and I wish to extend special thanks to Gary McKeone, Finola O'Doherty, Colette Nelis, and Hilary Fletcher. I am grateful to my colleagues Lucinda Cole, Nancy Gish, Gerry Peters, and Rick Swartz for their astute commentary and assistance. Gena Pelletier, Tess Davis, Rosina Menna, and Marie Cogswell were invaluable in helping me prepare the manuscript.

I also appreciate the support of the University of Southern Maine in providing me with research time and financial resources. The Faculty Professional Development fund of the College of Arts and Sciences helped to fund several trips to Ireland. The Provost also provided some funding, and the Faculty Senate Research Fund provided a grant in 1990. I am also grateful to The American Council of Learned Societies, who provided a Grant-in-Aid to fund portions of my research for this book.

My greatest debt is to Barbara Hope, who provided me with much valuable commentary on the manuscript and without whose understanding and unqualified support completing this book would have been impossible.

Excerpts from *After Bable: Aspects of Language and Translation,* by George Steiner, copyright © 1975 by George Steiner, are reprinted by permission of Oxford University Press.

Excerpts from *Molly Sweeney,* by Brian Friel, copyright © 1994 by Brian Friel, are used by permission of Dutton Signet, a division of Penguin Putnam, Inc.

Excerpts from *Outside History: Selected Poems 1980–1990,* by Eavan Boland, copyright © 1990 by Eavan Boland, are reprinted by permission of W. W. Norton and Company.

Excerpts from the poetry of W. B. Yeats are reprinted with the permission of A. P. Watt Ltd. on behalf of Michael B. Yeats and with the permission of Scribner, a Division of Simon and Schuster, from *The Collected Works of W. B. Yeats, Vol. 1: The Poems,* revised and edited by Richard J. Finneran, copyright © 1924 by Macmillan Publishing Company, renewed 1952 by Bertha Georgie Yeats.

The following copyright holders have kindly granted permission to reprint excerpts from Brian Friel's works: Faber and Faber for *The Loves of Cass McGuire, Crystal and Fox, Selected Plays, Making History,* and *Dancing at Lughnasa;* Gallery Press for *The Loves of Cass McGuire, Crystal and Fox, The Gentle Island, Volunteers, The Communication Cord, Making History, Dancing at Lughnasa,* and *Molly Sweeney;* Brian Friel for *The Mundy Scheme, The Gentle Island, Volunteers,* and *The Communication Cord;* Catholic University of America Press for *Selected Plays;* and Penguin Ltd. for *Molly Sweeney.*

Permission to reprint copyrighted material is also gratefully acknowledged: Attic Press, Vincent Browne, *The Canadian Journal of Irish Studies,* Catholic University of America Press, *The Crane Bag,* Field Day Theatre Company, Brian Friel, Gallery Press, *Irish Independent, Irish Times, Literary Review,* Mercier Press, Fintan O'Toole, Penguin Ltd., Random House / Knopf, Routledge, Oliver Sacks, *Times Literary Supplement,* Verso.

Earlier versions of portions of *Brian Friel's (Post)Colonial Drama* have appeared in *Colby Quarterly, Comparative Drama, Contemporary Literature, Éire-Ireland,* and in *Brian Friel: A Casebook* (New York: Garland, 1997).

Abbreviations

The following abbreviations are used for editions of Friel's plays and stories cited throughout the text.

CC *The Communication Cord.* 1983. London: Faber and Faber.

CM *The Loves of Cass McGuire* 1984. Oldcastle: Gallery Press.

DL *Dancing at Lughnasa.* 1990. London: Faber and Faber.

GI *The Gentle Island.* 1973. Oldcastle: Gallery Press.

MH *Making History.* 1989. London: Faber and Faber.

MS *Molly Sweeney.* 1994. New York: Penguin.

SL *The Saucer of Larks.* 1962. Garden City, N.Y.: Doubleday.

SP *Selected Plays.* 1986. Washington, D.C.: Catholic Univ. of America Press. (Includes *Philadelphia, Here I Come!, The Freedom of the City, Living Quarters, Aristocrats, Faith Healer,* and *Translations.*)

SS *Selected Stories.* Ed. Peter Fallon. Introd. Seamus Deane. Dublin: Gallery Press, 1979.

TP *Two Plays: Crystal and Fox and The Mundy Scheme.* 1970. New York: Farrar Straus.

VO *Volunteers.* 1989. Oldcastle: Gallery Press.

Chronology

1966   *The Gold in the Sea* published in New York and London

       Philadelphia, Here I Come! produced on Broadway at the
        Helen Hayes Theater

       The Loves of Cass McGuire premiered in New York at the Helen
        Hayes Theater

1967   *Lovers* premiered in Dublin at the Gate Theatre

       Moved to the village of Muff, County Donegal

1968   *Crystal and Fox* premiered in Dublin at the Gaiety Theatre

1969   *The Mundy Scheme* premiered in Dublin at the Olympia Theatre

       A Saucer of Larks: Stories of Ireland published in London

1971   *The Gentle Island* premiered in Dublin at the Olympia Theatre

1972   Became member of Irish Academy of Letters

1973   *The Freedom of the City* premiered in Dublin at the Abbey Theatre

1975   *Volunteers* premiered in Dublin at the Abbey Theatre

1976   *Farewell to Ardstraw* and *The Next Parish* produced by
       BBC Northern Ireland TV

1977   *Living Quarters* premiered in Dublin at the Abbey Theatre

1979   *Aristocrats* premiered in Dublin at the Abbey Theatre

       Faith Healer premiered in New York at the Longacre Theater

       Selected Stories published in Dublin

1980   Founded Field Day Theatre Group with Stephen Rea

       Translations premiered in Derry at the Guildhall

       American Welcome premiered in Louisville at the Actors Theatre

1981   *Anton Chekhov's "Three Sisters": A Translation* premiered
       in Derry at the Guildhall

1982   *The Communication Cord* premiered in Derry at the Guildhall

       Became a member of Aosdana, the "national treasury
       of Irish artists"

       Appointed to the Arts Council

       Received Christopher Ewart-Biggs Memorial Award
       for *Translations*

1983   *The Diviner: Brian Friel's Best Short Stories* published in
       Dublin and London

1984 *Selected Plays* published in London (Includes *Philadelphia, Here I Come!, The Freedom of the City, Living Quarters, Aristocrats, Faith Healer,* and *Translations.*)

1986 Nominated as the first writer since Yeats to a seat in the Irish Senate

1987 *Fathers and Sons: After the Novel by Ivan Turgenev* premiered in London at the Lyttleton Theatre

1988 *Making History* premiered in Derry at the Guildhall

1990 *Dancing at Lughnasa* premiered in Dublin at the Abbey Theatre

1991 *Dancing at Lughnasa* won awards for best play of the season in London

1992 *Dancing at Lughnasa* won awards for best play of the season in New York

      The London Vertigo premiered in Dublin at the Andrews Lane Theatre

      Ivan Turgenev's "A Month in the Country" premiered in Dublin at the Gate Theatre

1993 *Wonderful Tennessee* premiered in Dublin at the Abbey Theatre

1994 Resigned from Field Day

      Molly Sweeney premiered in Dublin at the Gate Theatre

1997 *Give Me Your Answer, Do!* premiered in Dublin at the Abbey Theatre

Brian Friel's (Post)Colonial Drama

1

Introduction

DESPITE THE BROADWAY SUCCESS OF *Philadelphia, Here I Come!* in 1966, Brian Friel did not mature as a playwright until the production in 1973 of *The Freedom of the City*. As Seamus Deane points out, "All of Friel's major work dates from the mid-1970s. Before that, he had been an immensely skillful writer who had found himself being silently exploited by the ease with which he could satisfy the taste for Irishness which institutions like the *New Yorker* and the Irish Theatre had become so expert in establishing" (1986b, 16). *The Freedom of the City,* however, marked a new level of awareness about language, and it is Friel's awareness of the intimate relations among language, discourse, illusion, myth, politics, and history that distinguishes his mature work from his early work. Not coincidentally, *The Freedom of the City* is the first piece of writing that explicitly articulates Friel's sense of colonial oppression. Some earlier stories and plays had alluded to the North, but Northern Ireland was never the focus of this early work. It was as if Friel's gaze from his standpoint in Derry faced westward toward Donegal, as in many of his stories, southward toward the Republic, as in *The Mundy Scheme* and *The Gentle Island,* or beyond the Atlantic, as in *Philadelphia, Here I Come!* and *The Loves of Cass McGuire.* In these early texts the border between North and South played no significant role in Friel's literary imagination; it was virtually nonexistent or transparent. Like many Northern nationalists in the first several decades after partition, Friel cocooned himself in his own community, and in his early writing he largely ignored the political and social realities of his divided state. There is very little in his early published work that suggests that Friel is from Northern Ireland.

After the civil rights movement of 1968–69 it was no longer possible for Northern nationalists to pretend that there was no border, that Stormont and unionist oppression did not exist, or that they belonged to the Republic, which was beginning to distance itself from the Northern situation. After *The Freedom of the City* Friel's plays became more politically conscious and at the same time they became more and more obsessed with the operations of language and the images that it creates. Of the nine plays he wrote in the decade following 1970, three justify ranking Friel among Ireland's foremost playwrights and among major twentieth-century dramatists—*Aristocrats, Faith Healer,* and *Translations*—and these three appeared in rapid succession between March 1979 and September 1980. Although *Faith Healer* arguably is his finest play, *Translations* became the instant classic of his canon and one of his most performed plays.

Several critics have linked Friel's views of language with George Steiner's book *After Babel: Aspects of Language and Translation* (1975), which Friel read in the late 1970s. These critics have focused primarily on Steiner's influence on *Translations* and other late plays. Richard Kearney (1983 and 1987) first explored language issues in Friel's plays. Kearney, however, limited his investigation to *Faith Healer, Translations,* and *The Communication Cord* and he merely listed in an appendix certain passages from *After Babel* relevant to these three plays. My own essay (1989) analyzed more carefully the nature of Steiner's influence on *Translations,* as did Robert Smith (1991) from a different perspective. Helen Lojek (1994) applies Steiner's notion of translation to Friel's plays in general.

Brian Friel's (Post)Colonial Drama culminates this strand of Friel criticism. Arguing that the Heideggerian views on language Friel found in *After Babel* were incipient in his own work from his early short stories, I examine Friel's entire published oeuvre from the perspective of his orientation toward language and its relation to the illusions, myths, and narratives we construct to negotiate psychological and social experiences. Most Friel critics misread his texts because they ignore his preoccupation with language and focus primarily on the social and political issues raised in them. A focus on language, however, offers fresh interpretations of the texts and, far from narrowing the significance of Friel's work, opens it up to some of the major intellectual issues of our time.

Steiner's book did not so much form Friel's views of language as help him to formulate them more precisely and with more authority. It also gave him the confidence to exploit those views in his plays with more power and ingenuity. It was no accident that Friel's annus mirabilis that produced *Aristocrats, Faith Healer,* and *Translations* occurred immediately after his exposure to Steiner. Steiner's theory of language and translation helped Friel to achieve something he had always desired for his work—a process I try to chart in this book—"the patient assembly of a super-structure which imposes a discipline and within which work can be performed in the light of an insight, a group of ideas, a carefully cultivated attitude" (1972b, 21). This "superstructure" could also be characterized as a discourse on language for which Steiner's book provided Friel access. This discourse has a genealogy in Western culture, but it also has a specific Irish genealogy. Friel's idealist views on language situate him within a tradition of Irish language theories that includes George Berkeley, Oscar Wilde, W. B. Yeats, J. M. Synge, and James Joyce.

A focus on language alone, however, cannot explain why linguistic idealism has appealed to Irish intellectuals from the late nineteenth century to the present. A narrow focus on language also runs the risk of aestheticizing and universalizing Friel's texts and the orientation toward language they exhibit. As Kearney points out, "Friel brilliantly contrives to refashion Steiner's academic research in the form of a drama concretely situated in his native cultural and historical context" (1983, 38–39). Although Steiner himself insists on the historical specificity and contingency of any act of communication or translation,[1] he does not provide

---

1. Steiner says, for example, "A text is embedded in specific historical time; it has what linguists call a diachronic structure. To read fully is to restore all that one can of the immediacies of value and intent in which speech actually occurs" (1975, 24). Although Steiner's theory of language and translation is postmodern without being poststructuralist, he agrees with the poststructuralist emphasis on the ultimate indeterminacy of any text or utterance: "The determination of the dimensions of pertinent context (what are all the factors that may have genuine bearing on the meanings of this statement?) is very nearly as subjective, as bordered by undecidability in the case of the historical document as in that of the poetic or dramatic passage" (1975, 136).

the means for theorizing that contingency. That theoretical power is available, however, in postcolonial theory.

Unfortunately most postcolonial theory has not been able to account satisfactorily for Ireland's unique colonial history.[2] Unlike most other colonies and former colonies, Ireland is located geographically and racially within the first world. Consequently its culture is characterized by first-world as well as by third-world affinities and structures. Also, part of Ireland's population—Northern nationalists—remains in a colonial situation (at least until the full implementation of the Belfast Agreement), so that there are within Ireland at least two distinct phases of national consciousness. Moreover, the Northern unionist community, despite their protestations of being British, are also part of a continuing, albeit arguably anachronistic, colonial structure. In terms of cultural identity, the Irish consider Ulster unionists to be British, whereas the British consider them Irish. Today they are instruments of a colonial power that has become very ambivalent about Northern Ireland, as ambivalent perhaps as the Republic of Ireland.

Despite limitations, several postcolonial studies particularly are germane to this study of Friel—Homi Bhabha's *The Location of Culture* (1994), Declan Kiberd's *Inventing Ireland: The Literature of the Modern Nation* (1995), David Lloyd's *Anomalous States: Irish Writing and the Post-Colonial Moment* (1993), and Terry Eagleton's *Heathcliff and the Great Hunger: Studies in Irish Culture* (1995). Bhabha provides a theoretical apparatus that is sufficiently flexible and nonprescriptive to account for the complexities of the Irish situation, while Kiberd, Lloyd, and Eagleton offer the most thorough postcolonial analyses to date of the Irish situation.

For an account of Ireland's colonial and postcolonial experience Bhabha's theories accomplish several things. First of all, they can account for the popularity of, indeed the necessity for, idealistic linguistic philosophies in colonial situations—they are the means by which the colonized imagine an alternative to their condition. For Kiberd art in a colonial context tries to create "a different order of reality": "against the

2. Postcolonial analyses of Irish culture include: Anderson 1994, Eagleton 1988, Eagleton 1995, Gibbons 1992, Jameson 1988, Kiberd 1995, Lloyd 1987, Lloyd 1993, S. Richards 1997, Said 1988.

ability to imagine things as they are, it counterpoises the capacity to imagine things as they might be" (1995, 118). In the case of Ireland, although Berkeley's language philosophy provided a potential foothold for a colonized imagination to reimagine its situation, from the time of Berkeley to the late nineteenth century Ireland suffered first under the century-long oppression of the penal code and then, as nationalism advanced haltingly after 1798, the devastation of the famine inhibited cultural and political progress toward liberation. By the last two decades of the nineteenth century, however, a number of factors contributed to a climate in which it was possible to imagine Ireland as other than a British-dominated possession. Catholic emancipation in 1829 and the subsequent growth of a Catholic middle class had laid the political foundation. By late in the century political institutions, like the Irish Republican Brotherhood, the Land League, and Parnell's Irish Parliamentary Party, along with new cultural institutions like the Gaelic Athletic Association, the Gaelic League, the Irish dramatic movement, and the Irish literary renaissance, had provided institutional discourses that could sustain the reimagining of the Irish nation.

In situations of colonial nationalism mimetically oriented theories of language and aesthetic realism are useless because the colonized do not agree with the imperial power on what constitutes representational norms. In the light of Bhabha's theory linguistic idealism would have appealed to Irish writers as a means of cultural survival, a means of imagining alternative histories and alternative worlds to those provided by the colonizing power. Steiner acknowledges as much. He says, "*Language is the main instrument of man's refusal to accept the world as it is.* Without that refusal, without the unceasing generation by the mind of 'counter-worlds' — a generation which cannot be divorced from the grammar of counter-factual and optative forms — we would turn forever on the treadmill of the present" (1975, 217–18; Steiner's emphasis). Bhabha, however, goes well beyond Steiner's observation by theorizing a reinscribed, non-mimetic narrative of identity that emerges performatively from the boundaries of conflicting cultures.

Bhabha's theoretical stance can also account for Ireland's complex and unique situation as both a past and present colony located within the boundaries of the first world. Bhabha proposes to analyze colonial and postcolonial cultures in terms of a rewriting of the grand narratives of Western culture that wrote all kinds of people out of history — women, minorities, subalterns, migrants, diaspora cultures, and the colonized across the globe — all of whom became people without histories. Bhabha would replace those grand narratives, along with the Western traditions of ontology and epistemology that support them, with performative enunciations that reinscribe the symbols of Western culture from the postcolonial perspective of the marginalized. By focusing on performative enunciations from the boundaries between cultures, Bhabha avoids the oversimplified binaries of much postmodern theory and he is able to move beyond the narrow confines of the orthodox poststructuralist categories of race, class, and gender. The complexity of the Irish situation especially mandates an analysis that is neither limited to simplified Irish/British binaries nor confined to conventional deployments of race, class, and gender, categories whose integrity in Ireland is disrupted by other political and ideological imperatives.

Finally, as with Friel, Bhabha's perspective rests ultimately on a post-Heideggerian approach to language. Bhabha, in fact, illustrates in very concrete ways the "pathbreaking" nature of language Heidegger articulates in his late essays. The introduction to Bhabha's *Location of Culture* opens with an epigraph from Heidegger's *Poetry, Language, Thought*: "A boundary is not that at which something stops but, as the Greeks recognized, the boundary is that from which *something begins its presencing*" (1994, 1; Heidegger's and Bhabha's emphasis). Drawing from a wide variety of postmodern and poststructuralist sources, Bhabha's profoundly eclectic perspective deploys a notion of enunciation whose genealogy can be traced from Heidegger through the performative function of language developed in the speech-act theory of Austin and Searle and its modifications by DeMan and Judith Butler.[3] In *The Location of Culture* Bhabha theorizes in a nonprescriptive, concrete way the liminal presencing of a colonial cultural identity as a historically specific time and site of enunciation. This enunciatory site, which involves both personal

3. Bhabha also draws key notions from Barthes, Derrida, Foucault, Walter Benjamin, Freud, Lacan, Frantz Fanon, Hortense Spillers, Deborah McDowell, Paul Gilroy, Houston Baker, Henry Louis Gates, Jr., Cornell West, Stuart Hall, Toni Morrison, Salman Rushdie, and Derek Walcott.

and communal agency on the part of the oppressed and dispossessed, inscribes anew not only the history of the oppressed but also, in challenging the seamless continuities of the hegemonic national culture, the history of that hegemonic culture. Heidegger's notion of language as pathbreaking enables Bhabha to claim that the articulatory moment at the boundary of conflicting cultures constitutes the hybrid space and the historical present occupied by the colonized and the colonizer alike.

Because of its flexibility and its Heideggerian approach to language, Bhabha's orientation avoids, for example, the limitations of Jameson's emphasis on spatial binaries and class, of Eagleton's persistent ironizing of binary relations, of Frantz Fanon's underestimation of the bourgeois role in liberation movements, of Benedict Anderson's requirement of a homogenous imagined community, and of both Fanon's and Said's anachronistic dependence on universals of liberal humanism. Bhabha's enunciative notion of cultural difference also avoids two extreme views of cultural diversity—the liberal notion of multiculturalism, which sublates difference within an ethos of tolerant relativism, and radical separatist movements, which resist identification with the hegemonic, universalized Western self by substituting a purified, totalized ethnic self.[4]

While both Lloyd and Eagleton draw from Bhabha's theories, neither of them limit themselves to Bhabha but draw from a wide range of postcolonial and poststructuralist theorists. In the process they both complicate and refine some of Bhabha's positions, but they also sacrifice some of his flexibility. Some of their more enlightening observations derive from their application of Gramsci's notion of hegemony to the Irish sit-

4. Bhabha says that in both these cases "Cultural diversity is the recognition of pre-given cultural contents and customs; held in a time frame of relativism it gives rise to liberal notions of multiculturalism, cultural exchange or the culture of humanity. Cultural diversity is also the representation of a radical rhetoric of the separation of totalized cultures that live unsullied by the intertextuality of their historical locations, safe in the Utopianism of a mythic memory of a unique collective identity" (1994, 34). Regarding liberal multiculturalism in particular, Bhabha notes how the ethic of liberal tolerance imagines "opposition in order to contain it and demonstrate its enlightened relativism or humanism" (1994, 24) and how such a strategy can never empower, indeed disempowers, the "non-Western other" (1994, 192).

uation. Lloyd's rigorous study, which is heavily indebted to Fanon, Deleuze, and Guattari in addition to Gramsci, critiques Irish nationalism and Irish identity politics as a new hegemonic formation that replicates the hegemonic structures of the former imperial power. According to Lloyd, because nationalism requires a monologic voice to create its subjects in opposition to the imperial power, after liberation that monologic voice continues in operation, often with the assistance of the apparatuses it inherited from the former imperial state, and by continuing disenfranchises other voices within the new nation. Thus, the subaltern still cannot speak. In opposition to that new hegemony Lloyd favors "occluded" cultural practices, such as street ballads and folk songs, that are resistant or recalcitrant to the new hegemonic culture and thus unrepresentable by it. Rather than pursuing identity politics, which for Lloyd tend toward hegemonic dynamics and negate recalcitrant, antihegemonic, unassimilable elements in a society, Lloyd prefers to attempt to "understand the complex dynamic of the interaction between subaltern groups and the state formation" (1993, 8). Whereas nationalist hegemony and identity politics substitute one hegemonic master narrative for another, Lloyd wants to keep the "historical narrative" open to "undeveloped possibilities" (1993, 10).

Although Lloyd's argument is compelling at points, he clearly tries to theorize how Ireland might have conformed to Fanon's ideal of a national liberation that remains in the hands of the people rather than appropriated by a bourgeois elite. Like other Fanonites, at the same time that Lloyd espouses the right of the colonized to self-determination, he also would prescribe the shape that liberation should take. Consequently he is not content that subaltern voices speak for themselves in performative enunciations at the boundaries of conflicting cultures and he feels the need to "repoliticize" Bhabha (1993, 123–24, n. 49). Lloyd also does not suggest why some practices were assimilated into the master narratives and why others were excluded. He also does not indicate what sort of a national narrative would eliminate the possibility of occluded social and cultural practices and how such a narrative could have supplanted the master narratives of imperialism. Moreover, Lloyd's argument does not really distinguish between nationalism in its prehegemonic form, when it functioned as one of the occluded voices, and in its postindependence hegemony. Nor does he show how hegemonic practices emerge from an unrepresentable, and thus presumably undifferentiated, matrix of occluded practices. Lloyd's critique of nationalism seems valid for postindependence Ireland, particularly in its first few decades, where what might arguably be called a monologic official Gaelic Catholic nationalism, enshrined in the 1937 Constitution, tried to suppress other voices. Irish nationalism, however, before or since independence, was never monologic. On the contrary, as Lloyd is aware, since 1798 there have been many different varieties of Irish nationalism, some of them more open than others to alternative voices. In any case, other voices have always asserted themselves in the face of a putative monologic nationalism. In many ways the canon of modern Irish literature, as Lloyd himself ably demonstrates, is largely a record of dissident voices in relation to nationalism. Yet Shaw, Yeats, Joyce, O'Casey, O'Faolain and others have hardly remained "occluded." In the end Lloyd's postulation of a monologic nationalism to shore up his argument about occluded voices and practices weakens that argument.

Eagleton also focuses on hegemony in Ireland, particularly on the failure of the Anglo-Irish Ascendancy to create a hegemonic society in Ireland. Unlike Lloyd, Eagleton does not find Ireland to be merely an example of a monologic bourgeois nationalism. Eagleton is much more sensitive to the paradoxes and oxymorons of Irish nationalism, British colonialism, and Anglo-Irish relations. Although he acknowledges that "the mantle of revolutionary modernism in Ireland passed to the rural middle class—passed, in a word, to one of the most conservative formations in Western Europe" (1995, 277), for Eagleton Irish nationalism, like the literary modernism he associates with it, is a hybrid of the archaic and the avant-garde. Rather than simply replicating imperial hegemony, "The 'modernist' time of nationalism" moves "in two directions at once. Turning its back on a callow British modernity, it sets off in search of its own ancient spirituality; but in doing so it takes a modernizing leap forward, one which will break beyond the history of the merely recent into an authentic future" (1995, 281). Within nationalism itself Eagleton detects a progressive and modernizing emphasis on self-determination and civic rights along with the more conservative Romantic emphasis on modeling the present on a traditional past: "Both nationalism and modernism . . . in striving for some post-bourgeois form of life, finds [*sic*] its [*sic*] models for this in the pre-bourgeois world" (1995, 285). Because "revolutionary nationalism unites the archaic and the avant-garde, inflecting what is in fact a modernizing project in the rhetoric of ancient rights and pieties . . . the revolutionary nationalist is at once the most primitive and progressive of creatures" (1995, 285). Spawned by the "spiritually disinherited children of the bourgeoisie" (1995, 284), both nationalism and modernism are forms of radical conservatism.

Although Eagleton acknowledges the predominance of the performative in Irish writing, his analysis is still locked into sets of binary oppositions he uses to structure his analysis of the Irish situation (Irish/British, Ascendancy/native, archaic/modern), and these binaries inhibit the emergence of self-articulated, hybrid enunciations, as with Bhabha's more Heideggerian approach. In every instance Eagleton can resolve these binaries only aesthetically under the sign of irony, which he typically illustrates by the example of Joyce's *Ulysses*.

For the purposes of my present study, the theories of Steiner and Bhabha along with the criticism of Kiberd, Lloyd, and Eagleton open up a space, in the Heideggerian sense, in which Friel's linguistic and postcolonial concerns can appear, particularly in relation to the Irish tradition of linguistic idealism evident in his predecessors Wilde, Yeats, Synge, and Joyce. The point of my analysis, especially in chapter 2, is not to conflate the linguistic sites of Wilde, Yeats, Synge, Joyce, Friel, Steiner, and Bhabha, but rather to situate Friel within a genealogy of revolt against mimetic theories of language, a genealogy that begins with Romantic, neo-Hegelian expressive theories of language, including late nineteenth-century symbolism, and manifests itself most recently in poststructural theories of language. Implicit in this genealogy of linguistic idealism is a parallel genealogy of style that resists ontological mimetic notions of style as transparent window or polished mirror on the world. This genealogy would begin with epistemological notions of style as the distorting mirror of individual consciousness and include postmodern and poststructuralist notions of style/discourse as constitutive of the "realities" it constructs. These genealogies, generated typically by frustration with, dissatisfaction with, or (in colonial contexts) resistance to, mimetic orientations, are replicated in the history of Irish culture from Wilde to Friel and within the development of Friel's oeuvre itself.

Beginning with Wilde, Anglo-Irish theories of symbolism appeal to neo-Hegelian, autobiographical aesthetics of expression that are centered in the individual consciousness of the artist. Although this symbolism, particularly in Wilde and Yeats, retains remnants of an ontological metaphysics in its appeal to Platonic archetypes, it actually marks a transition to post-Kantian epistemology by positing the artist as the source of those archetypes. Despite their occasional anticipations of postmodern and poststructuralist views of language, Wilde's "The Decay of Lying," Yeats's early symbolism and his doctrine of the mask, and Joyce's Stephen Dedalus in *Portrait* and the first half of *Ulysses* all manifest this stage of a symbolic aesthetics of expression. The second half of *Ulysses* marks a transition from a consciousness-centered aesthetics of expression to a decentered, discourse-oriented aesthetics.

Steiner's linguistics in *After Babel*, which provide an epistemological frame for the Irish tradition of linguistic idealism I chart in the next chapter, derive from the German phenomenological tradition rather than from Saussurean structuralism. This phenomenological tradition exhibits a similar genealogy of revolt. As Romantic aesthetics of expression replaced mimetic aesthetics and were in turn supplanted by poststructuralist semiotics, so consciousness-centered Romantic hermeneutics replaced the text-oriented exegesis of the Enlightenment and in turn were replaced by the more culturally and historically oriented hermeneutics of the postmodern period. Although Steiner articulates a postmodern hermeneutic of indeterminacy,[5] he still assumes a consciousness-centered process of translation and so remains within Western epistemological traditions.

Bhabha's eclecticism, which historicizes Steiner's epistemological frame, reinscribes both the hermeneutic and poststructuralist traditions within postcolonial theory. Bhabha proposes to replace Western ontology and epistemology with enunciative practice. For Bhabha epistemology "insists on the subject as always prior to the social" (1994, 185), whereas

5. I am using the term postmodern here to distinguish post-Romantic hermeneutic practices that do not share the major premises of discourse-oriented poststructuralist theories that descend ultimately from Saussure.

enunciative practice "alters the subject of culture" by focusing on "signi-fication and institutionalization" rather than on "function and intention" (1994, 177). The epistemological for Bhabha is "locked into the herme-neutic circle, in the description of cultural elements as they tend towards a totality." The enunciative, in contrast, is "a more dialogic process that attempts to track displacements and realignments that are the effects of cultural antagonisms and articulations — subverting the rationale of the hegemonic moment and relocating alternative, hybrid sites of cultural negotiation" (1994, 177–78). Enunciative practice for Irish writers often meant subverting both the hegemonic narratives and the hegemonic practices of British culture with their own nonmimetic narratives of identity. Friel was no exception.

2

Friel and the Irish Art of Lying

W E ARE PRODUCTS OF STORIES we tell about ourselves. We are the protagonists in narratives we have internalized and, like Coleridge's ancient mariner, we repeatedly tell these stories about ourselves both to ourselves and to others. These stories negotiate our relations with others and with our circumstances. When others accept our narratives of ourselves or when we interact with our environment in accord with them, we feel authenticated, validated. When others refuse or fail to accept our narratives or when circumstances resist them, our sense of self often becomes unstable. These stories and narratives are driven by our most fundamental needs, for example, our need for love, hope, dignity, self-esteem, meaningfulness, or sometimes just the need to escape an existence that is mundane, meaningless, or painful. The needs themselves are products of conscious or unconscious narratives shaped by the many discourses in our society and culture that we have internalized and accepted as our own. Both the narratives and the discourses are constituted by language, in the broadest poststructuralist sense of the word. Consequently our own identity, our own sense of self is ultimately constituted by language. As Heidegger points out, we do not speak language, it speaks us. Identity, then, is structured as a fiction, as a story or a number of stories, about who we are.

Narratives and the principles that govern them apply not only to individuals but also to collections of individuals—families, communities, organizations, tribes, ethnic groups, nations, civilizations. Groups of individuals are identified by narratives they share, narratives about who they are, where they came from, what their purpose and destiny is.

These stories, too, are driven by fundamental needs, by other underlying narratives, and they are shaped by existing discourses internalized by the group.

What happens when our narratives, individual or collective, are not validated? What happens when the narratives of mutually dependent individuals conflict? What happens when individual narratives conflict with group narratives? What happens when the narratives of two groups sharing the same physical space are mutually antagonistic to each other? These are the central preoccupations of Brian Friel's writing.

Over the course of his career Friel developed a Heideggerian sense of the immanence of all experience in language, a sense that our realities are constructed out of discourses and narratives we have internalized, that the very facts of our existence are construed within the frameworks of these discourses and narratives. Living in Northern Ireland as a member of the minority Catholic nationalist community provided Friel with the experience of trying to negotiate his daily existence between the Scylla and Charybdis of two mutually antagonistic narratives. Each community had its own narrative for who they were, where they came from, what they stood for, and where they were going. Accompanied by two sets of equally antagonistic social and political discourses, these conflicting narratives constituted the history, geography, and polity these communities shared with each other. It is no wonder that the dysfunctional family became a major trope in Friel's plays.

Like many Irish, Friel experienced what it meant to be construed by conflicting narratives and discourses from the day he was born; his identity, like that of his state, was inscribed with conflicting narratives. Births in Ireland are recorded by both church and state and their records do not always agree. Sometimes ideology structures the disagreement. Friel's birth records are a case study in miniature of Northern Ireland relations.[1] He was born in 1929 in Killyclogher near Omagh, County Tyrone, but the exact date of his birth and his name of record are matters of interpretation. The Knockmoyle parish register lists the birth of Brian Patrick Ó'Friel as January 9 and his baptism on January 10, but the Gen-

---

1. For details on the controversy over Friel's birth records see Pine 1990, 13 and 15, and Dantanus 1988, 220 n. 1.

eral Register Office in Belfast lists his birth date as January 10 and Angli-
cizes his name to Bernard Patrick Friel. Richard Pine points out, "At the
time of Friel's birth the Protestant bureaucracy discouraged the registra-
tion of 'Gaelic' names" (1990, 15). The parish registry, in contrast, obviously preferred the more Gaelicized forms of its parishioners' names.
According to Ulf Dantanus, the name Friel, a variant of Farrell and un-
common outside Donegal and its borderlands, derives from the Irish
ÓFirghil ("man of valour") (1988, 31). Friel's self-identification conforms
neither to the parish register nor to the Belfast register but is a hybrid of
the two. Friel has always celebrated his birthday on January 9, and he
uses the Christian name on the parish register, which inscribes him
within a Gaelic heritage, and the surname of the Belfast public register,
which inscribes him within a British context. Friel also has used Bernard,
his given name on the Belfast register, as a name for a youthful protagonist in his short stories. Friel's identity of record, then, is a fictional construct inscribed within two conflicting authoritative discourses, much as
in the "Wandering Rocks" episode of Joyce's *Ulysses* the daily existence of
Dubliners is inscribed between the discourses of church and state. Obviously, the whole issue of naming and the British misnaming of Owen as
Roland in *Translations* has deep personal meaning for Friel. As Pine suggests, he may have felt like his dual protagonist of *Philadelphia, Here I
Come!* Friel himself has said to Pine, "Perhaps I'm twins" (1990, 15).

Homi Bhabha provides us with a useful postcolonial perspective for
looking at the discrepancies on Friel's birth records. For Bhabha there is
always a Derridean displacement, in the sense of both difference and
temporal deferral, in translations between colonizer and colonized. This
displacement articulates a hybrid identity that is neither that of the colonizer nor that of the colonized, but an identity of an "in-between" site
that is historically contingent and specific. Thus Friel's name articulates
neither the Irish Brian Patrick ÓFriel nor the British Bernard Patrick
Friel but a hybrid of the two that is neither the one nor the other. As
Bhabha would put it, Friel's identity is both "split and doubled" or "less
than [either] one and doubled." Friel's hybridity, of course, extends well
beyond his name. As a member of the minority Northern nationalist
community who has moved across the border into the Republic of Ireland without relinquishing his ties to the North, Friel, like Seamus

Heaney and other Northern writers, is part of both the postcolonial environment of the Republic and the still colonized situation of the Northern nationalist community. This hybrid quality, as we shall see in subsequent chapters, becomes crucial to understanding the significance of Friel's work, particularly a text like *Translations,* in relation to the cultures he inherited.

Friel's hybridity often shows up as a critical ambivalence. He describes the political and cultural sympathies of his upbringing as typical for a Northern Catholic. He says, "I was reared in a very traditional, Catholic, nationalist home. I came to Derry in 1939 when war was beginning. We believed then that Germany was right and that England was wrong, that sort of thing" (Boland 1970, 12). Friel's father had been a nationalist member of the Derry City Corporation, and Friel himself was active in the Nationalist Party for several years. He was by no means an unthinking, chauvinistic nationalist, however. His sympathies were tempered by a cautious and questioning skepticism about his heritage, a skepticism that anticipated Field Day's brand of new nationalism. During his years as a school teacher Friel says,

> I first began to wonder what it was to be an Irish Catholic; in short this was when for the first time in my life I began to survey and analyse the mixed holding I had inherited — the personal, traditional and acquired knowledge that cocooned me, an Irish Catholic teacher with a nationalist background, living in a schizophrenic community, son of a teacher, grandson of peasants who could neither read nor write. The process was disquieting — is disquieting because it is still going on. (1972b, 19)

Although he belonged to the Nationalist Party for a while, he remained ambivalent without relinquishing his allegiances. He says that he has a tendency to "get involved in sporadic causes and invariably regret the involvement" (1972b, 17). His description of his own involvement with the Nationalist Party echoes Joyce's view of feckless nationalist politics in "Ivy Day in the Committee Room": "I suppose it held on to some kind of little faith, you know. It wasn't even sure what the faith was, and it was a very despised enterprise by everybody. We used to meet once a month wherever it was in a grotty wee room and there'd be four or five old men who'd sit there and mull over things. It was really hopeless" (1982a, 22).

Friel's early work was largely apolitical, however, and was not self-conscious about the role of language and discourse in shaping our perceptions of experience and history. But as the political situation in Northern Ireland heated up in the late sixties and early seventies, Friel and other Northern writers came under increasing pressure to take a stand in their writing. Friel resisted at first, but then his own participation in Derry's Bloody Sunday march in January of 1972 broke down his resistance, and a play he had in progress at the time quickly coalesced into *The Freedom of the City*. Loosely based on the 1972 Bloody Sunday incident and cast in a theatrical form that resembles some of Joyce's more radical stylistic experiments in the second half of *Ulysses,* the play deals overtly with contemporary political material in representing the various discourses, both Irish and British, that contributed to the tragedy.

Since the first production of *Freedom of the City* in February of 1973, Friel has been accused of abetting the nationalist cause in the North. Sympathetic and hostile readers alike often distort his texts, particularly his more political plays, either because they focus on political and social issues without taking into account Friel's complex concerns about the interrelations of language, politics, and culture or because they focus on purely formal aesthetic concerns to the neglect of others. Also, they often fail to acknowledge the commitment of Friel and Field Day to demythologizing the traditional pieties that contribute to the sectarian divisions in the North. For example, without abandoning his sympathy for the Catholic minority he was born into, *Freedom of the City* demonstrates how discourses on both sides produced the attitudes responsible for the tragedy of Bloody Sunday. Richard Kearney articulates one of the most eloquent defenses of Friel against the charges of political propaganda levied against him by antinationalist critics such as Edna Longley and Brian McAvera. Kearney bases his defense on Friel's concern with the role of language in our experience:

> Several of Friel's later plays do indeed have a political content—in the sense that they address the nature of Irish nationalist ideology in both its historical and contemporary guises. But they do so in a way that is profoundly anti-propagandist. One of Friel's primary concerns in such recent plays as *Translations* and *The Communication Cord,* is to explore the

complex relationship between political ideology and the problematic nature of language itself. Like most artists influenced by the modernist movement, Friel is deeply preoccupied by the workings of language. And like most genuine artists he is aware that language does not exist in a timeless vacuum but operates in and from a specific historical situation. It is not surprising then that Friel should display a particular attentiveness to the ways in which different political ideologies—i.e., those of British colonialism and Irish nationalism in particular—have so often informed or deformed the communicative function of language. Those who accuse Friel of propagandistically supporting the cause of political nationalism are grossly misconstruing his work. For they fail to appreciate that his overriding concern is to examine the contemporary crisis of language as a medium of communication and representation. (1987, 510)

Friel's own particular hybridity, then, stems partly from his linguistic awareness. For Friel the "crisis of language" takes the form of his complex Heideggerian sense of the immanence of all experience in language, the sense that we do not speak language but that language speaks us. In his early plays and stories this sense begins as an exploration of the psychological and social functions of necessary illusions, functions such as providing mundane or deprived existences with meaning, dignity, hope, or simply escape. For Friel, these illusions are persuasive because, like the illusions of art, they appeal to deep emotional needs. In the early stories illusions typically are compensatory and necessary to the psychic health of the individual. The early plays, however, are darker and open up to larger social and cultural contexts. In these plays illusions and myths typically fail to negotiate satisfactory relations between the individual and the social, cultural, or political context. Although the dissatisfactions that make illusions necessary imply, perhaps unconsciously, a colonial syndrome, none of these early stories and plays overtly acknowledges the links among language, illusion, and politics.

With *The Freedom of the City* Friel began to see how prevailing discourses shape our illusions and myths and ultimately determine individual destinies and the course of history. From this point on, Friel's plays become much more complex and probing. Although it took Friel several years to totally relinquish some reference point beyond language as a check against the free play of language and illusion, with the productions of *Aristocrats* and *Faith Healer* in 1979, his annus mirabilis, Friel embraces an orientation in which illusion, myth, identity, and even history are products of language, discourse, and narrative. In embracing this view Friel places himself within a tradition of Irish writers who have elevated blarney (in the form of linguistic idealism) to aesthetic and philosophical distinction. Synge and Joyce are Friel's most important predecessors in this tradition, but behind them we must also include Yeats and Wilde.[2]

Wilde was one of the first since Berkeley to give an Irish character to the epistemology that eventually produced the linguistically sophisticated philosophies of thinkers like Heidegger, Derrida, and Foucault. Wilde had assimilated that epistemology from the ancestors of poststructuralism in German thought, including Kant, Schiller, and Hegel, who were popular at Oxford when Wilde was an undergraduate. Although Wilde's views fall within a tradition that can be traced from Vico through Foucault, it has had special force in colonial and postcolonial Ireland since the last decades of the nineteenth century when political and cultural nationalism began to move Irish national consciousness toward liberation from colonial oppression. In many ways Wilde's "Decay of Lying" (1889) sets the stage for the linguistic concerns of Yeats, Synge, Joyce, and Friel. Written in the form of a Platonic dialogue, "The Decay of Lying" defends Wilde's famous thesis that "Life imitates art far more than Art imitates life" (1973, 74). Great art for Wilde anticipates life and molds its shape; it invents the archetypes by which we perceive nature and history. Consequently nature and history are human constructions, and what makes them credible is primarily a matter of style. Despite the typical Wildean phrasing designed to astonish, bewilder, and outrage with paradox after paradox, there is a remarkable rigor to the logic of Wilde's argument.

By lying Wilde does not mean common everyday lying, such as the misrepresentations of politicians (1973, 58–59) or lying to gain some immediate personal advantage, what Wilde calls "lying with a moral purpose" (1973, 84). The lies Wilde advocates are the fictions of art or "lying for its own sake" (1973, 85). "Lying, the telling of beautiful untrue

2. Terry Eagleton projects this tradition of antimimetic idealism even further into the Irish past, "as far back in Irish thought as the ninth-century theology of John Scottus Eriugena" (1995, 334 n. 39) and "the fantastic hyperbole of the ancient sagas" (1995, 333).

things," Wilde insists, "is the proper aim of Art" (1973, 87). Wilde blames the "commonplace character" of much of the literature of his time on the "decay of Lying as an art, a science, and a social pleasure" (1973, 60).

Wilde's treatise on lying was part of the turn-of-the-century debate between realism and Romanticism. "The Decay of Lying" defends Romanticism against realism in art. Post-Kantian Romanticism had opposed poetry and the aesthetic imagination to science and the world of fact, and since the Romantic revolution the rise of realism had become associated with science. According to Wilde, by the end of the nineteenth century the art of lying had decayed because society had bartered its soul for a drab, commonplace world of scientific fact. Wilde prophesies that the "worship of facts" will lead to sterile art and the death of beauty (1973, 61). Refuting Matthew Arnold, he says, "No great artist ever sees things as they really are. If he did, he would cease to be an artist" (1973, 82). For Wilde, art is not disinterested and objective, it does not depict "the object in itself as it really is." On the contrary, all art is ultimately subjective and autobiographical. Wilde says, "The only portraits in which one believes are portraits where there is very little of the sitter, and a very great deal of the artist" (1973, 83). As an artistic method Wilde judges realism to be "a complete failure" (1973, 69).

Wilde's attack on realism centers on two long-revered Aristotelian principles—mimesis and probability. Wilde flatly denies mimesis as an aesthetic principle: he says, "Life and Nature may sometimes be used as part of Art's rough material, but before they are of any real service to Art they must be translated into artistic conventions" (1973, 86). If life dominates the artistic process beyond a certain degree, it "drives Art out into the wilderness" (1973, 68).

For the imitative ideal of realism Wilde would substitute a creative ideal. In Wilde's fin-de-siècle Platonism, art does not imitate life but invents the archetypes by which we perceive it. Anticipating contemporary theories of the social and cultural construction of reality, Wilde claims that what we find in life or nature is not something that exists there already but what our great artists have taught us to find there.[3] London fogs, for example, are the products of art not nature:

3. Despite Wilde's anticipation of poststructuralist discourse theory, he was bound by the philosophic traditions of his time, and his Neoplatonism acts in the

Where, if not from the Impressionists, do we get those wonderful brown fogs that come creeping down our streets, blurring the gas-lamps and changing the houses into monstrous shadows? . . . At present, people see fogs, not because there are fogs, but because poets and painters have taught them the mysterious loveliness of such effects. There may have been fogs for centuries in London. I dare say there were. But no one saw them, and so we do not know anything about them. They did not exist till Art had invented them. (1973, 78–79)

Wilde's aesthetics of lying, with its nonmimetic conception of art as archetypes, have important implications for the relation of truth and style. If Wilde rejected Aristotle's emphasis on mimesis, he embraced his principle of probability as an antidote to excessive realism. He says that a writer can rob "a story of its reality by trying to make it too true" and that some novels "are so life-like that no one can possibly believe in their probability" (1973, 61). Echoing Aristotle's aesthetic preference for probable impossibilities over improbable possibilities, Wilde pontificates, "Man can believe the impossible, but man can never believe the improbable" (1973, 84). Emphasizing probability over the realistic criterion of possibility, Wilde concludes that only style can make something believable (1973, 83) and that "Truth is entirely and absolutely a matter of style" (1973, 72).

Wilde's rejection of realism can be read as a necessity of his colonial situation. Kiberd claims, "Wilde refused to write realist accounts of that degraded Ireland which he only partly knew, and he took instead Utopia for theme, knowing that this would provide not only an image of revolutionary possibility for Ireland but also a rebuke to contemporary Britain" (1995, 50). Style, according to Kiberd, was "potentially redemptive" for Irish writers, "charged with the power to lift the fallen material of the given world to a new place of consciousness" (1995, 126), and "this explains the tremendous emphasis on style in Irish writing from the time of Yeats onward" (1995, 120).

The Irish rejection of realism, however, is not merely voluntary but structurally compelling. Realism, objectivity, and a worship of facts are

---

service of a Hegelian aesthetics of expression: "the self-conscious aim of Life is to find expression," and "Art offers it certain beautiful forms through which it may realize that energy" (1973, 87).

possible only within a homogenous, consensual community; consequently the mimetic mode typically is unavailable to the marginalized identity of the colonized. As Kiberd explains, "A writer in a free state works with the easy assurance that literature is but one of the social institutions to project the values which the nation admires, others being the law, the government, the army, and so on" (1995, 118). The colonized writer lacks this assurance. Moreover, to write in a mimetic or constative mode requires a writer to identify with the institutions of the colonizer. Wilde's Romanticism and linguistic idealism substitute a performative for a constative model of language. As Eagleton says, "when Wilde speaks of language as the parent rather than the child of thought, he is adopting a performative rather than representational epistemology which has a lengthy Irish provenance" (1995, 333). Because the hybrid articulation of the colonized operates in an enunciative or performative mode, its meaning is established not in relation to some imitated content of an uttered sentence but in relation to a context that exists outside the sentence. For Bhabha this performative "Third Space," unrepresentable mimetically [i.e., as content], "constitutes the discursive conditions of enunciation" [i.e., the historically specific context, as in an ironic or performative statement] (1994, 37). Eagleton notes that what matters to the colonized is the addressee, whereas what matters to the colonist is the referent: "Language is strategic for the oppressed, but representational for their rulers" (1995, 172). Where realism pretends to be oblivious of its occasion and audience, the performative genres of Irish writing strategically took both into account. This "split-space of enunciation" opens up the possibility of "conceptualizing an *inter*national culture" anew (Bhabha 1994, 38–39). Thus the appeal of Romanticism in colonized Ireland, as opposed to the strength of the realistic tradition in the colonial metropole of London, lies in the opportunities it offers to construct a new identity, as Wilde did quite self-consciously, to escape the stereotyped identities imposed by the colonizer.

Mimesis is unavailable for other reasons also. According to Bhabha, when the colonized mimics the colonizer (that is, when the colonized tries to act in accordance with the social and cultural dictates of the hegemonic culture), even amongst the colonized who have been educated in the colonial metropole, as Wilde was, there is never an exact replication; there is always a displacement, temporal and spatial. Mimesis can only be partial. Or to put it another way, since a part substitutes for the whole, colonial mimicry has the structure not of mimesis but of metonymy. When the mimic culture is played back to the colonizer it appears strange, unnatural, and threatening. Thus when Wilde, after, or perhaps as a result of, excelling at Oxford, presented his own self-consciously constructed persona as the epitome of Britishness and English aestheticism, the hegemonic culture was amused, threatened, and appalled. It responded by parodying him, indicting him, and incarcerating him. If Wilde's English model was Walter Pater, the pose of English aestheticism Wilde constructed from that model was, in Bhabha's terms, a colonial doubling, a doubling both incomplete and in excess ("less than one and doubled"), one that involved splitting, translation, transformation, displacement. Viewed from Bhabha's perspective, in the figure of Wilde "culture's double returns uncannily—neither the one nor the other, but the imposter—to mock and mimic, to lose the sense of the masterful self and its social sovereignty. It is at this moment of intellectual and psychic 'uncertainty' that representation can no longer guarantee the authority of culture; and culture can no longer guarantee to author its 'human' subjects as the signs of humanness" (1994, 137). To put it another way, Victorian Britain incarcerated Wilde because his mimicry of Englishness challenged the hegemonic culture's authority to author its subjects.

This fundamental miscognition involved in any translation between the colonizer and the colonized constitutes colonial hybridity, the challenge to power in the very exercise of that power. And the partialness of any enunciation, that is, its hybridity, its quality of being "less than one and doubled," constitutes a metonymy, not a mimesis of a plenitudinous presence. Subject to Derridean *différance* (that is, both difference and deferral), the hybrid enunciation, such as Wilde's "The Decay of Lying," is simultaneously repetition and difference. This hybridity Bhabha calls the "name for the strategic reversal of the process of domination through disavowal"—"strategies of subversion that turn the gaze of the discriminated back upon the eye of power" (1994, 112). We find just such a strategic reversal of the gaze in Wilde's disavowal of Arnold's mimetic ideal for criticism as a disinterested effort "to see the object as in itself it really is."[4]

Like Wilde, Yeats also defended symbolism against nineteenth-century realism and, despite significant differences of temperament and philosophy from Wilde, a number of issues from "The Decay of Lying" became central to Yeats's own aesthetics, including a bias against imitation and an emphasis on aesthetic archetypes and masks.[5] Yeats's theories of symbolism and the mask share Wilde's post-Romantic premise that consciousness creates its own reality, that, as he phrases it in "The Tower," "Death and life were not/Till man made up the whole" (1983, 198). Wilde even may have sent Yeats off in search of Byzantium, which Wilde describes in "The Decay of Lying" as a place where the imitative arts were rejected in favor of the decorative. Wilde's notion that the "proper school to learn art in is not Life but Art" (70) is reflected in the lines from "Sailing to Byzantium" "Nor is there singing school but studying/Monuments of [the soul's] own magnificence" (1983, 193).

Like Wilde's Neoplatonism, Yeats's early symbolism was based on a notion of archetypes, which Yeats had assimilated from various sources, including Wilde, Plotinus, Shelley, Blake, occult doctrines, Irish fairy lore, and French symbolism. Central to Yeats's early symbolism is his notion of the *Anima Mundi* or the Great Mind and Memory of Nature. Based on a Neoplatonic theory of archetypes, Yeats's *Anima Mundi* (literally the "Spirit of the World") in many of its features resembles Jung's notion of the collective unconscious, except Yeats's concept involves both the conscious and the unconscious mind.

Yeats's Jungian theory of symbolism eventually evolved into his doctrine of the Mask, which also was inscribed in terms of Wilde's colonial

4. As Lloyd and Eagleton have shown, Wilde's performativity had a counterpart in the Irish novel of the nineteenth century. Because social and political life in colonial Ireland was so fractured and disruptive, the stable social formations of a hegemonic culture required for verisimilitude in the novel were lacking. See especially the chapter in Lloyd 1993 "Violence and the Constitution of the Novel" and the chapter in Eagleton 1995 "Form and Ideology in the Anglo-Irish Novel."

5. Ellmann 1967, 3–27 discusses the influence of Wilde's "Decay of Lying" on Yeats.

aesthetics of lying. Wilde insisted, "what is interesting about people in good society . . . is the mask that each one of them wears, not the reality that lies behind the mask" (1973, 63–64). Yeats's poem "The Mask" virtually paraphrases Wilde:

> It was the mask engaged your mind,
> And after set your heart to beat,
> Not what's behind. (1983, 95)

and his doctrine of the Mask elaborates considerably on Wilde's observation, particularly in the poem "Ego Dominus Tuus," which, like Wilde's "Decay of Lying," dramatizes his doctrine as a dialogue between two characters.

Incorporating his earlier symbolist aesthetics into a more complex theory, Yeats characterizes the mask as an imaginative, idealized, and stylized image that exists in the "deeps of the mind." More, specifically, it is an image of one's antithetical or anti-self, which is most unlike oneself in that it possesses all that the self lacks. So seeking the mask is an attempt to perfect the self, and achieving the mask unites the self and the anti-self in what Yeats calls Unity of Being. The mask, then, is the image of a humanistic ideal that becomes one's goal or destiny in life. In "Ego Dominus Tuus" two characters Hic and Ille (the Latin words for *this* and *that*) debate the notion of mask as an aesthetic/psychological ideal. Hic is engaged in the conventional quest of finding himself "and not an image," whereas Ille seeks not himself but his anti-self, a nonmimetic image that is most unlike himself and possesses all that he lacks. Ille asserts that the perfected art of Keats or Dante came, not from finding themselves, as Hic claims, nor out of what they had in themselves, but out of what they most lacked, by fashioning an opposite image, by setting their chisels "to the hardest stone." As with Wilde, their art does not reflect their lives but exists in opposition to it. Emphasizing the contrast between Dante's life and his art, Ille says,

> Being mocked by Guido for his lecherous life,
> Derided and deriding, driven out
> To climb that stair and eat that bitter bread,
> He found the unpersuadable justice, he found
> The most exalted lady loved by a man.

Likewise, about Keats he says,

> . . . he sank into his grave
> His senses and his heart unsatisfied,
> And made—being poor, ailing and ignorant,
> Shut out from all the luxury of the world,
> The coarse-bred son of a livery-stable keeper—
>
> Luxuriant song. (1983, 161–62)

The underlying principle of the Mask (and of Yeats's whole aesthetic vision) is struggle, the conflict of warring antithesis. One could read Yeats's doctrine of the mask in terms derived from Bhabha and Frantz Fanon as the displaced desire of the colonized to supplant the colonizer (Bhabha 1994, 44; Fanon 1963, 52). In Yeats colonial struggle and conflict is sublimated into cultural forms. Struggle is not only the essence of life and death, but it is out of struggle that beauty, especially tragic beauty, is born. Through struggle we forge our beings, and great beauty is born from the ecstasy and passionate heat produced by the fusion of self and Mask. In "Leda and the Swan," for instance, all the beauty and glory, as well as the struggle and destruction of classical civilization is figured in a violent rape of a mortal by an immortal that conceived the beauty of Helen.

Yeats's quintessential colonial poem "Easter 1916" (1983, 180–82) also inscribes the figure of the Mask. In this poem Yeats characterizes Ireland prior to the Easter Uprising and the executions that turned that abortive military bungle into a national martyrdom as a fool's paradise, a place "where motley is worn" and where life consisted of exchanging "polite meaningless words." The leaders of the uprising were part of this "casual comedy," but they also had a dream, an image diametrically opposed to the motley of the casual comedy, and their efforts to fashion a new image from the hardest stone produced the "terrible beauty" of tragedy with all its transfiguring power. The Mask of these rebels was their dream of an independent Ireland, for which they sacrificed their lives. Despite Yeats's reservations that "Too long a sacrifice / Can make a stone of the heart," he concludes by affirming the beauty of tragedy in pursuit of one's Mask: "enough / To know they dreamed and are dead." "Easter 1916" not only illustrates Yeats's doctrine of the Mask operating in history and on a national scale but also vindicates his belief in the power of symbols to move people, even a nation, figured here in the stone that resists all transitory impulses, as did the historically persistent dream of an independent Ireland:

Hearts with one purpose alone
Through summer and winter seem
Enchanted to a stone
To trouble the living stream.

In Bhabha's terms the Easter Uprising and the Proclamation that accompanied it constitute a hybrid moment of enunciation, an "insurgent act of cultural translation" that is discontinuous with its colonial past and opens up a future of possibility. For Bhabha as for Yeats, these enunciations from the margins do not "merely recall the past" but renew it and refigure it "as a contingent 'in-between' space, that innovates and interrupts the performance of the present" (1994, 7). Eagleton makes the same performative claims for Yeats's poem, in which, he says, the Rising "is constituted as real by the performative power of Yeats's fiction." Eagleton says Yeats wished to "structure the revolution rather than reflect it," and so "the poem imitates the action of the Rising itself, which proclaims into being something which plainly does not exist" (1995, 307–8). For Bhabha this process of cultural negotiation and translation produces a hybrid culture and a "new" reinscribed history that "poses the future, once again, as an open question" (1994, 235) — a future that "makes available to marginalized or minority identities a mode of performative agency" (1994, 219) through which survival as a subject once again becomes possible. As in Yeats's poem, "The changed political and historical site of enunciation transforms the meanings of the colonial inheritance into the liberatory signs of a free people of the future" (1994, 37).

Like Yeats and Wilde, Synge also operates linguistically in a performative mode and defends turn-of-the-century Romanticism against the competing aesthetics of realism. In *The Well of the Saints* and *The Playboy of the Western World* he asserts the Wildean aesthetic that life imitates art. *The Well of the Saints* is not as successful a play as *Playboy,* nor does it articulate the aesthetics of lying as effectively, but it served as an important prelude to Synge's masterpiece. In *The Well of the Saints* an elderly blind couple, Martin and Mary Doul, have their sight restored by an itinerant saint only to discover that they were much happier inhabiting the illusions of their blind world than enduring the ugliness and derision of the sighted world. In other words, the imaginative world they had created for themselves while they were blind was much more accommodating to them than the sighted world of ordinary experience. After they lapse into blindness again, they refuse to allow the saint to restore their sight a second time and they proceed to create a new set of fictions that enable them to create another satisfactory "reality" for themselves. As the Irish had for centuries refused to accept the reality imposed on them by their colonizer, their only recourse was to seek to create alternative worlds in their own performative enunciations.

In *The Playboy of the Western World* Synge creates a much more successful and dynamic metaphor for the aesthetics of lying, one where the "real" world eventually conforms itself to an imaginative fiction. In *Playboy* the feckless Christy Mahon, through his ever more elaborate stories about how he killed his da, creates an imaginative fiction of himself that is most unlike the cringing, submissive creature that fled and left his father lying in a field. As Christy's story becomes more elaborate with each retelling, his own role as protagonist in the story becomes more dominant and self-assertive. As a result of telling his story and observing the reactions of the young women who hear it, Christy gradually becomes the hero of his story by romancing Pegeen Mike and beating all the young men of the village at games of riding, running, and jumping. Christy, in other words, proceeds to become the fiction of himself that he has created, to realize it in his behavior and attitudes to the point that when his father eventually returns Christy is able to turn the tables in their relationship and dominate him.

Not only does Christy turn life into art, but he also serves as a figure of the artist. Christy's powers of language are central to his role as hero. Pegeen clearly establishes his connection with the traditional image of the poet: "I've heard all times it's the poets are your like, fine fiery fellows with great rages when their temper's roused" (1960, 23). Christy's powers of language grow with each retelling of his story until toward the end he is wooing Pegeen and defending himself against the villagers with his most eloquent language: "for there's torment in the splendour of her like, and she a girl any moon of midnight would take pride to meet, facing southwards on the heaths of Keel. But what did I want crawling forward to scorch my understanding at her flaming brow?" (1960, 73).

In *The Well of the Saints* the world of imagination created by Martin and Mary Doul, although it suffices for them, remains apart from the ordinary reality of others. In *Playboy*, too, Synge acknowledges the difference between reality and imagination; as Pegeen says, "there's a great gap between a gallous story and a dirty deed" (1960, 77).[6] Synge even dramatizes this difference by having Christy reenact his famous deed in front of the townspeople and by showing Christy the ballad hero biting the cowardly Shawn Keough on the leg. But unlike the Douls's fictions in *The Well of the Saints,* in *Playboy,* as in Yeats's "Easter 1916," fiction has power over reality; Christy brings his imaginative construct to bear on the ordinary world around him and transforms it. By the end Christy is capable of asserting himself without the prop of his story. Through experiencing himself in his fiction and in his growing rhetorical powers, Christy has in effect transformed himself. He has elevated his self-esteem and he has recognized what that self-esteem has enabled him to achieve in the world: "If I am an idiot, I'm after hearing my voice this day saying words would raise the topknot on a poet in a merchant's town. I've won your racing, and your leppin" (1960, 74). Christy's new perspective on himself not only reverses his relationship with his father but also enables him to see the villagers, in whose eyes he had become transformed, as much greater fools than himself. As the curtain closes, Christy envisions himself as someone who will "go romancing through a romping lifetime" (1960, 80), become the heartthrob of women, and be immortalized in ballads sung about him, for, as Christy exclaims, "you're after making a mighty man of me this day by the power of a lie" (1960, 74).

Synge, like Wilde and Yeats, acknowledges that imaginative fictions may not be accurate mimetically, but he suggests that they nevertheless have genuine power over the real world. This is *Playboy*'s major aesthetic

---

6. Eagleton argues that the prevalence of the performative mode in Irish writing was a consequence of the "traditional gap between rhetoric and reality in Ireland," and eventually in Joyce's *Ulysses* that gap became "incorporated into the very forms of the fiction," to the point of being "the substance of an entire text" (1995, 257).

insight. In Wilde's terms, by becoming the hero of his own stories, Christy "realizes in fact what has been dreamed in fiction." In the process he both becomes a work of art himself and illustrates how life imitates art and not the other way around. In terms of Yeats's doctrine of the Mask, Christy imagines an image of himself that is most unlike him and then strives to become that image. Beauty results from the struggle to fuse self and Mask. Although influenced by Wilde and Yeats, Synge is actually closer to a Heideggerian view of language than either of them. With a much less abstract mind than either Wilde or Yeats, Synge avoids both the epistemological abstractions of Wilde and the occult ontological abstractions of Yeats in favor of a Heideggerian immanence in language. Christy's aestheticized self-image is simply the effect of the fictions he tells about himself. Viewed in Bhabha's perspective, Christy's fictions in *Playboy* inscribe the same transformational dynamic as Yeats's "Easter 1916": as a mode of performative agency Christy's eloquent enunciations intervene in his present and open up a liberated future of new possibilities where he translates his oppressive past under the yoke of his father into a projective future where, as the subject (in both senses) of his own narratives, he writes his history anew. From this perspective it is easy to read Christy's transformation as the kind of transformation colonial Ireland needed to undergo to write its history anew, to become master of its own historical narrative.[7]

Joyce also belongs to this distinguished Irish tradition of lying. In "The Dead," following Gabriel Conroy's after-dinner speech, all the guests sing "For they are jolly gay fellows . . . Unless he tells a lie" (1976a, 205). The jolly gay fellows are the dinner hosts, Gabriel's aunts and their niece, and the reader knows as the dinner guests sing their appreciation that in his speech Gabriel lied about his real feelings toward his aunts. This is ordinary lying, what Wilde calls "lying with a moral purpose." Joyce, however, was equally adept at the other kind of lying—amoral or aesthetic lying.

---

7. Kiberd goes so far as to suggest that the tripartite structure of Synge's *Playboy* "corresponds very neatly with Frantz Fanon's dialectic of decolonization, from occupation, through nationalism, to liberation" (1995, 184).

Unlike Wilde, Yeats, and Synge, in the debate over realism and Romanticism Joyce did not reject realism in favor of Romanticism but rather he rejected both in favor of a hybrid of the two. The hybrid, however, was still defined in Wildean terms. Not only does *Portrait* fulfill Wilde's criterion that all art is autobiographical, but Stephen Dedalus is modeled on the Wildean aesthete, and his theories of artistic creation in both *Portrait* and *Ulysses* bear the imprint of Wilde's aesthetics. For Wilde, "Romanticism is always in front of Life" (1973, 87). The same is true for Joyce's Stephen, even though he would wed the Romantic image to an image from the sensible world. At the end of *Portrait* Stephen rejects Yeats's latter-day Romanticism in favor of a forward-looking Romanticism that will marry Stephen's soul to an image in the real world that adequately responds to it. Referring to one of Yeats's fictional characters from his stories and poems, Stephen says, "Michael Robartes remembers forgotten beauty and, when his arms wrap her round, he presses in his arms the loveliness which has long faded from the world. Not this. Not at all. I desire to press in my arms the loveliness which has not yet come into the world" (1976b, 251). Stephen's quest throughout *Portrait* is "to meet in the real world the unsubstantial image which his soul so constantly beheld" (1976b, 65). This quest is a classic case of the imagination of the artist anticipating life. It is also a classic case of a nonmimetic colonial enunciation. Both Yeats's backward-looking Romanticism and Stephen's forward-looking Romanticism summon into existence a world that is other than the colonial world they inhabited. The closest Stephen comes in *Portrait* to finding his soul's image in the world is his momentary epiphany of the bird-girl on Sandymount Strand. She is the "life that had cried to him," an "envoy from the fair courts of life," and "her image had passed into his soul for ever" (1976b, 172).

Stephen's discovery in *Portrait* that his vocation is to "create life out of life" (1976b, 172) also is couched in Wilde's terms on the relation of mimesis to imagination in art. According to Stephen, the artist forges "anew in his workshop out of the sluggish matter of the earth a new soaring impalpable imperishable being" (1976b, 169). Or as he puts it in *Ulysses*, "In woman's womb word is made flesh but in the spirit of the maker all flesh that passes becomes the word that shall not pass away.

This is the postcreation. *Omnis caro ad te veniet* [All flesh will come to thee]" (1961, 391). This formulation conforms to Wilde's notion of the proper relation of mimesis and imagination in art: "Art takes life as part of her rough material, recreates it, and refashions it in fresh forms, is absolutely indifferent to fact, invents, imagines, dreams, and keeps between herself and reality the impenetrable barrier of beautiful style, of decorative or ideal treatment" (1973, 68).

Ulysses too is saturated with the Wildean aesthetics of lying. The novel opens with allusions to Wilde's opposition of Romanticism and realism. In the opening episode Buck Mulligan holds a mirror up to Stephen's face and cites Wilde's definition of Romanticism as "The rage of Caliban at not seeing his face in a mirror."[8] Stephen's reply — that the mirror "is a symbol of Irish art. The cracked lookingglass of a servant" (1961, 6) — alludes to Wilde's comment in "The Decay of Lying" about how the realist's analogy of art as a mirror of life reduces genius "to the position of a cracked looking-glass" (1973, 73–74). Stephen's remark, which characterizes Irish art as a form of degraded realism, mimics the central antirealist bias of "The Decay of Lying" as well as the fractured reality of colonial Ireland detected by Eagleton and Lloyd in the Irish novel.[9]

8. From Wilde 1965, xvi: "The nineteenth-century dislike of Realism is the rage of Caliban seeing his own face in a glass. The nineteenth-century dislike of Romanticism is the rage of Caliban not seeing his own face in a glass."

9. Eagleton, for example, argues in "Form and Ideology in the Irish Novel" that the Irish novel is "ambiguously realist" (1995, 154) because Irish writing has been dominated by an antimimetic, antirepresentational aesthetic. In Ireland language was not so much representative or reflective of an agreed upon truth as strategic, rhetorical, and performative, as in sermons, political pamphlets, and ballads. In the nineteenth century the Irish novel could only present a fractured realism where the conventions of realism are often disrupted by schematic devices, strategic moralizing, polemics, bombast, preaching, and propaganda. Consequently nineteenth-century Irish novels were hybrids of realism and other genres, such as fantasy, fable, oral tales, romance, melodrama, naturalism, and gothic. Moreover, these formal contrasts were "signs of the resistance of [Irish] history to the cultural forms of its rulers" (1995, 224). Kiberd adds the insight that "rather than adapt themselves to the inherited genres, [Irish] writers tried to adapt the genres to themselves" (1995, 300).

Stephen's most elaborate aesthetic lie becomes the focus of the "Scylla and Charybdis" episode of *Ulysses*. Here Stephen articulates an autobiographical theory of Shakespeare's art and Wilde is invoked several times in relation to it. Earlier in the novel, when Mulligan touts Stephen's theory to Haines, he says, "We have grown out of Wilde and paradoxes" (1961, 18). Whether Stephen's theory goes beyond Wildean paradoxes or not (in a sense Stephen out-paradoxes Wilde), Mulligan's statement nevertheless establishes Wilde as Stephen's starting point. To make sure we do not miss the connection between Stephen's theory and Wilde, as Stephen warms to his argument in "Scylla and Charybdis," Joyce has John Eglinton, one of Stephen's audience in the National Library, remind the reader of Mulligan's comment: "I was prepared for paradoxes from what Malachi Mulligan told us" (1961, 194). And toward the end of Stephen's performance, Mr. Best, another librarian listening to him, says, "You ought to make it a dialogue, don't you know, like the Platonic dialogues Wilde wrote" (1961, 214). Of course, "Scylla and Charybdis" is a dialogue and, like Wilde's "Decay of Lying," it renders an aesthetic theory in dialogue form.

Stephen models his theory on the Sabellian heretical doctrine of the Trinity that claims "that the Father was Himself His Own Son" (1961, 208). Likewise, the artist begets himself in his own works or, like God the Father, begets his works in his own image (1961, 194, 197). Literary characters like Hamlet, then, are consubstantial with their father/artist Shakespeare (1961, 197). Since the artist fathers himself, he is "Himself his own father" (1961, 208), he is the "all in all" (1961, 212). According to this Sabellian theory of art, Shakespeare, like Joyce, put his own life into his work and created his characters in his own image. Thus, Mulligan can say to Haines about Stephen's theory, "It's quite simple. He proves by algebra that Hamlet's grandson is Shakespeare's grandfather and that he himself is the ghost of his own father" (1961, 18). Since as artist Shakespeare is the father of the ghost of Hamlet's father (whom Shakespeare is known to have played in performances of *Hamlet*), then Shakespeare is Hamlet's grandfather as well as his father. But then if Shakespeare created himself in Hamlet, he is also his own son and grandson. When Stephen recalls Mulligan's comment, he recalls a slightly less exaggerated but no more accurate formulation of his theory: "He proves by algebra that Shakespeare's ghost is Hamlet's grandfather" (1961, 28). In addition to the Sabellian heresy, Stephen's theory depends on his definition of a ghost as "One who has faded into impalpability through death, through absence, through change of manners" (1961, 188). Thus, Shakespeare became a ghost of his former self when he left Stratford for London and it is Shakespeare's ghost (the London Shakespeare as opposed to the Stratford Shakespeare) who wrote the plays. If the artist is the "all in all" — Father, Son, and Holy Ghost — then Mulligan's exaggerated formulation is just as valid as Stephen's. As Stephen says, when Shakespeare wrote *Hamlet* "he was not the father of his own son merely but, being no more a son, he was and felt himself the father of all his race, the father of his own grandfather, the father of his unborn grandson" (1961, 208). Shakespeare, in other words, achieved Stephen's artistic goal, articulated at the end of *Portrait,* of forging in the smithy of his soul the uncreated conscience of his race. Or to put it another way, Shakespeare is not the supreme example of mimetic art, the realist holding up a mirror to nature; rather he is more like God and colonized artists who bring new worlds into existence.

Like Wilde's "Decay of Lying," Stephen's exaggerated theory of autobiographical aesthetics about Shakespeare provides a powerful metaphorical model for neo-Hegelian, expressive theories of art, of which Joyce's *Portrait* and the first half of *Ulysses* are prime examples. Yet when asked if he believes his own theory Stephen readily says "No" (1961, 214). Stephen's theory, in other words, is a lie. But it is an aesthetic lie, a creative fiction. Like "The Decay of Lying," Stephen's theory is rigorously logical. In fact, Stephen's rigor, given the explicit allusions to Wilde, could be read, as Mulligan suggests, as an attempt to outdo Wilde's outrageous paradoxes. But despite the rigor of Stephen's logic, his theory ultimately is based on two fictional premises: a parthenogenetic, autobiographical theory of art (i.e., the artist reproduces himself in his art) and the definition of a ghost, which Stephen compares to Aristotle's "dagger definitions" (1961, 186). Given these two premises, Stephen's logic is airtight. But because it is based on two fictions, Stephen's autobiographical theory about Shakespeare's art has the truth, not of fact, but of metaphor; that is, it is not mimetically accurate but

rather its metaphorical consistency gives it the status of Aristotle's probable impossibility. Metaphors communicate quite effectively without re-
quiring literal belief. After all, as Stephen says, paternity itself "may be a
legal fiction" (1961, 207).

The second half of *Ulysses* pushes the theory of literature as lying
even further, and even more than Stephen's autobiographical theory of
art, moves beyond Wilde's neo-Hegelian paradoxes. In a sense, "Scylla
and Charybdis" is Joyce's good-bye to the character he modeled on the
Wildean aesthete. Stephen appears in later episodes, but never center
stage with his own virtuoso performance as in "Scylla and Charybdis." In
this episode Joyce also bids good-bye to a Romantic notion of style as
centered exclusively in individual consciousness. Although sections of
"Wandering Rocks," the second half of "Nausicaa," and Molly Bloom's
monologue in "Penelope" still employ a consciousness-centered narrative, everywhere else in the second half of *Ulysses* consciousness itself
has been dispersed over various discourse forms that construct the realities inhabited by the characters. Nature is no longer created by the minds
of artists, as Wilde insisted, but by language and discourse, which construct or re-present both mind and nature. In the second half of *Ulysses*
the characters' individual styles of expression become subsumed under a
bewildering variety of discourse forms, what Bakhtin calls incorporated
genres (1981, 320–23). Much of the "Cyclops" episode, for example, is fil-
tered through parodies of various styles that were readily available in
print to the average middle-class Dubliner in 1904. Joyce parodies several
literary genres popular in late-nineteenth-century Dublin, including
translations of Irish myth and legend (such as those by Lady Gregory
and Standish O'Grady), popular prose versions of medieval romance
(modeled on Tennyson and William Morris), and sentimental genteel fiction. He also parodies newspaper accounts of various types of events as
well as documents, records, and reports that would interest middle-class
Dubliners, such as legal documents, trial records, medical journal reports, minutes of Gaelic society meetings, reports of occult experiences,
and proceedings of Parliament. And he parodies the religious discourse
of prayers and the Bible, a child's primer, and adult childtalk. Taken together, the discourses represented include the most common written
sources available to the average middle-class Dubliner. The "Cyclops"

episode suggests the cumulative effect of being exposed daily to the modes of perception represented by these discourse forms. Succeeding episodes, except for "Oxen of the Sun" and "Penelope," present their material through extended parodies of single discourse forms: in "Nausicaa" Joyce allows us to see and experience Bloom through the eyes of Gerty McDowell, or rather through the discourse of popular romance stories that this Irish Emma Bovary has internalized as her own; in "Circe" everything is perceived through the hallucinatory effect of Freudian dream work; in "Eumaeus" we stumble through an old man's tired prose; and in "Ithaca" we submit to the catechistical inquisition of scientific discourse.

Joyce's dominant mode of handling these discourse forms in the second half of *Ulysses* is parody, the mode par excellence of colonial mimicry. Joyce parodies not only the language of the imperial colonial power—in the "Oxen of the Sun" episode a series of parodies proceeds through the entire history of English prose style from its Latin and medieval roots to modern slang—but also the daily discourses of the colonial capital, including the discourses of anticolonial nationalism. A discourse like journalism might be considered a mimetic use of language, but if discourse constructs reality, as Joyce's parodies suggest it does, then all language is performative rather than mimetic and *Ulysses* truly has rewritten the world from the colonial margins as a hybrid, performative enunciation.[10]

10. Lloyd argues that Joyce's constant stylistic modulations in *Ulysses* mimic the parodic hybrid discourses of the colonial subject and the colonial culture (1993, 110) and by refusing "any normative mode of representation" (1993, 106) "deliberately dismantles voice and verisimilitude" (1993, 109) to the point that any particular discursive mode is prevented "from occupying a position from which the order of probability that structures mimetic verisimilitude could be stabilized" (1993, 109). Consequently "*Ulysses* as a whole refuses the narrative verisimilitude within which the formation of representative man could be conceived" (1993, 110).

Eagleton calls *Ulysses* a "magnificent parody of fictional realism" (1995, 150–51) in which Joyce "uses his mythological framework to ironize and estrange that more tenacious modern myth which is realism itself" (1995, 225). In *Finnegans Wake*, according to Eagleton, "Joyce turns the medium of English against the nation which nurtured it, thus reversing the colonial power relation at the level of discourse" (1995, 269).

Joyce's notion of aesthetic lying, as with that of Wilde, Yeats, and Synge, has important implications for a theory of style. Western culture has produced three dominant orientations toward style. Classical and neoclassical theories of language and rhetoric were fundamentally mimetic and conceived of style as a transparent window to the world. Style could dress up or enhance substance or content but not fundamentally change it. Pope's notion of literature as "What oft was thought, but ne'er so well expressed" is typical of this orientation. Romantic and modernist views of language underlying the aesthetics of lying tended to view style as a lens that colors or distorts what it views. The substance or content may be altered considerably depending on perspective, vantage point, or emotional disposition, but it remains as the source or focal point of language. More contemporary theories of language, however, often insist that style is neither transparent nor does it merely distort, but rather it constitutes what it perceives. In this last sense style is more like a scientific instrument designed to detect or measure something we cannot observe directly, such as the wave length of light or the behavior of atomic particles. Thus, wave lengths of light and subatomic particles exist as measurable effects of instrumentation and theoretical discourse. Style, as such an instrument of perception, operates in a more Heideggerian fashion in that it not only makes things appear but also determines how they appear. And like any scientific instrument, every style has its capabilities and limitations, its points of illumination and its blind spots.

In *Ulysses* there appear to be two views of style contending with each other. One is a modernist view that suggests that each character (for example, Stephen, Bloom, and Molly) has a distinct style of expression and their various modes of expression provide multiple perspectives on the experiences portrayed in the novel. Throughout *Ulysses* Joyce uses the metaphor of parallax (the apparent displacement of a heavenly body when viewed from two divergent points on the earth's surface) to suggest this notion of multiple perspectives. The stylistic parodies of the second half of *Ulysses,* however, suggest a radically different view of language and discourse. These styles, which represent prevailing discourses of the time, are the instruments of perception that grant access to what otherwise would remain unseen. In other words, the "styles" represented by these discourses make things appear and determine how they appear. Things can be made apparent only through one style or another. There is no transparent or neutral style, nor is there any preexistent reality that is distorted by style. Derridean indeterminacy notwithstanding, language (as Heidegger has shown) makes things appear, and style determines how they appear. Wilde is not simply being outrageous in "The Decay of Lying" when he says, "Truth is entirely and absolutely a matter of style" and "It is style that makes us believe in a thing—nothing but style." Things in themselves, as Kant pointed out, are beyond our ken; and outside of style, that is, outside the ways in which things appear to us, we can know nothing of them.

Friel inherits this distinguished tradition of Irish mendacity. Developed over the course of his career, Friel's views on language link him with the idealist language philosophies of his predecessors Wilde, Yeats, Synge, and Joyce. Like them, Friel acknowledges how the word becomes flesh through the power of a lie. At the level of individual perception and memory, for example, Friel dissolves the traditional distinction between fact and fiction. For Friel facts themselves are factitious. In an autobiographical essay Friel asks, "What is a fact in the context of autobiography?" He goes on to answer his own question: "A fact is something that happened to me or something I experienced. It can also be something I thought happened to me, something I thought I experienced. Or indeed an autobiographical fact can be pure fiction and no less true or reliable for that." He illustrates this point with a Wordsworthian spot of time he describes from his childhood, a memory he uses in *Philadelphia, Here I Come!* with all the implications of its factual inaccuracy. He remembers walking home one day with his father along a dirt road, after fishing in the rain. But then he realizes that some of the facts in his memory of that scene could not have been accurate. "The fact," he concludes, "is a fiction." He asks,

> Have I imagined the scene then? Or is it a composite of two or three different episodes? The point is—I don't think it matters. What matters is that for some reason . . . this vivid memory is there in the storehouse of the mind. For some reason the mind has shuffled the pieces of verifiable truth and composed a truth of its own. For to me it is a truth. And because I acknowledge its peculiar veracity, it becomes a layer in my subsoil; it becomes part of me; ultimately it becomes me. (1972b, 18)

For Friel then, as for Synge's Christy Mahon, reality is something we construct out of our fictions of ourselves.

Friel also has followed the lead of Joyce into distinctly postmodern modes of perception and into developing literary forms appropriate to them. In *The Freedom of the City* (1973), for example, Friel adapts techniques for the theater that are similar to what Joyce developed in the "Cyclops" episode of *Ulysses*. Here Friel gives us multiple perspectives on an incident of political violence through various forms of public and private discourse; and no perspective coincides with another and all of them distort the event with fatal consequences.

In his play *Faith Healer* (1979) Friel has, in a sense, recast Synge's *Playboy*. *Faith Healer* characterizes individual memory as a verbal fiction of the past. In the course of four separate monologues three characters remember their lives together as part of a wandering faith-healing mission in Wales. Their memories all differ on important points about who did what and who wanted what. They each had constructed images or fictions dictated by their own compelling needs. Frank Hardy, the faith healer, says that in their memories "the whole corporeal world . . . had shed [its] physical reality and had become mere imaginings." The characters themselves "had ceased to be physical and existed only in spirit, only in the need [they] had for each other" (*SP,* 376). In *Faith Healer* Friel gives us no account of events apart from those given by the characters. The only truth available, in other words, is the truth of their deepest needs as reflected in the versions of events they construct, their images of the past.

Friel's perceptions about language, autobiography, and individual memory also apply to his views of the larger social context. As Seamus Deane says, Friel exposes the "fictive nature of the social contract" by suggesting that "society itself is a fiction in which we all must persuade ourselves to live, always acknowledging that these selves are also fictions" (1981, 9). For Friel, then, social contracts are grounded in fictions. The contract works when the fiction is mutually agreed upon, and it breaks down when there is no agreement. Most of Friel's writing, like *Faith Healer,* focuses on that lack of agreement in our social fictions. Friel's career-long focus on the lack of agreement among our collective fictions may have something to do with the facts that for centuries Ireland refused to accept its colonizer's fiction of itself and that since independence in 1922 conflict between competing fictions for the new political entity have resulted in very tangible, tragic consequences. In Ireland competing social and political fictions have been marked by a colonial structure. Articulating this structure, Seamus Deane says, "in divorcing power from eloquence, Friel is indicating a traditional feature of the Irish condition. The voice of power tells one kind of fiction—the lie. It has the purpose of preserving its own interests. The voice of powerlessness tells another kind of fiction—the illusion. It has the purpose of pretending that its own interests have been preserved" (1986b, 18).

For Friel fictions are constitutive of the only realities we have. In the world of his later plays no independently verifiable reality ever appears; every reality is somebody's fiction, and his tragedies result from one fictitious construction of reality overpowering another. His plays, in other words, are very much like the "real" world, where people routinely bludgeon each other with their own fictive truths, whether in marital discord or discord in Northern Ireland, Bosnia, or the Middle East. Married couples fight to establish their own versions of the truth or to defend their own self-images, just as Northern unionists, Serbs, and Israelis want their version of a homeland to dominate the versions of Irish nationalists, Kosovars, and Palestinians. In world politics, particularly postcolonial politics, asserting the right to become one's own fiction of oneself is a serious and often bloody business.

Friel's later views on language owe a good deal to George Steiner's book *After Babel: Aspects of Language and Translation* (1975). Friel read *After Babel* in the late 1970s as part of his preparation for "translating" Chekhov's *Three Sisters* into Irish English. (The word "translating" here is both accurate and misleading. Since he does not know Russian, Friel worked from five standard English translations of *Three Sisters* [1980b, 59]). *After Babel* provided Friel with a thorough and contemporary theory of translation, but Steiner's Heideggerian notions of translation extended far beyond translating between languages to investigate the fundamental nature of all language and communication. Steiner undoubtedly reinforced and solidified Friel's own sense of the fictive powers of language, which had been incipient in his early stories and plays.

Among the issues of language and translation dealt with in *After Babel,* the most germane for Friel's work is the power of language to conceal and dissimulate. From Steiner's postmodern viewpoint we speak as much to conceal as to communicate (1975, 46). He says, "Only a small portion of human discourse is nakedly veracious or informative in any monovalent, unqualified sense." He explains how in many different ways discourse often "conceals far more than it confides," how communications always includes "what is *not* said in the saying, what is said only partially, allusively or with intent to screen" (1975, 229; Steiner's emphasis).

Steiner, however, pursues this issue far beyond the capacity of language to conceal. He sees the capacity of language to lie as fundamental to its function and power: "The human capacity to utter falsehood, to lie, to negate what is the case, stands at the heart of speech and of the reciprocities between words and world. It may be that 'truth' is the more limited, the more special of the two conditions. We are a mammal who can bear false witness" (1975, 214). Even more emphatically, it is this capacity for untruth that has given the animal who speaks an evolutionary advantage. And that advantage is tied to a capacity to imagine that which is not the case. This power of language to "'un-say' the world, to image and speak it otherwise" (1975, 218), amounts to nothing less than our escape from time. Far from being an abuse of language, this ability to "hypothesize and project thought and imagination into the 'ifness,' into the free conditionalities of the unknown . . . is the master nerve of human action" (1975, 217). In Steiner's analysis our capacity for lying is our passport to both past and future. It is commensurate with our capacities for remembering and construing and for dreaming and forecasting.

The power of language to un-say the world, to speak it otherwise, is crucial in a colonial situation. Whether defined as a social imaginary, an imagined community, or a performative enunciation, it is the only route to liberation. In *Imagined Communities* (1991) Benedict Anderson describes how the elite among the colonized traveled to the metropole for education and training and then were sent back to the colony to help administer it. This educated class typically produced the leaders of revolt against the colonial power. In other words, what they learned in the metropole about how the world was organized and how it came to be that way ultimately became unsaid, inverted, turned against the colonizer.

Bhabha offers an especially sophisticated analysis of how lying functions in a colonial context. For Bhabha the very structure of communication between the colonizer and the colonized makes lying inevitable. He notes how the colonized's typical response to the demand of the colonizer for narrative (truth), was "sly civility," an answer that never satisfied the interlocutor (1994, 93–101). Because any iterative enunciation by the colonized necessarily transposes the context of any statement, truth is always beside the point, that is, it is "outside the sentence," as it is in any performative utterance. The colonized, in other words, focus on the occasion of any statement and on the addressee rather than on the referent. Thus, any truth or fact from the point of view of the hegemonic culture always undergoes a splitting, a translation, a displacement. The two contexts guarantee an incommensurability in any communication between them. Thus, the insistence of the colonizer that the colonized imitate and identify with the hegemonic culture always results in a residue of colonial silence or nonsense, the Horror of Kurtz, the Ouboum of Forster's Marabar caves. This residue remains untranslatable, and constitutes an incommensurability at the point of enunciation, an incommensurability that acknowledges difference that cannot be reconciled by a transcendental, universal subject position (as in relativism, multiculturalism, or Eagletonian irony). For Bhabha this is not simply a question of cultural codes but a problem of the structure of the signifier (1994, 126). Colonial enunciation necessarily produces "lies that never speak the 'whole' truth" (1994, 138): "in the moment of the discursive splitting, it oversignifies; it says something beside the point, something besides the truth of culture . . . a truth that is culturally alien" (1994, 135). From these marginalized enunciatory spaces "the work of signification *voids* the act of meaning in articulating a split-response" (1994, 132; Bhabha's emphasis).

In plays Friel wrote after reading Steiner, he dealt much more confidently and explicitly with lying as fundamental to language. In *Translations,* for example, the characters of Hugh and Jimmy Jack are well attuned to the mendacious quality of language. Lt. Yolland remarks at one point that he has heard them "swapping stories about Apollo and Cuchulainn and Paris and Ferdia—as if they lived down the road" (*SP,* 416). Jimmy Jack particularly escapes his present into an ancient classical past. This aging, unwashed, "Infant Prodigy" lives so thoroughly in the world of Greek heroes and gods that by the end of the play he has betrothed himself to Pallas Athene. The immediacy with which Jimmy

Jack experiences the ancient classics is a product twice over of the capacity of language to construct a world out of words. First Homer did it and then Jimmy Jack projects himself into that Homeric world, or perhaps more accurately, Jimmy Jack appropriates Homer's world into his own. One wonders if Friel's Jimmy Jack is not James Joyce displaced a century into his Gaelic past. They both have the same initials, both were "unwashed" child prodigies, and both bring Homer's gods and heroes to life in a contemporary present.

In the light of Steiner's analysis, Jimmy Jack's privatization of Homer is not an aberration of language but an exercise of its most ennobling power: "At every level," Steiner says, "from brute camouflage to poetic vision, the linguistic capacity to conceal, misinform, leave ambiguous, hypothesize, invent is indispensable to the equilibrium of human consciousness and to the development of man in society" (1975, 229). This is particularly true of colonial situations. For Steiner, not only does mendacity distinguish us from the beasts on the evolutionary ladder, it also guarantees our survival: "We secrete from within ourselves the grammar, the mythologies of hope, of fantasy, of self-deception without which we would have been arrested at some rung of primate behaviour or would, long since, have destroyed ourselves. It is our syntax, not the physiology of the body or the thermodynamics of the planetary system, which is full of tomorrows" (1975, 227). For Bhabha the survival value of this power of language is amply evident in colonial situations. The "newness" that enters the world through the process of hybrid enunciation produces a reinscribed history that opens up a future through which survival for the wretched of the earth once again becomes possible (1994, 235).

The character of Hugh in *Translations* becomes Friel's most articulate spokesman for Steiner's insights. He is much more consciously aware than Jimmy Jack of how the deceits of language are tools of survival, and he expresses that awareness in terms of the Irish colonial context and pretty much in Steiner's own words: referring to Gaelic, Hugh says to Lt. Yolland, "Yes, it is a rich language, Lieutenant, full of the mythologies of fantasy and hope and self-deception—a syntax opulent with tomorrows. It is our response to mud cabins and a diet of potatoes; our only method of replying to . . . inevitabilities" (*SP*, 418–19). For both

Steiner and Hugh cultural survival under chronically adverse conditions such as colonialism often depends on an inverse relation between capacity for linguistic elaboration and material well-being. Virtually quoting Steiner, Hugh says to Yolland, "You'll find, sir, that certain cultures expend on their vocabularies and syntax acquisitive energies and ostentations entirely lacking in their material lives. I suppose you could call us a spiritual people" (*SP*, 418; cf. Steiner 1975, 55). As Eagleton says, the "bathetic gap between form and content" is "an index of the condition of the colonial writer, wryly conscious of the discrepancy between the exuberance of the signifier and the meanness of the referent" (1995, 150).

In addition to the characters of Hugh and Jimmy Jack, in *Translations* Friel acknowledges the power of dissimulation in language through his metaphor of Lying Anna's Poteen. Hugh's favorite pub is Anna na mBreag's, whose name means "Anna of the lies" (*SP*, 417). When Owen and Yolland rename all the locations in Baile Beag as they Anglicize it into Ballybeg, they are sustained and assisted in their project by Lying Anna's Poteen (*SP*, 409–22). Anna's heady brew is a very appropriate metaphor, as Anna is an appropriate muse, for all the deceptions, self-deceptions, concealments, and erosions that were involved in translating and transforming Gaelic Ireland into modern Anglicized Ireland.

The most productive lies in a colonial situation relate to the past and the future. For the colonized a seamless continuity of past, present, and future is impossible. Following Walter Benjamin, Eagleton characterizes the colonial present as a "weightless moment," a "mere empty passageway" suspended between a past that cannot be relinquished and a transfigured future that has not yet arrived (1995, 280). The arrival of the colonizer was an interdiction of the history of the colonized. Resistance to that interdiction is likewise an intervention in the colonizer's history. To arm itself culturally for resistance, a colonized people selectively invents or re-members its past strategically — "a painful re-membering, a putting together of the dismembered past to make sense of the trauma of the present" (Bhabha 1994, 63). The hybrid enunciations theorized by Bhabha do not "merely recall the past" but renew it, refigure it, and restage it so that it necessarily "estranges any immediate access to an originary identity or a 'received' tradition" (1994, 2, 7). This new hybrid national narrative converts a "nostalgic past" into a "disruptive 'anterior'" that "displaces the historical present" and "opens it up" to alternative histories and narrative subjects (1994, 167). Bhabha's enunciative present is also a lie, one that "can no longer be simply envisaged as a break or a bonding with the past and the future, no longer a synchronic presence" (1994, 4). Rather than being continuous with the past and the future, a hybrid enunciation is "a return to the present," a "space of intervention in the here and now," an "insurgent act of cultural translation" (1994, 7). Combined, this past which is "not originary" and this present which is "not simply transitory" produces the lie of the future, "an interstitial future, that emerges *in-between* the claims of the past and the needs of the present" and that becomes open once again to a rewriting of narratives and subjectivities (1994, 219; Bhabha's emphasis). Christy Mahon, for example, rewrites his own subject and narrative of the future at the end of Synge's *Playboy of the Western World,* a future formed discontinuously with his past within an asynchronous enunciative present.

Likewise, for both Steiner and Friel, history is an act of creative lying. For Steiner, history is a highly selective use of the past tense (1975, 29), with which historians literally *make* history (1975, 136), and the histories they make are not necessarily commensurable with each other (1975, 29). For Steiner, ascertaining the meaning of history is no more assured than ascertaining the meaning of a literary text (1975, 136). Friel's *Making History* (1988) dramatizes this insight by juxtaposing two historical versions of the Gaelic chieftain Hugh O'Neill. During the course of the play Archbishop Lombard composes his famous account of O'Neill as the last hero and defender of Gaelic Ireland, while the onstage action in effect dramatizes Sean O'Faolain's portrait of O'Neill as neither Irish hero nor traitor to the British crown, but as a profoundly ambivalent man torn between his allegiance on one hand to his native Ulster and on the other hand to England, where he had been reared and educated, whose culture he admired, and whose queen he had once loyally served.

Translations also demonstrates a keen awareness of the relations between fiction and history. In a key passage Hugh, the erudite hedge-school master about to become obsolete, says, "it is not the literal past, the 'facts' of history, that shape us, but images of the past embodied in language. . . . we must never cease renewing those images; because once we do, we fossilize" (*SP,* 445). We can see more clearly what is at stake for

Friel in Hugh's comment if we look at a statement he made in an interview in 1980, the year *Translations* was first produced:

> In some ways the inherited images of 1916, or 1690, control and rule our lives much more profoundly than the historical truth of what happened on those two occasions. The complication of that problem is how do we come to terms with it using an English language. For example, is our understanding of the Siege of Derry going to be determined by Mac-Cauley's [sic] history of it, or is our understanding of Parnell going to be determined by Lyons's portrait of Parnell? This is a matter which will require a type of eternal linguistic vigilance. (1980b, 61)

Obviously for Friel, history is not a matter of a disinterested, "objective" account. It matters to him who constructs Ireland's historical images and what are their allegiances, prejudices, and assumptions. Likewise, Seamus Deane sees much of Irish historical writing over the past century as attempts by the Anglo-Irish Ascendancy and their descendants in the Free State and the Republic to highlight their own contributions at the expense of the Gaelic Catholic majority population: he says, "From Lecky to Yeats and forward to F. S. L. Lyons we witness the conversion of Irish history into a tragic theatre in which the great Anglo-Irish protagonists—Swift, Burke, Parnell—are destroyed in their heroic attempts to unite culture of intellect with the emotion of multitude, or in political terms, constitutional politics with the forces of revolution" (1986a, 48).

Friel further develops his thinking about language as lie in *The Communication Cord* (1982), written the year after *Translations*. The play is a wild farce of mistaken identities and fabricated images, all deliberately contrived to satisfy the immediate needs of each of the characters. One of the characters, Tim, is writing a thesis on discourse analysis based on the popular assumption that people converse by exchanging units of information that constitute a message according to an agreed code. The lies, charades, and wild fictions that follow completely refute this naive, positivist model of discourse. Tim begins to suspect, "Man as communicator—doesn't always work, does it? I mean in a situation like this we can hardly explain the individual as being simultaneously creator and creation of his own communicational possibilities, can we?" (*CC*, 34). Tim's suspicion here hints at a notion of language like Bhabha's performative enunciation where meaning occupies a "Third Space" of "communicational possibilities" and can never be read off the content of a proposition because meaning is always located "outside the sentence" in its contingent context. Likewise, this contingent context of "communicational possibilities," which forms part of our political and cultural unconscious, can not "be mimetically read off from the content" (1994, 36). Bhabha says,

> The pact of interpretation is never simply an act of communication between the I and the You designated in the statement. The production of meaning requires that these two places be mobilized in the passage through a Third Space, which represents both the general conditions of language and the specific implication of the utterance in a performative and institutional strategy of which it cannot "in itself" be conscious. (1994, 36)

If, like Tim in *The Communication Cord,* "you seek simply the sententious or the exegetical, you will not grasp the hybrid moment outside the sentence—not quite experience, not yet concept; part dream, part analysis; neither signifier nor signified" (Bhabha 1994, 181). Furthermore, the hybrid site of enunciation is, in Spivak's terms, a "catachrestic space," like the cottage setting in *The Communication Cord,* where "words or concepts" are "wrested from their proper meaning" (Bhabha 1994, 183).

At the end of *The Communication Cord* Tim realizes he may have to rethink his thesis, as he arrives at some conclusions that typically characterize the language of colonials and postcolonials who are accustomed to focusing, not on the content of an utterance, but on the addressee or the occasion, conclusions such as "maybe the message doesn't matter at all" and "it's the occasion that matters" or "the reverberations that the occasion generates"; or perhaps what matters is "the desire to sustain the occasion," or "saying anything, anything at all, that keeps the occasion going."[11] He even suspects another conclusion most colonials, as well as Beckett and Heidegger, have arrived at, that "maybe even saying nothing . . . maybe silence is the perfect discourse" (*CC,* 85–86).

The Communication Cord also poses Steiner's suggestion that "possibly we have got hold of the wrong end of the stick altogether when ascrib-

---

11. It is interesting to note that the plays of Harold Pinter support some of these same conclusions about language.

ing to the development of speech a primarily informational, a straightfor-wardly communicative motive" (1975, 229). "It is not, perhaps," Steiner says, "'a theory of information' that will serve us best in trying to clarify the nature of language, but a 'theory of misinformation'" (1975, 218), which is precisely what Wilde and poststructuralists like Derrida have given us. For all its farcical nonsense, *The Communication Cord* is just such a theory of misinformation in compact dramatic form.

Beyond his own plays, Friel's views on language inform the various projects of the Field Day Theatre Group, which he cofounded with actor Stephen Rea. Friel and his Field Day colleagues have focused attention on images and myths that have shaped Irish consciousness, especially those that have helped form the prejudices that divide the country today. Friel and other Field Day writers hope to alter these long-standing preju-dices that inhibit cultural and political harmony by demythologizing tra-ditional images and myths and supplanting them with more productive ones. And they expect to articulate this new hybrid reality through the power of a lie. For example, in "Anglo-Irish Attitudes," one of Field Day's pamphlets, Kiberd explores the uniquely posed thesis that the "English did not invade Ireland—rather, they seized a neighbouring island and in-vented the idea of Ireland. The notion 'Ireland,'" he says, "is largely a fic-tion created by the rulers of England in response to specific needs at a precise moment in British history." Likewise, he claims that the "Irish no-tion of 'England' is a fiction created and inhabited by the Irish for their own pragmatic purposes" (1986, 83). One of Ireland's retaliations against England's myth of Ireland, Kiberd implies, was Oscar Wilde becoming more English than the English (1986, 86). In Bhabha's terms Wilde's pos-turing can be seen as an unsettling and threatening mimicry of the Eng-lish, a reversal of the gaze that stereotypes the colonized native.

3

Enabling Fictions
The Short Stories

F RIEL BEGAN WRITING SHORT STORIES while he was teaching school
during the 1950s. His stories were good enough that he soon had a
contract with *The New Yorker* for first refusal on whatever he wrote. The
money from this contract enabled him to quit teaching in 1960 and devote full time to his writing (Friel 1965, 9–11, 14; and Friel 1980a).

The stories are largely traditional, all written in the manner of O'Faolain and O'Connor, particularly O'Connor, whom both Friel and his critics acknowledge as the dominant influence on him.[1] Although a few of
the stories are set in the Northern cities of Omagh and Derry, most of
them are set in rural areas of County Tyrone and Donegal. Even when
set in the cities, however, Friel's stories have a distinctly small town atmosphere. Written in the relatively halcyon days before the outbreak of
the recent troubles in the North, the stories are not overtly political or
historical like his later plays. They ignore the border between North and
South and they eschew the social issues that separate Catholic and
Protestants in the North. Instead they focus on revealing incidents in the
lives of the rural and small town Catholics among whom Friel grew up.
Friel once explained that "when you write for the American market . . .
there are certain aspects of Irish life that you ignore lest you upset the
traditional concept of Irish life which Americans have" (1957, 510).

Friel once said "nothing important ever happens to you after you're
ten or so" (1965, 7). Friel said this in 1965, and subsequent events altered
this opinion; but his stories, all of which were published by 1965, conform to it. Most of the incidents they are based on were probably wit-

1. Friel 1982a, 21; Dantanus 1988, 21; Fallis 1977, 272; Foster 1974, 64–65.

nessed or experienced by Friel as a boy, and many of the stories are written from the point of view of a young boy.

Most of Friel's stories are straightforwardly realistic, well crafted, and offer generous and sympathetic insight into his characters. They often focus on charming or quaint idiosyncracies of Irish rural life. But taken as a whole no dominant, organizing vision governs them. Beyond the craftsmanship of the writer himself, they contain nothing special to recommend them over the stories of any other extremely competent Irish realist. Thematically, the stories deal with a broad spectrum of concerns within the rural and small town Catholic milieu that Friel claimed then for his aesthetic domain.[2] Despite this thematic range, however, as a corpus these stories lack a cohesive thematic core comparable, say, to what Joyce provides in *Dubliners*. D. E. S. Maxwell intimates this lack when he praises "the vibrant solidity of the settings" as "perhaps the strongest single impression left by the world of these stories" (1973, 31). Even though Friel once said about his stories that the writer must persuade the reader "to the particular vision of these people that you're writing about" (1965, 4–5), no particular vision of Friel's people emerges in these stories.

Milton Levin offers the most balanced appraisal of Friel's stories: he says they "are deftly put together, but most are very close to the standard *New Yorker* pattern: a bit of local color; a low-keyed narrative only little more than an anecdote; a well-placed symbol or pattern; and a half-ironic, bitter-sweet conclusion. It is not quite a formula, and Friel is never a mere manufacturer, but he is not among the top rank of Irish writers of fiction" (1972, 132). Friel is even harsher on himself than his critics are: he says, "I've written a lot of short stories that are bad. Very bad. Stories that appeared in the collection *The Saucer of Larks* should never have gone into it. Many of them are not good at all" (1965, 8–9).

Friel's own comments about his writing during this period reveal the source of his aesthetic problems with the short story—a limited conception of the genre that inhibited his power to mold the form to a stronger

2. Commentators on the stories have characterized their thematic content variously: "the nature of disappointment and desire" (Deane 1981, 7); elegiac views of "loves, friendships, observances" in particular Irish communities (Maxwell 1973, 17, 47); and more generally, the "close observation of the people who inhabit [Friel's] well-known local habitat" (Dantanus 1985, 75).

purpose. At that time the "basis" of the short story for Friel was nothing more than "these particular people, caught in these particular circumstances at this particular time" captured "with sufficient vividness and sufficient understanding" (1965, 6). This view, which conforms to the emphasis of Anglo-American formalism on particularity, hardly constitutes the stuff of a sustaining aesthetic vision. Friel's lack of vision might suggest, especially in light of his subsequent development, that he acquiesced in his position as a colonial subject, that he had not yet achieved that critical consciousness that characterizes the process of decolonization, a process which Fanon says inevitably succeeds (1963, 37).

There is one motif, however, that Friel explores in approximately half of his stories that later became central to the mature art of his drama — the theme of illusion and its role both in the psychic life of the individual and in connecting that psychic life to the social environment — that suggests that in these stories, at least, Friel was exploring, perhaps unconsciously, the crippled psyche of a colonized people. In this light the stories and some of the early plays could be seen as a phase in Friel's career that served as a prelude to arriving at the critical consciousness that inaugurates decolonization. Friel himself appears to have recognized the importance of this thematic for his career when he chose the pieces for his *Selected Stories* (1979), where eight of the ten stories focus on the psychological and social functions of illusion.

Illusion and Friel's Narrative Art

Most of these stories deal with the necessity of illusions to the psychic health of the individual, especially when circumstances deprive that individual's existence of meaningfulness or dignity. As several critics have pointed out, illusions compensate for these deprivations in the characters' lives and make life bearable for them.[3] Sometimes the illusions provide escape from grinding poverty ("The Potato Gatherers," "Mr. Sing My Heart's Delight," "The Gold in the Sea"). In other stories illusions provide escape from a routine, commonplace existence without meaning or grandeur ("My True Kinsman," "A Man's World," "Everything

3. Dantanus 1985, 66; Deane, 1986b, 17–18; and Foster 1974, 64.

Neat and Tidy," and "Foundry House"). In other cases illusions enable a character to preserve a fundamental dignity in the face of some fear or adversity ("The Saucer of Larks," "The Diviner"). At other times illusions give meaning to the present or the past ("Among the Ruins").

"Foundry House," which has received more critical attention than any other Friel story,[4] gives an especially poignant example of an illusion that relieves a life of its oppressive banality. The illusion in this case plays a variant on the Irish big house tradition. The variant element here is that the aristocrats are Catholic rather than Protestant. In "Foundry House," Joe Brennan finds grandeur and beauty in his memories of a Catholic big house in whose gate lodge he grew up. Foundry House has fallen on hard times, however, and it now lies "in the green patch that lay between the new housing estate and the brassiere factory" (*SS*, 59). Mr. Bernard (Hogan), the master of Foundry House, is a decrepit hulk of his former self. He has been crippled by strokes and has to be led like a giant child learning to walk. Mrs. Hogan is a tall ungainly wraith from the past. She constantly works her mouth and lips even when not speaking and when she does speak she often appears to be absentmindedly oblivious to a good half of what is before her. The only two Hogan children, Declan and his sister Claire, both chose to enter religious life, thus ending the family line. Declan, a Jesuit who is Joe's age and his former playmate, treats Joe with insincere, formulaic heartiness and appears to be amazingly detached from the decay of his parents and their household. The occasion of the story is a reunion of sorts at which Declan and his parents play a tape sent by Claire from an Africa mission from which she will never return. Joe is present as the technician to operate the tape recorder. (He repairs radios and televisions for a living.) Sister Claire's tape is a painful cliché of such communications. She is obviously unaware of the family's situation, and although she addresses each one personally, she offers only the sprightly platitudes of a relative long out of touch.

Joe is appalled by what he witnesses. His former memory of Foundry House had made him feel humble, unworthy, and deferential. Although his own life is the fecund antithesis of the present life of Foundry

4. Dantanus 1985, 48; Deane 1979, 13; Foster 1974, 68–71; Maxwell 1973, 41–42.

House — nine children all lively and healthy, as Mrs. Hogan notes — in contrast it seems like the "sensual music" of Yeats's "mackerel-crowded seas." When Joe returns home his gate house is teeming with chaotic activity. Joe cannot bring himself to tell his wife what he has seen. He can only repeat that everything was nice, lovely, and the same as ever. As his ever practical wife puts out her cigarette and sticks the butt behind her ear, Joe can only repeat that the Hogans are still "A great family. A grand family" (*SS*, 70). He clings to a memory that makes life bearable for him, a vision of life as grand and lovely and never changing, a vision that makes him forget that his life is spent repairing machines and producing babies. A Yeatsian perspective might depict "Foundry House" as imagining an aristocratic past that gives meaning to the tawdry present. John Wilson Foster, for example, says, "Joe is caught between the stagnation of the land with its compensating echoes of a grand past and the philistine impersonalisation of the urban industrial present." Echoing Yeats's disparagement of the bourgeois culture that replaced the Anglo-Irish culture, Foster calls the housing estate and the brassiere factory that border on Foundry House the "twin images of modernity and of the price paid by Joe and his ilk for their liberation from the paternalism of the Foundry Houses of the last century." While for Foster, Mr. Bernard "represents the decline of the old order," he also represents "its lithic endurance, grandeur raised to the power of history, of myth" (*SS*, 70–71). To give up his illusion of Foundry House Joe must admit that his soul is "fastened to a dying animal" and that all the loveliness of the world is reduced to birth, copulation, and death. Joe's memory of an aristocratic past to which his family was connected, however menially, provides him with a mythical foundation that gives meaning to his life and relief from his own mundane existence. But unlike Joe and Foster, Friel avoids Yeatsian nostalgia for a lost past by depicting the Hogan family in irremediable decline, as incapable, except somewhat pathetically for Joe, of redeeming the "filthy modern tide." However betrayed Joe may feel by his postcolonial present, yearning for a colonial past provides at best a Band-Aid for Joe's damaged psyche.

In Friel's stories the illusions harbored by the characters are not necessarily unconscious. Often the characters are quite aware that their illusions do not correspond to anything in their external circumstances. But that does not thereby relegate the illusions to the realm of delusion or unreality. Although an illusion may not correspond to anything external, it nevertheless frames external circumstances and mediates the interaction of the characters with them. Several critics have pointed out that these conscious illusions are a form of "imaginative compensation" that does not "supplant reality but make[s] it tolerable."[5] In many ways the subject matter of these stories is the necessity of illusion in negotiating our relationship with what is Other or outside of ourselves.

Illusions in these stories often have a social as well as a psychological function. Although the psychological and social functions are not always distinguishable, some stories are more oriented toward the social than others, for example, "The Barney Game," "The Highwayman and the Saint," and "The Diviner." Seamus Deane notes how in Friel's stories "the failure to wholly be oneself . . . is not simply the place's fault or the individual's. It is a failure in the transaction between individual and society" (1979, 12). He insists elsewhere, however, that Friel's focus is not simply the "tension between self and society" but the more subtle insight "that the formation and the fostering of illusion is one of the means by which the relationship between the individual and society is preserved when there is nothing else to support it." As Deane acknowledges, these social fictions are not merely a "form of escapism" (1981, 9), but neither do they operate only when there is nothing more substantive to support the social contract. The social contract is always a fiction of some sort. Tension arises when people do not share the same fictions, that is, when fictions conflict or are mutually exclusive.

The most powerful story that deals with the social function of illusion is "The Diviner." In "The Diviner" the death of Nelly's first husband releases her from the humiliation and indignity of being married to an alcoholic for twenty-five years. She then becomes a well-respected charwoman who works for the best families in the village. When she remarries she tells nothing about her new husband and they lead a reclusive life together: "The grinding humiliation of having her private life made public every turnabout in bars and courthouses for twenty-five years had made her skilled in reticence and fanatically jealous of her dignity" (SS, 18). When her new husband drowns, Nelly keeps her vigil in "dignified

5. Dantanus 1985, 66; Deane 1979, 11; Maxwell 1973, 42.

resignation" as the townsfolk look for his body. Father Curran, the local parish priest, keeps the vigil with her, but offers only repeated sayings of the rosary and "ponderous consolings" (SS, 19). After all search efforts fail to recover the body, they send for a diviner who "could find anything provided he got the 'smell of the truth in it'" (SS, 21). When the diviner arrives he mysteriously knows more about Nelly's husband than she is comfortable with. The parish priest sees the diviner as a whiskey-besotted fake, but then he does find the body. When they lay it on the shore McElwee, the postman who suggested the diviner, tries to hide from Nelly and the priest two pint whiskey bottles he found on the corpse. Fr. Curran first pronounces a pious, formulaic obituary over the body and, after asking McElwee to see if Nelly's husband had been carrying rosary beads, he insists on seeing everything they found on him. On realizing his blunder, the priest calls for a rosary as Nelly cries, "helplessly, convulsively, her wailing rising above the drone of the prayers. Hers, they knew, were not only the tears for twenty-five years of humility and mortification but, more bitter still, tears for the past three months, when appearances had almost won, when a foothold on respectability had almost been established" (SS, 26).

In "The Diviner" Nelly's reticence toward everyone is a desperate attempt to preserve her own dignity by maintaining the illusion of respectability. She hoped this illusion would erase the humiliation of her first marriage and camouflage the fact that her second husband also was an alcoholic. What is at stake is her self-image, which she tries to preserve through her reticence. The villagers gossiped incessantly about her new husband, but until the drowning Nelly successfully preserved the privacy that protected her dignity. Once the secret is out, however, her dignity and respectability will be sacrificed to the town gossip mill. She will no longer be the "perfect servant" (SS, 17), the charwoman the best society desires; instead she will be poor Nelly, the woman with an unfortunate predilection for alcoholic husbands. Unlike Synge's Christy Mahon, in her attempt to negotiate a more desirable self-image Nelly fails. Her best version of herself will not be accepted in the end by the villagers as her primary identity. Instead she has an undesirable image foisted upon her. Notice that the illusion of respectability her dignity requires is not totally divorced from the possibilities of her circumstances (although this is not always the case in Friel's stories). She herself is respectable, but the social contract of small villages taints the wife with the sins of her husbands. As Deane points out, in "The Diviner" "individuality is shown to be a social achievement; society is shown to be the home of individuality" (1979, 12).

Although the setting for "The Diviner" is rural Ireland and Nelly is frustrated by the attitudes of her own village, the structure of her dilemma repeats the colonial dilemma of Ireland saddled for centuries by unflattering stereotypes foisted upon it by Britain. It is as if Cathleen ni Houlihan, respectable charwoman to the best ascendancy families, is inevitably married to a drunken Irishman.

Friel's concern with illusion has been misread by some critics as a conventional attempt to distinguish between reality and illusion.[6] While the disjunction of external circumstances and the world of illusion is often clear in these stories, Friel's interest lies less in discriminating between reality and illusion than in asserting their necessary interaction. As Deane points out, the illusions central to so many of the short stories "do not simply disappear when their surrogate quality is acknowledged. Instead, they seem to exemplify the necessity of illusion in a society which so severely distorts the psychic life" (1979, 11). Deane recognizes that Friel's interest lies not in distinguishing reality from illusion but in exploring the social and psychic needs these illusions fulfill, particularly the need for dignity: "To recognise the squalor and insufficiency of one's life by the creation of an alternative fiction is its[e]lf an expression of dignity, not simply a flight from reality" (1979, 14). Dignity, however, is only one need that illusions fulfill.

"The Illusionists" illustrates the complexities of the problem better than most of the other stories. In this story the annual visit of M. L'Estrange, illusionist, delights the children in a small rural school with his magic tricks. Because he always came around the first week in March, he was viewed as a harbinger of spring. Each year, after he thrilled the children by making rabbits disappear, pulling huge wooden molars out of his mouth, and other such sleights of hand, M. L'Estrange and Mr. Boyle, the school teacher and father of the narrator, would retire to the family cottage and reenact another annual ritual, accompanied by a bottle of

6. Dantanus 1985, 66; Foster 1974, 64; Maxwell 1973, 37; Pine 1990, 61.

whiskey, in which they reminisced about their respective careers of magician and schoolteacher. Mr. Boyle would tell how he had come in first in all Ireland in the qualifying exams for the teaching profession, how he could have had any post in Ireland, and how he was sought after in all the major cities but chose the village of Beannafreaghan because he felt they needed a teacher who could offer more than the others. L'Estrange, for his part, would tell how he had played before distinguished audiences in the capitals of Europe. As the whiskey bottle became emptied these reminiscences tended to degenerate into separate simultaneous monologues about a past that was obviously a much desired "might have been" for each of them where their minor, local talents became national and international successes.

The young narrator was as fascinated with these tales as he was with L'Estrange's tricks. The boy, who was told he would be sent to a Jesuit boarding school in Dublin next year, tried to escape this unpleasant prospect by fantasizing about running off with L'Estrange as his apprentice. But his no-nonsense mother, like many of the mother figures in Friel's stories, introduced the voice of sober realism and did her best to distract the boy, much to his frustrated dismay, from the drunken ramblings of the "pair of bletherskites" (SS, 75), as she called them. Each year Boyle became more mean-spirited and sarcastic the more drunk he became. L'Estrange usually ignored him and departed when Boyle began to taunt him, but that year ("when my whole future depended on him" [SS, 77], the narrator tells us) L'Estrange lost his temper and the ritual between the two men degenerated into a drunken shouting match in which they debunked each other's most cherished illusions. The ever practical mother dealt fiercely and rudely with both her husband and L'Estrange. Upon ejecting L'Estrange, whose real name is Barney O'Reilly, she called him a sham and bid him never to return. After L'Estrange departed they discovered his hat and the mother sent the boy after him. He found L'Estrange sprawled by the road next to his bicycle. He helped him up and retrieved his rabbit, which although released from its box made no attempt to escape. It had been sitting passively beside the spinning wheel of the bicycle. As young Boyle picked it up he noted, "Its dull, weary eyes, mother's eyes, stared back at me, beyond me" (SS, 79). L'Estrange gave the boy a penny and wobbled off. Upon returning to the cottage, the boy was greeted with the sober, practical advice of his mother to eat his supper to ward off hunger and the cold. His immediate response was an elaborate fantasy about his encounter with L'Estrange, in which the illusionist gave him a half crown rather than a penny, promised to visit him at boarding school in Dublin, and when he was grown to take him on as an apprentice illusionist and travel the world. Then he began to cry as he recanted the illusion and admitted that L'Estrange only gave him a penny and was so drunk he could barely walk. Realizing how bereft her son was when left only with the reality of two drunken shams, Mrs. Boyle abandoned her own graceless realism and reminisced about their good times the previous spring and summer and how they would repeat them again this year. In other words, she offered her own myth of spring renewal. The story concludes with the boy saying, "I stopped crying and smiled into her breast because every word she said was true. But it wasn't because I remembered that it was true that I believed her, but because she believed it herself, and because her certainty convinced me" (SS, 81).

"The Illusionists" makes clear that Friel's focus is not on demarcating reality from illusion. After all, we never learn whether Boyle did qualify as first in Ireland or whether L'Estrange did perform in London and Europe. For Friel illusion is not, as Deane suggests, simply a matter of compensation for deprived circumstances or a social fiction deployed when there is nothing else to support the contract between the individual and society. Rather the illusions in the short stories serve the same function as myths — they are necessary illusions that promote the health of our psychic and social life. Illusions are necessary because they give meaning, significance, or hope to existence. Even the realist illusion of the mother — the illusion of not having any illusions — serves this function. A realist might speculate that the mother's myth of spring is more effective because, unlike the myths of Mr. Boyle and L'Estrange, it corresponds to certain facts and circumstances of the past. Friel, however, does not allow this view to be decisive — young Boyle is not comforted by his mother's vision of spring because he "remembered that it was true" but because of her own sense of certainty about it. The power of illusion, in other words, depends not on its truth but on some other quality of conviction. Wilde had claimed that only style "makes us believe in

a thing—nothing but style," but in Friel's short stories that credible quality is never clearly defined. What is clear is that despite the realistic form
of the short stories, philosophical realism is not the alternative to the
world of illusions they explore.

In many ways "The Illusionists" itself is a fictional metaphor for the
necessary illusions of art, which persuade us, not because they refer accurately to a world of external circumstance or fact, but because, like
Mrs. Boyle's myths of spring, they appeal to our deepest emotional
needs and convince, as Wilde understood, by virtue of their own sense
of certainty about themselves. The self-aggrandizing illusions of Mr.
Boyle and L'Estrange, in contrast, self-destruct. These illusions are not
replaced by an unmediated reality, however, but by another illusion that
mediates more effectively between desire and the world of the Other.

As Friel's career developed, his recognition of the role illusion plays in
our psychic and social life became more profound and complex. In the
later plays the nature of illusion itself changed as it became more and
more enmeshed in Friel's growing awareness of its implication in language. In the stories, as Seamus Deane points out, "the author's insistence on the actuality of event and on the reality of imagination is quite
impartial. His linguistic diplomacy is directed towards gaining recognition for both sides" (1979, 9); but in the later plays Friel's allegiance to the
"reality of imagination" has completely overshadowed his "insistence on
the actuality of event." Moreover, in the later plays Friel represents imaginative reality as a linguistic construct. *Faith Healer,* for example, whose
theme is anticipated by "The Illusionists," also characterizes individual
memory as a verbal fiction of the past. But in *Faith Healer* there is no reality of event that is not produced by some discourse of desire. George
O'Brien notes how in the plays "the typical protagonist is inevitably a
man of language, composing and recomposing his identity in the light of
the cultural options to which his language provides access" (1989, 29).
The passage from *Translations* about the Irish language being "full of the
mythologies of fantasy and hope and self-deception—a syntax opulent
with tomorrows" suggests not only the function of illusion in a colonial
culture, as do the stories, but also how in his later plays Friel's concern
with the nature and function of illusion has shifted to a focus on language itself as the creator of our illusions. This shift from individual illu-

sions to the power of language in general marks a major development in Friel's perspective from his early work to his mature plays.

The later plays are also more pessimistic about the power of illusions and the social contracts our fictions bind us to. Seamus Deane points out that in the stories the separation of the social and the imaginative is "often threatened" but "never permitted," whereas in the plays this separation is "enforced." In the later plays Deane says, "the relationship between community, familial and social, and the individual, alienated and stricken, has finally crumbled. Interaction between the two leads only to mutual destruction. . . . The friction between individual and group, between the demand for internal freedom and the system of embodied values is now intolerable. Here, in the development from stories to plays, Brian Friel's work registers a characteristic and irreversible development in modern Ireland" (1979, 9, 13). In the stories illusion usually succeeds in preserving individual dignity or maintaining viable relations between individual and society; but in the later plays the illusions typically fail, no adequate substitute is found, and the social contracts do not work to the mutual benefit of all parties concerned. When "Foundry House" is rewritten as the play *Aristocrats,* for example, nothing salutary or redeeming is salvaged, however tenuously, from the myth of the Catholic big house. The memory lingers, to be sure, but stripped of any redemptive power. The conclusions to the more pessimistic stories, such as "The Highwayman and the Saint," "The Diviner," "Stories on the Verandah," and "Everything Neat and Tidy," are more indicative of his later mood than stories like "The Illusionists." Even what pessimism exists in the early stories is deepened in the later plays.

From Story to Stage

Even though he had written eight plays for radio, television, and stage between 1958 and 1964, a number of things conspired to produce the popular misconception that Friel began his writing career as a short story writer. One reason, of course, was Friel's early success with *The New Yorker.* But also many of Friel's plays echo the stories in various ways. The themes of most of his early plays (prior to 1973) resemble those of the stories, particularly the theme of love and its disappointments. Several critics have pointed out how Friel's early plays suffered more than they gained from the influence of his story writing.[7] *Lovers* limply recast a previously published story—"The Highwayman and the Saint"—into dramatic form, but other plays also suffered from a conception of their subject matter that was more appropriate to storytelling than to dramatization. Friel himself also fostered the misconception; as late as 1965 he identified himself primarily as a short story writer: "I live on short stories. This is where my living comes from. As for playwriting it began as a sort of self-indulgence and then eventually I got caught up more and more in it. But the short story is the basis of all the work I do" (1965, 4).

Although it would be accurate to say that he first became known as a story writer, the actual sweep of his early career belies his self-identification as a story writer. Friel's first six publications, appearing between 1952 and 1960, included two stories, two radio plays, a stage production, and a nonfiction piece. The contract with *The New Yorker* undoubtedly had a lot to do with his emphasis on stories between 1960 and 1964, but in the midst of his *New Yorker* story-writing spree he produced two more stage plays (*The Enemy Within* and *The Blind Mice*) and decided that he needed to study playwriting in a more formal way. So in 1963 he took his family off for several months to Minneapolis to study with Tyrone Guthrie, who had just opened a new regional theatre there. Guthrie was working on *Hamlet* and Chekhov's *Three Sisters* at the time. Friel explains his situation then:

> I found myself at thirty years of age embarked on a theatrical career and almost totally ignorant of the mechanics of play-writing and play-production apart from an intuitive knowledge. Like a painter who has never studied anatomy; like a composer with no training in harmony. So I packed my bags and with my wife and two children went to Minneapolis in Minnesota where a new theatre was being created by Tyrone Guthrie and there I lived for six months. . . . I learned about the physical elements of plays, how they are designed, built, landscaped. I learned how actors thought, how they approached a text, their various ways of trying to realise it. (1972b, 19–20)

This sounds more like a frustrated playwright than someone who identifies himself with story writing. From his association with Guthrie Friel gained considerable self-confidence and assurance in his stagecraft. He

---

7. Deane, 1986b, 15–16; Fallis 1977, 272; Leary 1983, 130–33; Linehan 1967, 26.

said the experience "gave me courage and daring to attempt things" (1991, 56). The results were immediate and overwhelming. The first play he wrote after studying with Guthrie was *Philadelphia, Here I Come!*. It was unquestionably more assured in its dramaturgy than any previous play and after premiering in Dublin it went on to a long Broadway run. As the *New Yorker* contract enabled Friel to give up school teaching in 1960, the successful Broadway run of *Philadelphia, Here I Come!* enabled him to give up another not wholly satisfying career as a short story writer and devote his energies exclusively to his first love — the theater. He was beginning to recognize the limitations of his stories, particularly their derivative quality. He realized that he had not found his own voice and that he was mostly echoing O'Faolain and O'Connor (1982a, 21). He published his last story with *The New Yorker* in 1965 and has published none since.

Despite Friel's recognition about his limitations as a short story writer, his storytelling instincts nevertheless have continued to be the "basis" of many of his plays; they have, in fact, become a trademark of his dramaturgy. Throughout his career Friel often has employed narrative devices of one sort or another. As Tom Kilroy has noted, in Friel's plays "many of his effects are close to those of the novelist and short story writer. His plays consistently test the histrionic adaptability of these techniques, whether or not they can be made to work on stage" (1993, 91). Friel's penchant for narrative effects has been traced to an anecdotal tradition in Irish literature and to the Irish tradition of the *seanchaí* (Kilroy 1993, 98; Roche 1994, 115), as well as to his stint as a story writer. Kilroy says, "while our culture may have had no indigenous, native theatre prior to the eighteen-nineties it did have the *seanchaí*, a distinctively histrionic artist with his repertoire, his own audience. It was inevitable with such an oral tradition that the told-tale should be subsumed not only into the literary short story . . . but into the novel and emerging drama as well" (1993, 98).

As Friel's stagecraft matured he was much more successful at adapting his storytelling instincts to the stage. Sometimes the later adaptations are wholly successful and merit Kilroy's praise that "More subtly than any other Irish playwright Friel has transcribed this national skill into the theatrical medium" (1993, 98). "Foundry House," for instance, underwent a much more thorough and successful transformation into dramatic form than "The Highwayman and the Saint" when it was recast as *Aristocrats,* and Kilroy's favorite examples of Friel's storytelling art—*Living Quarters* and *Faith Healer*—achieve stunning narrative effects without sacrificing dramatic impact. Other late plays, however, never emerge as successful dramatic forms from their narrative materials—*Making History,* for example.

4

Apprenticeship
The Loves of Cass McGuire and the Early Plays

RIEL BEGAN WRITING PLAYS FOR RADIO IN 1958, but his earliest attempts were uncertain and not very accomplished in their dramaturgy. His first significant stage play was *The Enemy Within*, produced by
the Abbey in 1962. He had his first commercial success with *Philadelphia,
Here I Come!* (1964), which was followed in rapid succession by *The Loves
of Cass McGuire* (1966), *Lovers* (1967), *Crystal and Fox* (1968), *The Mundy
Scheme* (1969), and *The Gentle Island* (1971).

The typical pattern of criticism to date has tended to focus on the
links between these early plays and the short stories as a source of weak-
ness in Friel's dramaturgy, although some critics acknowledge that in
comparison with the stories the early plays are more psychologically
complex and technically more innovative (Leary 1983, 130; Ormsby 1970,
31). More important for the purposes of this book, however, is Friel's
treatment of myth and illusion in these early plays.

In these early plays Friel continued to explore the function of illusion
in psychic and social experience. The role of illusion is explored somewhat tentatively as leitmotif in *Philadelphia* and *Lovers;* then it is explored in detail in *Cass,* only to be resoundingly renounced in *Crystal and
Fox.* Of the seven stage plays produced between 1962 and 1971 (excluding
the unpublished *Blind Mice*), the earlier of them tend to focus primarily
on the illusions of individuals and how their illusions bind them to or
alienate them from their immediate social environment. Social, cultural, or historical backgrounds are sometimes present but secondary.
In *The Mundy Scheme* and *The Gentle Island,* however, the primary focus
shifts to broader social, cultural, and historical registers with the indi-

vidual characters becoming more illustrative or representative of these larger concerns.

After *The Gentle Island* most Friel critics agree that his plays open up more consistently toward the larger canvases of Irish history and culture (O'Brien 1989, 75–76). Whereas the short stories and the early plays typically explored various individual and social dimensions of rural life in the Irish republic, most of Friel's later plays focus on more public and political issues. The individual and social registers are not neglected, of course, but the public and the political registers become much more prominent in the plays. It appears that Friel came to conceive of drama as more appropriately functioning on these latter registers as opposed to the more limited horizons of the stories.

The overriding concern of Friel's plays on the public, political register is the inadequacy of the various myths or public illusions that the Irish republic chose to sustain itself, myths that try to create what Benedict Anderson (1991) characterizes as a homogenous imagined community. Having grown up in a traditional nationalist environment, Friel was especially well situated to examine these myths and their effects, and his plays taken as a whole constitute a profound exploration and critique of those myths as well as an attempt, on the cultural and symbolic register, to articulate some of the contradictions within those myths and between those myths and historical narratives of postcolonial Ireland. The central contradictions arose from the typical postcolonial desire to assert the difference between the emergent native culture and that of the former colonial power. Asserting this difference has been the primary function of the Gaelic, Catholic, peasant identity that has governed cultural productions since the beginning of the cultural revival in the 1880s, that guided the political ideology of the 1916 revolutionaries, and that shaped social and economic policy in the first decades of the Irish Free State after 1922. Irony and contradiction arose immediately, however, because, as Friel's *Translations* acknowledges, for better or worse the cultural, social, and political institutions of modern Ireland are profoundly and irrevocably Anglicized. This contradiction at the heart of Ireland's symbolic self-representation evidences itself in effects on the various registers from the individual to the social, the cultural, and the political. This contradiction also produces effects in the unresolved, and perhaps unresolvable, conflicts in cultural traditions that are playing themselves out most noticeably in Northern Ireland today. Friel began this process of examining Ireland's myths and self-representations in *The Mundy Scheme* and *The Gentle Island,* but it became the dominant focus of subsequent plays.

Friel's treatment of myth and illusion in these early plays anticipate the later plays. Often in the earlier plays myth and illusion are associated with nonrealistic experimental theater techniques, another mark of their postcolonial function in resisting the hegemonic realism of the imperial power. At this stage in his career, however, Friel had not yet articulated how language itself plays a constitutive role in the production of myths and illusions.

As with the short stories, Friel's early plays also suffered from underdeveloped aesthetics. Friel saw his function as a playwright rather conventionally as encouraging "sympathy and intelligence and understanding" for his characters through emotional identification. At this point he did not see the writer's job as getting across a social message or breaking down political or religious barriers. He specifically did not advocate a political drama like Osborne's (1965, 5).

Despite the lack of overt political content in these plays (excepting *The Mundy Scheme*), running through all of them is a distinct current of postcolonial malaise. The death or failure of life-sustaining illusions is a motif common to these plays. One of the syndromes seldom dealt with in postcolonial criticism is what might be called the postpartum depression of former colonies in the period following liberation. The period prior to liberation is characterized by intense nationalist mythologizing that projects a precolonial past into a future full of possibilities free from imperial interference. The euphoria that precedes and accompanies liberation soon must be replaced with the gritty, sobering negotiations of nation building. With the common enemy and cause of all colonial unhappiness removed, the newly liberated often turn on each other, as the Irish did in their civil war after the Anglo-Irish treaty. Even after the civil war the promise of nationhood became transformed into the much more sobering ideal of DeValera's frugal independence with its claustrophobic social policies and isolationist economic policies. It did not help that Irish independence soon was followed by worldwide economic depression. In a sense all Friel's plays articulate various forms of postcolonial disillusionment.

Besides articulating disillusionment, the early plays are postcolonial rather than colonial in another sense because in them, at the conscious level at least, Friel's subject position, with the exception of *The Enemy Within,* is that of a citizen of the Republic of Ireland rather than of Northern Ireland. In its constitution the Irish republic still claims the territory of Northern Ireland and extends citizenship to all its inhabitants, and in 1967 Friel and his wife moved from Derry to Donegal. Even before the move, however, as a writer Friel identified more with his Irish citizenship than with his British citizenship of Northern Ireland.

Six Early Plays

The Enemy Within, first performed at the Abbey in 1962 and the earliest play Friel wrote that he cared to publish, focuses primarily on the struggle within St. Columba (suggested by the title) between his allegiance to his family, which draws him into their political and military squabbles, and his allegiance to his religious calling. In the end spirit triumphs somewhat conventionally over worldliness. Illusion does not play a significant role in this play, but Friel does cast the internal struggle of Columba between his allegiance to his family and his allegiance to his spiritual vocation as a contrast between competing discourses, between a nationalist rhetoric of nostalgia and a biblical rhetoric of spiritual aspiration. Unfortunately for the play's conclusion and its thematic thrust, the discourse of spiritual aspiration lacks the energy and emotional power of the traditional Irish nationalist discourses of kinship and of nostalgia for the land. Even though Columba is the most sympathetic portrait of a priest in Friel's published canon, Friel's more powerful identification with the nationalist tradition than with the Maynooth tradition he once rejected seems to inhibit an effective dramatic balance here. Even though we may understand in the end why Columba rejects the nostalgic appeal of home and family, because of the rhetorical imbalance we are not made to feel the passion of the struggle. Moreover, Friel's awareness of the link between discourse and identity is rudimentary in this play. It remained for Friel in later plays to articulate the link between illusion and self-image, and in still later plays to see the more complex links among language, illusion, and identity. Nevertheless, in its central concern with conflicting self-images, the play anticipates in form as well as in theme the conflict between two competing allegiances represented in Friel's portrait of Hugh O'Neill in *Making History*.

On the thematic register, it is not difficult to see Columba's dilemma as a thinly disguised figure for the dilemma of the artist in a highly charged political atmosphere like Northern Ireland. Torn between his God and his *patria* (as Joyce dubbed the combined temptation of family and country), Columba, like Joyce, refuses the call of Cathleen ni Houlihan to sacrifice his soul for his country. Thus Columba also anticipates Frank Hardy of *Faith Healer* as a type of artist. In this sense Columba's struggle could be read metaphorically as the plight of writers, particularly Northern Irish writers, caught between the demands of a virulent political ideology and the demands of their art. Although the latest round of troubles had not yet begun in Northern Ireland, Friel may already have internalized the tensions and in the figure of Columba resolved, intellectually at least, to resist the lure of politics in his art. The rhetorical and emotional register of the play, however, turns out to be a better indicator of Friel's future direction.

It has already become commonplace in Friel criticism to see the next four plays *Philadelphia, Here I Come!, The Loves of Cass McGuire, Lovers,* and *Crystal and Fox* as a quartet in which Friel explores the theme of love from various angles. Friel himself has lent credence to this view (Bell 1972, 106; Friel 1982a, 22). Such a view of these four plays, however, tends to isolate them from other Friel texts. By contrast, a focus on illusion integrates this quartet into a more continuous development by linking them to the stories that preceded them as well as to the more mature plays that succeeded them.

If *The Enemy Within,* by virtue of its production at the Abbey, gave Friel his first significant recognition as a dramatist in Ireland (Dantanus 1988, 83; Maxwell 1973, 61), *Philadelphia, Here I Come!* announced his entry onto the international scene. Although critical consensus favors *Philadelphia, Here I Come!* as the outstanding play of these early texts, and notwithstanding its commercial success, *Philadelphia* is perhaps Friel's most overrated play.[1] Reviewing a 1994 revival of the play in New York, Vincent Canby accounts for its popularity in the face of its limitations: "*Philadelphia, Here I Come!* is not a great play, but it's a bewitchingly actable one" (1994, H 5). Its actability marked a considerable advance in Friel's stagecraft that undoubtedly can be attributed to his sojourn with Tyrone Guthrie. The assurance Friel gained from his stay with Guthrie showed up most notably in a willingness to experiment with dramatic form that has characterized all his subsequent plays. *Philadelphia, Here I Come!* has two experimental components, both of which concern us here — the splitting of the protagonist into two characters played by two different actors and the illusions of memory that highlight the conflict between father and son.

The split protagonist in *Philadelphia* has nothing to do with the modernist interest in the divided self and schizophrenic personalities, or, as Elmer Andrews claims, with the postmodern concern with "dismantling the unified subject" (1995, 76), but rather with a much more conventional post-Romantic conception of an inner and an outer self, which Friel explains in stage directions that preface the play:

> The two Gars, PUBLIC GAR and PRIVATE GAR, are two views of the one man. PUBLIC GAR is the Gar that people see, talk to, talk about. PRIVATE GAR is the unseen man, the man within, the conscience, the *alter ego*, the secret thoughts, the id. PRIVATE GAR, the spirit, is invisible to everybody, always. Nobody except PUBLIC GAR hears him talk. But even PUBLIC GAR, although he talks to PRIVATE GAR occasionally, never sees him and *never looks at him*. One cannot look at one's *alter ego*. (*SP*, 27; Friel's emphases)

The confusion of conscience, ego, and id suggests the rudimentary quality of Friel's post-Romantic conception of the self here. Even though this dramatic device provides all the liveliness and humor of the play, the notion of identity operating here is distinctly a premodernist unitary personality split into two voices, one which utters what is acceptable and the other which utters what one would really like to say if one were not

1. For overestimations see E. Andrews 1995, 84–95; Levin 1972, 132–33; O'Brien 1989, 51. For a negative assessment see Kaufmann 1966, 28.

so inhibited. There is no real conflict between these two selves. In addition to its actability, that this device also represents a fairly common and conventional notion of the self undoubtedly accounts for much of the popularity of the play.

The central struggle in the play, however, is not between the public and the private self, but between Gar, both public and private, and his father S. B. Unfortunately the structure of the play focuses primary attention on neither the split protagonist nor his troubled relationship with his father but on the issue of emigration. Although the emigration motif is not unrelated to the struggle for the father's affection, by foregrounding it Friel disperses the emotional energy of the play and denies the son's struggle for paternal affection the depth and intensity it deserves.

What power and depth there is to the father-son relationship in *Philadelphia, Here I Come!*, is built around a memory device modeled on Friel's own childhood memory of the fishing trip with his father he discusses in "Self-Portrait." This is the most important moment in the play, yet rather than culminating the previous series of incidents, it culminates what has been essentially a leitmotif in the previous two episodes. Both Gar and his father remember scenes with each other from the past, or rather they misremember them because both have apparently altered details of the scenes. But as Friel realized with his own personal memory, the accuracy of details is not important. What is important is the desire they express, the lack they represent — Gar's desire for a father he never had and S. B.'s desire for a son he never had. Gar's memory represents an intimate connection with a father who exhibits tender solicitousness and is happy just to be with his son fishing. S. B.'s memory represents a son who wishes to emulate his father. The irony is that the connection fails in part because Gar *is* much like his father — an emotional cripple incapable of intimacy. This is a typically Irish disability born perhaps of generations of colonial servitude in which fathers, deprived of self-respect and self-confidence, were particularly inept or inhibited in providing a role model for their sons and all the intimacy that would entail. Even some Irish-American father-son relationships have inherited this disability.

For all its innovative stagecraft, *Philadelphia, Here I Come!* remains within the milieu of the stories aimed at an American audience. The play deals with all the charming clichés of Irish life Friel thinks American audiences are interested in. He was right. *Philadelphia, Here I Come!* had the longest Broadway run of any Irish play up to that time (326 performances) (1980a). As Seamus Deane points out, *Philadelphia, Here I Come!* "was a virtuoso performance of the kind of Irish eloquence which had come to be expected from Irish playwrights" (1986b, 16). But the subject matter was very familiar territory and the play's theatrical innovations are flawed. The split protagonist is eminently actable and charming, but it is based on a rather superficial notion of the self. The misremembered memories highlight the emotional alienation of Gar from his father, but the power of that alienation is dissipated among other elements of the play. Despite these problems, the play's success gave Friel a great deal of confidence as a playwright and he soon ceased to identify himself as a short story writer.

The Loves of Cass McGuire is a much more profound and complex exploration of the deprivations of love than *Philadelphia*, and its experimental devices are both more extensive and more sophisticated. Although *Cass* opened on Broadway, it never had the popular success or appeal of *Philadelphia, Here I Come!*. Compared to *Philadelphia*, *Cass* is more pessimistic, less sentimental, less inclined to assuage painful emotions with light comedy, more experimental, and more demanding of a sophisticated and thoughtful audience. Broadway was not the right venue for this play. *Cass* also has a much more complex protagonist than *Philadelphia*. I disagree with the assessment of Ulf Dantanus that *Cass* "does not possess the same steady and fluent integrity that characterizes *Philadelphia, Here I Come!*" (1988, 106). On the contrary, the play has much more structural integrity in developing its central focus, which like *Philadelphia* deals with frustrated love, with desire that can find no appropriate love object. Despite its tragedy and pessimism, however, there is also much humor in *Cass*, but compared to the humor in *Philadelphia* it is harder, grimmer, more biting, more Beckettian. More so than *Philadelphia, Here I Come!*, *The Loves of Cass McGuire* is the gem of Friel's early plays, and it deserves to be included in his *Selected Plays* alongside *Philadelphia* if not in its place. *Cass* also serves much better than *Philadelphia* as a bridge between the early stories and the later plays. Moreover, its intellectual sophistication, dense texture, more disciplined structure, and extensive theatrical experimentation are better indications of Friel's mature strengths in later plays, such as *The Freedom of the City*, *Aristocrats*, *Faith Healer*, and *Translations*. A detailed discussion of *Cass* appears at the end of this chapter.

Like *Philadelphia, Here I Come!* and *The Loves of Cass McGuire*, *Lovers*, which premiered at Dublin's Gate Theater in 1967, continues to explore various facets of love in contemporary rural Ireland. *Lovers* focuses primarily on romantic love and its inevitable withering within the institution of marriage. The play has two experimental devices: 1) the play is divided into two parts, "Winners" and "Losers," that are linked thematically but not narratively; and 2) "Winners" uses two impersonal narrators. *Lovers* is a slighter play than either *Cass* or *Philadelphia*, perhaps because its tone, mood, and handling are still rooted too much in Friel's short stories. "Losers," in fact, is simply a stage adaptation of the story "The Highwayman and the Saint"; but "Winners" too has more the feel of the stories rather than of the plays that immediately preceded it. Taken together, "Winners" and "Losers" suggests that pious conventions and the pressures to conform to social mores strangle whatever limited potential there may be for fulfilling love relationships in Irish society. In the world of this play winners are those who have not yet had the hopes, dreams, and illusions love feeds upon crushed by a social environment so barren and bleak that only twisted and perverse simulacra of healthy hopes and dreams can survive. The winners escape because they die young. The survivors lose anything worth living for, but their fate appears more pathetic than tragic because the protagonists of "Losers" lack any capacity for feeling and suffering. The device of the narrators in "Winners" contextualizes what is happening in the stage present in terms of both past and future, but the device has none of the resonance of the narrative devices in later plays, such as *Living Quarters* and *Dancing at Lughnasa*. The profound mood of disillusionment in *Lovers* depicts the postcolonial Republic at the end of the age of DeValera as claustrophobic and suffocating.

Friel's next play *Crystal and Fox* explores the possibility of life without illusion. Fox Melarkey, who runs an itinerant variety show, is determined to strip away all redeeming illusions. As a traveling showman who traffics in illusion, he anticipates Frank Hardy of *Faith Healer* as a type of artist whose tricks of the trade give him an intuitive if inarticulate un-derstanding of life's tricks. When Fox plays at his own game of life, he carries over his awareness of how things are rigged and how illusions are made. Despite his profession, or perhaps because of it, and notwith-standing the connotations of his surname, Fox has a vague, undefined yet powerful desire to face life down without props. Like many of Beck-ett's characters, he strips life bare, but unlike Beckett's characters, he does it without humor and without the compulsiveness to continue the game. He wants to dismiss the rules and end the game. Friel leaves him at the end terribly alone with nowhere to go, nothing to do, no game to play, no show to go on. In some ways Fox is an extended development of Pat Quinn from *The Loves of Cass McGuire*, a character whose function is to unmask the illusions of others. But Fox, more percipient than Pat, de-mythologizes himself as well, an unmasking so complete that it leaves him and his life an empty shell. When Fox has peeled away the last layer of the onion, he is left face to face with the nothingness at the center of it all. In the face of such knowledge hope departs and love no longer suf-fices. Fox refuses to entertain any illusions that he can win again; he has been running the games too long for that foolish hope. Unfortunately for this play, the audience is no more enlightened than the uncomprehend-ing Fox at the end. We never understand Fox's motives; we never fathom his pathology.

As with other Friel plays, the role illusion plays in *Crystal and Fox* is typically misread by critics with conventional notions about illusion and reality. Maxwell, for instance, says, "In his own small community, Fox sees through the simple-hearted panaceas for human discontents" (1973, 94). Such a statement does not begin to perceive the ground Friel is working in this play. George O'Brien is closer to the mark when he says, "The play devours itself: when there are no more masks for Fox to wear, the play ends. Without illusion there can be no theater; without uncer-tainty there can be no reality" (1989, 55). In the end what Fox seems to discover is that when all plays are done, all tricks unmasked, the reality we are left with, the nothingness, the Joycean void that the magical illu-sions of language have masked from our vision, is nothing worth having.

Prior to that period characterized by the full power of his maturity as a writer, Friel wrote two other plays that belong to his early period of development — *The Mundy Scheme,* a political satire, and *The Gentle Island,* a play as dark and troubling as *Crystal and Fox.* Both these plays move beyond the function of illusion in negotiating between individuals and their immediate social environment to more public political and cultural registers. They both serve as a critique of certain political and social myths prevalent in postcolonial Ireland. They still belong to this early phase, however, because they lack the sophisticated awareness of how these myths are produced as effects of language and discourse.

The Mundy Scheme is a facile but entertaining satire on how the postcolonial Republic has realized the ideals of its 1916 martyrs. The premise of the play is established in a prelude spoken by a disembodied voice:

> Ladies and gentlemen: What happens when a small nation that has been manipulated and abused by a huge colonial power for hundreds of years wrests its freedom by blood and anguish? What happens to an emerging country after it has emerged? Does the transition from dependence to independence induce a fatigue, a mediocrity, an ennui? Or does the clean spirit of idealism that fired the people to freedom augment itself, grow bolder, more revolutionary, more generous? (*TP,* 157)

The play answers the last question in the negative and the penultimate question in the positive.

The protagonist of *The Mundy Scheme* is the Taoiseach F. X. Ryan. He is a former auctioneer with interests in real estate. In order to strengthen his political position he is seduced by an economic panacea proposed by a Texan, Irish-American, real estate millionaire by the name of Homer Mundy. His scheme would turn the unproductive mountains, hills, and bogs of the West of Ireland into a cemetery for the space-starved urban capitals of industrial countries. This scheme supposedly would bring prosperity, roads, tourism, and employment to Ireland's most economically depressed counties and it would be a much more palatable alternative than providing naval bases for the U.S., which would undermine Ireland's international position of strategic neutrality. The scheme would also enable Ryan and his relatives to make millions by buying up land in the West of Ireland. In the end Ryan double-crosses his collaborators by setting them up for public scandals so that he is left to reap the personal benefits of the Mundy scheme for himself.

The Mundy Scheme has had little appeal for critics.[2] Although it is competent satire, it is unremarkable. There is no technical experimentation and not much ingenuity of plot. Its effects are broad rather than subtle or refined, and its chief value is perhaps the insight it provides into Friel's political opinions at this point. Friel's satirical targets in this play include the character of politicians, the perennial economic problems of the West of Ireland, and, perhaps more importantly, the myths deployed by government officials to mask the crass commercialism and corruption of their enterprises. Those myths include the revolutionary hopes of 1916, the West of Ireland as the symbol of Irishness, and Ireland's neutrality as symbolic of its place among nations. Friel's view of the leaders of the Irish republic in *The Mundy Scheme* resembles that of Yeats, who railed against the paudeens and gombeen men the new democratic Free State produced as leaders. These views do not differ markedly from those of other Irish intellectuals since Yeats who have been dismayed by the impoverishment of intellect and imagination displayed by a succession of government administrations since 1922, by the betrayal of idealism, by the hypocritical, petty-minded, self-serving nature of the political animal, by the absence of statesmanship, by the prevalence of commercialism, and so forth. *The Mundy Scheme* also anticipates the dissatisfaction of postcolonial critics like Eagleton and Lloyd with the compromised idealism of bourgeois nationalism that has dominated postindependence Ireland. Although Friel's satiric perspective perceives Irish leaders as seriously compromising the idealism of 1916, Friel himself soon became more skeptical of the latter-day manifestations of that idealism in Northern Ireland. With the founding of Field Day in 1980 Friel aligned himself with the new nationalism of John Hume and the SDLP (Social Democratic and Labour Party) in Northern Ireland, which offered Northern nationalists a moderate bourgeois alternative to the more radical, working-class-based politics of Sinn Fein.

2. Milton Levin calls it "a clever cartoon, but not much more than a cartoon" (1972, 135), but that judgment is perhaps too severe. Maxwell may be closer to the mark when he says, "Its metaphorical felicity is not brought finally into line with the serious satirical purposes" (1973, 87). Metaphorically *The Mundy Scheme* is very thin and has little to offer.

Like *The Mundy Scheme, The Gentle Island* focuses on the myth of the rural West as the bedrock of Irish values, and like Patrick Kavanagh's poem *The Great Hunger,* it demystifies the myth of Gaelic rural innocence as the foundation for family and social values for the Irish nation. The play is nothing less than a savage attack on that myth. This time, however, the mode is not satire but rather a bleak, naturalistic tragedy that portrays peasant life in the West as visceral, vengeful, and without redeeming virtue. The technique of the play is straightforward naturalism with no experimental devices.

The romantic peasant ideal Friel unmasks in this play is articulated by a gay Dublin couple who arrive on the island of Inishkeen (whose Gaelic name means "the gentle island") on holiday just after it has been depopulated by all but one family. In mock imitation of the social ideals of newly independent Ireland, Shane extols "the simple, upright, hardworking island peasant holding on manfully to the *real* values in life, sustained by a thousand-year-old culture, preserving for my people a really worthwhile inheritance" (*GI,* 37; Friel's emphasis). Shane's partner Peter, who lacks Shane's sense of irony, romanticizes Inishkeen according to the common myth: "the sea, the land, fishing, turf-cutting, milking, a house built by your great-grandfather, two strong sons to succeed you — everything's so damned constant. You're part of a permanence" (*GI,* 53).

Peter's kind of tourist-board nationalism and nostalgia for the Gaelic peasant life maintained a considerable hold over the Irish imagination for decades after independence. It permeated art and literature, it was promoted by the Catholic Church, and it governed social and economic policy.[3] And it is by no means dead today. Shane, however, sees through the myth to something more disturbing and sinister. If debunking the myth of an idyllic Gaelic innocence is the thematic thrust of this play, sex and violence are the vehicles. In addition to many images of violence, the visceral nature of the peasant sexuality in this play is established from the beginning. In comparison with the peasant sexuality of Inishkeen, the homosexual relationship between Shane and Peter, based on mutual caring and respect, is depicted as sane and civilized.

3. See, for example, Brown 1985.   ·

Although there is no technical experimentation in the play, as a leit-motif Friel does emphasize how "There's ways and ways of telling every story" (*GI*, 56). There are alternative versions to stories and events in the play, and the audience is given no privileged information about them. The motif, however, does not have much resonance in this play as it does, for example, in *The Loves of Cass McGuire*. In the end it does not matter whose story we believe. Regardless of what actually happened, the characterization of rural Ireland in this play is devastating. It would be an even more powerful debunking of Irish social and political myths if it were a better play, for *The Gentle Island* also suffers from other tech-nical problems. In execution it is too straightforward and obvious; it lacks the subtlety Friel exhibits in other plays. In style its bleak natural-ism is closer to *Crystal and Fox* than any other play. Perhaps the major technical problem is with characterization. Much violence is foreshad-owed in the characters of Manus and Philly, but Sarah, whose character early in the play exhibited only a love of dancing and society, becomes the dark avenging angel while Manus wavers and Philly turns out to be harmless.

A more serious problem is the anger and bitterness with which Friel unmasks the myth of Gaelic innocence as the source for family and so-cial values. As Seamus Deane says, "in *The Gentle Island* . . . Friel turned on all the illusions of pastoralism, ancestral feeling, and local piety that had been implicit in his dramatization of the world of Ballybeg. . . . The delicate tensions which had been so finely balanced in *Philadelphia* are now surrendered in an almost vengeful spirit" (1986b, 15). In unmasking other myths Friel usually tempers his critical eye with a sympathetic un-derstanding that enables us to empathize more with the suffering of the characters. We do empathize with Shane and Peter, but this raises an-other problem with characterization: they are not the protagonists; this is not their play.

It appears that *The Gentle Island* along with *The Mundy Scheme*, and perhaps even *Crystal and Fox* and *Lovers*, were written during a period of Friel's development that gradually darkened with anger toward Irish so-ciety. In these plays he attacks repressions (particularly sexual repres-sions), pressures toward conformity (especially in religious and social mores), and political and social myths. A common theme in these plays appears to be the failure of hopes, illusions, and myths as sources of redeeming values and the author's growing anger in the face of recognizing that failure.

The Loves of Cass McGuire

Of all Friel's early plays his most profound and ambitious exploration of the social and psychological functions of illusion is *The Loves of Cass McGuire*. More so than the other early plays, it deserves as well as rewards a more detailed analysis.

Cass is about a returning emigré. She could be a female Gar returning to the old sod after fifty-two years working in a hash house on the edge of the Bowery. Her experience in New York bears out Gar's misgivings about America objectified in the shallow, garish vulgarity of his Aunt Lizzie. As Terence Brown points out, *The Loves of Cass McGuire* has "caught a poignant moment of transition in Irish/Irish-American relations focusing at just that point in social history when an economically resurgent country, with its eyes on membership of the European Community, was beginning to recover from its infatuation with all things American (that infatuation reaching hysterical proportions during John Kennedy's all too brief Presidency and a kind of orgasmic intensity during his visit to the land of his forbears in 1963)" (1993, 190).

Cass is vulgar if nothing else; however, she is not shallow. Friel's description of her in the stage directions captures her balance of vulgarity and emotional depth: "Ugly is too strong a word to describe her, and plain not nearly strong enough. If she ever had good features once, there is no trace of them now. A life of hard physical work has ravaged her. Only her spirit is strong and resilient" (CM, 14). Much of the humor of the play results from the insertion of Cass's frank vulgarity into the provincial respectability of her brother's well-to-do, upper-middle-class family. The setting is not Ballybeg, which is probably too remote for this play, but perhaps a somewhat more upscale town closer to Dublin.

The plot of *Cass* is simple: at age seventy Cass's options in New York, where she cohabited with the owner of the hash house, have run out. She returns to Ireland expecting to be welcomed by her brother's family, to whom she had sent ten dollars each month faithfully for fifty-two years plus gift money for the children at Christmas times and birthdays. Her brother Harry, however, is a very successful businessman-accountant, and he and his wife Alice find Cass's Bowery manners and style intolerable. It turns out that they have saved every penny Cass sent them, including her gift money, because they "never really needed it." Harry proudly informs Cass that, including accumulated interest, she has accumulated a tidy nest egg of more than $7,000 or £2500 that will make her "independent of everyone" (*CM*, 40–41). While Harry is proud of this callous bourgeois gesture and oblivious to its emotional impact, Cass is dismayed by the refusal of her love gesture and by the implications of that refusal, implications that are soon realized when she is sent to Eden House, a retirement home where she can live out her life "independent of everyone" with other equally deserted and desolate souls.

While the melodramatic plot is simple, its execution is complex, too complex for a Broadway production. The complexity results primarily from four experimental devices Friel employs in the play—characters seeking control of the narrative, repressed memory sequences, direct addresses to the audience, and a sequence of "rhapsodies" that rewrite the past. Friel did not invent these devices but adapted them from playwrights such as Pirandello, Arthur Miller, Eugene O'Neill, Tennessee Williams, and Samuel Beckett, who had used them successfully in the past. All these devices deal in some way with the nature, structure, and function of illusion and all of them, at the unconscious level at least, replicate structures of the (post)colonial psyche. These devices, more so than anything in the plot, explore the emotional and psychic needs of the characters much more profoundly than the two Gars device or the misrememberings in *Philadelphia, Here I Come!*. Indeed, the experimentation in *Cass* exceeds anything Friel had done before.

The first of these devices, echoing Pirandello's *Six Characters in Search of an Author*, has Cass and Harry operating at the levels of both character and author in fighting for control of the script. The play begins with Harry and his family revealing the sequence of events that led to their committing Cass to Eden House. Their representation, of course, suggests the inevitability of their decision—Cass got drunk, caused considerable damage at a local pub, called her deaf mother a big cow, and sang half the night in her room. Naturally, behavior of this sort is unacceptable for a respectable upper-middle-class family. As these revelations mount, Cass enters and insists that the story start "with me stuck in the gawddamn workhouse" (CM, 15), as Cass insists on calling Eden House. (It was built on the site of the old workhouse.) Like Manus in *The Gentle Island*, both Cass and Harry realize the importance of how a story is told. Control of the script obviously entails shaping its meaning and significance. Harry, who wishes to assert his patriarchal privilege of logocentric control of the discourse, says, "It must be shown slowly and in sequence why you went to Eden House." But Cass resists against all logic and temporality. When upon her first entrance her brother insists that the story has already begun, Cass, who wants to shift the direction and disrupt the temporal sequence of the narrative, replies, "The story begins where I say it begins" (CM, 15). After she successfully wrests control of the narrative from Harry, the play proceeds but not "slowly and in sequence." Instead the scene in Harry's living room suddenly becomes the common room at Eden House, a transition prepared for in the set directions, and the plot henceforth bumps along in nonlinear twists and turns that combine memory, illusion, action in the stage present, and monologues to the audience. At the very beginning Harry has his way, but in the end it is Cass's play. And Friel, with his Pirandellian device, has it both ways. The only difficulty with this device structurally is that Friel does not follow up on it. It never reappears, unless you count a couple of instances where Cass comments on the peculiarity of the title of the play (CM, 23, 44). Perhaps the device, once it accomplished its purpose for Friel, was no longer needed. Although it could be argued that the characters' self-consciousness about being in a play metamorphoses into another of the nonrealistic devices—Cass's addresses to the audience—an allusion to the struggle to control the plot toward the end would have been more satisfying aesthetically.

Although Cass successfully wrests control of the narrative away from Harry, she does not have full control of it. Her purported purpose in redirecting the narrative is not only to keep Harry on the hook about sending her to Eden House but also to repress the painful memories of the past, particularly her rejection by her family upon her homecoming. She says,

So we're going to skip all that early stuff, all the explanations, all the ex-
cuses, and we'll start off later in the story—from here. (*Light up bed area*)
My suite in the workhouse, folks. Drop in and see me some time, okay?
Where the hell was I? (*Remembering*) Yeah—the homecoming—back to
the little green isle. Well, that's all over and done with—history; and in
my book yesterday's dead and gone and forgotten. . . . And they'll [i.e.,
the audience] see what happens in the order *I* [Friel's emphasis] want
them to see it; and there will be no going back into the past! (*CM*, 16)

Although Cass insists that she lives only in the present, Harry, while he
may have lost control of the script, is right when he tells Cass, "You may
think you can seal off your mind like this, but you can't. The past will
keep coming back to you" (*CM*, 16). In fact, the painful scenes of the first
few days of her homecoming recur throughout acts 1 and 2, at first tentatively against Cass's resistance but then much more insistently as the
play progresses.

These memory sequences constitute the second nonrealistic device
Friel uses in *Cass*. They somewhat resemble those used by Miller in *Death
of a Salesman*. All the memory sequences deal with the portion of the
narrative Harry wanted to begin with and Cass wished to suppress, that
is, the homecoming period between Cass's return to Ireland and her
commitment to Eden House. Cass's painful rejection by her family obviously distresses her, especially given the loveless conclusion of her New
York experience. She says that she left after the death of Jeff Olsen, her
one-legged boss, lover, and cohabitant, but this version of her departure
is challenged by Pat Quinn, the resident Barthean mythographer of
Eden House who demystifies the myths of all the other residents for us.
According to Pat, Jeff Olsen threw her out. The memories, then, represent the loss of what Cass so desperately sought by coming home—family and acceptance by them.

One of her most painful memories is the discussion with Harry about
her father's death. She was especially close to her father, and one of the
few times Harry wrote to her was to inform her of his death, but she got
the news three weeks after he was buried. Her drunken spree at Sweeney's pub came on a day when she had visited her father's grave. In a
sense, she experienced his loss at least three times: first when he left
home for Scotland because he could not get along with her mother; a
second time when she was denied the purging ritual of attending his fu-

neral; and finally when visiting his grave evoked the lifelong loss yet again. Harry, who assumes the place of the father after his death, reduplicates the experience of paternal rejection for Cass. Cass's almost total lack of connection with her dotard mother causes her no difficulty at all in contrast with the dead father. This suggests that the maternal connection was much less important for Cass, as it appears to have been for Friel. Or perhaps it would be more accurate to say that the pain Cass must come to terms with in this play, as in *Philadelphia, Here I Come!* and other Friel texts, derives from the double necessity of the (post)colonial father to be and his failure to be an adequate object of desire.

Despite Cass's efforts to resist these memories—"I don't go in for the fond-memory racket," she says (*CM*, 19)—they are enacted on stage (the setting is Eden House) with the various family members appearing to replay them with Cass. When Cass resists these memories, she usually returns to an earlier memory either about her life in New York or about her life in Ireland before she left. Cass narrates these earlier memories to the audience as she tries to ignore the presence, in her mind and on stage, of the family members. Gradually Cass's resistance to replaying these memories breaks down. By act 2 almost no resistance remains to fight off the pivotal memory about the money she had sent home. By the end of the act she is completely at the mercy of these memories and is broken by them. By act 3 all the homecoming memories have been played out and they are replaced by an actual visit to Eden House by Harry and his family and by a rhapsodic delusion, the means by which other Eden House residents rewrite the intolerably painful experiences of their past into a revised history of happiness and fulfillment.

The delusions of Eden House become the focus of the third nonrealistic device—the "rhapsodies," which are reminiscent of O'Neill and Tennessee Williams (E. Andrews 1995, 99). In each act one resident of Eden House (Trilbe in act 1, Ingram in act 2, and Cass in act 3) sits in a special winged chair ("Downstage right, conspicuous in its isolation" [*CM*, 8]) reserved for that purpose. In an introductory note to the play Friel explains that he saw these three rhapsodies "as part of the formal pattern or ritual of the action" and that the musical term "rhapsody" seemed appropriate for a play he conceived musically as "a concerto in which Cass McGuire is the soloist." Friel says, "Each of the three characters who rhapsodize — Trilbe, Ingram, and Cass — takes the shabby and unpromising threads of his or her past life and weaves it [sic] into a hymn of joy, a gay and rapturous and exaggerated celebration of a beauty that might have been" (CM, 7). Trilbe converts a banal, penurious, spinsterly life as an unqualified, migrant elocution teacher into high romance, worthy of her fictional namesake,[4] where she marries a wealthy Scot in France (her "prince from Edinburgh in Provence" [CM, 30]), lives in a chateau on the Loire, and becomes a world traveler. In his fantasy Mr. Ingram marries eighteen-year-old Stella, a ballet dancer who drowned tragically on their rapturous honeymoon in the south of England. With the help of a German prince and his yacht they searched for her body for nine days but never found her. According to Pat Quinn, the resident cynic of Eden House who called Trilbe a "tramp with notions" (CM, 22), what actually happened was that Ingram, an organist in an English cathedral, fell in love with a music-hall dancer, followed her all over England, married her to the dismay of his family, and two days after the wedding his new bride eloped with a German count on his yacht, never to be seen again. In Cass's rhapsody she marries Jeff Olsen, who becomes a distinguished gentleman. Her father attends the wedding, and she and Jeff live in a huge apartment on New York's West Side. She remains close to her brother's family, and after Jeff dies, when she returns to Ireland she has a magnificent homecoming. Brother Harry sets up a parade of chauffeured limousines and she goes out walking with her old lover Connie. In her revised life Cass is the one who insists that she move out of Harry's home, but instead of Eden House she moves to a seaside cottage where she entertains the family frequently.

These rhapsodies lead to the question of what is real and how reality relates to the transformations of memory and desire. In Cass there are several competing levels of truth or reality and they are not necessarily compatible with one another. The rhapsodies, for instance, are clearly symbolic representations of desire; that is, they represent less what may have actually happened than the intense desire for love, or at least the desire for having been loved. We know that they are transformations of the

4. Trilby O'Ferrall is the protagonist of the 1894 romance novel Trilby. The name O'Ferrall, according to Dantanus, is another variant of Friel (1988, 31).

character's lived history because we have other versions of the events involved. In the case of Trilbe and Ingram we have Pat Quinn's alternative
version of their lives and loves. In the case of Cass we have her own earlier narratives that conflict with her rhapsody. But Pat's versions and
Cass's earlier narratives are also suspect to a certain extent. They are
probably closer to what we the audience would accept as actual history,
but they themselves are transformations of the real. Cass's narrative
about why she left New York (Jeff Olsen died) is contradicted by Pat who
claims Jeff threw her out. We don't know who to believe here, although
the vehemence of Cass's response to Pat suggests that Pat may be right.
We do believe him about Trilbe and Ingram because the alternatives—
the rhapsodies—are so much less credible. But even Pat's versions are
not certain—only more probable. Moreover, his versions need to be interpreted as well. All of Pat's counternarratives are transformed by his
own quality of cynicism that sets him apart from the other inhabitants of
Eden House and preserves him from their delusional fates. As Trilbe
says, "He never really belonged . . . he was never fully one of us" (CM,
64). But Pat himself is subject to a degree of delusion. Although his
claims about prospects for leaving Eden House turn out to be true, his
claim that his nephew cannot manage without him is countered by a
message from the nephew delivered by Tessa (the maid at Eden House):
"He says if you want to stay that suits him" (CM, 60).

Whatever claims to truth, reality, or actuality we wish to accept in this
play, then, must be read through the transformations of desire they undergo. In other words, we have no unmediated access to the truth. The
rhetorical features of the rhapsodies—that they take place in the isolated
winged chair, that they employ the exaggerated tropes and conventions
of romance novels like *Trilby*, that they are contradicted by other narratives—lead us to reject them as representations of actual lived history,
though not as representations of severe psychic deprivation.

We find Cass's own narratives more credible than the rhapsodies because her sardonic wit distances herself, at least initially, from the delusions of Eden House. But her narratives too are full of cracks and
contradictions. Through the stories she tells about Jeff and other New
York people and the connections she felt with them, we glimpse a
poverty of spirit and disaffection as well. She feels Jeff liked her though

he did not show it. One story she tells is about a cheap, garish Irish brooch Jeff gave her one Christmas. She was so touched at this rare demonstration of affection that she began to cry. Whereupon Jeff said he did not buy it but traded "some Irish bum a ham and cheese sandwich for it." "And, Gawd," says Cass, "I cried all the more then . . . must ov been real drunk . . . you know, he was so kind to me" (*CM*, 34–35). We have no way to verify whether Jeff bought the brooch or not. He may have said he traded for it out of embarrassment over her crying. Nor can we be sure that Jeff ever gave her a brooch in the first place. All the brooch incident represents is the quality of her relationship with Jeff, and the representation must be read and it can be read differently. To Cass the story represents how kind Jeff was to her. We the audience probably read it as a rather pathetic gesture of minimal affection with the pathos heightened by Cass's overeager response conditioned by a lifetime of emotional deprivation. Most of her stories about New York hint at the emotional poverty of her situation there: Jeff, we are told, "had a wife somewhere on the West Coast" (*CM*, 31).

Her chronic deprivation is part of the reason Cass prefers to discount history: she says, "I dunno . . . this gawddamn going back into the past! Who the hell knows what happened in the past!" (*CM*, 47). She claims to regret nothing. Despite her dismissal of the past, however, Cass plunges into the past and regrets everything—her relationship with her father, her relationship with her teen-age lover Connie, the New York scene, her homecoming with Harry. Clearly she desperately wants only to look ahead because the Skid Row washouts she knew seem dangerously close to her own destiny and threaten to drag her into identifying her own fate with theirs if she allows herself to reflect on her own past. But reflecting on her past is just what Friel forces upon her throughout the play, and when the weight of that past proves overwhelming, rather than face it or embrace it as her fate, her psyche opts for a delusional rewriting of it.

Each of the three rhapsodies concludes with lines from Yeats's poem "He Wishes for the Cloths of Heaven," lines that serve as a refrain for the play:

But I, being poor, have only my dreams;
I have spread my dreams under your feet;
Tread softly because you tread on my dreams. (1983, 73)

Trilbe and Ingram recite these lines after each of their rhapsodies and assert them as expressing "our truth." Cass, after her rhapsody, joins them in the recitation. These lines suggest that the play would not negate any of the various registers on which "truth" is represented in the play. In fact, no one in the play is free of illusions, and none of the illusions is devoid of truth at some level.

Besides the narratives of Harry and Cass, the rhapsodies of Trilbe, Ingram, and Cass, and the cynicism of Pat, other characters also have necessary delusions. In order to make her life bearable, Harry's wife Alice needs the illusion that all her children are doing well and that they will all come home for the holidays. By the time she expresses these desires, however, we have already heard from Harry that none of them will be coming home and that they all are unhappy.

Tessa, the maid at Eden House, is just beginning to dream her adult life. When she announces her engagement at the beginning of act 3, she begins by saying her fiancé is a building contractor. When pressed, however, she admits he is only an apprentice bricklayer. She projects her hopes for the future onto the engagement, as any young lover would do, and her imagination races from the honeymoon to the bungalow they eventually will build when her husband becomes a building contractor. This brief slice of a scene places Tessa at the beginning of the same process of dreaming a life for herself that Cass is concluding. The rhapsodies of Trilbe and Ingram represent the ultimate destination of life's dreams, which is none other than a continuation of the dreaming process but with all possibility of fulfillment annulled. The plays that immediately follow *Cass* (*Lovers* and *Crystal and Fox*) continue to explore this theme. Tessa anticipates the young couple of the first half of *Lovers* who die before their options are annulled.

If Tessa represents the place where adult daydreaming begins for all the characters in the play, Mrs. Butcher's arrival at Eden House in act 3 represents the place where we first met Cass in act 1. Like Cass, Mrs. Butcher sets herself apart from the other residents of Eden House and enlists the audience as her allies: "Lunatics is sane compared with these ones," she confides after walking on stage just after Cass's rhapsody. Despite her resistance, however, Trilbe and Cass recognize it as only a phase in her assimilation into Eden House: "She's still at *that* stage," says Trilbe

(Friel's emphasis), and Cass advises Mrs. Butcher "it's better to get into the routine here right away" (*CM*, 68).

Direct address to the audience by a character is the fourth experimental device Friel deploys in *Cass*. Cass herself addresses the audience in the first two acts and Mrs. Butcher does the same in act 3. Friel uses this device in two ways: first, as a narrative technique to convey information about Cass's past as well as her attitudes and feelings about what is happening on stage; and second, as a structural and thematic device that indicates Cass's gradual loss of contact with the world outside of Eden House. As a narrative technique these direct addresses fill us in on Cass's relationship with her father, who deserted his family, her teenage fling with Connie Crowley that led to her decision to emigrate, her experiences living and working in New York, her observations on Eden House and its residents, her attitudes about the past, the title of the play, and what seems most real to her. As a structural/thematic device Cass's contact with the audience serves as a barometer of Cass's connection with a world she is desperately trying to hang on to. At the beginning of the play she uses her monologue with the audience to keep the painful memories of her homecoming at bay. Focusing on her audience helps her to ignore the persistent and intrusive memories that appear on stage in the form of her brother and his family, memories that emphasize her almost total alienation from them. In act 1 she is quite comfortable with the audience and with the image of herself that she presents to them. By the end of act 2, however, her connection with the audience has become tenuous, and this is indicated by her difficulty in finding anyone when she looks out into the theater. After listening to Ingram's rhapsody in act 2 (she already witnessed Trilbe's in act 1), Cass is rather awed and perplexed and she begins to lose her grip on the reality she prefers to identify with. A few minutes later, after Pat Quinn challenges the veracity of her own narrative about New York, Cass addresses the audience but is no longer able to verify its presence: "Where are you?" she asks, and then she implores "Stick with me" (*CM*, 50). Cass realizes that to maintain her own narrative as socially viable she has to have other people who share it. Harry has his own version, Trilbe and Ingram constitute their own exclusive interpretive community of two, and when Pat refuses to accept Cass's version, she desperately tries to hang on to her friends in the audience. But at this point Cass is already slipping away from the audience and into the delusional reality of Eden House. In act 3 she cannot find the audience at all and, concluding that they were a dream, she ceases trying to communicate with them. At this point when she recounts a dream about herself on a ship in a wedding dress, she talks only to herself. She is now out of touch with everyone, except perhaps Trilbe and Ingram. Her former reality has become the dream and her dreams have become her reality. Mrs. Butcher, the new arrival at Eden House in act 3, assumes Cass's role as contact with the audience, and she uses that contact, as Cass did, to distance herself from the delusional temptations of Eden House.

Cass's relationship to the audience represents yet another level of the real in the play. It is this relationship that helps Cass maintain her grip on the here and now until she succumbs to the delusional realities of Eden House in the end. She enlists the audience on her side of the argument at her first entrance, when she enters the narrative Harry has begun. Friel explains about the audience: "They are her friends, her intimates. The other people on stage are interlopers" (*CM*, 15). The other characters are interlopers because they threaten the fragile identity Cass has fabricated for herself with the audience. Since her relationship with the audience is through monologue, she controls the discourse much like an author. Of course, in the end Friel denies her the control she desires, and Eden House provides her with the only alternative environment where she can construct a narrative of herself she can live with. The alternative of life without a narrative that gives some meaning to her existence (the option explored in *Crystal and Fox*) is apparently not an endurable option for Cass's psychic condition.

These monologues with the audience suggest the complex epistemology Friel is working with in this play, as he raises much more probing questions than in his short stories about the interrelations among experience, memory, art, and illusion. At one point in one of her monologues Cass asks, "Where have all the real people gone?" (*CM*, 26). The other characters (Harry and his family) have drifted off stage during her monologue, so we are not sure at this point whether Cass is referring to the audience or to the other characters. Immediately after she says this, the two characters we might conventionally call the most unreal enter—

Ingram and Trilbe. At this point in the play, then, Cass's confusion becomes our confusion, and that confusion itself draws attention to the different competing narratives in the play—those of Harry, Cass, Trilbe and Ingram, the playwright/audience—as various registers of the real.

All along Trilbe has been asserting the reality of Eden House against other possible versions. At one point in act 1 she says, "Catherine, m'dear, we are your only world now. We have the truth for you. . . . We know what is real, Catherine" (*CM*, 29). Trilbe then launches into her rhapsody. Trilbe's reverie triggers a memory in Cass of her nephew Dom pruriently inquiring about her living arrangements with Jeff Olsen. Although shaken by Trilbe's rhapsody, Cass is determined to resist the lures of Eden House, but not without uncertainty. She looks to cynical Pat for reassurances that she will not be worn down. But as Cass begins to lose touch with the audience, she becomes lured by Trilbe's call to forsake the world for Eden House. When at the end of act 2 Cass, seeking the audience, cries out "Where are you," only Trilbe answers (*CM*, 50). In act 3 Cass is almost completely circumscribed by the reality of Eden House, by "our truth," as Trilbe calls it, which she and Ingram claim is just as real as the world of the audience Cass is seeking.

Most critics of *The Loves of Cass McGuire* have perceived the role of illusion in the play in rather conventional terms as escape from or compensation for a painful reality.[5] Perceived in these conventional terms, however, the rhapsodies seem awkward and simplistic. D. E. S. Maxwell, for example, says, "These ritual excursions come off as a dramatic contrivance because the body of the play so firmly establishes, in realistic terms, the bewildered suffering of the participants" (1973, 77). Maxwell obviously assumes here a conventional notion of the difference between reality and illusion and of our ability to distinguish between them. *The Loves of Cass McGuire*, however, challenges conventional beliefs both about what is real and about our ability to distinguish between the real and the illusory.

The illusions in *Cass* are more than escape or compensation for a hard life; rather they are, like neurotic or psychotic symptoms, painful sym-

5. See, for example: E. Andrews 1995, 99–105; Dantanus 1988, 104; Maxwell 1973, 70–71, 76; O'Brien 1989, 57.

bolic negotiations with a reality principle. *Cass* focuses on the necessity of illusion for survival in the grimmest of psychological circumstances—deprivation of love, which is aptly symbolized in the garden at the rear of the stage by the continuous presence of an illuminated cupid statue "frozen [like Cass] in an absurd and impossible contortion" (*CM*, 8). Cass's transition from a crass realist to an inhabiter of illusory memory in order to survive is poignant and moving. She begins like the pragmatic mothers in the short stories and ends like the dreamers of the stories. The tragedy of *The Loves of Cass McGuire* is her discovery that her world is without love. At the end of her rhapsody she identifies the lack that drives her to distraction: "Connie and Father and Harry and Jeff and the four kids and Joe and Slinger . . . and I love them all so much, and they love me so much; we're so lucky, so lucky in our love" (*CM*, 67). Cass's tragedy, and the significance of the play's title, derives from her rejection by everyone she loves. Her rhapsody, then, fulfills the classic Freudian function of wish fulfillment. The dreaming process becomes inevitable not merely as a means of making life bearable through escapism but as a means of negotiating an identity with society that preserves dignity and gives some positive value to one's existence. No alternative reality exempt from such negotiations exists in the world of *Cass McGuire*. Some may negotiate more favorable terms for themselves than others, but none inhabit a reality unmediated by dreams and illusions.

Negotiations in *Cass* are particularly bleak. Although the characters manage to construct saving illusions for themselves, the redemptive quality of these illusions is minimal and far from reassuring. When Cass rewrites her history at the end of the play she accepts Trilbe's rechristening of her as Catherine. (Trilbe refused to recognize the nickname Cass from the beginning.) In Cass's revised autobiography Jeff Olsen and Connie Crowley merge into one husband—General Cornelius Olsen, a hero "in the last war" (*CM*, 68)—and she appropriates her brother's material success as her own: "I was the one that made it," she says, and "he never got nuthin' much outa life" (*CM*, 70). Like Beckett's Murphy, she inhabits a zone of the mind characterized by "the pleasure of reprisal, the pleasure of reversing the physical experience. Here the kick that the physical Murphy received, the mental Murphy gave. It was the same kick, but corrected as to direction. . . . Here the whole physical fiasco became a howling success" (1957, 111). In fact, Beckett's description of Murphy's hermetically sealed Cartesian mind shares some of Friel's epistemological premises.[6]

Cass's last words in the play are "Home at last. Gee, but it's a good thing to be home" (*CM*, 70). Cass's final resting place as Catherine McGuire is a creation of her imagination driven by desire. She is able to sustain her final illusion because she has a social context that is willing to reinforce it. We feel at the end, however, that Cass's illusions are not shared by the larger community represented by the role of the audience in the play. We had a connection with Cass early in the play, but we lose her in the end. One measure of the power of the play is the degree to which we feel this loss. George O'Brien expresses this response very well: "There is an irresistible sense of defeat when Cass opts for the world of rhapsody . . . . Illusion may be a saving grace. The imagination may be the ultimate form of resistance. But the models of illusion and imaginativeness are so bloodless and sexless, in comparison to Cass, that it is difficult not to think of her survival on the terms available as a defeat" (1989, 58).

While critics have felt the poignancy of Cass's plight, they typically have viewed the ending in the same conventional light they viewed the role of illusion. Consequently they find the ending (and the play) unsatisfying. Milton Levin, for example, finds the resolution of the play "an evasion" (1972, 133), and Elmer Andrews, who says Cass "gives up on reality altogether" finds the play's complexity incoherent (1995, 103–4). These critics have failed to recognize, however, that Friel structures *The Loves of Cass McGuire* so that we really cannot measure Cass's loss in terms of her distance at the end from some conventional notion of reality. The real never appears in *Cass* in any independently verifiable form but only as various representations of desire. If there is any privileged reality in this play it appears only as a relation between Cass and the audience. That the real appears as a relation between a fictional character with the status of a textual effect and a projection from that text of an

6. Tom Kilroy, without mentioning Beckett, recognizes the denouement of Cass as playing out her tragedy in a theater of pure mind similar to Murphy's (1979, 8–9).

observer of the fiction says something about the complexity of Friel's epistemology as well as about his conception of the play.

Although *The Loves of Cass McGuire* is not a play about the coloniza-tion of Ireland, Friel, as a member of the Catholic minority of Northern Ireland and a resident of the Republic has experience as both a colonial and a postcolonial. *The Loves of Cass McGuire* may be about an Irish emi-gré returning from America, but the structure of Cass's psyche is dis-tinctly postcolonial, particularly those aspects of her psyche that are linked to illusion and the four experimental devices in the play. I am not claiming here that Friel himself intended the play to serve as a metaphor for colonial or postcolonial Ireland, but rather that Friel's own psyche was structured by his colonial and postcolonial experience and he wrote that structure into Cass's psyche. Whether Friel was conscious of doing this is irrelevant. As playwright, Friel gave a dramatic form to this struc-ture, and if this happened unconsciously, so much the better, for it kept the play from becoming tendentious about it.

Contesting narrative authority is an important part of the colonial and postcolonial psyche, and the struggle between Cass and Harry over control of the narrative suggests the fictional nature of any narrative and how its meaning is shaped less by the purported "facts" that constitute the narrative than by its criteria for selecting germane facts and their order of arrangement, a kind of shaping process that is shared by histo-rian and playwright alike. As postcolonial critics have shown, control of the master narrative is central to any national liberation. In the imperial master narrative the colonized are mere objects of manipulation, pawns in the great design of a history written elsewhere. After liberation, con-trol of the historical narrative is seized and rewritten by the formerly colonized, who now assume the subject position within the narrative. Colonial Ireland was the subject of two competing master narratives, one written from the Gaelic perspective and one from the British per-spective. In Northern Ireland three narratives compete, a nationalist nar-rative, a unionist narrative, and a British narrative. The struggle between Cass and Harry could be read as analogous to the effort of the formerly colonized to assert narrative control over their own destiny. By contrast, a critic like David Lloyd might read it as a continuation on the part of the new nationalist hegemony, represented by Harry, to control the new narrative as the former imperial power did at the expense of minorities within the new nation. In the case of Ireland these minorities would include not only women and emigrés but Northern nationalists who have felt excluded since partition by what has come to be called "twenty-six county nationalism." Cass, in other words, becomes a displaced figure, in the Freudian sense, for anyone who feels excluded or objectified by a hegemonic narrative, as Friel, a member of the disenfranchised minority in the North, must have felt excluded and objectified by "official" narratives of the Northern Ireland statelet. At the same time he also found little solace in the new narratives of the Irish Republic, neither the nationalist narrative developed during the decades of the Free State nor the commercialism and consumerism of the post-Lemass Republic, as *The Mundy Scheme* and *The Gentle Island* so vividly illustrate.

The inevitable resurgence of the past as a determinant of the present is also a prominent colonial syndrome. Cass's insistently recurrent memories constitute not only a return of the repressed, but also a replication of this colonial syndrome. As Bhabha has argued, it is not an actual past the colonized remember but a refigured or re-membered past that paves the way for a transfigured future. The recent past under colonial rule tends to be repressed in favor of a more distant precolonial past, which provides the materials for a transformed future. In Bhabha's model both the ancient precolonial past and the more recent colonial past are refigured in a way that opens up a future in which survival as a subject again becomes possible. Cass engages in precisely this dynamic. She tries to repress her homecoming memories with memories of New York and of her life in Ireland before she left for New York. Also, in her rhapsody she reconstructs both her immediate past and her distant past in a way that structures a vision of a future in which she is sustained by love and controls her own destiny. Cass knows that the actual past is inaccessible: "Who the hell knows what happened in the past!" she exclaims. Moreover, because of her chronic deprivation, she prefers to discount history, as do the other inhabitants of Eden House, and they all transform their chronic deprivations into rapturous triumphs that lend meaning and dignity to their existences and open up a future in which survival as a subject is again possible. Cass's tragedy, however, is that her actual liberation is interdicted and her future forestalled by her effective incarceration in

Eden House. Lurking beneath Cass's fate, perhaps in the shadows of Friel's unconscious, is the interdicted future of Northern Ireland. In the early 1960s, Friel and his fellow Northern nationalists must have felt much like Cass living in the Eden House of her dreams with all possibility of fulfillment annulled. They were sustained only by fading republican dreams of a united Ireland that became more remote with each passing decade.

The device of direct address to the audience, like the other devices in the play, also highlights the nature and structure of illusion and its (post)colonial function. It serves Cass as a validating device for her version of things at the same time it serves the play's audience as a measure of Cass's grasp on her reality. On another register it also posits an audience as a necessary illusion for the construction of any narrative. The (post)colonial twist is not hard to imagine. In Northern Ireland the minority nationalist community existed in a state where its sense of itself, not to mention its civil rights, were denied both by its unionist neighbors and by the larger union itself. In such a situation, where one's own narrative is never validated, one inevitably looks to an audience outside the conflict for validation. In the early 1960s, when even the Republic of Ireland seemed remote and inattentive, many Northern nationalists must have wondered about who, if anyone, was listening to them. During the Troubles after 1968 the nationalist community often appealed to outside audiences, such as Amnesty International and the European Human Rights Commission, to authenticate their sense of outrage and injustice, an authentication they could obtain neither from their unionist neighbors nor from the British government.

In short, the major experimental devices of *The Loves of Cass McGuire* all provide her with the structure of a (post)colonial psyche. Given that Trilbe insists on calling her Catherine, within the structure of Friel's own political unconscious, is Cass, we might ask, a disguised and displaced Cathleen ni Houlihan figure for Northern nationalists who found her identity authenticated nowhere—not in America, not in the Republic of Ireland, and certainly not at home in Northern Ireland, except within the narrow confines of an increasingly isolated nationalist community, isolated in its own Eden House of a gloriously refigured past?

These early plays exhaust Friel's early exploration of individual, social, and cultural illusion prior to his discovery of the constitutive role played by language and discourse in the construction of illusion and myth. In *Philadelphia, Cass,* and *Lovers* memories, hopes, and illusions fail to provide sufficient spiritual sustenance to redeem mundane existence in postcolonial Ireland. *Crystal and Fox* demonstrates the hopelessness and lovelessness of life without illusions, even rigged illusions, while *The Mundy Scheme* and *The Gentle Island* depict the hollowness of national myths and illusions. Only *The Enemy Within* arrives at a spiritually satisfactory resolution, but that thematic resolution is undermined by the rhetorical and emotional emphases of the play. Although Elmer Andrews claims that Friel's early plays are "concerned with the way the individual's identity is substantially constructed from the range of languages available to him or her" and with the "dismantling of the unified subject" (1995, 74, 77), Andrews's analyses of the plays offer no substantiation of these claims. At this point in Friel's career he had not yet articulated the role language plays in the construction of identity and he had made no assault whatsoever on the unified subject. All that changed, however, with the production of *The Freedom of the City* in 1973.

5

The End of Innocence
The Freedom of the City and *Volunteers*

The Freedom of the City marks the beginning of Friel's maturity as a major modern dramatist. Most critics agree that the play, which premiered at the Abbey in 1973, is a major departure for Friel in a number of ways.[1] From this point on, in addition to broadening his scope more consistently to include social, political, and cultural issues, Friel also enters a new phase in his awareness of how language and discourse function on those more public registers and how its functioning there impacts on individuals. More than anything else, this new awareness, what we might call a heightened linguistic consciousness, accounts for the greater complexity and sophistication we witness in Friel's later plays. Tom Kilroy says that Friel's mature plays "attempt to transfer to the stage the kind of density and complex inter-changes which we normally associate with the best prose fiction" (1979, 9). Of particular interest to this study is how this linguistic consciousness contributed to Friel's understanding of the role illusion plays in larger social, political, and cultural contexts. What he explored most notably in *Cass McGuire* at the level of the individual subject is now projected onto a broader canvas of collective subjects. *The Freedom of the City* also marks the first major artistic statement by Friel on the situation in Northern Ireland. *The Mundy Scheme* had satirized politics in the Republic a few years earlier, and taken together, these two political plays indicate a major shift in Friel's aesthetics.

Friel's aesthetics, as reflected in his public statements, actually evolved through three distinct stages separated from one another by political

1. See, for example, Dantanus 1988, 22; Deane 1981, 7; Deane 1986b, 16–17; O'Brien 1989, 77–78.

events: the first stage ends with the beginning of the civil rights movement in Northern Ireland in 1968 and the second stage ends with Bloody
Sunday (January 30, 1972).

Friel's early aesthetics consisted largely of several unexamined formalist assumptions that were commonplace in the 1950s and 1960s when he
began to publish his stories. In a 1965 interview for *Acorn*, a magazine
published by Magee College in Derry, Friel eschews the kind of political
commitment exhibited by dramatists like Osborne and Wesker and
prefers instead an art that elicits sympathy and understanding without
advocating action, which he says is the responsibility of the reader not
the writer. He says that the purpose of a play may be to move an audience, but it moves them "not through their head but through their
heart." "All any writer does," Friel claims at this point, "is to spotlight a
situation. In other words, he presents a set of people and a situation with
a certain clarity and understanding and sympathy and as a result of this
one should look at them more closely." This may lead to the writer "getting one section of the community to take a closer look at another," but
never as a crusader (1965, 5–6). In another early pronouncement a couple
of years later, Friel says that the function of dramatists is to be "concerned with one man's insignificant place in the here-and-now world.
They have the function to portray that one man's frustrations and hopes
and anguishes and joys and miseries and pleasures with all the precision
and accuracy and truth that they know; and by so doing help to make a
community of individuals" (1967, 17). Aesthetic assumptions such as
these can account for plays like *The Loves of Cass McGuire* or *Philadelphia,
Here I Come!*, but they are of limited use when applied to a play like *The
Freedom of the City*.

After 1968, when the civil rights movement was under way in Northern Ireland, Friel noticeably shifted his view of the artist's relation to politics. At this point Friel recognized that personal involvement was
inevitable, but he still wanted to maintain some distance between the
writer and the engaged individual. In an interview from the early 1970s
Friel comments on the role of the writer in the face of the civil rights dis-
turbances: he says, "I know of no Irish writer who is not passionately engaged in our current problems. But he must maintain a perspective as a
writer, and—equally important—he will write about the situation in

terms that may not relate even remotely to the squalor of here and now"
(Maxwell 1973, 29). In another interview from 1970 he said he did not
think he could write about "the situation in the North" because he was
"emotionally much too involved about it . . . A play about the civil rights
situation in the North won't be written, I hope, for another ten or fifteen
years" (1970a, 14). In an interview with Eavan Boland that same year,
Friel still refused, on the one hand, "to subordinate a literary craft to political or personal crisis" and advocated the distancing effect of a disciplined patience and literary skill, which he says "are more likely to give a
generous interpretation to personal experience than initial feelings of
outrage, fear or anger." Yet, on the other hand, he says,

> There is a state of crisis here and inevitably if one is part of this crisis at
> all, this is bound to affect my work and this is primarily my first concern.
> . . . The crisis is there, and I keep wondering how it can be of use to me.
> I know that may seem a very selfish attitude. But it is, after all, a profes-
> sional approach to the situation. On a personal level, of course, we're all
> terribly involved in it. But for the writer, I think his position is better as
> a sideline one, as against an involved one. (Boland 1970, 12)

There is a tension in these quotes, even a note of ambivalence, between a passionate personal engagement and a desire to retain some
aesthetic distance.

After Bloody Sunday, however, all ambivalence evaporates and the
whole tone and tenor of Friel's aesthetic pronouncements change. In an
essay published in the *Times Literary Supplement (TLS)* in March of 1972
Friel recalls the early days of the Abbey riots. The Irish people, he says,
"recognized then that the theatre was an important social element that
not only reflected but shaped the society it served; that dramatists were
revolutionary in the broadest sense of that word." Predicting much that
would occur intellectually and culturally as well as politically in Ireland
over the next two decades, including his own Field Day movement, he
adds,

> It requires no gift of prophecy to foresee that the revolt in Northern Ire-
> land is going to spread to the Republic; and if you believe that art is an
> instrument of the revolutionary process, then you can look forward to a
> spate of committed plays. I do not believe that art is a servant of any
> movement. But during the period of unrest I can foresee that the two al-
> legiances that have bound the Irish imagination—loyalty to the most

authoritarian church in the world and devotion to a romantic ideal we call Kathleen—will be radically altered. Faith and Fatherland; new definitions will be forged, and then new loyalties, and then new social groupings. It will be a bloody process. (1972a, 305–6)

Why Friel altered his aesthetics so dramatically can be judged from a comment he made about Bloody Sunday ten years after the event. Friel himself had participated in the march and he says,

It was really a shattering experience that the British Army, this disciplined instrument, would go in as they did that time and shoot thirteen people. To be there on that occasion and—I didn't actually see people get shot—but I mean, to have to throw yourself on the ground because people are firing at you is a very terrifying experience. Then the whole cover-up afterwards was shattering too. We still have some kind of belief that the law is above reproach. We still believe that the academy is above reproach in some way, don't we? (1982a, 22)

So looking back a decade later, after he had formed Field Day and after he had written *Translations*, Friel's feelings about the event are still very strong and he had not altered his committed stance. In fact, when asked about the writer's relation to the troubles in the North, although he felt he wrote *The Freedom of the City* too soon in the heat of passion after Bloody Sunday, Friel does not revert to his pre–Bloody Sunday position of cautiously warning writers to remain on the sidelines: "The experience is there," he says, "it's available. We didn't create it, and it has coloured all our lives and adjusted all our stances in some way. What the hell can we do but look at it?" (1982a, 23). He also said he was not worried about "crude" political misreadings of *The Freedom of the City*: invoking Yeats's fear that one of his plays had incited revolutionary violence, Friel says, "That wouldn't worry me anyway. 'Have I sent out certain young men?'—that sort of thing wouldn't worry me at all" (1982a, 22). Friel doesn't feel that he will eschew writing political plays in the future: "There are continuing obsessions, like the political thing is a continuing obsession, and I've written two or three demonstrably political plays. And I keep saying to myself I'm never going to write another political play because it's too transient and because I'm confused about it myself, but I know damn well and I'm sure I'll have another shot at it again sometime" (1982a, 22).

Obviously the Northern troubles, particularly the Bloody Sunday incident, compelled Friel to reevaluate his responsibilities as a writer. Seamus Deane has eloquently expressed Friel's accommodation as a writer to the political turmoil in the North:

> Strangely, it is when he comes closest to the actuality of the Northern crisis, and when he risks sententiousness and judgement, that he comes close to his best work. Brian Friel is one of the few writers we have whose sensibility is not bludgeoned by the fact of the North; rather it is heightened, especially in its awareness of the possibility of perceiving in it the inescapable relationship between tragedy and politics in which Friel has always, I think, believed, but the actuality of which he has at last met in a specifically Irish form that has deep and not merely provincial repercussions. (1974, 15–16)

The Freedom of the City

The Freedom of the City was the first product of Friel's third and most politically engaged period. The play, set in Derry at the Guildhall and the nearby city walls, makes no attempt to reproduce the events of Bloody Sunday in which thirteen people marching to protest internment were killed by British troops, but it quite deliberately evokes them. The character of the Judge, for instance, employs language from the *Widgery Report*, the official inquiry into the Bloody Sunday shootings that exonerated the military of all blame. Although the play is set in 1970 on a day on which nothing significant occurred in Northern Ireland, Elizabeth Hale Winkler has shown how Friel has drawn generally from characteristics of the period from 1968 through 1972, a period that included civil rights demonstrations, the introduction of British troops, the internment controversy, and the introduction of tanks and heavy weapons, as well as Bloody Sunday (1981, 15–16).

A number of readings of *The Freedom of the City* focus on its overt political content: it has been characterized as anti-British propaganda, as being about poverty (a view Friel has lent credence to) (Jent 1994; Winkler 1982, 412), about social injustice (Winkler 1981, 23; O'Connor 1989, 10), and as pleading the case of Derry Catholics (Winkler 1981, 16). All these readings, however, tend to oversimplify the play. If instead we focus on Friel's manipulation of discourse forms, the play immediately becomes more complex and intricate and less obviously partisan. In terms of language, the play is strangely bifurcated to begin with. Linguistic events occur on two registers. One is the register of literary realism that portrays the three victims and their activities inside the mayor's parlor in the Guildhall. The other is the register of public discourse represented in the forms of a judge, soldiers, a constable, a general, a military press officer, a forensic expert, a pathologist, a priest, a balladeer, a TV news commentator, and a sociologist. These public discourses fall into at least three ideological categories — those that assume allegiance to the British government, those that sympathize with the Irish victims, and those that purport to a disinterested objectivity. The significance of the play derives primarily from the differences among these registers and discourses. This distinction between private and public discourse forms, while it creates some aesthetic problems I will discuss later, neatly mirrors the shifting emphasis in Western aesthetics over the past few decades. In this play it is as if Friel glimpses the inadequacy of either the public or the private register to represent experience, but stops short of a fully conscious articulation of the problem.

On the register of literary realism, the audience knows shortly after the opening of the play that Skinner, Lily, and Michael are marchers who stumbled inadvertently into the Guildhall and the mayor's parlor after the military fired on the demonstrators with tear gas, water cannons, and rubber bullets. The scenes in the mayor's parlor with these three characters alternate throughout the play with the exterior scenes that employ the various public discourses. In the parlor scenes we come to know the victims according to the conventions of traditional realism that encourage emotional identification with the characters. The three all come from the oppressed Catholic community of Derry, although they represent different elements of it and express very different attitudes toward the march and the civil rights movement in general.

Michael is a humorless, bourgeois idealist. Inspired by Gandhi, he believes firmly in nonviolent protest and in its efficacy. He has been on every civil rights march since 1968. While he opposes the social injustice in Northern Ireland that victimizes him, he otherwise identifies with the prevailing middle-class values about property, respectability, and the good intentions of government officials. He objects to Skinner's disrespect for the property of others and he marches because he wants the same opportunity for a decent job and a decent home enjoyed by his Protestant counterparts. Like Skinner, he is unemployed, but unlike Skinner, Michael wants to work and become a productive member of his society. Michael also has a naïve trust in established authority. Since he considers his motives to be dignified and peaceful and since his conscience tells him he has nothing to be ashamed of, he feels that he has nothing to fear from authorities in power. In fact, Michael trusts and identifies with established authority more than he does with Skinner and Lily, who he thinks discredit "dignified, peaceful protest." He perceives Skinner as a representative of the "hooligan" element that takes advantage of peaceful protests and turns them to their own purposes. Since *hooligan* is one of the terms frequently employed by authorities to discredit the political motives of protesters, whether violent or nonviolent, in blaming the hooligans for inciting authorities to excessive force, Michael inhabits the perspective authorities had hoped to create with the word. In the end Michael experiences his death as a tragic mistake, and he dies in disbelief and astonishment.

Skinner, who calls Michael a "boy scout," is at the other end of the ideological spectrum from Michael. Skinner is ironic, cynical, witty, and disrespectful. When Michael asks if he is for civil rights, he says "I'm crazy about them" (*SP*, 129). Unlike Michael, he prefers to be unemployed. He has no fixed address and he lives by his wits. He also has a great sense of irony and fun. While in the Guildhall he drinks the mayor's whiskey, wears his robes, smokes his cigars, uses his phone to place bets, and defaces one of his portraits with a ceremonial sword. Where Michael trusts the government, Skinner is very cynical about its self-serving interests. He says that if he is sick or dead the government provides very well for him, but alive and well he is a problem for them. He has no illusions about his fate. He knows that a price will be exacted for what they have done, inadvertent or not, and that "the poor are always overcharged." He dies as he lived—"in defensive flippancy" (*SP*, 150).

Lily comes from another situation altogether. She is a charwoman with a disabled husband and eleven children. They all live in a run-down, two-room flat in a converted warehouse. She is superstitious, instinctual, and sees the world as patently unfair. Like Skinner, however, she has a sense of fun and she shares in some of his antics as they both manage to get as much enjoyment as they can out of what opportunities present themselves in their bizarre situation. Although at one point she confesses that she does not know why she marches, she later admits that she marches out of frustration and impotence for her Down's syndrome child. She knew she was going to die the minute they stepped outside; she sensed it like an animal. In the end she is filled with regret over the life that eluded her "because never once . . . had an experience, an event, even a small unimportant happening been isolated, and assessed, and articulated" (*SP*, 150). Her good instincts, in other words, could not save her from dying of grief.

Since the play opens with Skinner, Lily, and Michael dead on stage and since in their first appearance in act 2 they utter their dispassionate but poignantly eerie thoughts at the moment they died, there is no suspense about their fate. Their scenes are devoted to revealing their characters and establishing their relationship to the demonstration and the social circumstances it arose from.

The scenes within the Guildhall are framed by the public discourses outside. The discourses are uttered by characters, but they are not drawn according to the conventions of literary realism. Instead they are much more like character functions; they represent different groups of the principals involved in the Northern turmoil. We do not come to know them as people, only as public voices. These voices, however disembodied or nonparticularized in terms of conventional realistic portrayal, are major participants in the action. In fact, one could argue that, despite the violation of Aristotelian tenets about the cause-and-effect relationship between character and action, the discourses themselves function as major protagonists in the drama and become the sources from which the action springs. By comparison, Lily, Skinner, and Michael appear as hapless victims of the discourses of power that orchestrate their fate. Unlike classic tragic protagonists, these three characters contribute nothing to advance the plot and provide no motive from which the tragic actions proceed. Three other victims from the Derry minority community with different character traits could have served equally well as far as the dynamics of plot are concerned. The same would not be true of Oedipus,

Hamlet, or Macbeth. In a sense the real protagonists of the play are the discourses of power that frame the activities of the hapless trio in the mayor's parlor, limit their possibilities, determine the course of their lives, appropriate the meaning of their existence, and collaborate to snuff out that existence to suit the purposes of the respective discourses.

The most important of these discourses of power is represented by the Judge, who presides over the inquiry into the deaths of Skinner, Lily, and Michael. His discourse consists of interrogating witnesses and drawing conclusions from their testimony. He is English, elderly, and an old army man. It is soon evident that neither his interrogation nor his conclusions are disinterested, although he tries to cloak them in a rhetoric of objectivity. He explains near the beginning of the play that his "tribunal of inquiry . . . is in no sense a court of justice." This turns out to be true ironically but not in the sense that he intends. He says, "Our only function is to form an objective view of the events . . . it is essentially a fact-finding exercise." With his next statement, however, he is well beyond the facts. He says, "our concern and our only concern is with that period of time when these three people came together, seized possession of a civic building, and openly defied the security forces." The facts may indicate, he "objectively" surmises, that they were "callous terrorists who had planned to seize the Guildhall weeks before" or perhaps "the misguided scheme occurred to them on that very day" (*SP*, 109–10). Of course, the audience soon learns that the Judge's narrowly circumscribed inquiry has a kind of polaroid bias that screens out in advance pertinent "facts" about Skinner, Lily, and Michael. For the Judge the most significant question his tribunal must answer is who fired first. The very framing of this question assumes that the victims were armed and provides a rather egregiously cynical example of John Dewey's insight: "The way in which the problem is conceived decides what specific suggestions are entertained and which are dismissed; what data are selected and which rejected; it is the criterion for relevancy and irrelevancy of hypotheses and conceptual structures" (1981, 229).

Throughout his interrogations the Judge consistently assumes that the three victims were armed terrorists who planned to occupy the Guildhall in deliberate defiance of local authorities (*SP*, 148–49). The major thrust of his questioning endeavors to confirm these assumptions. He encounters problems, however, with conflicting testimony over who fired first and whether the victims were armed. Priests and civilians on the scene, including photographic journalists, saw no weapons in the hands of the victims. The army and police, by contrast, claim they saw the victims fire at them first, even though no weapons were recovered from the bodies of the victims and no military or police personnel were shot. The army claims that the weapons were removed before they could get to the bodies. The Judge chooses to believe the testimony of the military and the police in the face of counter testimony. Consequently he is forced to rely on indirect evidence from the forensics expert, who describes how the presence of gunpowder particles on skin and clothing, particularly in certain patterns on the hands, may indicate that someone could have fired a weapon. But Dr. Winbourne testifies that such evidence is not conclusive, for powder particles could have rubbed off the soldiers who shot them as they carried the bodies away.

Despite conflicting testimony and the lack of any hard evidence that the victims were armed, the Judge concludes that by defying the marching ban the marchers and their speakers made tragedy inevitable, that there was no evidence to believe that the security forces acted without restraint, that there was no reason to believe that the soldiers fired first, and that indirect testimony indicated that all three victims were armed and at least two of them fired their weapons (*SP*, 168).

In addition to tipping his inquiry in one direction, under the guise of objectivity and fairness, the Judge also suppresses information as pertinent to the incident as its tragic result. When a police witness begins to reveal information about Lily's impoverished circumstances, the Judge curtly says, "We are not conducting a social survey, Constable" (*SP*, 108). A little later he says, "it is none of our function to make moral judgements" (*SP*, 110). By excluding social and moral considerations, the judge excludes all consideration of the reasons for the march in the first place and he ensures that the marchers will not be perceived as people with legitimate concerns. These exclusions that supposedly preserve "objectivity," in other words, enable the Judge to portray the victims as armed terrorists unworthy of anyone's sympathy, a rhetorical strategy that is countered by the scenes in the Guildhall.

As other commentators have pointed out (Winkler 1981, 25; McGowan 1980, 300), Friel took much of the Judge's orientation and even some specifics of his language from the *Widgery Report,* the actual tribunal that investigated the Bloody Sunday incident. Like Friel's Judge, Lord Widgery claimed that his tribunal was "essentially a fact finding exercise" and "not concerned with making moral judgments" (1972, 1–2). Widgery also claimed that "'Who fired first?' is probably the most important single issue which I have been required to determine" (1972, 16). Like the Judge, Widgery allowed the police and the military to testify anonymously, and when civilian testimony conflicted with the soldiers' he chose to believe the soldiers in every case. The four conclusions of Friel's Judge at the end of the play are either directly quoted or adapted from the eleven conclusions at the end of the *Widgery Report.*

Much more than the Judge's character, language, and conclusions, however, comes from the *Widgery Report.* With the exception of the American sociologist Dodds and the balladeer, all the other figures representing the various forms of public discourse have counterparts in the list of witnesses who testified before the Widgery tribunal. As Widgery points out, the 114 witnesses "fell into six main groups": priests, other Londonderry citizens, press and media personnel, military, police, and medical and forensic experts (1972, 2). Friel's public discourses represent five of these groups, or perhaps all six if you allow that the balladeer and his entourage represent sentiments of the Derry citizenry. Another possible reading is to say that Friel let the three victims in the Guildhall speak for the views of Derry citizens, who in the *Widgery Report* testified overwhelmingly that the Bloody Sunday victims were unarmed and that the military initiated the gunfire. It is possible, then, to see the entire structure of the play as derived from the *Widgery Report.*

Other important elements of the play also have their origins in the *Widgery Report.* Reliance on paraffin tests as the sole means to establish whether any of the slain had used firearms, since no firearms were recovered by the army, was an important part of Widgery's evidence. Another interesting element of the Widgery report is Widgery's classification of the participants in the march. He identifies three types: 1) nonviolent marchers, 2) hooligans, and 3) gunmen (i.e., IRA operatives). The report barely mentions the nonviolent marchers nor does it mention any of the issues regarding civil rights and internment that motivated the march. Even when discussing the background of the incident Widgery refers only to earlier violence by IRA gunmen and rioting by hooligans without ever mentioning the social and political issues at stake. Friel captures this lacuna in Widgery's focus when he has his Judge interrupt the testimony of the policeman with his remark about "not conducting a social survey." This remark is the extent of his acknowledgment of the prime motivation for the majority of marchers. Although Widgery was concerned with establishing the presence of gunmen at the scene of the violence, since none were captured nor any weapons confiscated, he could not give them much play in his report. When he discussed the marchers he discussed primarily what he called "the hooligan element." Hooligans were those marchers who were neither peaceful protesters nor IRA gunmen but primarily youths who engaged in acts of rioting and violence, such as defacing property and throwing rocks and bricks (and sometimes nail and petrol bombs) at police and soldiers. Moreover, hooligans engaged in these disruptive activities gratuitously or perhaps for the sheer enjoyment of it; for no motivation for such actions was even hinted at in the *Widgery Report*. In fact, the *Widgery Report* could be said to be obsessed with hooligans, even though it never established whether any of the slain were hooligans, let alone gunmen. By creating the aura of hooliganism and insinuating IRA involvement both in the events of the years immediately preceding Bloody Sunday and during the incident itself, Widgery rhetorically justified the military response where he could not justify it with concrete evidence. In Friel's play the hooligan argument is introduced only by Michael with reference to Skinner, but Friel's Judge makes a somewhat stronger identification than Widgery did by repeatedly referring to the three Guildhall occupants as terrorists, a term usually applied by British and Northern Ireland officials to IRA gunmen. In any case, the Judge's repeated appellation of terrorists carries assumptions of guilt with it similar to the *Widgery Report*'s repeated allusions to hooligans. As Seamus Deane has pointed out, in certain discourses the repetition of certain loaded words such as *terrorist* [*hooligan* would be another] can be skillfully deployed to invoke "entirely pejorative meanings" (1974, 13). This is certainly what Widgery does to color the entire Bloody Sunday march with pejorative connotations. He creates an image of the event that discredits, or at least refuses to acknowledge, its higher aspirations, aspirations represented in Friel's play by the character of Michael, who was inspired by Gandhi's principle of nonviolence and identified by the Judge as the one most certainly armed.

Friel's handling of the Judge has elicited the charge of "nationalist propaganda" from viewers and readers of the play, particularly from the unionist community and in England.[2] But if we look at some of the other public figures, we discover that Friel's view of the tragedy is more complex than that. Whereas the Judge's inquiry takes place after the three victims have been slain, other public figures participate as the situation develops. It is a tribute to Friel's dramaturgical skill that he was able to weave the various time frames so effectively into the play sequence, which jumps back and forth between the different frames without regard to chronology yet without confusing the audience or interfering with their involvement or understanding. Two figures that become an important part of the dynamics of the unfolding events are the Army Press Officer and the Balladeer. While Skinner, Lily, and Michael are still in the mayor's parlor, the Press Officer announces at a press conference that a band of up to forty terrorists forced open the side door of the Guildhall and occupied the entire first floor. He also says that they have access to arms. When pressed for sensitive details, he refuses to answer any further questions (*SP,* 126). The Balladeer presents an even more exaggerated view. His first song, with the obligatory invocation of whiskey and past republican heroes, has one hundred Irish heroes taking the Guildhall in defiance of both the army and the Royal Ulster Constabulary (RUC) (*SP,* 118). The Balladeer's second song gets the numbers right, but the three heroes are now enshrined as martyrs to the centuries-old national cause. The phrases are stock republican ballad stuff—two lads and a mother, the Saxon bullet, "Mother Ireland, one and free," blood sacrifice, and so forth (*SP,* 148). I do not see how anyone could read this as other than a satire on Irish political ballads. Moreover, the effect of both the Press Officer and the Balladeer in terms of the dynamics of the unfolding events is the same—they both foster the official view of a deliberate plot to seize the Guildhall and they both elevate the stakes and the level of fear by exaggerating the numbers and labeling them either

2. E. Andrews 1995, 129; Dantanus 1988, 140; O'Connor 1989, 14.

terrorists or heroes. In this context the terms *terrorist* and *hero* refer to the same thing from opposite perspectives, and neither term accurately characterizes any of the three victims.

Liam O'Kelly, the RTÉ (Radio Telefís Éireann, Irish national radio and television) newsman, also contributes to the dynamics of the tragedy by unwittingly confirming the official view for his listening audience. At an early stage in the development of events he announces unconfirmed reports that fifty gunmen have seized the Guildhall. He points out that the Guildhall is a symbol of Unionist domination and that if it falls into the hands of terrorists, the government will be embarrassed. At this point the army refuses to confirm the report for O'Kelly, but a "usually reliable" source from the Bogside is willing to confirm it (*SP,* 117–18). The effect of O'Kelly's broadcast is to help spread rumors and lend credence to the official view of a terrorist plot that later motivates the Judge's inquiry.

The Priest, like the Balladeer, represents a partisan view, but Friel represents him, too, as a contributing factor to the social and political climate that produced the tragedy. Addressing his congregation after the deaths but before the funeral, he emphasizes the social issues that prompted the march in the first place, those same issues suppressed by the Judge's official inquiry; but his emphasis equally distorts what we have witnessed ourselves in the Guildhall. The Priest, who gave the victims their last rites, talks of the "deep and numbing grief" their deaths have spread over the parish and he encourages his parishioners to "sit back and take stock and ask ourselves the very pertinent question: Why did they die?" Not willing to leave such a pertinent question to the whims of individual conscience, the Priest undertakes to answer the question himself:

> They died for their beliefs. They died for their fellow citizens. They died because they could endure no longer the injuries and injustices and indignities that have been their lot for too many years. They sacrificed their lives so that you and I and thousands like us might be rid of that iniquitous yoke and might inherit a decent way of life. And if that is not heroic virtue, then the word sanctity has no meaning. No sacrifice is ever in vain. But its value can be diminished if it doesn't fire our imagination, stiffen our resolution, and make us even more determined to see that the dream they dreamed is realized. May we be worthy of that

dream, of their trust. May we have the courage to implement their noble hopes. May we have God's strength to carry on where they left off. (*SP*, 124–25)

The Priest creates Christlike sacrificial martyrs out of Skinner, Lily, and Michael as he translates social and political issues into religious and biblical terms. Since this sermon sanctions blood sacrifice, a key trope for the republican tradition of physical force nationalism, and undoubtedly will fan the flames of future violence, we are encouraged to infer that previous sermons have contributed to the present tragedy. In the end the message of the Priest is not much different from that of the Balladeer, only expressed in a different idiom—in flimsily disguised form the dream of Irish political unity is yoked here, as it often was in the speeches and writings of Pearse, to God's will. As with Columba's involvement with his family's squabbles in *The Enemy Within*, religion serves as catalyst and accompaniment to politics.

In his second sermon, given on the same day as the first, the Priest changes tactics entirely. Since preaching the first sermon he apparently (perhaps as a result of a communication from his superiors in the hierarchy) has bought the official line that the IRA was behind the seizure of the Guildhall. Consequently, although he still extols the goals of the civil rights movement as peaceful, dignified, and respectful, Skinner, Lily, and Michael are no longer Christlike martyrs who sacrificed their lives for the benefit of others but dupes of the IRA who contaminated the movement and proposed to sell out the Irish people to "Godless communism." Now instead of firing imaginations and stiffening resolutions, the Priest wishes to promote "that most revolutionary of doctrines"—"'Blessed are the meek for they shall possess the land'" (*SP*, 155–56). The implication is clear—the hierarchy can be quite Janus-faced when it comes to looking out for its own interests, and the discourse of the clergy has its own unique powers of misrepresentation.

By the time of the funeral the next day the church hierarchy has had another change of heart, or at least a change of tactics, for they are out in force. The mass is celebrated by no less than the four Northern bishops together, and the Cardinal Primate was flown in from Rome. Not to be outdone by the hierarchy, virtually the entire government of the Republic—the Taoiseach plus the "entire Dail and Senate"—attended the ceremony. All of this is described by RTE newsman O'Kelly with great gravity and great care to convey the magnitude of the dignity evident in this expression of "enormous grief" that has "furrowed the mind of this ancient, noble, suffering city of St. Colmcille" (SP, 167). O'Kelly conveys this atmosphere of grave dignity impeccably except for the one slip of getting Skinner's real name wrong. Again the spirit of gravity in this representation is completely at odds with what we have witnessed in the Guildhall. O'Kelly's rendition, greatly enhanced by the power and reach of his medium, is no less an exaggeration than the others. In fact, it tends to reinforce the Priest's first sermon as the broadcast sympathizes with the long-suffering city, besieged now (by unspoken implication) by the very ancestors of those who suffered the siege of 1688–89. The intimation here seems to be that the news media is an accomplice, unwitting or not, to the efforts of the church hierarchy and the politicians of the Republic to take advantage of the Derry tragedy to promote their own images. Three different discourses coincide here—religious, political, and journalistic—to distort by word and gesture the deaths of three people we have come to know.

Contrary to those who see *The Freedom of the City* as nationalist propaganda, Friel is as hard on the Irish sympathizers—the clergy, the press, Irish politicians, and the sentiment on the Derry streets represented by the Balladeer—as he is on the Judge and the other British sympathizers. As Elizabeth Hale Winkler says, "Friel shows us exactly how such factors as rumor and counter-rumor, fear and nervousness, mutual suspicion, sectarian assumptions and political punitive thinking combine to create a situation in which shootings are at least comprehensible, if not inevitable or justifiable" (1981, 21). This more balanced view of the play does not deny Friel's genuine sympathy for his three victims or for the Catholic cause in the North. It does claim, however, that Friel's tough-minded sympathy is not blind to the distortions of discourse on either side nor to how the distortions on both sides contributed to the tragedy. This kind of double vision is what is lacking in Friel's Judge and in the *Widgery Report*, where it was desperately needed. In this case, the commitment of art displayed more objectivity than the inquiry of justice.

Dr. Philip Alexander Dodds, "an elderly American professor with an informal manner" (SP, 110), presents the most difficult interpretive puz-

zle in the play. Critics have not been able to judge whether Friel is satirizing Dodds's ivory tower detachment from the personal tragedies he
comments on or whether through Dodds Friel directs our attention to
the issue of poverty (McGowan 1980, 298; Winkler 1981, 22–23). Some
credit Dodds with the most objective view of the events (Jent 1994, 577;
O'Brien 1989, 82; Rix 1980, 91), while others are not sure he is any closer
to the reality of the three victims than the Judge, even if Lily and Skinner
do illustrate some of Dodds's theses about the poor.[3] Winkler articulates
the problem most clearly:

> Are we to take him completely seriously, as a mouthpiece of a wider so-
> cial insight, perhaps identical with Friel's? His analysis is often chillingly
> accurate. But in total effect Dodds is too impartial to understand the
> particular manifestations of discrimination in Northern Ireland, and
> many of his remarks prove to be true of only one or two of the three
> protagonists. Above all, he never refers either to the action of the play or
> to any of its characters. He is completely uninvolved and presents his
> analysis directly to the audience. . . . If Friel's ultimate goal is to awaken
> not only intellectual understanding but also emotional sympathy for the
> underprivileged minority, then Dodd's role is an ambiguous one: his is a
> necessary cold and clear voice, but in his lack of feeling and involvement
> he is in the end closer to the establishment characters whom Friel sati-
> rizes. (1981, 23)

Although I offer no definitive arguments to solve the Dodds puzzle,
there are two perspectives that have not been considered yet. One is
gained by looking at the source for Dodds's theories, the American anthropologist Oscar Lewis, while the other is gained by examining how
Dodds's discourse interacts with other discourses in the play. Richard
Pine and William Jent both mention Lewis and provide pertinent quotes,
but neither probes very far into the Friel-Lewis connection. In an interview with Eavan Boland just prior to the opening of *The Freedom of the
City*, Friel said that when Bloody Sunday happened he was at work on a
play about evictions in the eighteenth century: "And then Bloody Sunday
happened," he said, "and the play I was writing, and wasn't succeeding
with, suddenly found a focus. I was stuck until this point and this was a
kind of clarification" (Boland 1973, 18). Apparently what *The Freedom of*

3. E. Andrews 1995, 135; Pine 1990, 111–14; Winkler 1981, 22–23.

the City and the play about evictions had in common was the issue of poverty, and this is what came into focus for Friel with Bloody Sunday. In fact, at the time he insisted that *The Freedom of the City* is "not about Bloody Sunday" but "a play which is about poverty" (Boland 1973, 18). Now we are under no obligation to accept a playwright's own understanding of his play; a very cogent case can be made for reading the play as one about political injustice in Northern Ireland. Nevertheless, the details Friel used to draw the characters of his three protagonists suggest that the impoverished condition of the politically disenfranchised in Derry was indeed a major concern.

If we grant that concern, then understanding the role of Oscar Lewis may be illuminating. A number of things about Lewis must have appealed to Friel. Lewis is known in anthropology both for his controversial theoretical concept of the "culture of poverty" and for his methodological innovations. Lewis's notion of a "culture of poverty" became the foundation for a number of Lyndon Johnson's Great Society policies and programs, such as Head Start. His methods emphasized extensive documentation in the words of the impoverished themselves, particularly in underdeveloped regions of the world, such as Mexico, Puerto Rico, Cuba, and India.

Of Dodds's three lectures, the first two consist entirely of material taken almost verbatim from the last section of Lewis's introduction to *La Vida* entitled "The Culture of Poverty," in which he explains the concept he was famous for. These two lectures essentially summarize Lewis's notion of the culture of poverty as an inherited "social and psychological condition" as well as an economic condition. Consequently poverty cannot be addressed through economic means only. The psychological and social conditions must also be addressed in order to disrupt the cycle of poverty that passes from generation to generation. The culture of poverty is also an inherited adaptive and reactive mechanism that enables the poor to cope with their hopeless and marginalized status in stratified, capitalistic society (*SP*, 110). Because the poor feel "inferior, marginal, helpless, dependent," they tend to be present oriented, and rather than plan for the future, they focus "with resignation and frustration" on the "here and now" (*SP*, 133). Consequently the poor are often more spontaneous, sensual, and fun-loving than the more repressed, future-oriented middle class.

Methodologically Lewis typically focused on family structures and his book *La Vida: A Puerto Rican Family in the Culture of Poverty—San Juan and New York,* the book Friel used, is a series of autobiographies by members of an extended family to which Lewis added a lengthy theoretical introduction. The autobiographies are based on taped interviews with the family members and they present a vivid and compelling family portrait in the unexpurgated language of the family members themselves. In these recorded stories, Lewis says,

> I have tried to give a voice to people who are rarely heard, and to provide the reader with an inside view of a style of life which is common in many of the deprived and marginal groups in our society but which is largely unknown, ignored or inaccessible to most middle-class readers. . . . It is my hope that a better understanding of the nature of the culture of poverty will eventually lead to a more sympathetic view of the poor and their problems and will provide a more rational basis for constructive social action. (1966, xii)

This statement could also apply to *The Freedom of the City,* which like Lewis's *La Vida* juxtaposes concrete illustrations of the Derry poor in their own voices with an elaborate abstract and theoretical structure. So *La Vida* may have provided Friel with more than just Dodds's ideas; it may have been, along with the *Widgery Report,* the inspiration for the structure and technique of the play.

In addition to the structure and technique of *La Vida* and its central ideas on the culture of poverty, other ideas of Lewis must have resonated with Friel's view of the impoverished and disenfranchised in Northern Ireland. For example, in his introduction Lewis says that the culture of poverty is "endemic in colonialism" (1966, l) and often results "from imperial conquest in which the native social and economic structure is smashed and the natives are maintained in a servile colonial status, sometimes for many generations" (1966, xlv). Friel's work from *The Freedom of the City* on, particularly *Translations,* demonstrates his growing understanding of the historical implications of Ireland's long colonial servitude to an imperial power.

Lewis's sympathy for the poor and his understanding of the connection between the culture of poverty and the forces that produce it, such as capitalism and colonialism, were only part of his legacy. Another part was the appropriation of the notion of the culture of poverty by political reactionaries to justify doing nothing for the poor, since, according to Lewis, eliminating poverty itself did not necessarily eliminate the psychological and social structures endemic to the culture of poverty, which he says "is a whole way of life" (1966, lii). Lewis himself did not share the reactionary view. In fact, his studies in Cuba reinforced his own socialist sympathies and made him "inclined to believe that the culture of poverty does not exist in the socialist countries" (1966, xlix). Lewis's own sympathies, however, did not prevent people from exploiting the reactionary potential of his notion of the culture of poverty.

Whether Friel's understanding of Lewis was based on the sympathies evident in his introduction to *La Vida* or on his controversial reputation is not clear. The portrait of Dodds, as Winkler has pointed out, could be read either way. More than one critic has pointed out that Dodds places the Derry incident in an international perspective (Jent 1994, 579; McGowan 1980, 298). But does Friel mean to imply here that the civil rights movement in Northern Ireland will extricate the Catholic minority from their culture of poverty? Skinner and Lily do not seem to have this level of awareness, and Michael is very naïve in his.

The ambivalence of Dodds's character has led Richard Pine to conclude that Friel's construal of Dodds is aesthetically flawed. He calls Dodds "the sociologist ex-machina" (1990, 113) and suggests that Friel subverted Lewis in an "unsuccessful attempt to universalise the condition of poverty" (1990, 111). Pine does not venture to guess whether the subversion was intentional or not, but he does feel that Friel shared the views of Dodds/Lewis but did not successfully implement them in the play: "Lewis's thesis remains implicit in Friel's thinking rather than fully-fledged in his play" (1990, 112).

Friel's handling of Dodds contributes significantly to the ambivalent response to him. If we examine how and where Dodds's lectures on the sociology and anthropology of poverty interact with the text, the impression of Dodds tends to be favorable, but this favorable impression is then countered by the degree of Dodds's detachment from the events of the play and by the academic ambivalence of his conclusions, which are presented in a third lecture that Friel did not take from Lewis's *La Vida*.

All Dodds's lectures are sandwiched between scenes in the mayor's parlor and scenes of the Judge's interrogations. This consistent juxtaposition seems to imply that Dodds mediates between the unjust bias of the Judge's assumptions and what we witness in the mayor's parlor. Indeed, Dodds provides exactly the sociological perspective the Judge refuses to consider. As William Jent points out, Dodds's lectures constitute the only public discourse in the play that focuses primarily on poverty and, as a Brechtian alienation device, they raise the issue in its relation to the march in the minds of the audience (1994, 576, 580). The information Lily reveals about her background certainly stresses its poverty, but without Dodds's lectures the issues of political injustice would have overwhelmed the issues of social injustice even more than they do in the play's present form.

Sometimes the positioning of Dodds's lectures serve to illustrate his points and therefore reinforce the authority of his views within the context of the play. For example, Dodds's second lecture, in which he says that the present-orientation of the poor makes them more spontaneous, sensual, and fun-loving than the more repressed, future-oriented middle class, is followed by the scene in the mayor's parlor in which Skinner and Lily thoroughly enjoy themselves masquerading in the robes of the mayor, aldermen, and councillors. Michael, who has internalized middle-class values, is very uncomfortable with such frivolity, and he asserts the necessity for peaceful, dignified protest. Because he is shaped by the culture of poverty but espouses middle-class values, Michael is denied the adaptive compensations of a here-and-now mentality capable of alleviating the psychological oppression, at least temporarily, with spontaneity and humor. Consequently he has the worst of both worlds. The second lecture is also juxtaposed to the scene in which the general in charge of the military operation justifies the excessively disproportionate force deployed before the Guildhall. This juxtaposition appears to reinforce Lewis's views that the values of the dominant culture, enforced by physical force if necessary, are largely responsible for enforcing the psychological and social as well as the economic conditions of the culture of poverty. When Lily, Skinner, and Michael finally walk out with their hands above their heads, this too seems to illustrate a Dodds / Lewis thesis—that the only certain future facing the poor is death. As with the worldwide culture of poverty, their fate has been known from the beginning.

The wisdom of Dodds's views on the culture of poverty, however, is countered by what Winkler has called the "lack of feeling and involvement" in his manner. He always addresses the audience with calm informality, which Friel underscores in his first lecture by accompanying Dodds's entrance with the offstage sounds of a civil rights rally in progress with a fiery Bernadette Devlin–type figure addressing the crowd. Dodds addresses the audience with the rally continuing in the background, thus creating a sharp contrast between Dodds's manner and the Devlin-type firebrand. This lecture is interrupted by the roar of tanks moving on the rally. The woman addressing the crowd urges them to stand their ground and shooting and pandemonium break out. When the noise subsides and fades into the background again, Dodds calmly resumes his lecture without acknowledging the interruption. What are we to make of this? Is Friel satirizing the disinterested "objectivity" of the American academic establishment in relation to Irish studies? Is Dodds an example of the objectivity the Judge travesties? Is his "objectivity" a mask for indifference?

Another Dodds puzzle revolves around his final lecture, most of which does not come from Lewis's *La Vida*. It occurs immediately after the Judge's interrogation of the pathologist, who describes in chilling clinical language the number of wounds to the three victims (thirty-four total) and the extent of the mutilation they caused. Dodds's lecture then gives some statistics about the inequitable distribution of wealth in Latin America and the United States. Is Dodds's statistical detachment analogous to the chill in the pathologist's language? Or does it suggest compassion for the poor throughout the world?

Dodds's conclusions in this third lecture raise even more problems. He notes that proposed solutions to the inequitable distribution of wealth have ranged from insisting that the poor help themselves to restructuring the "entire free enterprise system" (*SP*, 163). But Dodds's academic detachment expresses no preference of his own. Instead he concludes that until disagreement over possible solutions is resolved (as unlikely a possibility as one could imagine) the poor will become more numerous, more alienated, more insecure, and that the only certainty in their future is death. This prediction certainly has much greater rhetorical and emotional impact following, as it does, immediately after the pathologist's gruesome description of the bodies of Lily, Skinner, and Michael.

In the end we must ask ourselves whether Dodds's detachment under the circumstances is any less insidious than the more obvious injustice of the Judge. On the one hand, I would have to agree with Pine that if Friel's intent was to emphasize the social issues, his relative handling of the Judge and the forces marshaled against his protagonists in comparison with his handling of Dodds worked against that intent. On the other hand, perhaps the contradictions in Friel's handling of Dodds aptly represent the contradictions in the handling of poverty within a capitalist colonial structure, where, as Lewis suggests, poverty is endemic. Consequently any attempts to alleviate it are necessarily academic and abstract.

Although interpretations of *The Freedom of the City* have focused on the social and political issues raised by the play, the range of responses on those issues has varied widely, particularly about the relative balance between political and social issues in the play. Some political readings look right past the social issues the play raises. The English press, for example, found *The Freedom of the City* little more than anti-English Celtic propaganda.[4] Purely political readings on the Irish side also tended to ignore the play's concern with the plight of Derry's poor. Ulick O'Connor, who reads the play from a traditional republican nationalist perspective, says that in *The Freedom of the City* "Friel confronts the implications of the British Government's failure to apply the Rule of Law to the Executive in Northern Ireland and uses the events of Bloody Sunday to explore the problem which is at the root of the relationship between this country and England" (1989, 10). Others see the play as partisan but not propagandist (McGowan 1980, 301; Winkler 1981, 25).

The polarization among critical responses has not been helped by Friel's own ambivalence about the play. From statements he made before the premiere Friel obviously anticipated some political readings of the play, but hoped, perhaps wishfully, that people could read beyond them. In the interview with Eavan Boland he raises the formalist issue of aes-

4. E. Andrews 1995, 129; Dantanus 1988, 140; O'Connor 1989, 14.

thetic distance and hopes that the social issue of poverty will take precedence over political readings of the play:

> This play raises the old problem of writing about events which are still happening. It's the old problem of the distinction between the mind that suffers and the man who creates. The trouble about this particular play in many ways is that people are going to find something immediate in it, some kind of reportage. And I don't think that's in it at all. Very often an accident in history will bring about a meeting point, a kind of fusion for you. And this is what happened. This is a play which is about poverty. But because we're all involved in the present situation people are going to say "this is a very unfair play," and of necessity it has got to be unfair in this public kind of way. I hope that people will come to see this with an open mind. But, of course, they may come and see in it only a confirmation of some kind of prejudice in the play anyhow. (Boland 1973, 18)

Nonpolitical readings of *The Freedom of the City* have come mainly from critics who share a New Critical, formalist approach. Their strategies, which define art as disinterested, predictably find Friel more aesthetically detached and more interested in individuating his protagonists than in the abstract rhetoric of his other figures.[5] Winkler, for example, cites Friel's deviation from the actual events of Bloody Sunday as an act of "deliberate artistic distancing" (1981, 16), and she suggests that when Friel does express his personal views he does it with bad art, that is, by not fully realizing some of his figures, such as the Judge, as characters (1981, 23). In the end, however, Winkler's astute reading skills do make some of Friel's political concerns very evident and she is forced to contradict herself and her formalist aesthetic (1981, 27–28).

A reading of *The Freedom of the City*, however, need not be limited to formalist strategies nor to thematic readings focusing on poverty, the Catholic minority in the North, or politics in Northern Ireland. *The Freedom of the City* is the first play in which Friel displays an awareness of how discourse shapes the institutional realities that we inhabit. Figures like the Judge and Professor Dodds, in other words, are not just unrealized characters or abstract satirical figures; rather they, along with the

5. Dantanus 1988, 137–39; Maxwell 1973, 104; Winkler 1981, 16, 23.

military, the police, the expert witnesses, the media, the Priest, and the Balladeer, represent the various institutional discourses within whose horizons Lily, Skinner, and Michael must work out their fate. These discourses establish the arena of experience, so to speak, in which the victims are sacrificed.

If *The Freedom of the City* is read as a play about language and discourse and how they function in relation to each other and to the fate of individuals, then the issue whether the play is about poverty or politics is less crucial, as is the issue of Friel's personal politics. Friel's use of generic titles rather than names for some of the figures (the Judge, the Priest, the Balladeer) suggests that they are important not as individuals but because they represent the array of institutional discourses that interact, through both collision and collusion, in actual historical incidents like Bloody Sunday. Collusion, by the way, is not necessarily limited to nonopposing discourses. As we saw above, the Balladeer and the RTE newsman both contribute to the rumor shared by the military that the Guildhall was deliberately occupied in an act of political defiance, a view that later governed the Judge's official inquiry. Rather than perceiving the institutional discourses as "bogus" (E. Andrews 1995, 130), "dishonest" (Verstraete 1988, 88), or transparently inadequate (O'Brien 1989, 81) in comparison to the more "fully realized" dialogue of Lily, Skinner, and Michael, we should recognize that Friel has given us very powerful and "honest" realizations of the various discourses of power in Northern Ireland. Perhaps Friel's most important insight in this play is, as Winkler suggests, that these discourses create the lived history we all inhabit. As George O'Brien says, "Lily, Michael, and Skinner, are flayed in the crosstalk of language from the various 'framers' [i.e., institutional discourses] as surely as they are butchered by the soldiers' bullets" (1989, 79).

This reading of *The Freedom of the City* on the register of discourse is not without its lacunae. It does not explain the relationship of the various institutional discourses to the conventional realistic scenes in the mayor's parlor. It is easy to see the impact of the discourses on the three victims, but they themselves do not participate in them and they do not appear to be formed by them. Somehow they are immune to assimilating them at the same time they are destroyed by them. Instead of being shaped by the institutional codes that shape the public figures, they are drawn according to another code (that of literary realism) based on a fundamentally different epistemology that emphasizes and privileges their individuality rather than their institutional encoding. Of course they *are* encoded—Lily by her culture of poverty, Skinner by his personality type, and Michael by his bourgeois values—but they are also represented in a more traditional literary form with all of its assumptions about how character is constructed from within. The same kind of split characterizes Joyce's *Ulysses,* which is partly centered on the consciousnesses of its three protagonists and partly on social, cultural, and institutional discourse forms. And like Joyce's *Ulysses, The Freedom of the City* represents both of these modernist and postmodernist epistemologies in its structure and techniques. On the one hand, Maxwell, a modernist critic, notes how the characters Lily, Skinner, and Michael particularize different perspectives on reality (1973, 104). According to this reading strategy, they provide three different points of view on the situation. They do not necessarily distort the "facts," but the facts of the situation have very different meanings for them as they are folded into their experience and consciousness. In a poststructuralist reading, on the other hand, the institutional discourses fabricate their facts, and they are no less real for that. The military perceived themselves opposed by forty gunman and acted accordingly. The Judge saw three armed terrorists, the Priest three martyrs, and the Balladeer three Irish heroes.

This split between conventional characterization and discourse forms poses an interpretive challenge. Is the text deliberately schizophrenic? If so, what are we to make of it? Or is the text genuinely torn between modernist and postmodern modes of representation? That we can so easily measure the distortion between what goes on in the Guildhall and the representations of that activity by the various institutional discourses raises a serious problem. Both before and after *The Freedom of the City* (for example, in *The Gentle Island* and in *Faith Healer*) Friel seems to acknowledge that we have no privileged access to reality apart from our narrative representations of them. But in *The Freedom of the City* his portrayal of the scenes in the mayor's parlor in terms of the conventions of literary realism bestows a privileged status on that version of events and makes all the other versions appear distorted or untrue. For example, we in the audience know that they were not armed and that they were not organized terrorists who deliberately seized the Guildhall. Nor were they martyrs or heroes in the usual sense. Perhaps Friel at this point, like Western intellectual culture generally, was vacillating between modernist and postmodern views of language and the play questions the adequacy of institutional discourses to signify character and experience. In this play at least, Friel appears to privilege the code of literary realism as a norm against which the distortions of institutional discourses can be measured. The result is a contradiction, since the play also demonstrates an awareness of how institutional discourses are formative as well as deformative of actual events. And this contradiction has led to oversimplified readings, such as the suggestion that the play moves away from the reality witnessed at the beginning to the fictions contrived about it (Rix 1980, 85).

If *The Freedom of the City* did not entirely make the transition from a modern to a postmodern epistemology, it did mark a transition in Friel's oeuvre from a colonial to a postcolonial consciousness. Although some of the earlier plays did deal with postcolonial symptoms of the Republic of Ireland, the general invisibility in Friel's early work of the border between Northern Ireland and the Republic indicates that, as a British subject of Northern Ireland, Friel had not yet openly acknowledged his colonized status. As a writer his nationalist identification with the Republic enabled him to repress his colonial status, and when that status emerged, as it did in *The Loves of Cass McGuire,* it emerged in disguised and displaced form. Friel's heightened linguistic consciousness in *The Freedom of the City,* however, signals the emergence of his recognition of colonial status into the full light of consciousness. As Lewis argued about the poor, when mired within the culture of poverty they tend to be "provincial and locally orientated and have very little sense of history"; they do not understand that their problems and conditions are shared by the poor the world over. But when they do "acquire an objective view of their condition" (as presumably they would under socialism), "from that moment they have broken out of their subculture, even though they may still be desperately poor. And any movement . . . which gives them this objectivity . . . inevitably smashes the rigid caste that encases their minds and bodies" (*SP,* 111). This same argument applies to the colonized. Once they have become "objectively" aware of their situation, or in Fanon's terms, once they call their colonial situation into question, they begin the process of decolonization, and "all decolonization," Fanon insists, "is successful" (1963, 37). It cannot be said that Northern nationalists had little sense of history, but their sense of history, at least prior to 1968, could be said to be local and provincial, a narrow view of history from within their own tradition. The civil rights movement in Northern Ireland, however, made Northern nationalists realize that they shared a condition with the oppressed worldwide: the civil rights movement itself consciously modeled its techniques on those of Martin Luther King and sang "We Shall Overcome" at its rallies; Friel's play, through the character of Michael, invokes Gandhi and the struggle for independence in India; and republican murals in Derry and Belfast identify their plight with Palestinians, South African blacks, Native Americans, and women everywhere (Rolston 1992, 49–59). In a sense, *The Freedom of the City* marks the beginning of decolonization for Friel as a Northern nationalist writer, and so, as postcolonial theory suggests, it is no accident that the transformation in his colonial consciousness is accompanied by a transformation in his linguistic consciousness.

Volunteers

One somewhat puzzling issue about *The Freedom of the City* is the absence of any reference to the IRA. By 1970, the year in which the play is set, the IRA was active again, and by Bloody Sunday their extreme republicanism had become one of the discourses of power in the North. Perhaps one could claim that the references to the hooligan element by Michael and the priest encompass the IRA, but if the *Widgery Report* is any indication of local usage, there is a clear distinction between hooligans and gunmen. Widgery tried to make a case for the presence and influence of IRA gunmen on Bloody Sunday, but lacking any firm evidence, he had to content himself with focusing primarily on "hooligans" who had been observed throwing things at British troops. Several critics have noted Friel's omission of the IRA, but none offers any illuminating explanations (Maxwell 1973, 105; Winkler 1981, 17–18).

Whatever Friel's reasons for ignoring the IRA in *The Freedom of the City,* his next play compensates for the omission by giving them a leading role as social and cultural metaphor. *Volunteers,* which premiered at the Abbey in 1975, is set in a Dublin archaeological dig. In a situation that recalls the Wood Quay controversy, the dig must excavate the site of an ancient Viking settlement before a new hotel complex is constructed over it. The dig is staffed by a volunteer work crew of political internees and supervised by a warder and an archaeology professor. Because they volunteered for the dig, the prisoners on the work crew have been tried and convicted of collaboration by their fellow internees, who have planned a prison riot to camouflage the execution of one or more of them. Escape is no option because their comrades outside prison would enforce the executions as well. Their sentences, revealed at the end of act 1, hang over their activities on stage like a pall.

Beneath this pall events take place on two levels: the first is the archeological activity of the dig, and the second level consists of the interactions among the prisoners orchestrated by the incessant bantering and clowning of Keeney and his sidekick Pyne. Friel describes Keeney as "Quick witted, quick tongued, and never for a second unaware. Years of practice have made the public mask of joker almost perfect" (*VO,* 17). Keeney's banter includes bawdy rhymes and narratives about the Viking skeleton dubbed Leif, who was unearthed in the dig. Keeney provides a surface veneer of humorous and ironic commentary that tugs emotionally against the pall of death that hangs over them all. Keeney's stories and banter also serve the dramatic function of revealing things about himself and his fellow volunteers and of linking their fates (and the fate of the Irish in general) to the victimization of Leif, whose leather thong about his neck and small hole in his skull indicate that he suffered some kind of ritual execution. Leif's skeleton lies exposed on stage for most of the performance as a constant reminder of the fatal subterranean currents on which Keeney's comic routines float.

In one of his comic routines that mimics a history lesson by Dr. King, the professor in charge of the dig, Keeney suggests how the different registers on which the play operates interact with each other. Keeney notes that the excavations, which range from early Viking times to late Georgian Dublin, "a period of approximately a thousand years," provide "an encapsuled history, a tangible précis of the story of Irish man" (*VO,* 36). "The more we learn about our ancestors," Keeney pontificates, "the more we discover about ourselves . . . what we are all engaged in here is really a thrilling voyage in *self*-discovery" (*VO*, 37; Friel's emphasis). What these explorers into the Irish past discover about themselves is not reassuring: they are being used by the bourgeois society that interned them "because of attitudes that might be inimical to public security" (*VO*, 55), and when they have finished using them they will be returned to prison where execution by their fellow internees most likely awaits them. They are lost in every sense. No allegiance has any significance for them; no effort or activity has any meaning. Most of the activity of the play is a comic mask designed to disguise from themselves the ultimate meaninglessness of their fate. This is perhaps Friel's most Beckettian play, and Keeney's question about this "voyage in *self*-discovery" — "how many of us want to make *that* journey?" (*VO*, 37; Friel's emphasis) — is very apt.

Although *Volunteers* invokes the politically charged subject of internment, as Seamus Heaney has pointed out to critics who have read the play as being about the politics of internment, "The play is not a quarrel with others but a vehicle for Friel's quarrel with himself . . . It is more about values and attitudes within the Irish psyche than it is about the rights and wrongs of the political situation, and represents a further digging of the site cleared in his *Freedom of the City*" (1975, 806). Although Ulf Dantanus finds *Volunteers* "extremely difficult" to interpret (1988, 155), he has provided the best critique of the play to date. He agrees with Heaney and says the play "attempts to disentangle the complex web of loyalties that determines the political complications in the North," and in the process reveals "the confusion within the Irish psyche" (1988, 154).

Beyond representing the Irish psyche engaged on a voyage of self-discovery, however, *Volunteers* plays on another register that adds a further layer of exploration. As with its immediate predecessor *The Freedom of the City*, *Volunteers* is a play intimately concerned with the functions of language and narrative. Dantanus gives us only an intimation of this concern: he cites Keeney's prattle as evidence that "Friel may intend no more than an allusion to the hazards of communication" (1988, 154). But, as Keeney speculates on the cause of Leif's death, his most interesting speculation is that Leif (like the three victims in *The Freedom of the City*) was a "casualty of language," and "which of us here isn't?" he adds (*VO*, 28). In what sense is Lief a "casualty of language"? Likewise, in what sense are Keeney and the others casualties of language? To address these questions excavates another layer of Friel's *Volunteers,* a layer that perhaps challenges Fanon's assumption that "all decolonization is successful."

The role of *Hamlet* in *Volunteers* bears directly on these questions. Keeney asks several times in the course of the play, "Was Hamlet really mad?" One of those times occurs immediately after he speculates that Leif was a casualty of language. The function of *Hamlet,* it turns out, is crucial to understanding what Keeney calls the "hazards of language" (*VO,* 28), the explorations of which make *Volunteers* one of Friel's earliest language plays.

The superficial allusions to *Hamlet* are obvious. The excavation pit that constitutes the set is variously described as a bomb crater, a huge womb, a prison yard (*VO,* 35); but it also alludes to the grave digging scene in *Hamlet,* with Keeney and his cohorts, particularly Pyne, corresponding to the clowns Hamlet happens upon as they dig Ophelia's grave. But Keeney's clowning and posing, along with his "antic imagination" (*VO,* 71), generally make him a Hamlet figure as well. As with almost everything in *Hamlet,* Keeney warns us, with an allusion to the "Swan of Avon," that the diggers in *Volunteers* "are not what they seem" (*VO,* 36). Keeney in particular is not what he seems; as with Hamlet, his mad verbal antics mask a profound despair. At one point when an archaeology student asks him what his mad muttering is about, Keeney replies, "Just trying to keep sane" (*VO,* 31).

On a less obvious level *Hamlet* serves a more profound function in *Volunteers* that involves a sense of history and the relation of language and narrative to history, a topic Friel explores in more depth in *Translations* and *Making History.* Despite Keeney's posturings about the dig being an encapsulated history, Friel makes it clear that the notion of history he is playing with has nothing to do with positivist facts. At one point in the play the digger Butt challenges the dating of a twelfth-century Viking ship because they discover a bone carving of the ship on the same level of the dig as the tenth-century Viking clay-and-wattle house they have unearthed. The matter is never resolved. Friel's point apparently (a point he has made elsewhere) is that it does not matter. What is preserved as history in this play is preserved in language — in limericks, in comic banter, in invented narrative — and the history so preserved is what boxes in the five diggers. By digging into their national past they are uncovering the forces that bind them to their present destiny. In two senses then, they are digging their own graves—they are simultaneously exhuming their own past as they prepare their own burial.

The play on archaeology in *Volunteers* has an analogy with the historical Hamlet. The Viking finds in *Volunteers* range from the tenth-century clay-and-wattle house to the thirteenth-century jug the archaeologist George reconstructs. This period is roughly contemporaneous with stories about Hamlet that circulated from the tenth to the twelfth centuries and culminated in the *Historia Danica* of Saxo Grammaticus. These stories are the original sources of our knowledge about Hamlet. The "historical" Hamlet, in other words, exists, as far as we know, only in these narratives and others like them that constitute a history to which Shakespeare's version contributes. Hamlet, then, exists primarily as an effect of language and so can be said to be quite literally "a casualty of language."

Beyond the allusions to *Hamlet,* the limericks, songs, verbal banter, and narratives in *Volunteers* create, like the excavations themselves, an encapsulated version of Irish history that establishes the discourses, sets the horizons, and limits the possibilities within which the prisoners/diggers must work out their destiny, very much as the fates of Michael, Skinner, and Lily are determined by the discourses of *The Freedom of the City*. These verbal forms create something comparable to the history Hamlet inherits at the beginning of Shakespeare's play and the role he must play in it. Take, for example, Keeney's bawdy limerick about Parnell:

> There once was a bird called O'Shea
> Who was known as a fabulous lay.
> Then along came Parnell
> Who screwed her to hell
> And we feel the results to this day. (*VO,* 18)

This limerick does not have the air of historical profundity. Yet it invokes the history of internecine warfare that led Joyce's Stephen Dedalus, who felt the lingering results of the Parnell affair forcefully one Christmas dinner, to call Ireland "the old sow that eats her farrow" (1976b, 203). Like Parnell, Keeney and his fellow diggers, who faithfully served the republican movement, are persecuted, not for betraying the movement or for any antirepublican activities, but because they violated a code of behavior. The play represents, then, not so much the injustice of internment as the insensitivity of the Irish in their treatment of one another.

Other limericks function similarly. One about Leif casts him as a victim of sectarian warfare "between Jesus and Thor" (VO, 18); another casts the prisoner Knox as a Calvinist in a mixed marriage to a papist; one about the leftist student Des notes that his Marxist cant never realizes itself in action. The final limerick encapsulates the entire play as well as Keeney's final assessment of the diggers' desperate situation:

> On an archaeological site
> Five diggers examined their plight
> But a kangaroo court
> Gave the final report—
> They were only a parcel of . . . (VO, 88)

Two songs also comment on what the diggers lack most in the world—any source of love that might lead to concern (either personal or general) about their plight. "There is a Tavern in the Town" (VO, 79–80) depicts a relationship destroyed by insensitivity. Keeney and Pyne sing from the famous refrain:

> Fare thee well for I must leave thee;
> Do not let this parting grieve thee.
> And remember that the best of friends must part, must part.
> Adieu, adieu, kind friends, adieu, adieu, adieu.
> I can no longer stay with you, stay with you.

But the first stanza that sets up the refrain is equally relevant to the diggers' abandonment:

> There is a tavern in the town,
> And there my true love sits him down,
> And drinks his wine with laughter and with glee,
> And never, never thinks of me.

"The Bonny Labouring Boy" sung by Pyne depicts a girl whose parents disapprove of her love of a laborer and ask why she throws herself away on a "poor labouring boy?" (VO, 34, 54). "Powerful aul' song," remarks

Keeney (*VO*, 54), who apparently intuits in the rejection of the "labour-ing boy" an analogue to the abandonment of the diggers by every ele-ment of Irish society. Friel implies that the rejection of the diggers is comparable to the rejection of history implied in the precedence of the hotel business over archaeology.

The ceaseless banter of Keeney and Pyne, like the songs and limer-icks, masks at the same time that it reveals a substantive message be-neath its antic surface. Through this banter we learn about Dr. King's book on radiocarbon dating, a book dedicated to the site supervisor George. Keeney's mockery of King and George's later obsession with the vase he restored suggests that the focus of these archaeologists is less on the human than on the scientific and on artifacts for their own sake.

Keeney also philosophizes through his banter. He tells George that Eternal Verity is actually a Derry whore by the name of Vera McLaugh-lin who spends her nights "dodging about the quays" (*VO*, 55). When Keeney looks at the vase George restored, it is no mere artifact or testi-mony to the art of the restorer, but a symbol of Smiler restored to his original self before he was beaten out of his senses and sanity by the Dublin police for leading a demonstration to protest the internment of a workmate. When Keeney threatens to toss the fragile jug around, he asks pertinent questions about its ownership that were not raised by the archaeologists. Does Smiler, who found the fragments, own it, or does Dr. King the director of the excavation, or the nation, or Leif the skele-ton? These questions are both flippant and suggest some profound issues about authority, not just authority over the dig and who has the right to call it off to proceed with building the hotel but also authority over his-tory and who has the right to reveal and reconceal it, a debate still cur-rent over historical revisionism in Ireland today. Keeney asks, for example, what wisdom there is in digging a hole and filling it up again. Another banter routine mocks the face that Ireland, while persecuting its own and covering over its history in concrete, presents to the world, par-ticularly to the United States, through its tourist board images. In this routine two American women traveling in Ireland find none of the civil commotion they have heard about but only friendly Irishmen willing to frisk them wherever they went. Even the mad routine about Des having to have his stomach pumped after inadvertently making a cup of coffee with the cremated ashes of his Aunt Coco from California suggests that the American connection may look appealing at first, as a source of value in the Irish exploration of history, but offers ultimately only dead ends of that history. In Keeney's mock letter protesting the termination of the dig he lampoons the hypocrisy of Des's leftist values, along with the motives of Dr. King and his connivance with commercial interests. Finally Keeney's mock versions of George's after-action reports on each of them are delivered in the style of obituaries, thus linking their work at the dig with their fates back at the prison.

Taken together, the banter routines of Keeney and Pyne raise, in comic capsule form, a number of issues crucial to any exploration of Irish history. As Seamus Heaney implies in his poem "Bogland" when he says "Our pioneers keep striking / Inwards and downwards" (1990, 22), Friel seems to suggest that the Irish must look within rather than outside Ireland for solutions to its problems. But Friel also acknowledges how many contradictions, impediments, and values operate in Irish society and culture that block any promising archaeology of the Irish past and how they are likely to sacrifice its diggers to the convenience of the moment.

Although these banter routines are ingeniously pregnant with significance for the play, as a dramatic device they are probably much less effective on the stage than they are on the page. On the page they can be frozen momentarily, isolated from the rapid-fire pace of Keeney's speech, and contemplated with a leisure that would not be available to a theater audience. The routines work as comedy on the surface, but if their denser sublayers are missed, they wear thin long before the end of the play. Even Pyne, who participates in them, wearies of "Keeney's yapping" (*VO*, 81); but Pyne tires of the routines for the opposite reason—when they no longer provide an escape from facing inevitabilities.

In the limericks, songs, and banter Keeney and his fellow diggers, the people who supervise them, and the Irish society they represent all become "casualties of language" in the sense that language represents them all in present time and throughout Irish history as casualties. "Represented as" is the key here. Language makes things appear as something, in this case as victims or casualties. This designation is not inevitable, however. In *The Freedom of the City* Friel demonstrated how various discourses represented the three characters in the Guildhall.

Each discourse assigned a different designation for "representation as" — victim, hero, martyr, terrorist. *Volunteers* puts other Irish discourses into play — archaeology, business, tourism, republicanism, history (particularly certain motifs of Irish history — Parnell, sectarianism, Viking occupations, and so forth). Friel's deployment of the Viking motif illustrates how such a discourse might be manipulated. Like Heaney, Friel does not represent the Viking settlers of Dublin in the traditional manner as raiders and plunderers but as victims, particularly victims of their own culture.[6] In *Volunteers* insensitivity to one's own people and one's own history is the villain and not some outside invader, such as the Vikings, the English, or American economic power. As Dantanus says, "The social and political structure leaves the diggers at the bottom, isolated, misunderstood, confused and divided among themselves" (1988, 160).

More important than the limericks, songs, and banter to illuminating just how Leif, Keeney, and the others are casualties of language are the brief narratives in *Volunteers*, most of them invented by Keeney. These narratives are linked to specific characters in the play, but they also serve as emblematic narratives for Irish history. All the narratives in the play are told about Leif ostensibly, but they also bear resemblances to the lives of the prisoners and serve as metaphors for those lives and for the Irish generally.

The first narrative, told by Pyne, has Leif and his brother Ulf, after settling in Dublin and becoming Christians, set off to discover America. On the return voyage, tall, fair Ulf and his hoard of booty are lost at sea. Small, ginger-haired Leif survives the voyage with his Native American bride. Leif's family blames him and his "black pagan woman" for the fate of Ulf, and they burn the woman and execute Leif too. This narrative has many of the ingredients of Irish history — colonization followed by assimilation, emigration, sectarian suspicion and superstition, religious oppression, tribal retribution, and a femme fatale in the tradition of Dervorgilla and Kitty O'Shea. Pyne's story about Leif, in other words, evokes a long line of Irish figures who became sacrificial victims of their

6. See, for example, Heaney's poems "The Tollund Man," "The Grauballe Man," "Punishment," and "Kinship." For a comparison of Friel and Heaney on use of the metaphor of Viking archaeology see Dantanus 1988, 155.

own society. This narrative also reinforces the limericks about Parnell and about Knox's mixed marriage. After hearing the story, Keeney, knowing what his inmates back at the prison have planned for him, wonders why Leif came back at all. Later he fulminates about the return of Smiler, who has been reduced to an imbecile by one element of Irish society and marked for execution by another.

Another narrative about Leif told by Keeney and Pyne is modeled on Knox's life. In this version Leif, born of royal lineage, descends to the brink of beggary as a street musician after his father's death. He finds fulfillment, companionship, and financial security finally by becoming a runner for a subversive organization, which becomes the most important enterprise of his life. Knox had a privileged upbringing replete with silver service and weekly visits by an Italian cello instructor, but he has become a "snuffling, shuffling, grubby man . . . Not far removed from the kind of man one sees at night wrapped in newspapers and sleeping in the doorways of banks and cinemas" (VO, 15). This story plays on the cliché about all the Irish being kings or sons of kings, but in context, with Knox condemned along with the others by the subversive organization that gave a meaning to his life, it elicits only embarrassment and an obscene, vitriolic response from Knox.

Keeney tells yet another version of Leif's story that applies to the assiduous Butt, who threw himself into his archaeological work more than the others in an effort to ignore his desperate situation. In this version Leif is someone who served his masters loyally and well first as a slave oarsman, then as a blacksmith, a carpenter, and finally as a crofter or tenant farmer; but in the end he is discarded by those masters when he is no longer of use or when he asks for something for himself. Clearly this version of Leif's story highlights the centuries of colonial subjugation of the Irish and it strikes a resonant chord in Butt's psyche. Later when George informs Butt that Keeney is a troublemaker without loyalties and will not be given a good report after his clowning put George's precious restored jug at risk, Butt's response is to drop the jug and reconsign it to the fragmented condition in which they found it. Butt's gesture affirms he will no longer play the loyal servant to be discarded by the master. In destroying the jug Butt lashes out at his betrayal by his own society and symbolically suggests that history restored cannot save them and make them whole again; instead it has become a meaningless academic exercise to further the careers of the professors and their students.

Butt's own rendering of Leif's story draws quite specifically from Keeney's life. In this version Leif is described as being much like Michael Collins, a bank clerk whose courage and brains made him one of the best men in the movement. Like the diggers in the play, Collins was marked for elimination by his former colleagues. In Butt's narrative Leif/Keeney knew where he stood as recently as several months ago when he volunteered for the dig more vociferously than the others. At this point Leif's narrative has shed even its thin camouflage and has taken on the actual details of Keeney's life. Keeney is now Leif and Leif is Keeney, whereas the other versions of Leif's narrative preserved at least a semblance of fiction. Keeney sees himself as someone who is unable to sustain a passion, especially in contrast to Butt, whom he describes as capable of "a consistent passion fueled by a confident intellect." These differences do not matter in the end, however; for Keeney imagines himself and Butt as "spancelled goats complementing each other, suffering the same consequences" (VO, 71).

What we see happening in this play under a seemingly frivolous surface of comedy and make-believe is an archeological excavation layer by layer of an Irish psyche bound to a miserable fate by the stories it tells about itself, by the language games it plays. Like the victims of *The Freedom of the City*, Keeney and his friends (and the Irish through history they have come to represent) become casualties of their own competing, conflicting, and contradictory discourses. Yet a full recognition of their fate is simultaneously distanced by the language, stories, and discourses. What reveals also conceals. As Keeney says when Pyne begins the first narrative about Leif, "'Once upon a time' — ah sure thanks be to God, lads, it's only an aul' yarn" (VO, 61). What Keeney realizes is that "once upon a time," as he says, will "keep up the protection of the myth" (VO, 62). Except for Keeney, the prisoners quite willingly conspire in the various strategies of concealment by refusing to recognize, except in fleeting glimpses, what those strategies simultaneously reveal. Only Keeney appears to be constantly aware of what lies beneath the surface levity of the language. Appropriately the Leif narrative told by Butt about Keeney is denied the "protection of the myth." Keeney's heightened awareness, however, puts his sanity at risk. Smiler represents those who have passed beyond the border of sanity in this voyage of personal and national self-discovery, and this is perhaps why Keeney identifies so much with his near escape. When Smiler returns Keeney refuses to celebrate with the others, whom he calls "imbecile acolytes fluttering about a pig-headed imbecile victim" (VO, 75). Keeney feels Smiler has blown his one feeble chance to escape his final victimization symbolized by the skeleton Leif, and he refuses to participate in the characteristically Irish cult of the victim. "For Christ's sake is there no end to it?" Keeney asks (VO, 75). It is a question Friel seems to pose with this play, which in many ways is as cynical and bleak as Crystal and Fox.

In many ways Keeney is an archetypal colonial figure. He is like Oscar Wilde—the colonial as clown who speaks in riddles his supervisors hardly comprehend. Keeney's limericks, songs, banter, and narratives all mimic Irish history in ways that involve, in Bhabha's terms, splitting, translation, transformation, and displacement. They are like the forms of colonial doubling, hybrid enunciations that are simultaneously repetition and difference, that are both incomplete and in excess ("less than one and doubled"), and that challenge the hegemonic culture by reversing the gaze that subjugates the volunteers as victims. Only in this case, the colonial oppressor is not an offshore imperial power, but rather, as in Joyce's writings, the Irish appear as oppressors of themselves. A new hegemony has created a form of internal colonization that has marginalized those who opposed the old imperial power, a repetition of what happened during and after the Irish civil war. In a sense, Friel again is exploring a postcolonial psyche that has replicated and perpetuated many of the structures of the colonial situation so that the Irish, in the stories and narratives they tell about themselves, continue to perpetuate the victim mentality of colonial times. Unlike Synge's playboy, they have not rewritten their history sufficiently to transform their character and fate. Thus Smiler does not escape, but returns to submit to the fate imposed on him by his country and his colleagues.

6

Family Matters
Living Quarters and *Aristocrats*

FRIEL'S NEXT PLAY, *Living Quarters*, which opened at the Abbey in 1977, returns from the public registers of *The Freedom of the City* and *Volunteers* to further probe the disturbed relations of Irish family life. In this play Friel subordinates a sketchily developed plot to a Pirandello-like technique that introduces thematic concerns beyond those that arise from the melodramatic plot. Played out on the register of a metanarrative and its relation to memory and desire, those concerns continue to explore various functions of language and illusion.

The plot, modeled on *Hippolytus*, is simple. An Irish army officer, Commandant Frank Butler, has just returned a hero from the Middle East, where his unit served as part of the UN peacekeeping forces during the 1970s. His entire family has assembled at his living quarters in Ballybeg, near his home barracks, to help him celebrate the honors bestowed on him for carrying nine of his wounded men to safety. As the family gathers, long-standing tensions between Butler and his children emerge, tensions resulting partly from his own stern personality and partly from his relationship with his equally stern first wife, whom he dutifully if not cheerfully nursed for years before her fatal illness claimed her. While he was gone, Butler's second wife Anna, thirty years younger and married to him only ten days before he left for five months in the Middle East, had an affair with his son Ben. Ben was her own age and full of vengeful anger toward his father. The affair was not carried out with any discretion and the whole town and barracks knew of it except for the Butler family. Shortly after the ceremony bestowing military honors on Butler, Anna informs him of her infidelity with Ben, whereupon Frank laments his unjust fate and to escape his pain puts a bullet through his own head. Despite opportunities, no one makes any attempt to prevent Frank's suicide. At the critical moment all the family members remain "isolated" and "cocooned in their private thoughts," remote from the pleas of Frank (*SP*, 241). The characters' collective guilt provides the premise and the impetus for the play's action.

The plot has the simplicity of its Greek model along with some of its themes. In Euripides's play the son, who is unjustly accused, and the lovestruck wife, his accuser, die in a plot orchestrated by the goddess of love, Aphrodite; but the variations in plot aside, the motifs of revenge, the destructive powers of love run amok, the injustice and mutability of fate are common to both *Hippolytus* and *Living Quarters*. Friel, of course, turns the Greek original toward his own understanding of the crippling and destructive relations between father and son, relations he has explored in other plays and stories, such as *Philadelphia, Here I Come!*, *Crystal and Fox*, *The Gentle Island*, and "The Illusionists." Friel adds a new wrinkle in this play with an equally crippling relationship between a mother (Butler's first wife) and her children. Usually Friel's mothers, if they are present at all, are supportive refuges for their children from their destructive fathers. If Friel's thematic debt to *Hippolytus* could be reduced to a single thought in Euripides' play it would be Phaedra's remark, "Consciousness of a father's or a mother's sins enslaves a man, however stout his heart may be" (Euripides 1958, lines 419–20).

Frank Butler had been a distant and severe father. He himself wondered whether his "lifetime in the army" had not made him carry over into his domestic life a "too rigid military discipline." He was aware that this rigidity had interfered with his relationships with his first wife, with his son Ben, and with his daughter Helen (*SP*, 194). Ben had idolized him, but before long his father's inaccessibility made him feel rejected. Ben's love turned to hate and he became a "spoiled mother's boy" (*SP*, 187). Frank had nursed his first wife through a long and painful illness, and although he had admired her, the joy had gone out of their relationship and his love had "withered into duty" (*SP*, 197). On the day his mother died, Ben called his father a murderer. Frank responded by hitting Ben. When his sister Helen suggested to Ben that his anger and hostility could fade with time, Ben replied, "You can preserve it. . . . You can embalm it consciously, deliberately . . . in acts of terrible perfidy . . . which you do in a state of confusion, out of some vague residual passion that no longer fires you; hitting out, smashing back, not at what's there but at what you think you remember; and which you regret instantly . . . But then it's too late, too late—the thing's preserved in perpetuity" (*SP*, 212). In the end Ben hoped his father had been able to sense the love he had for him "even if it was only in [his] perfidy" (*SP*, 245).

Frank's first wife also had her uncompromising side. Helen blamed her for destroying her marriage to her father's batman Private Gerry Kelly. Before the marriage her mother subjected Kelly to a withering interrogation that reduced him to tears. The marriage lasted only a few months before Kelly "deserted and vanished" (*SP*, 182).

After his first wife died Frank married the much younger Anna, who restored the joy to his life. Frank found Anna refreshingly open, direct, and uncomplicated, completely unlike the rest of the family, whom he characterized as "measured, watching, circling one another, peeping out, shying back" (*SP*, 196).

In its modern context the plot barely escapes melodrama; the primary thematic concerns are elaborated on the register of the metanarrative. The metanarrative is orchestrated by the character of Sir, or I should say the character function of Sir, for, like the public figures in *The Freedom of the City*, he is not a character in the usual sense. He is a narrative and stage device that disrupts while at the same time controlling the plot. Sir seems to fuse some of the functions of author, narrator, director, stage manager, and script manager without being identified with any one of these roles. According to the convention established by the play, he is the creation of the collective memories of the characters, a sort of regulative principle that structures their collective experiences surrounding the suicide of Frank Butler. Sir tells the audience at the beginning,

> the people who were involved in the events of that day, although they're now scattered all over the world, every so often in sudden moments of privacy, of isolation, of panic, they remember that day, and in their imagination they reconvene here [at the Butler's Ballybeg home] to reconstruct it—what was said, what was not said, what was done, what was not done, what might have been said, what might have been done; endlessly raking over those dead episodes that can't be left at peace. . . . But reverie alone isn't adequate for them. And in their imagination, out

of some deep psychic necessity, they have conceived this (*ledger*)—a complete and detailed record of everything that was said and done that day, as if its very existence must afford them their justification, as if in some tiny, forgotten detail buried here—a smile, a hesitation, a tentative gesture—if only it could be found and recalled—in it must lie the key to an understanding of *all* that happened. And in their imagination, out of some deep psychic necessity, they have conceived me—the ultimate arbiter, the powerful and impartial referee, the final adjudicator, a kind of human Hansard [the verbatim record of the proceedings of the British Parliament—named after its printer] who knows those tiny little details and interprets them accurately. And yet no sooner do they conceive me with my authority and my knowledge than they begin flirting with the idea of circumventing me, of foxing me, of outwitting me. (*SP*, 177–78; Friel's emphases)

But even this description is not quite accurate because the "memories" of the dead man, or rather what must have been his "present" experiences prior to his suicide, are also part of the ledger in addition to the memories of the survivors who are condemned to relive the events.

We could say then that Sir has only a virtual existence in relation to the events represented by the melodrama. He never participates as part of the melodrama but serves the regulative function of preserving what was actually said and done on the occasion by the characters. He is a metafiction created by the characters of the melodrama in their attempts to comprehend it. The stage directions for playing Sir confirm his separation from the others: "Always in full control of the situation, of the other characters, of himself. His calm is never ruffled. He is endlessly patient and tolerant, but never superior. Always carries his ledger with him" (*SP*, 175). On this metafictional register Sir adds a level of signification beyond the melodrama that Friel critics have not explored in much depth.[1] On this register Sir exists as a narrative effect of the collective memories / consciousnesses (past, present, and future) and as a narrative device of the author.

Given what Friel has said about the factual accuracy of memory not being that important and given what he does in a play like *Faith Healer*, where memories conflict over what actually happened with no arbiter to

1. For example, see E. Andrews 1995, 140–43; Dantanus 1988, 146, 151; Kilroy 1993, 94; Niel 1987, 355–56; O'Brien 1989, 89–92; Peacock 1993, 114–15; Pine 1990, 130.

resolve the discrepancies, one wonders why Friel felt it necessary to control the vagaries of memory in *Living Quarters*. This ontological commitment to some foundation in fact is reminiscent of the ontological implications of the realistic scenes in the mayor's parlor in *The Freedom of the City*. In *Living Quarters* individual memory is circumscribed by the social or collective nature of the events. All the participants agree, however reluctantly, on certain particulars of what was done and said. This agreement, we are told, derives from "some deep psychic necessity" and it constitutes the authority of Sir and the ledger. Beyond these agreed particulars the characters are free to interpolate according to the dictates of their desire, their angst, their guilt. Although at times they try individually to subvert the ledger, the power of the collective "deep psychic necessity" that constituted it prevents them from subverting it.

Early in the play two encounters establish Sir's role in the play. Immediately after the long opening speech by Sir in which he describes his own function (cited above), the play begins with two of the characters, Father Tom Carty and Charlie Donnelly, trying to negotiate with Sir over their roles (*SP*, 179–81). Sir is unyielding. Charlie is Miriam Butler's husband and he plays a strictly minor role in the melodrama. In fact, all the scenes in which he appears are omitted from the onstage action and Sir never allows him to participate, even as a spectator. The encounter between Sir and Father Tom, the camp chaplain, family friend, and confidant of the Butlers, is more elaborate and effectively illustrates how Sir and his ledger work at the level of the metanarrative. Tom enters and asks Sir how he is portrayed in the ledger. Sir tells Tom, "You'll be yourself, Father." Tom, however, insists on a more detailed description and Sir proceeds to characterize him as friend of the Butler family who married Frank twice and baptized all his children and grandchildren and who accompanied the family virtually everywhere, along with the batman. Tom is generally pleased with this description, except for the reference that links him with the batman. On this last point he demurs, but Sir nevertheless continues reading from the ledger:

SIR. "—and that pathetic dependence on the Butler family, together with his excessive drinking make him a cliché, a stereotype. He knows this himself—"

TOM. Cliché? For God's sake—!

SIR. "but he is not a fool. He recognizes that this definition allows him to be witness to their pain but absolves him from experiencing it; appoints him confidant but acquits him of the responsibility of conscience—"

TOM. That's not how—! O my God . . .

SIR. "As the tale unfolds they may go to him for advice, not because they respect him, consider him wise—"

TOM. November 14, 1997 (*Sudden revolt.*) Because they love me, that's why! They love me!

SIR. "but because he is the outsider who represents the society they'll begin to feel alienated from, slipping away from them."

TOM. (*Beaten.*) Outsider?

(ANNA *goes to* TOM *and puts her arm around him.*)

SIR. "And what he says won't make the slightest difference because at that point—the point of no return—they'll be past listening to anybody. At that point all they'll hear is their own persistent inner voices—" And so on and so forth.

TOM. (*On point of tears.*) O my God—O my God—

SIR. It's your role.

TOM. No, it's not. No, no, no, it's not.

SIR. And to have any role is always something.

(ANNA *begins to lead* TOM *away.*)

When you've thought about it, you'll agree with me.

TOM. No, no, no—

SIR. And you'll do it.

TOM. No, no—

SIR. Oh, yes you'll do it. (*SP,* 180–81)

Tom, of course does conform to his characterization in the ledger, despite his resistance. His guilt stems from the fact that when Frank sought his counsel in his moment of crisis, Tom was incapacitated by a drunken slumber. Because of his guilt over not being there for Frank, in his replays of this scene at the level of the metanarrative Tom tries to rouse the other characters to stop Frank from killing himself, but they do not respond because they did not, and consequently it is not in Sir's ledger. Sir deals harshly with Tom and tells him, "You had your opportunities and you squandered them. . . . You should have spoken then. We'll have none of your spurious concern now that it's all over. So sit down and shut up!" (*SP,* 242).

This encounter between Sir and Tom establishes the conventions of Sir and the ledger as well as the function of the metanarrative. From the encounter several functions emerge. One of these functions is to exhibit on stage something that is usually difficult to dramatize — what did not happen, what might have been but wasn't, along with what did happen. The device is ingenious for this purpose. A second function is the Pirandellian project of employing the metaphor of the theater to explore relations among truth, reality, and fiction. A third function continues Friel's exploration, begun in earlier plays such as *Philadelphia, Here I Come!* and *The Loves of Cass McGuire*, of how memory operates in relation to desire.

In *Four Quartets* T. S. Eliot established the validity of what might have been, the path into the rose garden not taken, as a viable route to salvation. For Friel that same path can constitute one's own purgatory on earth. Like Coleridge's ancient mariner, all the characters of *Living Quarters* are compelled to relive Frank's suicide in their memories because they were all, actively or passively, complicit in it. Part of the function of the metanarrative is to allow the characters to explore opportunities they passed up. For example, when Anna wants to proceed directly to the "point of no return" where she tells Frank of her affair with Ben, Sir insists that they explore intervening time when "different decisions *might* have been made" (Friel's emphasis): Sir says, "at this point it did occur to many of you to say certain things or to omit saying certain things. And it is the memory of those lost possibilities that has exercised you endlessly since and has kept bringing you back here, isn't that so?" (*SP*, 206). All the characters had some opportunity to do or not do something that might have altered the outcome. Ben once wanted to tell his father that he loved him and hated his mother, a revelation that might have altered the course of his relationships with his father and mother, but he did not say it. Anna wanted to tell Frank and the family about her affair with Ben at one point before the public ceremony. Since the whole camp knew about her affair with Ben, she would have spared herself and her husband the humiliation of the ceremony, where the troops sniggered "behind their hands all night" (*SP*, 235), and howled when the Taoiseach referred to Anna in his speech as "the Commandant's comely, composed and curvaceous consort" (*SP*, 234). She did not tell Frank and the family at that time, however, and Sir will not allow her to alter the chronological sequence in her memory of the event. She tries to tell them out of sequence anyway, but since it is not in the ledger, they continue as if they have not heard her.

In many ways Sir's role resembles the role of The Manager in Pirandello's *Six Characters in Search of an Author,* except that Friel's play does not have both actors and fictional characters. Sir deals only with fictional characters, but he deals with them as a director or stage manager might deal with actors. Consequently *Living Quarters,* like *Six Characters in Search of an Author,* operates simultaneously on a fictional register and on a metanarrative register of theatrical enactment of the fiction. There is a significant difference, however: in Pirandello's play the melodrama constitutes the fictional and the theater the real, although in terms of the modernist epistemological theme of the play the fictional is more "true" and alive than the theatrical enactment. In Pirandello's metaphor the actors are merely the shells of the eggs they are beating (1952, 213). In Friel's play Sir is an imaginary projection of the fictional characters, but the authority of his ledger implies that he acts more like a social reality principle that restrains individual flights of fancy, however driven they might be by need and desire.

In this metaphoric use of the theater as metanarrative, however, there is a certain ambiguity of roles. While most of the functions Sir performs are more appropriate to a director or stage manager, some are more appropriate to the playwright. Although he denies it, sometimes Sir acts like the author of the ledger. Sir tells the characters, for example, that he will organize their recollections for them and "impose a structure on them, just to give them a form of sorts." He also assures them that his selection and ordering of events "will be as fair and as representative as possible" (*SP,* 178). Moreover, Sir decides where they will begin in the chronology of events (*SP,* 179). In a sense Sir is like the writer who creates characters and a plot, but then the characters begin to assert a life of their own and try to subvert the authority of the author. But *Living Quarters* puts a poststructuralist twist on that common observation of writers. In *Living Quarters* the author has disappeared, has become invisible, and the author function has become inscribed in the text as Sir and the ledger. As Sir points out, he is a function of the collective narrative of the characters. The narrative, in other words, creates and speaks the author and not the other way around.

Most of the time, however, Sir's role resembles that of a director or stage manager dealing with actors and enforcing the authority of the author's script. When Sir reads the analysis of Tom's character from the ledger, he could be a director reading stage directions or interpreting a character for an actor. Sometimes Sir clearly is giving stage directions (*SP*, 183, 208, 209) and at other times he is interpolating the script without reading from it (*SP*, 206). At other times he discusses the emotional state of a character with that character as a director might discuss a character with the actor playing that role (for example, with Helen [*SP*, 183] and with Frank [*SP*, 192]). Sometimes Sir praises the characters' performances (*SP*, 205, 215), and then there are times when Sir simply provides narrative information necessary to the melodrama's plot. In at least one instance Sir comments like a Greek chorus on the situation ("They are not neglected children" [*SP*, 184]), but this could also be read as commentary to help actors understand their roles.

Sometimes it is not clear which role Sir is playing. His encounter with Tom, for example, could be read as a character pleading with an author to alter his portrayal or as an unhappy actor pleading with a director to alter the script. This same ambiguity of roles appears in other encounters with Sir. Immediately following his encounter with Tom, Sir rebuffs the efforts of Charlie to expand his role in the melodrama. This could be read as an author rejecting an expanded role for a character or as a director rejecting an actor's effort to enlarge his role beyond what is called for in the script.

Despite the ambiguities, in many ways Sir conforms to what Friel has described in interviews as the proper role of the director in theater. For Friel the most important relationship in producing a play is not between the director and the actors but between the playwright and the actors. The director's primary responsibility is to interfere in that primary relationship as little as possible. Disparaging the modern cult of the director, Friel says, "I'm very doubtful ab[o]ut the whole idea of a director interpreting a play in any kind of way that's distinctive to him" (1980a). In one interview he even went so far as to call directing "almost a bogus career" (1991, 61). For Friel a director should be more like an "efficient stage manager": he says, "I want a director to call rehearsals, to make sure the actors are there on time and to get them to speak their lines clearly and distinctly . . . I've no interest whatever in his concept or interpretation"

(1991, 61). For Friel the playwright's script is sacrosanct. He heaps anathema on the notion of either actors or directors altering the script: "It is not their function to amend, it is not their function to rewrite, or to cut, or to extend" (1972b, 21). Their only function is to be "obedient" to the script (1991, 61), "to interpret what is given them" (1972b, 21). According to Friel, "the dramatist ought to be able to exercise complete control over the realisation of his characters." He concedes that a "director can bring an objective view to the script that a writer can't have," but "a good director hones in on the core of what a play is about and realises that and becomes self-effacing in the process" (1980a). For Friel the script is "a final and complete orchestra score" and the stage directions are the musical notations (1991, 61). The director is the conductor and the actors the musicians: "They are all there to play the score as it is written" (1980a). Friel insists that he is "not going to re-write the second movement for the sake of the oboe player" (1991, 61).

In *Living Quarters* the ledger resembles an unusually detailed playwright's script, complete with stage directions, character descriptions, and even narrative background. And Sir seems to function as Friel's ideal director/stage manager. Despite the ambiguity of his function, Sir's most consistent traits are his objectivity and his fidelity to the ledger, his insistence that the characters do not deviate from its essentials. He refuses Charlie an expanded role, refuses to alter a scene to fit Helen's sense of it, he will not let Anna make her devastating revelation out of sequence, and he will not let any of the characters say anything that they may have wished to say at the time but did not say. So, in a sense, in *Living Quarters* Friel has used his notion of the ideal director as a central metaphor and an ingenious stage device.

Another function of this stage device of Sir and the ledger is to provide Friel with a counterpart to the role of fate in his Greek model. With Sir and his ledger Friel metaphorically explores what might serve as a check on the tendency of memory to alter and restructure facts and events. The nature of the collective memory of the characters acts as a reality principle that inhibits their desires to create more appealing scenarios for themselves. For example, Tom's attempt to rewrite his character, however more appealing it might be for him, would disturb the vicarious and voyeuristic relationship he had established with the Butler

family and the lack of responsibility it entailed. Also, when Anna tries to
utter her revelation to Frank out of sequence and the other characters do
not hear her, she apologetically asks Sir if she messed things up, but he
assures her that, while she "shuffled the pages a bit," nothing was
changed and no harm was done (*SP*, 203). In other words, in a collective
memory there are limits to how creative individual memory can be. As
with groups themselves, so with a group or collective memory, the reality principle tends to be enforced over the pleasure principle. And as his
enforcement mechanism, Friel summoned Sir, his ideal director/stage
manager, who could be trusted to interpret his script with firm, objective, self-effacing fidelity.

Thematically Friel's metafictional device in *Living Quarters* continues
to explore how memory functions. The authority of the ledger, however, conflicts with what Friel said earlier about how memory alters what
actually happens to create sustaining fictions of its own. In his next two
plays after *Living Quarters*, *Aristocrats* and *Faith Healer*, Friel continues to
explore the function of collective memory. In these two plays, however,
the rigidity of collective memory dissipates in two stages. In *Aristocrats*
the communal memory is not vested in any facts or events that necessarily occurred but rather in a collection of myths and lore shared by the
O'Donnell family. Casimir is the primary articulator of the family heritage, but membership in the group depends, not on any strict conformity of memory, but rather on varying degrees of subscription to the lore
and myths. It is almost as if in *Living Quarters* Friel posited a common
history that family members must accept as an indicator of group identity, whereas in *Aristocrats* the requirements for group membership are
much looser and more fluid. In *Faith Healer* collective memory breaks
down completely as individual memories diverge significantly about key
events in the characters' shared experiences. The lack of agreement is
such that no common or collective memory emerges that any of the
group can subscribe to. All of Friel's families are dysfunctional, but in
Faith Healer the degree of individual deprivation is so extreme that the
group reality principle has no power to enforce itself over individual
need and desire. There is even a question as to whether the three individuals in *Faith Healer* constitute a family, although they spend virtually
their entire personal and professional lives together. *Faith Healer* seems to

represent a situation much like that of Northern Ireland, where people live and work together without sharing any collective memories, myths, and lore. Like the characters in *Faith Healer,* the different communities in Northern Ireland do not even share similar memories of the same events, such as 1916, for example. *Living Quarters,* by contrast, deals with the opposite pathology and suggests more a single community locked into its narratives about the past and the endless rehearsal of them even after members of the community have scattered across the globe, just as the collective memory of Irish nationalism, with its own history of internecine betrayal and perfidy, has survived generations of diaspora and returns repeatedly to the original scenes of enactment. In this sense, *Living Quarters* continues the postcolonial Heideggerian exploration begun in *Volunteers* of how group identities become incarcerated in the narratives of betrayal and victimization a group tells about itself.

Aristocrats

Aristocrats, which opened at the Abbey in 1979 and won the New York Drama Critics Circle award for best foreign play in 1989, is another drama based on a family reunion and communal memory. In this case a wedding in the O'Donnell family of Ballybeg turns into a funeral. Like *Living Quarters, Aristocrats* deals with the decline of an Irish family from the traditional upper or upper middle classes, or at least as upper as Catholic families were capable of achieving since Penal Law days. In both *Living Quarters* and *Aristocrats* the families are from the professional classes: Frank Butler is an army officer and generations of the O'Donnell family have distinguished themselves in the legal profession. Ostensibly *Aristocrats* puts a new twist on the Irish "big house" tradition in literature by focusing not on a Protestant family but on a Catholic family that managed to acquire and retain its wealth and status. A family "without loyalty . . . administering the law for anyone who happened to be in power" (*SP,* 294), they would have been called "Castle Catholics" prior to 1922.

In this Catholic variation on the decline of the Irish "big house," the decline is charted in a number of ways, most obviously in the physical condition of father O'Donnell and of the house itself. The father, a district judge, has had several strokes and he is incontinent and incapable of caring for even his most basic needs. Ballybeg Hall is in serious disrepair: the roof leaks, the floors are rotted, the family can no longer afford its upkeep or even to heat it properly in the winter. Willie Diver, a local jack-of-all-trades from the village who is attracted to Judith O'Donnell, is a family benefactor by virtue of leasing land from them for which he has no use.

The decline also is reflected in the family's professional and social status. For the last four generations the O'Donnell family has descended the professional and the social as well as the economic ladder. Eamon, a villager who married into the family, has become the family historian, and he succinctly outlines the decline of the O'Donnell males in the legal profession; "Great Grandfather—Lord Chief Justice; Grandfather—Circuit Court Judge; Father—simple District Justice; Casimir—failed solicitor. A fairly rapid descent" (*SP*, 295). Marriage also has tarnished the luster of the O'Donnells's social status. Mother O'Donnell was an actress with a traveling company, "a raving beauty by all accounts" (*SP*, 295) whom the District Judge married after a five-day romance. Daughter Alice married Eamon, who was raised by a grandmother who spent her life as a maid at Ballybeg Hall. Casimir, the last of the O'Donnell males to grow up in Ballybeg Hall, after failing in the family profession, married a German spiritualist who supports Casimir and their two children by working as a cashier in a bowling alley. Casimir is nanny to his children and works part-time in a food-processing plant in Hamburg. Claire, the youngest O'Donnell, is about to marry a successful Ballybeg greengrocer, a widower with four children who is more than twice her age and who drives a "great white lorry with an enormous plastic banana on top of the cab" (*SP*, 269). Unmarried Judith, the oldest of the O'Donnell children, has fared no better. She runs the household for her invalid father and her manic-depressive, musically talented sister, Claire. She has an illegitimate child whom she has placed in an orphanage, a child conceived with a Dutch reporter while she was active in the civil rights movement in Derry during the late 1960s and early 1970s.

The family has gathered for Claire's marriage to the greengrocer, but father's final stroke supplants the wedding with his funeral. Thus, symbolically the wedding of Claire to a commoner becomes the funeral of the aristocratic tradition itself. The term *aristocracy* as applied to the O'-

Donnells is relative, of course. As Seamus Deane and W. J. McCormack have argued, the Anglo-Irish Ascendancy was primarily a bourgeois social formation. *Aristocrats* has the potential to be a nostalgia piece for aristocratic Ireland, but Friel is much less nostalgic and more realistic about the decline of the Irish aristocracy than, say, Yeats. Although Friel eschews nostalgia, nevertheless he is sympathetic to the plight and pain of these fading aristocrats. Friel avoids nostalgia by accepting the inevitability of the decline and by recognizing that the death of the tradition involves a liberation as well as a loss. Alice articulates this ambivalence in terms of the possibilities that the closing of Ballybeg Hall opens up for her: she says, "I don't know what I feel. Maybe a sense of release; of not being pursued; of the possibility of . . . of 'fulfillment.' No. Just emptiness. Perhaps maybe a new start" (*SP* 324). Commenting on the liberating prospects of aristocratic decline, George O'Brien says that the O'Donnells are "fortuitously freed into a future that catches them somewhat unawares but nevertheless willing to make a go of it" (1989, 92).

The suffocating confinement of the aristocratic tradition is powerfully represented by the domineering oppressiveness of the father, who as Casimir says, was very "adept at stifling things" (*SP,* 307). He refused to allow Claire to develop her musical talent because, even though he had married an itinerant actress himself, he did not want "an itinerant musician" for a daughter. His stifling of Claire suggests perhaps what drove his wife to suicide. He also oppressed and demeaned Judith, who took care of him and his household after the death of his wife, by constantly reminding her how she had "betrayed the family" (*SP,* 257) with her political and sexual escapades in Derry. Even more telling is the way he disabled his son's self-esteem. At age nine, as Casimir was discovering that people found him peculiar, his father drove home the insight by telling him, "Had you been born down there [in Ballybeg], you'd have become the village idiot. Fortunately for you, you were born here and we can absorb you." From that moment, at age nine, Casimir knew that he "would never succeed in life" (*SP,* 310).

At the end of the play all the O'Donnell children look forward to their release from Ballybeg Hall, however modest and tentative it might be. Judith plans to retrieve her child from the orphanage. Alcoholic Alice will return to "perhaps maybe a new start" in London with taciturn Uncle George as her only "keepsake" from Ballybeg Hall. Claire still looks forward to her postponed wedding to a man she senses she does not love. Moreover, she denounces Chopin, whose music she played so beautifully. Chopin's scherzos, ballades, waltzes, études, and nocturnes fill the air throughout the play and preserve, at the moment of its demise, the lyric, romantic atmosphere of Ballybeg Hall's aristocratic heritage. The only one who does not appear destined for a release of some kind is Casimir. He will return to his Helga in Hamburg, but he wants the family to come to Hamburg for another "party in Vienna," the family code phrase for the extravagant O'Donnell gatherings of their aristocratic past.

Unlike the others who will make the transition, however sordid, into postaristocratic Ireland, Casimir's personality is arrested in a social and cultural niche that has ceased to exist. He has acquired compensatory structures like the others. At age nine, for example, when his father made him realize he would never succeed, he very poignantly realized that there were "certain compensatory recognitions":

> once I acknowledged that the larger areas were not accessible to me, I discovered—I had to discover smaller, much smaller areas that were. Yes, indeed. And I discovered that if I conduct myself with some circumspection, I find that I can live within these smaller, perhaps very confined territories without exposure to too much hurt. Indeed I find that I can experience some happiness and perhaps give a measure of happiness, too. My great discovery. Isn't is so beautiful? (*SP*, 310–11)

But Casimir's "compensatory recognitions" do not liberate him. His rejection by his father has made him desire all the more the tradition his father inherited, and Casimir, more than anyone else in the play, succeeds in preserving the mythology of Ballybeg Hall.

Casimir's superb ability to invoke the mythology of Ballybeg Hall, and through that mythology the tangible atmosphere of its aristocratic past, is one of the triumphs of this play. Moreover, Casimir's mythologizing invokes another symbolic register on which the play operates— the register of language and discourse. Like *Living Quarters*, *Aristocrats* deals with a central epistemological question related to memory, only here there is no ledger to authorize even minimum agreement over what may actually have happened in the past. There is some agreement among family members, but only an agreement to subscribe to certain family myths.

Whether the past glory Casimir evokes ever actually existed is an open question. We can only be sure that it exists in Casimir's imagination, which is powerful enough to evoke it for others, especially with the piano accompaniment of his sister Claire, whose expert and frequent rendering of Chopin helps to sustain an atmosphere of lyrical, romantic elegance within which Casimir weaves his lush, mythical tapestry of Ballybeg Hall. Appropriately named after a Polish prince,[2] Casimir evokes the nineteenth-century, post-Romantic ambiance that Chopin so perfectly articulated for the elite of Vienna and Paris in the 1830s and 1840s.

Casimir's image of Ballybeg Hall filters out all the signs of disintegration and decay: he says, for example, "When I think of Ballybeg Hall it's always like this: the sun shining; the doors and windows all open; the place filled with music" (*SP,* 256). This vision of the Hall contrasts starkly with Judith's description later that details rotting floors, damaged roof, plastic sheets nailed to the rafters, the seventeen buckets they distribute around the house whenever it rains, and bank overdrafts necessary to keep up even this level of repair. Casimir cannot address this view of Ballybeg Hall and negative images like these typically dampen his spirits or provoke nervous idle chatter or activity in him. In response to Judith's description he loses his enthusiasm for guessing the title of the Chopin piece Claire just played, one of their favorite games, a game that comes to signify their childlike and innocent attachment to their aristocratic upbringing.

Almost everything Casimir says and does evokes his vision of Ballybeg Hall. He regales the visiting American professor Tom Hoffnung with sto-

2. Perhaps Friel meant to evoke the historical memory of Count Casimir Markievicz, the bon-vivant husband of Constance Markievicz. Constance and Casimir Markievicz lived the life of the fading gentry and Constance's forsaking of her aristocratic past in favor of her love for the Irish people effectively constitutes a historical analogy to the transition from an aristocratic past to a bourgeois future that Friel charts in *Aristocrats.* Casimir's surname also evokes aristocracy, the old Gaelic aristocracy that in Donegal was dominated by the O'Donnells until the flight of the Earls in the early seventeenth century.

ries about pieces of furniture that have become named after distinguished visitors to the Hall: G. K. Chesterton is a footstool he once fell
off; Gerard Manley Hopkins is a chair he once stained with tea; O'Connell the Liberator is a chaise longue that still bears the mark of his riding
boot; Yeats is a cushion he once laid his head on for three successive
nights waiting for the family ghosts to appear to him. Casimir's conversation peoples the Hall with the Irish intelligentsia and elite of the past
century, particularly the Catholic intelligentsia. Even his sister Anna was
renamed after one of these distinguished visitors: when she became a
nun she took the name Sister John Henry after Cardinal Newman, who
married their grandparents in Ballybeg Hall. Other visitors included the
great tenor John McCormack, whom Casimir remembers waltzing his
mother down the hall and out onto the tennis court. Even when he describes Claire's pedestrian greengrocer fiancé with the plastic banana on
top of his truck, he assimilates him into the mythology by making him
an accomplished trumpet player who will play duets with Claire in the
evenings. Having thus assimilated him, Casimir can then say with complete satisfaction, "Good. Good. It all sounds just—just—just so splen-
did and so—so appropriate. Everything's in hand. Everything's under
control" (SP, 269). Casimir's myth is what keeps everything in hand and
under control, however tentatively. It keeps Ballybeg Hall alive for him. If
he shared his sister Alice's view of the groom-to-be—a bespectacled,
pasty-looking, plump, balding "middle-aged widower with four young
children" who is old enough to be her father (SP, 269, 313)—life for
Casimir would simply not be worth living.

   In another imaginative bit of reconstruction that recreates the former
glamour of Ballybeg Hall, after Casimir has carefully searched the now
overgrown lawn to find the holes that marked the configuration of the
old croquet court, Casimir and Claire play croquet with imaginary mal-
lets, balls, and wickets. Even the realist Willie Diver is seduced into the
game.

   Casimir's most pressing need and desire is to preserve the atmosphere
and style if not the substance of his aristocratic heritage, to preserve the
sense that life is a succession of parties in Vienna like the one his grandfather (or perhaps it was his great-grandfather) attended when he told
Balzac to shut up while Chopin was playing one of his own pieces. "A
party in Vienna" in the O'Donnell family lore came to represent "any-

thing great and romantic and exciting that had happened in the past or might happen in the future" (*SP*, 306). Consequently every experience that comes his way Casimir must interpret in terms of how it contributes to his sense of life as a party in Vienna. Even his father's shabby funeral, in Casimir's rendition of it, becomes almost festive, especially compared to all the furtive whispering that accompanied his mother's funeral and the controversy over whether to allow her a Christian burial. Casimir saw "Every shop shut and every blind drawn; and men kneeling on their caps as the hearse passed; and Nanny sobbing her heart out when the coffin was being lowered" (*SP*, 309). Casimir thinks his father would have been gratified. In contrast, the more cynical Alice, when Casimir asks if she noticed that "the whole village closed down" for the funeral, remarks, "For the minute it took the hearse to pass through" and she adds that the church was nearly empty and the organist, who had expected to play at Claire's wedding that day, apparently wasn't told that the funeral had supplanted it and she played "This Is My Lovely Day." In her opinion, "Father would not have been amused" (*SP*, 313). As Alice paints this much more cynical view of the funeral, Casimir paces incessantly, as he does throughout much of the third act, in part because his father's death has profoundly shaken his confidence in his myth. For Casimir, "Somehow the hall doesn't exist without him" (*SP*, 311). Whenever an experience threatens to shatter Casimir's vision, it shakes and disturbs him, usually by subduing his effervescent enthusiasm, but he never admits it into conscious articulation. This is how he keeps at bay what Yeats called the "filthy modern tide." In the end Casimir recovers his spirits only by planning another "party in Vienna" for the O'Donnell tribe, this time in Hamburg, in order to continue their aristocratic past into the future.

Casimir's identification of his father with the tradition of Ballybeg Hall illuminates the source of his neurotic conflict. That glorious and extravagant past energizes Casimir, but at the same time it has enervated him. As Eamon remarks about the furniture named after the famous, it is "Like walking through Madame Tussaud's . . . Or a bloody minefield?" (*SP*, 274). Whenever his father's voice over the "baby alarm" catches him by surprise, Casimir goes rigid with fear, and when his father collapses in front of them, Casimir becomes catatonic—"on his knees, transfixed, immobile" (*SP,* 304). Even though his father crippled Casimir irrevocably at age nine, and even though he no longer remembered him when he visited, Casimir still identifies profoundly with all he represents. Casimir may have failed in the family profession, but he has not failed in preserving their imaginative legacy. Unfortunately for Casimir, this act of preservation proves to be self-destructive.

Casimir is not the only one seduced by Ballybeg Hall. Eamon has steeped himself in the tradition to the point that he knows more about it than the O'Donnells. He absorbed both his knowledge and infatuation with Ballybeg Hall from his grandmother, whose fifty-seven years as maid at the Hall made her a "fund of stories and information": "Carriages, balls, receptions, weddings, christenings, feasts, deaths, trips to Rome, musical evenings, tennis—that's the mythology I was nurtured on all my life," he says (*SP,* 276). When Eamon told his grandmother he was going to marry Alice O'Donnell, she called him a "dirty mouthed upstart" (*SP,* 277). Despite the financial implausibility of the family maintaining Ballybeg Hall, Eamon wants to keep it open for its symbolic value. He says its worth cannot be "assessed in terms of roofs and floors and overdrafts . . . Don't you know that all that is fawning and forelocktouching and Paddy and shabby and greasy peasant in the Irish character finds a house like this irresistible? That's why we were ideal for colonizing. Something in us needs this . . . aspiration" (*SP,* 318–19). Eamon, then, represents that strange nostalgia of the oppressed Irish to preserve one of the symbols of their oppression.

The central epistemological issues surrounding Casimir's mythmaking are raised by the character of Tom Hoffnung, an American professor visiting Ballybeg Hall to conduct research on the "Recurring cultural, political and social modes in the upper strata of Roman Catholic society in rural Ireland since the act of Catholic Emancipation" (*SP,* 265). His efforts to ascertain facts about the family history yield only conflicting memories and images created for him by the individual family members. He especially tries to verify Casimir's stories by politely cross examining him and by double-checking dates. He questions, for example, Casimir's memories of his mother playing the piano because Judith said something that implied that she did not play the piano. He also discovers that Casimir could not have remembered Yeats's visit since Yeats died two months before Casimir was born. Casimir typically responds by denying the counter evidence or by changing the subject. The audience, too, is given good reason to doubt the accuracy of Casimir's stories when he twists something Tom said into the grandiose assertion that Tom's uncle owns the Bell Telephone Company.

The rest of the family jokes about Tom's efforts to ascertain the truth about their situation. Alice says, "God help the poor man if he thinks he's heard one word of truth since he came here. . . . All you're hearing is lies, my friend—lies, lies, lies" (*SP*, 284). Eamon suggests that Tom might be better off writing a "gothic novel called *Ballybeg Hall—From Supreme Court to Sausage Factory;* four generations of a great Irish Catholic legal dynasty . . . a family without passion, without loyalty, without commitments; administering the law for anyone who happened to be in power; above all wars and famines and civil strife and political upheaval; ignored by its Protestant counterparts, isolated from the mere Irish, existing only in its own concept of itself, brushing against reality occasionally by its cultivation of artists; but tough—oh yes, tough, resilient, tenacious; and with one enormous talent for—no a *greed* for survival" (*SP*, 294; Friel's emphasis).

Because Tom is interested only in verifiable facts, as Eamon astutely observes, "There are certain things, certain truths . . . that are beyond Tom's kind of scrutiny" (*SP*, 309–10). The "facts" may all point to the final dilapidation and degradation of a tradition, and suggest perhaps that its only interest at this point would be historical. But these facts do not address the mythic significance of Ballybeg Hall, the self-conception of grandeur that is perhaps one of the most important "facts" about the aristocratic tradition. This self-conception is what Casimir tries so desperately to preserve. His name, his temperament, his enthusiasms, his out-of-touch sensibility are pure aristocracy, and could only flourish as such in that environment, as his father so crassly points out. Casimir's memories of Ballybeg Hall, though they may be factually inaccurate, have an authentic ring to them partly because of the vividness of their self-conception of his class. The portrait of the family Casimir constructs out of "lies" is "true" in the sense that the lies constitute both a family and a class mythology in which all the O'Donnells have participated and which has determined the values of their culture. It is a mythology that once exerted power in the world because it was supported by the structures of a material and political system.

That system has now passed out of existence, and Ballybeg Hall, as one critic has observed, "not only symbolizes an outmoded way of life, but also the outmoded perceptions of contemporary reality shared by all of its inhabitants" (Wiley 1987, 53). In the play everyone except Casimir is struggling to make the transition into another materially supported conception of society for which the O'Donnell's aristocratic mythology has ill prepared them.

The common villagers of Ballybeg are better suited for the new bourgeois world, which after all was created with them in mind. Willie Diver, Eamon, and Claire's greengrocer fiancé all represent this new species of survivor. Eamon is of particular interest because he is a villager who also has been caught up in the O'Donnell mythology, but he has not been blinded or crippled by it. He is both inside and outside the O'Donnell myth; he is both a consumer of the myth and its demystifying mythologist in Barthes's sense. Although like Casimir Eamon is not overly concerned with facts, he is no illusioned fool either. He even doubts Casimir's story about his German wife and children because no one has ever met them. He says Casimir's story has "the authentic ring of phoney fiction" (*SP*, 278). Eamon's point, and I think Friel's point, alludes to Oscar Wilde's distinction between authentic and phony fiction. As we saw in chapter 2, Wilde was convinced that truth was a matter of the conviction of style, that only style can make something believable, a claim based on Aristotle's "law of probability and necessity," according to which an artist should prefer probable impossibilities over improbable possibilities. In *Aristocrats* Casimir's mythmaking about the O'Donnells is convincing because its impossibilities are probabilities within the context of the myth, whereas Helga and the sausage factory are possibilities outside the range of probabilities contained by the O'Donnell myth, and consequently have the "authentic ring of phoney fiction."

Aristocrats may be the first play in which Friel fully embraces a post-Heideggerian view of language. Earlier he had done it briefly or retained a grip on some privileged version of reality (the mayor's parlor scenes in *The Freedom of the City* or the ledger in *Living Quarters*). The advance on Friel's epistemological and linguistic sophistication represented by *Aris-

tocrats can be gauged by comparing the play to its earlier incarnation as the short story "Foundry House." In the story, as we saw earlier, Joe Brennan, brought up in the gatekeeper's lodge, clung to his vision of the former grandeur of Foundry House as a refuge from his own commonplace existence. Preserving the illusion of past greatness somehow endowed life with more dignity and hope than Joe could derive from his own experience as a radio and television repairman and father of nine. In "Foundry House" Friel clearly demarks the line between illusion and reality. Joe's illusion has a psychological function in his mundane reality, but Joe never confuses it with that reality. The illusion enables Joe to believe in a mode of existence that has aristocratic grandeur and meaning beyond his own pedestrian world. Even though he is aware that that better world is not open to him, somehow its very existence is reassuring to him, and to live without the illusion is to live with the depressing awareness that salvation in this world is not a possibility for anyone.

In *Aristocrats* the illusion has achieved the status of myth, a myth that once had been validated by social practice, but now has few adherents or practitioners left. Casimir is the only remaining true believer. Eamon would like to sustain the material foundations for the myth, but in the end he submits to financial inevitabilities. The play catches the other O'Donnell children suspended between two worlds but groping toward accommodation with the new one. In *Aristocrats* the illusion is no longer merely personal. It is social and it once had a validity sustained by a complex social, economic, and political fabric. The foundations of that support have now crumbled; there is no longer a community of agreement to validate the myth; but its residue lingers on in the selective reconstructions of Casimir's memory. The truth of his reconstructions is not invalidated so much because they do not accurately represent the facts, although that may be the case in one sense, but rather because there is no longer a material, interpretive system within which those "facts" can be construed. Facts are created by systems of value, and the aristocratic system that produced Ballybeg Hall no longer has the power to validate Casimir's facts. *Aristocrats* captures, in the death of Judge O'Donnell and the consequent termination of his pension, the poignant moment when that power ceased altogether. Casimir is right to sense that "Somehow the hall doesn't exist without him." The sadness of the play lies in

mourning the passing of that signifying power the Judge's death represents and the pathos of the play lies in Casimir's failure to acknowledge
that passing.

Aristocrats also represents a historical recurrence, perhaps in the Niet-
zschean sense. That recurrence is contained in the name Casimir O'Donnell. One passing of an aristocratic culture is represented with the
departure from Ireland of O'Neill and O'Donnell in 1607, the "Flight of
the Earls" that has come to signify for Irish nationalists the end of the old
Gaelic culture, that is, the end of the material system that sustained the
old Gaelic aristocracy. After the departure of O'Neill and O'Donnell the
Ulster land they controlled was confiscated and given to the planters
who came over from England and Scotland. A second passing of aristocratic Ireland began with land reform in the late nineteenth century and
was effectively completed with the establishment of the Irish Free State
in 1922. Constance Markievicz, wife of Casimir, undoubtedly the best
known Polish aristocrat in Ireland, was intimately associated with the
historical process that led to Irish independence. Prior to independence
the Protestant Ascendancy was the material system that sustained the
O'Donnells of Friel's play, even though the O'Donnells's religion prevented them from being actual members of that Ascendancy. Thus,
Casimir's name and the play as a whole evoke both a colonial and a postcolonial transition for Ireland. Each transition is marked by both repetition and difference, just as Casimir's belated, out-of-context evocation of
Romantic Ireland is yet another repetition with a difference, or in
Bhabha's terms, another hybrid enunciation. This latest hybrid, however,
is not the Anglo-Irish hybrid the days of colonization produced but the
marriage of aristocrat and bourgeoisie that marked the demise of the
former as it was assimilated and appropriated by the latter. So in a sense
Aristocrats is another attack on postcolonial bourgeois Ireland, but it is an
attack that suggests no alternative. Instead the play views with both sympathy and detachment the translation of the material culture of Ascendancy Ireland into the material culture of a bourgeois democratic
republic, a transition that Aristocrats gives the Irish little to be optimistic
about.

7

Postmodern Memory
Faith Healer

I N *Faith Healer* Friel deepens and sophisticates his understanding of how language, narrative, and desire construct our sense of self as well as the experience of that self in relation to alternative constructions of itself by others. In technique this play combines Beckett-like monologues with a Pinteresque use of language in a structure that, as Kiberd (1985, 106) has pointed out, resembles Faulkner's in *The Sound and the Fury*. In four separate monologues three characters — Frank Hardy, the faith healer; Teddy, his manager; and Frank's wife Grace — remember their lives together as part of a wandering faith-healing mission in Wales. Their memories, however, do not coincide on key events they shared, because each one's memory is structured according to a different complex of compelling desires. Unlike *Living Quarters* or *The Freedom of the City*, *Faith Healer* provides no ledger or privileged register of representation to help us sort out the discrepancies among the three narratives. These discrepancies are crucial nevertheless, for in these gaps of memory and interpretation lies the significance of the play.

Several events in the play emerge as the most important poles of differentiation. One of these is the song "I love you/Just the way you look tonight" and how it became established as the opening theme song of Frank's performance each evening. Frank remembers that Teddy insisted on using an amplifying system and playing the song as "atmospheric background music" for the performance. Considering that the audience usually consisted only of the crippled and the diseased, Frank remarks about the song, "Yes; we were always balanced somewhere between the absurd and the momentous." Frank claims that he fought Teddy on the sound system and the music, but "finally gave in to him" (*SP*, 336).

Teddy's version of how the song was established as their theme differs from Frank's but also includes it. His monologue opens sometime after Frank and Grace have died, and Grace died a year after Frank. It opens with the song still playing on his phonograph and Teddy saying,

> I could listen to that all day . . . . It was Gracie insisted on that for our theme music. . . . Because that was the big hit the year she and Frank was married. . . . But of course as time goes by she forgets that. And of course he never knows why it's our theme—probably thinks I've got some sort of a twisted mind. So that the two of them end up blaming *me* for picking it! But by that time I really like the tune, you know; and anyway it's the only record we have. So I keep it. And old Teddy he's the only one of the three of us that knows its romantic significance. (*SP*, 354–55)

Grace, however, throws everything into question with her version. She says she hated the record and "begged Frank to get something else, anything else. But he wouldn't. It had to be that. 'I like it,' he'd say, 'and it confuses them.'" (*SP*, 350). Since Friel gives us no independent verification of any of these three different memories, how do we read them? Why wouldn't Frank remember Grace's objections to the song? Why would Grace suppress Teddy's interest in the song? Why would Teddy say Grace insisted on the song when she says that she hated it? Answers to these questions probe deeply into the recesses of the play.

Frank, whose monologue tends to focus on his own wrestling with his gift of healing, tends to suppress anything romantic between himself and Grace. Consequently he would filter out of his memory anything like Teddy's explanation, because it would not fit his paradigm for his relationship with Grace. That paradigm perceived Grace as a loyal, devoted appendage to his faith-healing mission. Frank did not even acknowledge Grace as his wife, which she apparently was, judging from what we might call the preponderance of evidence in the play. Frank always referred to her as his mistress, even in his own memory, where he also erased her original surname and place of origin. Frank's paradigm of Grace also associated her with the tidy, orderly values of her father, which Grace says she rejected when she left her family and a legal career to run off with Frank. He says of her,

> And there was Grace, my mistress. A Yorkshire woman. [She was from Northern Ireland.] Controlled, correct, methodical, orderly. Who fed

me, washed and ironed for me, nursed me, humoured me. Saved me,
I'm sure, from drinking myself to death. Would have attempted to reform me because that was her nature, but didn't because her instincts
were wiser than her impulses. . . . She never asked for marriage and for
all her tidiness I don't think she wanted marriage—her loyalty was adequate for her. And it was never a heady relationship, not even in the
early days. But it lasted. A surviving relationship. And yet as we grew
older together I thought it wouldn't. Because that very virtue of hers—
that mulish, unquestioning, indefatigable loyalty—settled on us like a
heavy dust. And nothing I did neither my bitterness nor my deliberate
neglect nor my blatant unfaithfulness could disturb it. (*SP,* 335)

This portrait of Grace as loyal drudge did not match her own self-
image. According to Grace she twice rejected and fled from the tidy, orderly existence represented by her father and the law profession.
According to her mother, what Grace wanted was not the role of loyal
mule Frank imagined for her, but to be the object of devotion herself
(*SP,* 373). Grace's own self-portrait resisted Frank's attempts to subject
her needs to his own. She says that she felt humiliated and wounded by
his repeated references to her as his mistress and by his perverse memory
lapses when it came to her surname and place of origin. She also contradicted his image of her compliant loyalty in the face of his neglect and
unfaithfulness. She deeply resented his neglect of her, particularly the
way he shut her out and obliterated her when he was possessed by his
gift of healing. She says that in his "moments of complete mastery" before a performance

when you speak to him he turns his head and looks beyond you with
those damn benign eyes of his, looking past you out of his completion,
out of that private power, out of that certainty that was accessible only
to him. God, how I resented that privacy! And he's reciting the names of
all those dying Welsh villages . . . And then, for him I didn't exist. Many,
many, many times I didn't exist for him. But before a performance this
exclusion—this erasure was absolute: he obliterated me. Me who
tended him, humoured him, nursed him, sustained him—who de-
bauched myself for him. Yes. And when I remember him like that in the
back of the van, God how I hate him again. (*SP,* 343–44)

Grace's bitterness extended to Frank's gift of healing itself. She felt alienated from his gift, which she did not understand. She was also wary of it
and would gladly have "robbed him of it" if she could have been certain

that its loss would not have altered Frank. She mistakenly thinks Frank knew how she felt, "and in his twisted way read into it the ultimate treachery on my part" (*SP*, 349). In her view, what threatened their relationship in its later years was not her ponderous, mulish loyalty but Frank's insistence "on dragging me into [the] feud between himself and his talent" (*SP*, 350). Since this view did not match Frank's self-perception, we might say that just as Frank read his need for unquestioning loyalty into his image of her, so she read her own feud with Frank's talent into their relationship. The effect of the nightly playing of "I love you/Just the way you look tonight" on Grace must have been the effect Frank wanted it to have on his audience—it confused her because Frank did not accept her as she was, or at least as she perceived herself to be.

Despite her bitterness and resentment, Grace loved Frank and they provided mutual sustenance, however perverse, for each other. In fact, the degree of Grace's bitterness and resentment is a good measure of her love for Frank and her dependence on him. At the end of her monologue, after Frank's death, she says "how I want that door to open—how I want that man to come across that floor and put his white hands on my face and still this tumult inside . . . I need him to sustain me . . . O my God I don't know if I can go on without his sustenance" (*SP*, 353). Frank too acknowledgeed his dependence on Grace—for cooking, washing, ironing, nursing, humoring, and for saving him from death by drinking—but his greatest debt to her was his own fiction of her loyalty, his most important emotional sustenance. As with Grace, Frank's dependency also was measured by an inverse proportion: Grace says she knows he found "some kind of sustenance in me—I'm absolutely sure of that, because finally he drained me, finally I was exhausted" (*SP*, 342).

These conflicting needs and images played a big role in their fights. Frank, of course, with one exception, did not remember any fights, since he required his image of Grace as mulishly loyal for his own emotional stability, such as it was. Both Grace and Teddy, however, describe frequent, bitter, vicious fighting. According to Grace, "things were said that should never have been said and that lay afterwards on our lives like slow poison" (*SP*, 350). Teddy confirms this view. He describes their fighting as "really sticking the old knife in and turning it as hard as they could" (*SP*, 360). When Grace describes their fights, however, she describes only

Frank's aggression and bitterness and not her own. She says Frank's as-
saults were not as intense "when his talent was working for him": she
says,

> after he'd cured someone he'd be satisfied just to flaunt himself, to taunt
> me: "And what does the legal mind make of all that? Just a con, isn't it?
> Just an illusion, isn't it?" . . . But when he couldn't perform . . . then he'd
> go for me with bared teeth as if I were responsible and he'd scream at
> me, "You were at your very best tonight, Miss O'Dwyer, weren't you? A
> great night for the law, wasn't it? You vengeful, spiteful bitch." And I'd
> defend myself. And we'd tear one another apart. (*SP*, 350)

Teddy's description of one of their fights, however, shows Grace
equally adept at taunting and slashing. One night when no one had arrived by the time the performance was scheduled to begin, Teddy describes how Grace walked through the door and flung a challenging
taunt at Frank: "'Where's the genius?' she shouts. 'I came to see the great
Irish genius. Where is he?' And he hears her and he screams, 'Get that
bitch out! Get rid of that bitch!' 'Oh, he's here, is he?' she says. 'Physi-
cian, heal thyself!' she says with this great, mad, mocking voice. 'Out!
Out!' he shouts. 'The genius!' she screams" (*SP*, 358). And so it goes on
and on.

Teddy's assessment of these fights begins to probe into the interstices
of their relationship. He asks, "And what was the fighting all about in the
end? All right you could say it was because the only thing that finally
mattered to him was his work—and that would be true. Or you could
say it was because the only thing that finally mattered to her was him—
and I suppose that would be true, too. But when you put the two propo-
sitions together like that—I don't know—somehow they both become
only half-truths, you know" (*SP*, 360). Teddy is right as far as he goes, but
he is also right that more can be said about the pattern of their fights.

From the descriptions of the fights we can see why the fights centered
around Frank's performances. His monologue makes it clear that his primary obsession was his talent, its consistency, its significance, and his
profound doubts about it. Equally clear from Grace's monologue was
her obsession with Frank and her jealous resentment of his talent. The
issue of Frank's talent, in other words, was a vulnerability both of them
could exploit, albeit from different perspectives. When Frank's talent

failed him, that was when he most needed Grace's loyal support; but that was also when she could hurt him the most by withholding that support and by preying on his self-doubts to boot. But Frank also used his successes to demean the orderly, controlled world of Grace's father. When he failed, however, that same orderly, controlled world was unbearably threatening to the habitual, unpredictable chaos of Frank's own life and profession, in part because he secretly envied it.

Teddy's memory about how the theme song came to be established, like Frank's and Grace's, was shaped by his emotional investment. Frank suspected that Teddy was either a romantic or a very pragmatic business manager who knew what his clients needed to hear. Given what we know about Teddy's history of managing Rob Roy, the Piping Dog, and Miss Mulatto and Her Pigeons, and about his theory of how the critical intelligence interferes with artistic talent, we can safely conclude that Teddy was definitely a romantic. As a practical business venture, Frank's faith-healing mission was a flop from the start. Teddy stayed with Frank and Grace because he loved them both and because he fulfilled his desire for Grace vicariously through Frank. His unrequited love for Grace also suggested the extent of his romantic impracticality. Teddy played almost no role in her emotional life, which was focused entirely on Frank. Her monologue barely mentions Teddy, except as the "devoted servant, dedicated acolyte to the holy man" (*SP*, 345). She evidenced no awareness whatsoever of Teddy's devotion to her, nor did Frank, whose egocentric view assumed that Teddy was devoted to him and to being associated with a spiritual enterprise. Teddy was aware of his devotion to both Grace and Frank, but he suppressed the extent to which that devotion had shaped his life. In fact, Teddy was quite blind to the power love had over him and he prided himself in his ability to separate his personal from his professional concerns:

> if you're going to handle great artists . . . you must handle them on the basis of a relationship that is strictly business only. Personally, in the privacy of your heart, you may love them or you may hate them. But that has nothing to do with it. Your client he has his job to do. You have your job to do. . . . But let that relationship between you spill over into friendship or affection and believe me, dear heart, the coupon's torn. The one rule I've always lived by: friends is friends and work is work, and as the poet says, never the twain shall meet. (*SP*, 357)

Even when he acknowledged his love of Frank and Grace, Teddy suffered from the illusion that he had been able to compartmentalize that love: at one point in his monologue he says, "she is this terrific woman that of course I love very much, married to this man that I love very much—love maybe even more. But that's all. Nothing more. That's all. And that's enough" (*SP*, 368). Teddy was unaware at the end why he exploded at the man who accused him of stealing the Frank Hardy banner from Grace's trash pile after he had just identified her body at the morgue and had just discovered that she had lived four streets away for the past year since Frank died without ever contacting him. At the morgue when a policeman asked how well he knew Grace, he said they had "a professional relationship going back twenty-odd years"; but then he felt compelled to ask himself, "'Cause that's what it was, wasn't it, a professional relationship? Well it certainly wasn't nothing more than that, I mean, was it?" (*SP*, 369). This question ends his monologue, sums up his life with Frank and Grace, and confirms his identity as a hopeless romantic, a modern, demotic knight in the courtly love tradition. That he remembered their theme song was chosen because it was a big hit the year Frank and Grace were married, that Frank and Grace only remembered disliking it, and that Teddy still loved to play the record testifies to his romantic involvement and to his ability to preserve his unrequited love unscathed from the ravages of consummated love that tore Frank and Grace apart.

The most emotionally charged and revealing memory about which they differed concerned the Scottish village of Kinlochbervie and what happened there. Grace and Teddy remembered it as the place where Grace had her stillborn child, although their memories of the details differed significantly. Teddy had the most detailed memory. He remembered coming out of a misty fog after climbing a long steep hill and then seeing below them in the valley, "bathed in sunshine," "this fantastic little village sitting on the edge of the sea, all blue and white and golden, and all lit up and all sparkling and all just heavenly. And Gracie she turns to me and she says, 'Teddy,' she says, 'this is where my baby'll be born'" (*SP*, 362). Teddy remembered that they became stuck there for several days because an axle on the van broke. As Grace was about to give birth

Frank walked away, despite Teddy's attempts to call him back, and Teddy delivered the baby in the back of the van with Grace calling for Frank:

> Her lying on my old raincoat in the back of the van . . . shouting for him, screaming for him . . . all that blood . . . her bare feet pushing, kicking against my shoulders . . . "Frank!" she's screaming, "Frank! Frank!" and I'm saying, "My darling, he's coming—he's coming, my darling—he's on his way—he'll be here any minute" . . . and then that—that little wet thing with the black face and the black body, a tiny little thing, no size at all . . . a boy it was . . .
>
> And afterwards she was so fantastic—I mean she was so bloody fantastic. She held it in her arms, just sitting there on the roadside with her back leaning against the stone wall and her legs stretched out in front of her, just sitting there in the sun and looking down at it in her arms. And then after about half an hour she said, "It's time to bury it now, Teddy." And we went into a nearby field and I had to chase the cows away 'cause they kept following us and I dug the hole and I put it in the hole and I covered it up again. And then she asked me was I not going to say no prayers over it and I said sure, why not, my darling, I said; but not being much of a praying man I didn't know right what to say; so I just said this was the infant child of Francis Hardy, Faith Healer, and his wife, Grace Hardy, both citizens of Ireland, and this was where their infant child lies, in Kinlochbervie, in Sutherland; and God have mercy on us all, I said. . . . And when the little ceremony was concluded, she put her two white hands on my face and brought me to her and kissed me on the forehead. Just once. On the forehead. (*SP*, 363–64)

Later in the evening Teddy placed a white cross on the grave. Frank returned just before dark and, although he glanced toward the van, he did not allude to what had happened. Teddy did not blame Frank, however. He thought Frank "had suffered all that she had suffered" and was near collapse. He concludes, "well, maybe he had to have his own way of facing things . . . None of my concern, thank the Lord, except in so far as it might affect the performance of my client" (*SP*, 365).

Clearly Teddy's version preserved both the illusory separation of his personal and professional lives and the courtly love romance (although delivering babies for the unattainable beloved is a rather radically modernized trial for a questing knight). In this incident Teddy actually moved beyond a vicarious relation with Grace to playing out the roles of husband and midwife. The degree of satisfaction this memory provided for Teddy's psychic sustenance can be measured by the quantity of vivid detail that accompanies it. Teddy managed to excuse Frank's desertion of Grace at her moment of greatest need for at least two reasons: first, it permitted him to act as a surrogate husband, and second it allowed him to preserve his attachment to Frank both personally and professionally.

Grace's version of what happened at Kinlochbervie, like her monologue generally, erased Teddy's role and gave Frank much of the prominence in the incident Teddy had given himself in his version. She remembered Kinlochbervie as a rainy dismal place where they just happened to be. She tells of having the baby in the back of the van without a doctor or nurse in attendance, but she does not mention whether Frank or Teddy helped her deliver the child. She does say that Frank "made a wooden cross to mark the grave and painted it white and wrote across it *Infant Child of Francis and Grace Hardy*" (*SP,* 344), actions and words that Teddy attributed to himself. She also says that Frank "never talked about it afterwards; never once mentioned it again; and because he didn't, neither did I" (*SP,* 345). For Grace, Teddy was barely part of the scene. What was important to her was what it said about her connection with Frank—he made the cross for their child—or her lack of connection with him—neither ever mentioned it again. For her emotional well-being Teddy's role was irrelevant.

Frank's memory erased the incident altogether and displaced it with an egocentric crisis that ostensibly had nothing to do with Grace, except to provide her with another opportunity to exhibit her mulish loyalty to him. He remembered Kinlochbervie as "a picturesque little place, very quiet, very beautiful" (*SP,* 337); and what he remembered happening there was receiving word that his mother had had a heart attack. He says, "when the news came, Teddy drove me down to Glasgow. Gracie wanted to come with me and couldn't understand when I wouldn't take her. But she used her incomprehension as fuel for her loyalty and sent me off with a patient smile" (*SP,* 337).

The rest of the memory involved his trip home and his unfulfilling relationship with his father. He recalled that his father did not recognize him when he arrived at the door and treated him more like an acquaintance than a son. His father did, however, manage to induce a measure of familial guilt by mentioning that Frank had "missed" his mother by one hour and ten minutes. Only when his father finally cried did Frank experience "overwhelming relief," and Frank cried with him (*SP*, 338). The focus of this memory is Frank's unresolved alienation from his father, as is the focus of another memory of his father with a mouth full of rotten teeth, a symbol of sexual impotence in Freudian lore. Grace confirms the significance of these memories for Frank in her monologue when she remembers that they were in Wales, as opposed to Kinlochbervie, when Frank received word of his father's death. And when he returned from the funeral "he spoke of the death as if it had been his mother's." "His mother," Grace says, "had been dead for years when I first met him" (*SP*, 346).

Given what we know about Frank's egocentric obsessions (he is as egocentric an artistic type as Stephen Dedalus), we can imagine that he might well have walked away from Grace at the one moment in their relationship when he had to acknowledge his own needs as secondary to hers. Perhaps as he wandered around until the baby was delivered and disposed of, he did muse on his own crippled relationship with his father, a memory triggered by the possibility of becoming a father himself. At one point he did say that he wanted a child; but he put the blame off on Grace for being barren. He imagined a son who might have had his gift of healing, and he also imagined that he would have asked nothing of him but would simply "have got pleasure just in looking at him" (*SP*, 372), a kind of admiration Grace desired and the kind suggested in the theme song "I love you/Just the way you look tonight."

Significantly Frank thinks about having a child after remembering Grace's father. Like Frank, Grace suffered because of alienation from her father, who considered Frank a mountebank. Frank never met Grace's father, but he experienced a curious connection with him through a phrase in a letter to Frank accusing him of "implicating my only child in your career of chicanery" (*SP*, 371). He remembers Grace collapsing with laughter over the phrase — "I suppose to demonstrate her absolute loyalty to me," he muses — but he thought her laughter was cruel "because by then my anger against him had died and I had some envy of the man who could use the word 'chicanery' with such confidence" (*SP*, 371–72).

Clearly, complex layer upon layer is piled up in these memories of

Frank's: his feeling about Grace's father invoked his feelings about his own father, about a father's feeling for a child, and about his fears of the orderly existence Grace's father represented to him, an order signified by the mastery of words which both appeals to Frank and intimidates him. This love-fear, attraction-repulsion dynamic carried over into his feelings about Grace, whom Frank never was able to dissociate from her father's values even though Grace herself had successfully rejected them, at least after her final trip home.

Thus, by playing variations on the Kinlochbervie incident, Friel ingeniously orchestrates his emotional triangle around a single event. The variations suggest that what actually happened is less important than what is remembered to have happened and that the facts are less important than their emotional significance within the psychic structures of memory. With this play Friel has realized in its most articulate form the significance of the misremembered fishing trip with his father when he was a boy, a significance he first approached when he used the memory in *Philadelphia, Here I Come!* With regard to how his own memory may have altered the facts about that fishing trip, Friel has said, "What matters is that for some reason . . . this vivid memory is there in the storehouse of the mind. For some reason the mind has shuffled the pieces of verifiable truth and composed a truth of its own. For to me it is a truth. And because I acknowledge its peculiar veracity, it becomes a layer in my subsoil; it becomes part of me; ultimately it becomes me" (1972b, 18).

Formally the contrasting memory device is a tour de force as well. Each character introduces each shared memory with identical or almost identical phrasing that acts like a refrain in poetry, particularly in good poetry, where the refrain accumulates meaning or alters in significance with each repetition. For the major incidents the characters repeat certain phrases that introduce the memory. Teddy's phrasing, for example, contains all the common elements for the introductory refrain for the Kinlochbervie incident: "very small, very remote, right away up in the north of Sutherland, about as far north as you can go in Scotland, and looking across at the Isle of Lewis in the Outer Hebrides" (*SP,* 362). These phrases serve to alert the theater audience to something they have heard before and to prepare them to recognize the significant differences. The coherence of the play depends not on any causally related series of events but on the consistency of each of the three psychic structures in editing and shaping their memories.

Another memory that illustrates how desire edits and censors memory concerns the night Frank cured an entire audience of ten. All three characters mention this night. Again Teddy's memory is the most detailed. He remembered that the people Frank cured were strangely quiet and content afterwards and that only one farmer who had been lame returned to thank Frank and he gave him his entire wallet. Stunned at first, Frank "went crazy with delight" and then sang and danced Grace down the aisle of the church and out into the snowy street. Then Frank and Grace hopped into the van and took off, leaving Teddy behind: "they went off to some posh hotel in Cardiff and lived it up until the wallet was empty." Teddy masked his pain at being left behind by rationalizing that their excitement was "understandable" and there was "no cruelty intended." The only reproach he allows himself is the remark "Just a little bit thoughtless—that's all" (SP, 359–60). When Grace remembered this scene she edited out Teddy and the fact that Frank cured ten that night. She focused primarily on their celebratory retreat: "I can think about the night the old farmer outside Cardiff gave him £200 for curing his limp—just handed him his wallet—and we booked into the Royal Abercorn and for four nights we lived like kings" (SP, 342–43). Frank carried around a press clipping about him curing ten that night as a kind of reassurance about his identity. When he mentions the incident, he recalls that only one of the ten returned to thank him and that he said jokingly to Grace "Where are the other nine?" (SP, 371). He does not mention the wallet, the £200, or the spree in Cardiff. Clearly the same obsessions shape their memories of this incident that shaped the contours of their various memories of Kinlochbervie: Frank is obsessed with his talent, Grace is obsessed with Frank, and Teddy is obsessed with them both but prevented, under the guise of his professional credo about mixing business and personal matters, from recognizing and articulating his real feelings. Typically Teddy's wish fulfillment regarding Grace plays a major role in the structure of his memory, but his desire is expressed only indirectly because his professional credo operates like a taboo in censoring his feelings toward his "clients." In this case Teddy's indirection manifests itself when, immediately before and after describing his desertion, Teddy describes fights between Frank and Grace and wonders whether artists "should ever be married" (*SP*, 360). He then cites a very humorous illustration of his attempt to breed his primary paradigm of the artist Rob Roy, the Piping Dog.

The final crucial memory is the return to Ireland and Frank's last performance. As with Kinlochbervie, Friel signals the importance of this memory by having each of the three versions begin with the same refrain: "So on the last day of August we crossed from Stranraer to Larne and drove through the night to County Donegal. And there we got lodgings in a pub, a lounge bar, really, outside a village called Ballybeg, not far from Donegal Town" (*SP*, 338).

In Frank's version of the story when he, Grace, and Teddy arrived at the pub, at first they remained apart from another group of men returning from a wedding. Then Teddy broke the ice with the other group and the two groups merged and much convivial drinking and chatter ensued. After hearing about Frank's marvelous achievements from Teddy, Donal, who had a crooked finger, challenged Frank to straighten it. Frank did. Later, "sometime before dawn," the wedding guests remembered their paralyzed friend McGarvey, who had not been able to attend the wedding, and insisted on bringing him to Frank. After Teddy had gone to bed and Grace had tidied up, Frank met with the wedding guests and McGarvey in a courtyard outside the pub just after dawn. Frank knew in advance, as he always did when he would fail, that he would not cure McGarvey.

Grace remembered that after arriving at the Ballybeg pub Frank was unusually relaxed and charming. He even introduced her as his wife. She also recalled that it was Frank, not Teddy, who approached the group of wedding guests and initiated the conviviality by volunteering to cure Donal's finger. She remembered Teddy staying outside the group looking on somewhat bewildered. She also remembered the crippled McGarvey as being part of the group at the pub and that after straightening Donal's finger Frank then set his sights on McGarvey, never taking his eyes off him. She said that she knew instinctively "that before the night was out he was going to measure himself against the cripple in the wheelchair" (*SP*, 352). She pleaded with him not to do it, but, as he often did to her dismay, he just looked right through her as if she were not there. She watched what happened in the courtyard from an upstairs window.

Teddy's memory of that evening outside Ballybeg says nothing about wedding guests, crooked fingers, or cripples in wheelchairs. What he remembered about that night was seeing Frank and Grace as they once were before all the fighting and bitterness. He recalled standing apart watching them the whole night be easy, relaxed, chatting, laughing, exchanging private remarks, touching each other, everyone wanting to talk with them and them talking with everyone. As he watched Grace singing "All those endearing young charms," Teddy was brought to the brink of a crisis that threatened to destroy the illusory wall between the personal and the professional in his life:

> she stands up there in that Irish pub, in that red dress and with her hair all back from her face; and she's looking at him as she's singing; and we're all looking at her; and the song—it sort of comes out of her very simple and very sweet, like in a way not as if she's performing but as if the song's just sort of rising out of her by itself. And I'm sitting there just outside the circle, sitting there very quiet, very still. And I'm saying to myself, "O Jesus, Teddy boy . . . O my Jesus . . . What are you going to do?" (*SP*, 368)

At this point Teddy noticed Frank watching him watch Grace, and he imagined that Frank "cured" him of the professional and personal impropriety in his mind: "and there he is, gazing across at me. And the way he's gazing at me and the look he has on his face is exactly the way he looks into somebody he knows he's going to cure . . . a very compassionate look. It's a look that says two things. It says: No need to speak—I know exactly what the trouble is. And at the same time it says: I am now going to cure you of that trouble" (*SP*, 368). It is at this point that Teddy realized that he loved them both, Frank maybe more than Grace, and he says, "for the first time in twenty years I was so content . . . I got drunk in celebration—slowly, deliberately, happily slewed!" (*SP*, 368). The next thing he remembered was Grace waking him up telling him something terrible has happened.

Frank's version of the Ballybeg memory again emphasized his lifelong wrestling with his talent, with all its triumphs and failures, and especially its debilitating unpredictability, which Frank sought to escape with this final failure. For Grace this memory represented her final failure too—her failure to woo Frank away from his obsession with his talent, an obsession that finally claimed him and left Grace bereft. For Teddy this was the moment when, on the verge of breaking faith with his guiding credo, he was able, with the help of the healing gaze of Frank, to strike an exquisite balance between his two loves and between his personal life and his professional life. It was as if in this fleeting moment of balance his most ardent desires were reconciled with his failure to achieve the objects of those desires.

Faith Healer demonstrates the role desire plays in the shaping of memory, desire that manifests itself in narratives about events. These narratives and the language out of which they are constructed are typically governed by an image, most commonly an image of the self or an image intimately related to the self. This image is constantly in the process of being confirmed, threatened, or challenged by our experience of events and by images of ourselves encountered in others. For people who are particularly open to influences of the other, these self-images can be very unstable, and a great deal of psychic energy may be devoted to attempts to stabilize them. The same is true for people whose environment continuously feeds back an image that the self, for whatever reasons, finds undesirable. Frank's self-image as artist/performer/faith-healer, for example, was threatened with every performance, some of which confirmed the image and some of which did not. Grace's refusal to be satisfied with the loyal drudge image Frank had of her resulted in her continuous battle with him against what she perceived to be the primary impediment to his recognition of a more desirable image of her—his obsession with his own self-image and the devoted loyalty it required from her as sustenance because of its instability.

Faith Healer implies that memories for Friel are fictions, but nonetheless real for that. As with Wordsworth, memory is a self-verifying, heartfelt truth. "And because I acknowledge its peculiar veracity," Friel says, "it becomes a layer in my subsoil; it becomes part of me; ultimately it becomes me" (1972b, 18). Grace says that Frank's fictions about her, about his father, and about the people he cured, and particularly his fictions about her marital status, her surname, and her place of origin, came out of "some compulsion he had to adjust, to refashion, to re-create everything around him" (*SP*, 345). This compulsion is frequently associated with artists, and Frank Hardy's temperament and his vocation as faith healer are frequently read as metaphors for the artist.[1] In a rare moment of explicit commentary on his own work, Friel also has encouraged this reading. He says that *Faith Healer*

> was some kind of metaphor for the art, the craft of writing, or whatever it is. And the great confusion we all have about it, those of us who are involved in it. How honourable and how dishonourable it can be. And it's also a pursuit that, of necessity, has to be very introspective, and as a consequence it leads to great selfishness. So that you're constantly, as I'm doing at this moment, saying something and listening to yourself saying it, and the third eye is constantly watching you. And it's a very dangerous thing because in some way it perverts whatever natural freedom you might have, and that natural freedom must find its expression in the written word. . . . I mean the element of the charlatan that there is in all creative work. (1982a, 22)

In its treatment of memory as fiction written by desire, however, *Faith Healer* also suggests that the artists' images become part of everyone's equipment in negotiating experience. Grace realized, for example, that despite her resistance to Frank's fiction of her, it had established the terms of her relationship to him, which in turn was the defining relationship of her own existence. At the end of her monologue she exclaims, "O my God I'm one of his fictions too, but I need him to sustain me in that existence—O my God I don't know if I can go on without his sustenance" (*SP*, 353). With Frank's death she had lost the source of her defining fiction and, unable to survive without it, she eventually committed suicide. Teddy's romantic fiction of her, in contrast, provided no sustenance for her, nothing to test the reality of her own existence against, no inverse proportion by which to measure her own dependency on him. The implication seems to be that while everyone is capable of producing fictions, some fictions exert more power over people's experience than others.

Fictions embedded in memory are not limited in their sphere of influence to the individual psyche. As with Frank and Grace, they provide a means of negotiating social relations. Social relations themselves be-

---

1. By far the most thorough and penetrating of these readings is Kiberd 1985.

come collective fictions that individuals subscribe to. Most of Friel's writing, like *Faith Healer*, focuses on the lack of agreement among social fictions. In "The Diviner" and *The Loves of Cass McGuire*, for example, social contracts break down because of a lack of agreement among individuals about the fictions governing those contracts. *Faith Healer*, in fact, marks the fullest articulation of this thematic on the register of the private and the social (as opposed to the public and the political). *Faith Healer* also belongs to the tradition of Irish "lying" outlined in chapter 2 that extends back through Joyce, Synge, and Yeats to Wilde. *Faith Healer*, in fact, is in a direct line of descent from Synge's *Playboy*, where Christy Mahon through social interaction creates a fictional identity for himself and then proceeds to inhabit that identity.

The implications of *Faith Healer* need not be limited to individual and social fictions, however. As I suggested in chapter 2, international tensions and conflicts often result from incompatible national narratives. The incompatible fictions of Frank, Grace, and Teddy, for example, suggest the long-standing incompatible fictions England and Ireland have had of each other in relation to the narratives each had constructed of itself.[2] Tony Roche, who calls *Faith Healer* "a drama of national identity," points out that the three characters are Irish (Frank), Northern Anglo-Irish (Grace), and English (Teddy) and that the narrative setting, which is mostly Wales and Scotland, serves "as a medial zone between the two excluded parameters represented by the characters themselves: Ireland and England." He persuasively argues that the stories of the three characters are "contending, conflicting dramas of national identity." He reads the conflict between Grace and Frank, who wears vivid green socks (*SP*, 331), in terms of the stereotypical Arnoldian contrast between the rational, orderly, practical, materialistic, civilized English and the vague, dreamy, idealistic, irresponsible, drunken Irish. Grace's Englishness is represented primarily by her father's values and her upbringing in a "typical Protestant Big House." Even though Grace has rejected these values, Frank continues to be threatened by them and to attribute them to

2. Kiberd 1984 is an insightful essay on the topic of Ireland's and England's mutually incompatible fictions of each other. Many of these insights were incorporated into Kiberd's 1995 book, where he says, "even in their fictions of one another, a strange reciprocity bound colonizer to colonized" (1995, 279).

Grace. Frank's insistence that Grace is a Yorkshire woman at once crystallizes her cultural significance for him. Frank's jealous admiration of her father's command of language suggests his own postcolonial insecurities. Roche acknowledges that Friel plays down Grace's religious affiliation, thus emphasizing her betrayal of her class by marrying beneath her. Her father objects to Frank not because he is a Catholic but because he is a "mountebank," and when Grace on a trip home rejects her father's judgment of her and Frank she does it with "words he never used; a language he didn't speak; a language never heard in that house" (*SP*, 348). Roche reads Teddy as "Friel's revenge on centuries of stage misrepresentation of the Irish by concocting this stage Englishman, the loquacious lovable cockney comedian" drawn from the milieu of the music hall comedian and the yellow tabloid press (1994, 117–24).

The postcolonial currents in *Faith Healer*, however, run deeper than Roche suggests. The monologues of the three characters constitute hybrid enunciations in Bhabha's sense. This is particularly true of Grace, whose identity is composed by means of a complex negotiation between her own self-image and need to be an object of devotion and Frank's image of her as loyal drudge. Frank's identity is also composed of complex negotiations — negotiations with his Scottish and Welch audiences through his performances, negotiations with Grace's own self-image which he transforms into the image of loyal drudge, negotiations with his image of Grace's father whom he both fears and admires. Teddy's self-image, too, of the consummate professional who is able to keep his personal feelings out of his business affairs, results from complex negotiations with Grace and Frank, or perhaps it would be more accurate to say with Grace through Frank. As with Cass McGuire and most other Friel protagonists, the characters of *Faith Healer* replicate the structures of the postcolonial psyche in these hybrid enunciations. Although one need not push a reading of *Faith Healer* to the level of political allegory, as Roche does, it is difficult to resist the temptation. Frank can be read as metaphor and metonymy for an insecure Sinn Fein Ireland who mightily wishes to believe in the self-sustaining autonomy of his talent and genius and would like to relegate the Anglo-Irish and the English to strictly supporting roles in the assertion of that self-sustaining autonomy. But, as his admiration of and aggression toward Grace's father suggests, he is more dependent on and more defined by his relations with the Anglo-Irish and the English than he cares to acknowledge. Grace suggests an Anglo-Ireland who seeks the acknowledgment and devotion of the Irish but is destined to be perpetually frustrated in that desire. Teddy is an England that prides itself on an impersonal professionalism, but this self-image serves to mask not only an intense underlying desire for both Irelands but also the fact that its own identity is partly formed by that desire. In the end, however, *Faith Healer*'s most profound postcolonial insight does not depend on the validity of the political allegory, and that is the insight that all notions of identity, personal or national, are the result of complex historical negotiations with others and that these hybrid identities are made manifest, at both the conscious and the unconscious level, in the narrative fictions we construct about ourselves in relation to others.

8

(De)mythology

Translations, The Communication Cord, and Field Day

IN MANY WAYS *Faith Healer* marks the culmination of the development of Friel's stagecraft and of the evolution of his postmodern understanding of language as lying. No play written since *Faith Healer* has equalled its concentrated power and intensity nor matched the fineness of its writing. Although it is a difficult play to perform—it must be staged and acted superbly to work at all—it deserves to be ranked among the great plays of the twentieth century. *Faith Healer*, however, is not Friel's most popular or best-known play. In the United States he still is better known for the successful Broadway runs of *Philadelphia, Here I Come!* and *Dancing at Lughnasa*. The next play he wrote after *Faith Healer*, however, was *Translations*, and it became the instant classic of his oeuvre. It is already being anthologized with other canonical texts of the Irish theater.[1]

Translations

Translations (1980) became an instant classic and the central text in Friel's oeuvre for a number of reasons. First of all, a number of Friel's concerns and preoccupations coalesced in this play: his interest in language and various historical and cultural discourses; his interest in Ireland's colonial and postcolonial history from a nationalist perspective; and his concern with the social and political turmoil in Northern Ireland. In addition to

---

1. For example, in Owens and Radner 1990 and in Harrington 1991.

fusing a number of Friel's long-standing preoccupations, *Translations* also emerged out of the political and social struggles that followed the Northern Ireland civil rights movement, which began in Derry in 1968. Out of this civil rights movement arose the Social Democratic and Labour Party (SDLP) and the new nationalism that characterized that party under the leadership of John Hume. This new nationalism also spread to the Republic and informed the ideology of cultural organizations like *The Crane Bag.* This new moderate, bourgeois nationalism inspired the 1984 report of the New Ireland Forum that led to the Anglo-Irish Agreement of 1985. In many ways *Translations* is an excellent metaphor for this new nationalism. The premiere of *Translations* in 1980 also launched Field Day in the public eye amid much hoopla in Derry over hopes for the reconciliation of the two Northern communities. The premiere followed a series of significant political events over the previous decade that included the fall of Stormont, the breaking of the gerrymander in Derry that had ensured unionist political dominance in a predominantly nationalist area, and the foundation of the SDLP in the wake of the civil rights movement. In other words, at its opening performance in Derry *Translations* was already dripping with cultural and political significance and it still remains an important cultural and political statement in the context of Northern Ireland and Anglo-Irish relations.

In a more practical academic vein, *Translations* is also an excellent text with which to begin a course in twentieth-century Irish literature because it effectively dramatizes (albeit from a nationalist point of view) so many different issues that have been important to Irish culture, history, and politics over the past century and a half, including the loss of the Gaelic culture and language, Anglo-Irish relations, colonialism and its legacy, and civil rights.

A number of important texts also intersect with *Translations* and contribute significantly to an understanding of the play and its intellectual, political, cultural, and social contexts. The postmodern view of all language as fundamentally implicated in various processes of translation, which provides the central metaphor and intellectual thesis for the play, derives from George Steiner's *After Babel* (1975), which Friel read in the late 1970s as part of his preparation for "translating" Chekhov's *Three Sis-*

ters into Irish English. Texts on Ireland's hedge schools also inform the play. While contemplating some of the matters that eventually became *Translations,* Friel discovered that one of his great-great-grandfathers had been a hedge-schoolmaster, and this discovery sent him to Dowling's *The Hedge Schools of Ireland.* He also drew from those writings of William Carleton that deal with his experiences in the hedge schools. For the map-making metaphor in *Translations* Friel drew from the histories of the nineteenth-century ordnance survey that created the Anglicized map of Ireland as we know it today. He particularly relied on John Andrews's *A Paper Landscape* (a history of the survey published in 1975), on the memoirs of Colonel Colby, who was in charge of the survey, and on the letters of John O'Donovan, an Irish civilian, native Gaelic speaker, and antiquary who worked on the survey with primary responsibility for standardizing the place names and their spellings (Friel n.d., 57). The program for the Derry premiere of *Translations* alludes to many of Friel's sources, including Steiner, Andrews, Dowling, Carleton, Colby, and O'-Donovan, as well as to other documents connected with the ordnance survey (Field Day 1980).

Friel set *Translations* in the townland of Baile Beag, County Donegal, in 1833, just as the new national schools, where lessons were to be taught exclusively in English, were about to replace the hedge schools, where instruction was often in Gaelic, particularly in the west of Ireland. Legislation passed in 1831 established a system of national schools throughout Britain. In Ireland students in these schools would no longer be taught in Gaelic and all the official place-names would no longer be Gaelic. The political advantages of this for the British were obvious. The schools taught in Gaelic also taught the Gaelic version of Irish history and preserved and fanned the traditional historical prejudices against the British. In the new national schools Irish schoolchildren would learn the history of Ireland from texts written in English from the English point of view. The hedge schools, although they varied widely in quality, kept Irish culture and language alive during a century of severe political and cultural oppression. Some of them even offered a decent classical education. The new national schools, however, were about to accomplish what the notorious Penal Laws had failed to accomplish—the eradication of Gaelic Ireland. Historians seem to agree that the national schools were more effective than any other means the British had used to eradicate Irish language and culture (J. C. Beckett 1966, 313). They needed only the famine to accelerate the change. While historians disagree over the precise number of Gaelic-speaking Irish in 1800 and in 1850, most agree that, although the official language had been English for centuries, between these two dates Ireland changed from a predominantly Gaelic-speaking nation to a predominantly English-speaking nation.

Friel discovered that the nineteenth-century ordnance survey had set up its first trigonometrical base in 1828 across the river Foyle from where he was living outside Derry in Muff, County Donegal. Then in 1976 he encountered John Andrews's *A Paper Landscape,* the recently published history of that survey. "And suddenly," Friel says, "here was the confluence—the aggregate—of all those notions that had been visiting me over the previous years: the first half of the nineteenth century; an aspect of colonialism; the death of the Irish language and the acquisition of English. Here were all the elements I had been dallying with, all synthesised in one very comprehensive and precise text. Here was the perfect metaphor to accommodate and realise all those shadowy notions—map-making" (Barry 1983, 123). Begun in 1824, the ordinance survey had produced its six-inch maps of Ireland (i.e., six inches to the mile) by 1846. These maps established the face of modern Ireland. Moreover, the survey standardized and Anglicized all the names and spellings of locations throughout the country. In many instances, prior to the survey neither place-names nor spellings were consistent. In *Translations* Friel focuses on that part of the ordnance survey that attempted to standardize and Anglicize all the Gaelic place-names, and his characterization of that process does not substantially distort O'Donovan's experience as rendered in his letters.

So the 1833 setting of the play symbolizes a major transition in Irish culture. Since both the national schools and the ordnance survey helped to eradicate what remained of Gaelic culture in Ireland, its language, and its place-names, *Translations* captures, in terms of its impact on the people of Ballybeg in County Donegal, a critical passage in Irish history as a living Gaelic culture is about to become Anglicized. As Friel once put it, *Translations* is "about how this country found a certain shape" (1982b, 8).

If one focuses purely on plot and characterization in *Translations*, then the play is a classic political/historical melodrama in the tradition of Boucicault. But the play does not remain on that level. Friel infuses it with linguistic concerns that transform the melodramatic plot and characterization into a much more sophisticated play. On the surface these concerns are signaled by an ingenious and deftly executed dramatic convention that indicates when an actor, while actually speaking English, is understood to be speaking Gaelic. This device is completely unobtrusive and it works flawlessly. It is also part of the structural and metaphoric logic of the play. Friel, for example, has refused to allow a bilingual production of the play for Gaelic-speaking audiences. He would allow the play to be done entirely in Gaelic, but he insisted that a bilingual play would violate the metaphorical integrity of the linguistic device: he said "I think you'd have to invent a different theatrical conceit if you did away with it. Otherwise, it doesn't make sense in a way; the conceit is part of the strange logic of the play" (Kiely 1981). The device highlights the issue of language as culturally and politically central and it provides a structure within which Friel can play numerous variations on the title metaphor of translation.

Many readings of *Translations* have tended to focus on the political, historical, and cultural issues the play raises and to emphasize the erosion, suppression, or replacement of one culture by another. Very few readers have explored the play's more central concern with language.[2] Friel himself has said that, while the political and historical thematics are obviously relevant to the atmosphere of the play, he had no desire "to write a play about Irish peasants being suppressed by English sappers," or "to write a threnody on the death of the Irish language." It is not that Friel lacked interest in Ireland's Gaelic past. On the contrary, he knew that for the play to work he had to capture "the wholeness, the integrity, of that Gaelic past." But he constantly worried about turning *Translations* into a political play, because for him "the play has to do with language and only language. And if it becomes overwhelmed by that

2. The chief exceptions are Kearney 1983, Kearney 1987, Lojek 1994, McGrath 1989, and Smith 1991.

political element," he says, "it is lost" (Friel n.d., 58–59). In the end, his concerns about the politics of the play were justified.

The text most crucial to understanding Friel's concerns about language in *Translations* is George Steiner's *After Babel*. Even though Friel had been groping for decades toward insights about language similar to what he found in *After Babel*, it is difficult to overestimate the impact Steiner's book had on *Translations*. I have dealt with this in some detail in "Irish Babel," but in general Friel wove many of Steiner's theoretical insights pervasively and ingeniously into the narrative fabric of *Translations*. Steiner's general epistemological orientation dominates the play, and the speech of Hugh, the hedge-school master, is peppered with direct quotations and near quotes from *After Babel*. Moreover, certain scenes and characters appear to have their genesis in passages from *After Babel*, including scenes and characters that would seem the least likely to have originated in scholarly linguistic abstractions.

Friel constructs the intellectual framework of *Translations* out of the central thesis of *After Babel* and several of its corollaries. Steiner organizes his book around the conviction that all communication, even within a single language, involves translation. The corollaries that Steiner derives from this thesis and that Friel deploys in his play include lying and concealment as central to language (discussed in chapter 2 above), the relation of language to Eros, the nature and difficulty of translating between cultures, and history as translation from the past to the present. These central insights from *After Babel* serve to orchestrate all the other materials of Friel's play.

If Steiner's *After Babel* provided a theoretic formulation around which Friel's views of language could coalesce, the historical contingency that motivated that coalescence, that provided the impulse toward agency, was Friel's colonial and postcolonial experience of both Irish states. Consequently, if *Translations* gave dramatic form to Steiner's linguistic abstractions, it also exhibited many of the major features of Bhabha's postcolonial theory, in which the concept of translation also is central. For Bhabha performative hybrid enunciations from the margins of colonial cultures are acts of translation, particularly translations of a native past into a cosmopolitan present and translations between cultures. Bhabha also recognizes the necessity of translating within cultures and temporalities, and so, like Steiner, acknowledges that any act of communication involves translation. In addition, Bhabha theorizes the inevitability of mistranslation between times and cultures and the inevitable existence of untranslatable residues.

Once we move beyond the obvious cultural and political themes in *Translations,* we can see how much more is going on with language and how Friel subordinates the cultural and political materials to the larger concern with language. Virtually every character and scene involves a translation of some kind. Even the title *Translations* refers less to the obvious tensions in the play between the English and the Gaelic-speaking Irish than to Steiner's linguistic epistemology centered on the notion that all communication, even within the same language, involves translation.

The first act of the play introduces several key issues about translation. The central dramatic action is set in motion when Owen, the younger son of the hedge-school master Hugh, returns after six years to his native townland of *Baile Beag,* a Gaelic-speaking community in Donegal. Owen has returned as a civilian translator employed by a British regiment of engineers charged with conducting an ordnance survey to modernize and Anglicize the map of Ireland. His first official duty is to translate Captain Lancey's introductory remarks to the *Baile Beag* residents. Owen's loose translation of Lancey's words, however, transforms the utterances in at least two ways: first, he reduces Lancey's ponderous officialese to simple speech; and second, he masks some of the more sinister implications of his words. For example, when Lancey says, "His Majesty's government has ordered the first ever comprehensive survey of this entire country—a general triangulation which will embrace detailed hydrographic and topographic information and which will be executed to a scale of six inches to the English mile" (*SP,* 406), Owen translates this statement as "A new map is being made of the whole country." But when Lancey says that the purpose of the survey is "so that the entire basis of land valuation can be reassessed for purposes of more equitable taxation" and "has for its object the relief which can be afforded to the proprietors and occupiers of land from unequal taxation," Owen translates these remarks as "This new map will take the place of the estate-agent's map so that from now on you will know exactly what is yours in law" and "the new map will mean that taxes are reduced" (*SP,* 406).

Owen's elder brother Manus translates Lancey's remarks quite differently, however; for he reads them in light of Ireland's past experience with England perceived from the Gaelic point of view. He immediately takes Owen to task: "What sort of translation was that," he demands. When Owen makes the smart response, "Uncertainty in meaning is incipient poetry," Manus retorts, "There was nothing uncertain about what Lancey said: it's a bloody military operation." Manus questions why the Gaelic place-names of their townland need to be changed and why the British soldiers persist in calling Owen Roland. Owen's response "It's only a name" does not mollify Manus (*SP,* 408), and it serves to underscore Owen's naïveté about his own collaboration as well as the differences between him and his brother. Later Owen's naïveté is smashed by the tragic consequences of his work. At the end of the play he must translate Lancey's resolve, if they do not find the missing Lt. Yolland, to destroy all the local townlands they have just renamed (*SP,* 439). As Lancey ticks off the new Anglicized names of the villages to be destroyed, Owen must translate them back into Gaelic. Owen realizes too late what he has been willing to barter away in order to advance himself in his colonial situation.

Owen's translations of Lancey raise a number of issues central to how language works to negotiate between two cultures in colonial circumstances. Most obvious is the temporal and spatial displacement involved in Owen's versions of what Lancey says. In Bhabha's terms, both Owen's and Manus's translations of Lancey are hybrid performative enunciations at a site on the margins between cultures, a site where the hybrid Anglo-Irish begins its presencing: "Translation is the performative nature of cultural communication. It is language *in actu* (enunciation, positionality) rather than language *in situ* (*énoncé,* or propositionality). And the sign of translation continually tells, or 'tolls' the different times and spaces between cultural authority and its performative practices. The 'time' of translation consists in that *movement* of meaning" (1994, 228; Bhabha's emphases). For Bhabha translation, like Friel's play, is "the staging of cultural difference" (1994, 227), and "Cultures come to be represented by virtue of the processes of iteration and translation through which their meanings are very vicariously addressed to—*through*—an Other" (1994, 58; Bhabha's emphasis), the Other in this case being Captain Lancey. Bhabha's theory emphasizes the interstices or borderlands of cultures as sites from which new histories of nations will be written by minorities, the colonized, migrants, and refugees. These "reinscribed" enunciatory histories will create a new internationalism that will not be limited to national traditions nor will they be universal but contingent and transnational—a "transnational and translational sense of the hybridity of imagined communities" that opens up a hybrid space of translation and negotiation in-between cultural difference (1994, 5). This articulatory, enunciatory process is not merely theoretical but an insurgent, subversive interrogation and intervention in world politics: Bhabha says, "Cultural translation desacralizes the transparent assumptions of cultural supremacy, and in that very act, demands a contextual specificity, a historical differentiation *within* minority positions" (1994, 228; Bhabha's emphasis). In this instance the translations of both Owen and Manus are acts of subversion, one subverting his own culture and the other subverting the culture of the Other. In the process, both cultures are being rewritten and neither survives intact.

In addition to suggesting these colonial implications of translation, Owen also illustrates Steiner's insights about the power of language to conceal. Owen's translations of Lancey conceal as much as they reveal both from himself and from the others, except for his shrewder brother. Also Owen's glib responses to his brother are obviously designed to conceal and evade rather than to communicate.

Another scene structured on a different kind of translation is the love scene between Maire and Lt. Yolland. The scene is both ingenious and moving. After a dance Maire and Yolland go off together. Even though neither can speak the other's language, they manage to communicate their love for each other primarily through their desire to utter words in the other's language, especially each other's name and their places of origin. Despite the language barrier, they insist that the other go on talking because the erotic message is getting through: they both say in their own language, "Don't stop—I know what you're saying" (*SP*, 429–30). The scene ends with them both focusing, without knowing it, on the same word in each other's language. The word is "always." Yolland says he wants to live always in Ireland with Maire and she says that she wants to live always with him anywhere (*SP*, 429–30).

Steiner also seems to have suggested this love scene to Friel. Besides postulating lying as the chief function of language, another fascinating connection Steiner makes is the relation of language to Eros. Steiner claims that our seminal and semantic functions "determine the genetic and social structure of human experience. Together they construe the grammar of being" (1975, 39). "Eros and language mesh at every point," says Steiner: "Intercourse and discourse, copula and copulation, are subclasses of the dominant fact of communication. They arise from the life-need of the ego to reach out and comprehend, in the two vital senses of 'understanding' and 'containment,' another human being. Sex is a profoundly semantic act" (1975, 38).

The word "always" suggests the ultimate erotic commitment for the propagation of both language and race, and the word itself has its source in Steiner. He raises it in connection with the problem of language and future time. He notes that while the relation between language and history is problematic enough, we have no history at all of the future tense, only our verbal projections of it (1975, 141). In this context he asks, "What logical validation can be found for statements of future contingency? What is the status of 'always'?" (1975, 145). The fate of Maire and Yolland raises this problem as well; for their pledge of perpetual commitment does not survive the play. Yolland mysteriously disappears, and the disconsolate Maire resolves to emigrate to America.

The love scene as a whole appears to represent the implicit but ill-fated ideal of the play. The attempt by Maire and Yolland to express their love for each other by trying to use, insofar as they are able, each other's language suggests the ideal of two cultures reaching out to each other, trying to communicate with each other and to understand each other—a naïve and romantic ideal that, as Friel well knows, has rarely if ever been achieved in world history and politics.

Lieutenant Yolland's desire to assimilate into Irish culture and society raises another issue illuminated by both Steiner and Bhabha—the problem of incommensurability in translating between cultures. Lieutenant Yolland articulates the cultural divide between Ireland and England when he realizes that, despite his desire to remain in Ireland, he will never be assimilated: "Even if I did speak Irish," he says, "I'd always be an outsider here, wouldn't I? I may learn the password but the language of the tribe will always elude me, won't it? The private core will always be

. . . hermetic, won't it?" (*SP*, 416). Yolland's statement acknowledges a cultural "idiolect" that will forever elude him beneath the surface of the Irish language, something that tangibly inhabits the language for its native speakers but remains ghostly for the non-native, concealed behind a veil never lifted. Yolland's comments essentially paraphrase a passage in *After Babel*. Steiner illustrates his point with different examples, but the idea is the same:

> There are innumerable near-identities or, more strictly speaking, overlaps of associative content which Englishmen share by virtue of historical or climatic experience but which an American, emitting the same speech-sounds, may have no inkling of. The French language, as self-consciously perhaps as any, is a palimpsest of historical, political undertones and overtones. To a remarkable degree, these embed even ordinary locutions in a "chord" of associations which anyone acquiring the language from outside will never fully master. (1975, 172)

For Bhabha, in translating between cultures there is always an untranslatable residue, an incommensurability at the point of enunciation that acknowledges difference that cannot be reconciled by a transcendental, universal subject position. This is why "cross-cultural identity" is as impossible as relativistic multiculturalism. This is not simply a question of cultural codes, as Yolland implies, but, as Bhabha points out, a problem of the structure of the signifier (1994, 126, 130): "The complementarity of language as communication must be understood as emerging from the constant state of contestation and flux caused by the differential systems of social and cultural signification. This process or complementarity as the agonistic supplement is the seed of the 'untranslatable'—the foreign element in the midst of the performance of cultural translation" (1994, 227). Bhabha cites two famous examples of this untranslatable residue in Kurtz's statement of "the Horror, the Horror" from Conrad's *Heart of Darkness* and the echo "Ouboum" in the Marabar caves from Forster's *A Passage to India* (1994, 123–30). For Bhabha Marlow's lie to Kurtz's Intended at the end of *Heart of Darkness*, is less a deliberate suppression of the truth than an acknowledgment of the incommensurability of two cultures. Bhabha says,

> Marlow does not merely repress the "truth" . . . as much as he enacts a poetics of translation that (be)sets the boundary between the colony and the metropolis. In taking the name of a woman—the Intended—to

mask the daemonic "being" of colonialism, Marlow turns the brooding geography of political disaster—the heart of darkness—into a melancholic memorial to romantic love and historic memory. Between the silent truth of Africa and the salient lie to the metropolitan woman, Marlow returns to his initiating insight: the experience of colonialism is the problem of living in the "midst of the incomprehensible." (1994, 212–13)

Owen's response to Yolland's misgivings—"You can learn to decode us" (*SP*, 416)—is obviously meant to sound naïve. Had he lived, Yolland's children might have approached the hermetic core, or perhaps their children; for, as Steiner says, "only time and native ground can provide a language with the interdependence of formal and semantic components which 'translates' culture into active life" (1975, 470).

While he was reading *After Babel,* there must have been times when Friel thought that Steiner was referring specifically to the cultural conflict between the Irish and the English. Steiner says, for example, "Time and again, linguistic differences and the profoundly exasperating inability of human beings to understand each other have bred hatred and reciprocal contempt . . . languages have been, throughout human history, zones of silence to other men and razor-edges of division" (1975, 56). For Steiner, of course, linguistic differences do not refer simply to verbal misunderstandings: he says, "It may be that cultural traditions are more firmly anchored in our syntax than we realize, and that we shall continue to translate from the past of our individual and social being whether we would or not" (1975, 467). This certainly seems to have been the case historically in Ireland and remains the case in Northern Ireland today.

For Bhabha misunderstanding or mistranslation is endemic to colonial situations. The Word of the imperial power is never interpreted "transparently" but in terms of the context of another culture. This fundamental miscognition interrogates its source and the source of its power. This reception of the word—transformed, displaced, misinterpreted, partial—constitutes colonial hybridity, the challenge to power in the very exercise of that power. The reception of the Word is always subject to Derridean difference and deferral. It is simultaneously repetition and difference, a reversal of the colonial gaze, a "strategic reversal of the process of domination through disavowal" (Bhabha 1994, 112). As examples of this process Bhabha cites the introduction of the English Bible to

India (1994, 102–22) and the "blasphemy" involved in Salman Rushdie's transplanting of the Koran into the context of the Western novel in *Satanic Verses*. Of the latter Bhabha says, blasphemy is "a transgressive act of cultural translation": "by revealing other enunciatory positions and possibilities within the framework of Koranic reading, Rushdie performs the subversion of its authenticity through the act of cultural translation—he relocates the Koran's 'intentionality' by repeating and reinscribing it in the locale of the novel of postwar cultural migrations and diasporas" (1994, 226).

The central metaphor for cultural conflict and linguistic transformation in *Translations* is the ordnance survey. As mentioned above, Friel's reading in 1976 of John Andrews's *A Paper Landscape*, by providing the "perfect metaphor," became the catalyst for fusing the other elements of the play that had been floating around independently in Friel's imagination. At one point Steiner links metaphor and mapmaking in a way that poignantly illuminates Friel's use of it. Metaphors, says Steiner, "are new mappings of the world, they reorganize our habitation in reality" (1975, 23). In *Translations* the remapping of Ireland amounts to nothing less than a reorganization of reality for the Irish. The scene where Owen and Yolland Anglicize the various place-names, for example, demonstrates the impossibility of conveying the precise significance of a place in one language into another language. They rename one place called *Bun na hAbhann*, which in Gaelic literally means "the mouth of the river." *Bun na hAbhann* had been variously known to the Anglo-Irish as Banowen, Owenmore, and Binhone, all of which Owen and Yolland reject. They tentatively consider Anglicizing it to Bunowen, but then reject that too as "neither fish nor flesh" (*SP*, 410). They finally settle quite arbitrarily on Burnfoot, which bears little relevance to anything. The letters of John O'Donovan suggest that Friel's characterization of the renaming process here was fairly typical of the ordnance survey.

Bhabha would see this process of renaming as metonymic rather than metaphoric because the translation of meaning in the new names is always necessarily partial. This partiality, however, is part of the structure of metaphor as well. No metaphor fully replaces what it refers to; the analogy is always partial. Only certain attributes of the metaphoric object substitute for its referent. Nevertheless, the miscognition involved in the renaming process well illustrates how translation produces an entirely new meaning that is neither of one culture nor the other but a new entity that is a hybrid, that duplicates with a difference, that replicates both cultures without being either one, "less than one and double."

Despite the various kinds of translation in the play and despite Yolland's observation that "something is being eroded," the play is not simply about the erosion of one civilization and language by another. The issues raised about language in the play are much more complex than this. Friel, for example, is neither naïve nor simplistic in attributing the erosion of Gaelic Ireland to the obvious distortions caused by Anglicizing the names. There are more subtle kinds of erosion at work as well. Even within the Irish language the connection between the names and the significance of places has begun to erode. Owen points out that *Tobair Vree*, the Gaelic name for a crossroads, is a corruption of "Brian's Well" (*Tobair Bhriain*); but the well, long since dried up, was never at the crossroad's anyway and the story of the Brian connected to it has been all but forgotten (*SP*, 420).

The most articulate character in the play on the issue of language is Hugh, the erudite hedge-school master about to become obsolete; and his remarks help to orchestrate the thematics of language Friel has set in motion. Despite his impeccable Gaelic credentials, Hugh's views of language are anachronistically contemporary with Steiner's. A protostructuralist of sorts, Hugh reminds Yolland, in an oblique comment on the renaming process, that words are not immortal but merely signals and counters (*SP*, 419). In other words, for Hugh language is governed by conventions that are ultimately arbitrary and subject to change and even atrophy. Steiner says,

> In certain civilizations there come epochs in which syntax stiffens, in which the available resources of live perception and restatement wither. Words seem to go dead under the weight of sanctified usage; the frequence [*sic*] and sclerotic force of clichés, of unexamined similes, of worn tropes increases. Instead of acting as a living membrane, grammar and vocabulary become a barrier to new feeling. A civilization is imprisoned in a linguistic contour which no longer matches, or matches only at certain ritual, arbitrary points, the changing landscape of fact. (1975, 21)

Although Steiner is talking about how a language can fossilize from within, perhaps on the *Tobair Vree* model, Friel obviously found Steiner's analysis equally apt for characterizing Ireland at the point when the Gaelic culture and language was about to become Anglicized beyond reclamation. Using Steiner's words, he has Hugh say, "a civilization can be imprisoned in a linguistic contour which no longer matches the landscape of . . . fact" (*SP*, 419). In the context of the play this statement is ambiguous. A reading that emphasizes politics over language might take it to mean that Hugh is referring to the English language not matching the facts of Gaelic Ireland, a reading suggested by the new Anglicized placenames. But Hugh could also be referring to Daniel O'Connell's view that the Gaelic language no longer matches the facts of an Anglicized Ireland. As Seamus Deane says, Hugh's statement "cuts both ways": "Ballybeg seems to have the invidious choice of speaking an old language that cannot be mapped onto the new country or of speaking a new language that cannot be mapped onto the old country" (1993, 107). If we look at this issue from Bhabha's perspective, a third possible interpretation arises — that neither Gaelic nor English matches the facts of the hybrid Anglo-Ireland.

Hugh appears to resign himself to O'Connell's view. Pointing to the book in which his son Owen and the ordnance officer Lt. Yolland have inscribed the new Anglicized place names for *Baile Beag* (now in the process of becoming Ballybeg), he says, "We must learn where we live. We must learn to make them our own. We must make them our new home" (*SP*, 444). Hugh, in other words, understands that the ordnance survey is remapping Ireland in many ways other than geographically and that Gaelic, despite the richness and spiritual qualities he finds so alluring in it, must give way to the political and economic realities of an Anglicized Ireland. A passage from *After Babel* is a good paraphrase of the O'-Connell view: Steiner says, "Numerous cultures and communities have passed out of history as linguistic 'drop-outs.' Not because their own particular speech was in any way inadequate, but because it prevented communication with the principal currents of intellectual and political force" (1975, 56).

The effects on a culture of losing its language and the potential for that culture to disappear into history are suggested in *Translations* with particular poignancy in the character of Sarah. She is the mute student whom Manus brings to the threshold of speech only to be terrorized into silence again by Captain Lancey's threat of violence at the end of the play. Not surprisingly this motif also appears in *After Babel,* and Steiner provides a useful gloss on Sarah's problem. He says, "The patronized and the oppressed have endured behind their silences" (1975, 33). "In the event of autism," he adds, "the speech-battle between child and master can reach a grim finality. Surrounded by incomprehensible or hostile reality, the autistic child breaks off verbal contact. He seems to choose silence to shield his identity but even more, perhaps, to destroy his imagined enemy" (1975, 35). Seamus Heaney has extended Sarah's significance to represent Ireland herself. In his allegorical reading he says, "It is as if some symbolic figure of Ireland from an eighteenth-century vision poem, the one who confidently called herself Cathleen Ni Houlihan, has been struck dumb by the shock of modernity" (1980, 1199). Combining the insights of both Steiner and Heaney, we might say that perhaps Sarah's problem suggests the "hidden Ireland" that in 1833 had begun to emerge after a century of oppression by the penal laws only to be devastated in the next decade by the famine years. Bhabha's theory would suggest yet another reading of Sarah, that like Kurtz's "the Horror, the Horror" and the Ouboum of the Marabar caves, Sarah's silence in the end constitutes that untranslatable residue between incommensurable cultures.

As we saw in chapter 2, Steiner also influenced Friel's view of history as an act of translation. Hugh's comment, "it is not the literal past, the 'facts' of history, that shape us, but images of the past embodied in language. . . . we must never cease renewing those images; because once we do, we fossilize" (*SP,* 445), reflects Friel's poststructuralist orientation toward history at the same time that it suggests one of the key effects of *Translations.* The play itself, particularly with its metaphoric stage convention of representing Irish as English, renews an image of Irish history at the point when the old Gaelic culture was being translated (as Friel translates it) into another language. Friel's evocation of the integrity of the Gaelic past in *Translations* is a typical colonial strategy. But like any other text, the past can never retain its original meaning when it is translated into the new context of the present. Like Rushdie's Koran, in its new context Friel's Gaelic past becomes something of a historical blasphemy. While this blasphemy may violate some original meaning, as a hybrid performative enunciation the selectively re-membered, refigured,

and restaged past opens up the present to what Bhabha calls "an interstitial future, that emerges *in-between* the claims of the past and the needs
of the present," a future in which the rewriting of colonial narratives and
subjectivities becomes possible (1994, 219; Bhabha's emphasis).[3]

It is no small irony that Friel synthesized his image of Irish history
in *Translations* from writings in English by Dowling, Carleton, Andrews,
O'Donovan, Colby, and others. But as Bhabha says, liberated people
"construct their culture from the national text translated into modern
Western forms of information technology, language, dress. The
changed political and historical site of enunciation transforms the
meanings of the colonial inheritance into the liberatory signs of a free
people of the future" (1994, 37).

The complexity of this form of cultural translation is suggested by
the conclusion of the play. At the end of *Translations* Hugh leaves us with
a complex and ambivalent image, although I do not think it is inconclu-
sive, as some have found it (Murray 1982, 440). He quotes a passage from
the beginning of Virgil's *Aeneid* that alludes to the goddess Juno's fears
that a race descended from Trojan blood (that is, Aeneas's race of Romans) will destroy her beloved Carthage:

> *Urbs antiqua fuit*—there was an ancient city which, 'tis said, Juno loved
> above all the lands. And it was the goddess's aim and cherished hope
> that here should be the capital of all nations—should the fates per-
> chance allow that. Yet in truth she discovered that a race was springing
> from Trojan blood to overthrow some day these Tyrian towers—a peo-
> ple *late regem belloque superbum*—kings of broad realms and proud in war
> who would come forth for Lybia's downfall—such was—such was the
> course—such was the course ordained—ordained by fate . . . (*SP*,
> 446–47)

3. Bhabha says, "The enunciation of cultural difference problematizes the binary
division of past and present, tradition and modernity, at the level of cultural representation and its authoritative address. It is the problem of how, in signifying the
present, something comes to be repeated, relocated and translated in the name of
tradition, in the guise of a pastness that is not necessarily a faithful sign of historical
memory but a strategy of representing authority in terms of the artifice of the archaic. That iteration negates our sense of the origins of the struggle. It undermines
our sense of the homogenizing effects of cultural symbols and icons, by questioning
our sense of the authority of cultural synthesis in general" (1994, 35).

In the third Punic War (149–146 B.C.) the Romans did destroy Carthage with a thoroughness rare in the history of the West. Friel clearly draws a parallel in the passage to England's erosion of the Irish language and civilization, the terrible intimation of which makes Hugh stumble over his translation of it. But the irony is that Latin, the language Hugh is quoting and translating, the language that signifies his own erudition, is the language of the conquering Romans; and Virgil wrote the *Aeneid* not to lament the destruction of Carthage but to celebrate the triumph of Roman civilization. In Hugh's quote and in *Translations* as a whole, there is a fatalistic inevitability about the domination of the conqueror's language, as fatalistic as the destiny of Aeneas to found Rome and of the Romans to destroy Carthage. Friel shares this fatalism. He has said about the Irish being educated in the English language and literature, "there is no possibility of escaping from this. We must accept this" (1980b, 60).

Within *Translations* there is a diversity of response to the cultural and linguistic conflict. Manus, who departs under a cloud at the end to eventually continue in his father's footsteps as a hedge-school master on the Aran Islands, maintains his allegiance to the old Gaelic traditions. His contrasting counterpart is Owen, who leaves his native culture behind in order to advance himself in the Anglicized world. He later realizes the enormous price he pays for his cultural conversion, but he nevertheless represents the many Irish who heeded O'Connell's advice to learn English to get ahead. Maire also desires to learn English. At one point she wishes she could communicate with her newfound love Lt. Yolland, but primarily she wants to equip herself for emigration. As Owen and Manus complement each other, so Owen also complements Yolland, who becomes a convert in the opposite direction. Upon his arrival in Ireland Yolland quickly becomes a Hibernophile and wants to learn Gaelic. Had he lived he undoubtedly would have been one those Englishmen who become "more Irish than the Irish."

The attitudes of Manus, Owen, Maire, or Yolland, however, do not correspond to Friel's. Hugh is much closer to Friel, who neither accepts a futile allegiance to the old Gaelic traditions (the position of Manus and, in Irish history, of someone like Daniel Corkery and the Irish Ireland tradition); nor does he approve of converting to the culture of the colonial power (the position of Owen and of writers like Shaw and

Wilde); nor would he choose the route of exile or emigration (the choice of Maire in the play and of Joyce and Beckett in their lives). Instead Friel would remain in Ireland and reappropriate the English language for Irish culture. Friel's Field Day Theatre Group explicitly articulates this goal in their cultural projects that are designed to appropriate English into a distinctively Irish idiom, as in their productions of world classics translated into Irish English and in their proposal for a dictionary of the Anglo-Irish language. In other words, the thematics of the play recognize and accept the cultural and linguistic consequences of Ireland's historical colonization, but without either nostalgia for the old Gaelic traditions or continued submission to British cultural imperialism.

Even though Friel himself has said, "Of course a fundamental irony of this play is that it should have been written in Irish," (1980b, 59), *Translations* itself suggests that the old Irish language and culture need not be plowed under and sterilized with salt, as the Romans did to the city of Carthage, and that Irish writers can appropriate their own past in English, as many writers of the Irish Literary Renaissance did. With its experimental representation of Irish in English, the play revives and renews the old Gaelic culture in the image of the hedge school as it translates it into another language and another time. Like Yeats and Synge, Friel translates a Gaelic past into an Anglo-Irish present. In this way *Translations* ingeniously preserves Irish history, literature, and culture through what Steiner calls the "poetic recreation or translation of a given language-world" (1975, 76). For Bhabha such an "insurgent act of cultural translation" becomes a "mode of performative agency" that liberates a subjected people into a future in which they rewrite their own subjectivities and narratives of identity (1994, 7, 219).

The Communication Cord

Not everyone agrees that what *Translations* preserves is worth preserving. While Friel and his Field Day colleagues tend to view *Translations* as a linguistic critique of traditional nationalist assumptions from within nationalism, others have seen it as simply recycling traditional nationalist perspectives. Edna Longley says the play "refurbishes an old myth," that it "does not so much examine myths of dispossession and oppression as repeat them" from a distinctly Northern nationalist perspective (1985, 28–29). Lynda Henderson, editor of *Theatre Ireland,* agrees with Longley and finds *Translations* a "dangerous" play because it oversimplifies the cultural and political oppression of an "innocent," "untroubled," "good-humoured" people by the "militarily superior, imaginatively undernourished and relatively illiterate English" (1986). Others have accused Friel of historical misrepresentation.[4] In particular, they claim that the kind of British reprisals depicted in *Translations* would be more appropriate to the age of Cromwell or to the 1790s than to the 1830s and that the uncouth Lancey is as much a distortion of historical realities as the urbane, sophisticated Hugh. They also claim that Friel does not sufficiently acknowledge forces that were eroding the Irish language and culture from within.

Typically critics who perceive *Translations* as simply pleading the Northern nationalist cause fail to recognize the concern with language that was more important to Friel than the colonial politics of the play. I do not think Friel would deny that the play is written from a Northern nationalist perspective, but he would claim that his perspective was not an uncritical nationalism that simply recycles the old myths. He says, for example, "I have no nostalgia for [Celtic Ireland]. I think one should look back on the process of history with some kind of coolness. The only merit in looking back is to understand, how you are and where you are at this moment" (1980b, 61). He has also said that he does not believe in "the wholeness, the integrity, of that Gaelic past" (Friel n.d., 58).

Seamus Heaney has said, "Friel knows that there were certain inadequacies within the original culture that unfitted it to survive the impact of the English presence and domination" (1980, 1199), and the play does bear this out. On the one hand, the characters of Hugh, Manus, and Jimmy Jack, despite their charm and learnedness, obviously represent a certain dead end of Gaelic culture; they have no prospects and no future in the world of the play. Manus's removal to the Aran Islands only postpones his obsolescence. Also the play does not simply blame the British; Owen has collaborated in the decline of his own culture and language. On the other hand, the play does not pretend that the colo-

4. J. Andrews 1983, Connolly 1987, Connolly 1993, and McAvera 1985.

nial presence and Ireland's colonial history had nothing to do with the disintegration of Gaelic culture.

Friel, in other words, exhibits more awareness than his critics of how the native past functions in a colonial and postcolonial environment. Longley and Henderson read *Translations* as a purely nationalist enunciation that is still trying to counter the old colonial narratives. In one sense it is a preliberatory narrative. Friel's characterizations of Lancey and Hugh effectively reverse the classic colonial stereotypes of the cultured English and the uncouth Irish. In another sense, however, *Translations* also is a postcolonial play, as Friel's own experience as a citizen of both Northern Ireland and the Republic of Ireland make him both a colonial and a postcolonial. The play is postcolonial in its acceptance of its hybrid Anglo-Irish heritage, in the linguistic sophistication that frames that acceptance, and in its performative role of rewriting Irish subjectivities and narratives of identity. It may be that because Friel retained certain symbols of nationalist culture, such as the hedge school, they were taken at face value and read as "more of the same," while Friel's nuances in his treatment of these symbols were lost. It is possible that for many antinationalist critics any invocation of nationalist symbols is a vice to be avoided, but many more readers than the antinationalists have responded to the colonial politics of *Translations* without recognizing how Friel's concern with language complicates any colonial thesis. Obviously the play does not always elicit the response Friel hoped for. The reason is not far to seek. *Translations* suffers from a rhetorical imbalance similar to the one that marred *The Enemy Within,* where the nationalist discourses of kinship and nostalgia for the land overwhelmed the discourse of spiritual aspiration. In *Translations* the colonial politics are presented very clearly with considerable emotional impact. The insights about language, in contrast, are much more cerebral and less obvious, often lurking in Hugh's cryptic comments.

Friel and his Field Day colleagues became very sensitive to this problem with *Translations,* and while they did not relinquish their views of the play as a critique of nationalist ideology from within, in their discussions of Friel's next play, *The Communication Cord* (1982), they at least acknowledged that *Translations* may have evoked certain "pieties" that should not remain unchallenged. Friel says that he wrote *The Communi-*

cation Cord as a farcical antidote to *Translations* because the latter "offered pieties that I didn't intend for it" and because he felt uncomfortably categorized by critics of *Translations,* as if he were being "corralled into something" he wanted to resist (1982a, 21). If *Translations* was "about how this country found a certain shape," then for Friel *The Communication Cord* is a "look at the shape this country is in now." That shape he finds somewhat absurd (1982b, 8). Also, if *Translations* suffered from having its linguistic issues obscured to some extent by its political content, Friel compensated with a vengeance in *The Communication Cord,* which he quite accurately calls "an attempt to illustrate a linguistic thesis" (1982a, 21).[5]

  The Communication Cord suggests Friel's self-reflective cautiousness about his own work in particular and about the Field Day enterprise in general. As Yeats once feared that one of his plays sent men out to die, Friel and the Field Day writers are aware of their own responsibilities in wielding language to create new myths for Ireland. Friel himself has advocated a "strong element of cynicism about the whole thing" (1982a, 23), and in a review of *Translations* Seamus Heaney says that while Friel exhibits "a constant personal urgency upon the need we have to create enabling myths of ourselves," he is also aware of "the danger we run if we too credulously trust to the sufficiency of these myths" (1980, 1199). *The Communication Cord* is Friel's skeptical counterbalance to *Translations,* and he wants the later play to be seen "in tandem" with the earlier one.

  The Communication Cord is a hilarious farce at the expense of traditional Irish nationalism. In the play Tim, a young linguist, has been persuaded by his friend Jack to "borrow" his family's restored thatched cottage in Donegal to impress Senator Donovan, the nationalist, antiquarian father of Susan, Tim's current girlfriend. Tim may only have the cottage for an hour, however, because Jack has invited his new romantic interest Evette to spend the weekend with him there. When Tim and Jack arrive at the cottage they discover that Claire, a friend of Jack's sister and a former girlfriend of both Jack and Tim, is already staying there. In one continuous sweep of action, the plot revolves around the many

---

5. The linguistic aspects of the play are discussed in chapter 2.

complications and obstacles that frustrate Tim's and Jack's scheme of deception.

The setting of *The Communication Cord* is crucial to any reading of the play. It both alludes to *Translations* and establishes a visual rhetoric quite different from the setting of the earlier play. In contrast to the attempt at authenticity with the hedge-school set in *Translations, The Communication Cord* translates the interior of a traditional thatched peasant cottage into a slightly too perfect modern reproduction. After describing the "'traditional' Irish cottage" set in extensive detail, Friel's stage directions tell us, "one quickly senses something false about the place. It is too pat, too 'authentic'" and has the distinct feel of a reproduction, "an artefact of today making obeisance to a home of yesterday" (*CC*, 11). This artefact has its psychological counterpart in the pietistic attitudes of the traditional nationalism the cottage represents. In the play these attitudes are held mainly by the older generation, represented by Jack's father, who restored the cottage, and Senator Donovan. According to the discourse of traditional nationalism, as rendered sardonically by Jack, "Everybody's grandmother was reared in a house like this . . . This is where we all come from. This is our first cathedral. This shaped all our souls. This determined our first pieties" (*CC*, 15). For Senator Donovan the cottage is "the touchstone," "the apotheosis," "the absolute verity" (*CC*, 31), "the true centre" (*CC*, 43). At one point Donovan, who was born in a thatched cottage himself, describes milking the family cow at the milking post inside the cottage as "a little scene that's somehow central to my psyche" (*CC*, 55). In the process of demonstrating how the cow was chained to the post, he chains himself literally to his memory when the rusty clasp on the chain refuses to open. Despite the broad farcical humor of the play, the implications of Senator Donovan's literal attachment to the set are clear: traditional nationalism is an anachronistic reproduction that chains the Irish unproductively to their past.

But even those who do not share the Senator's enthusiasm for his peasant past cannot escape its destructive effects in the present. Like the Yeatsian symbol that it is, the cottage itself seems to have a will and a power of its own; and, like the house set in Stewart Parker's *Pentecost* (produced by Field Day five years later) and the Marconi radio in Friel's *Dancing at Lughnasa*, it acts almost like a character in the play. With a loose-latched door and a fireplace subject to frequent blowdowns, the cottage intrudes at opportune moments to help keep the confusing farce of mistaken identities in motion. Tim feels that the cottage, whose chimney blowdowns and blown-open door repeatedly frustrate his scheme, harbors malevolent intent toward him: he says, "Did you ever have a sense that a place hates you?—that it actually feels malevolent towards you? I think this house hates me. I'm convinced that the genii of the house detest me. . . . Maybe it's because I feel no affinity at all with it and it knows that. In fact I think I hate it and all it represents . . . it's the willing, the conniving instrument of a malign presence" (*CC*, 40). The play concludes with the house, appropriately and symbolically, collapsing on Tim and the other characters of his generation. Again the suggestion is clear: both chaining oneself to the past and antipathy to that past are equally risky approaches to one's heritage.

Another anachronism in the play is the character of Nora Dan, whose name and speech suggests that she is a character out of a Synge play. She speaks in the rhythms of Synge's peasants—"He is surely. And it'll be the big wages he'll earn in a place like that"—and her speech is peppered with colloquialisms like "stirk," "gulder," "deaved," and "yous," all of which suggests that her peasant quality is as contrived as that of the cottage. The stage directions describe her as "A country woman who likes to present herself as a peasant" and Jack calls her "the quintessential noble peasant—obsessed with curiosity and greed and envy" (*CC*, 21). Like the cottage, she is too pat and false, and like the cottage she represents an ersatz, tourist-board nationalism that often passes for the real thing in Ireland. Both she and the cottage represent the Irish Ireland nostalgia that dominated nationalism from the days of the late nineteenth-century revival through the first several decades of independence.

Some critics agree that *The Communication Cord* subverts the attitudes toward history and language supported by *Translations*. They claim that by ridiculing the "metropolitan utopia of thatched-cottage-nostalgia which the production of *Translations* had seemed to excite" (Barry 1983, 118), the *Communication Cord* "undermines the pieties" and the potential sentimentality "sponsored by the earlier play" (Deane 1986b, 21). Richard Kearney argues, "If *Translations* tended to mythologize language, *The Communication Cord* demythologizes it . . . [and] de-centers all easy assumptions about the retrieval of such lost, cultural origins" (1983, 52). For Kearney *The Communication Cord* "satirizes the contemporary attitude of certain sentimental nationalists who seek to revive the old culture, which is now irretrievably lost" (1987, 511). Other critics, however, remain skeptical about Friel's skepticism. Edna Longley says *The Communication Cord* "comfortably fails in its intention to subvert the pieties of *Translations*" (1985, 29) and Brian McAvera characterizes *The Communication Cord* as "a rerun of *Translations* as farce" (1985, 20). For antinationalists like Longley and McAvera, the presentation of nationalist symbols, even for the purposes of subverting them, is not to be countenanced.

Actually *The Communication Cord* does more than provide an antidote for the pieties raised in *Translations;* it also serves to position the critical nationalism espoused by *Translations* in relation to two of its alternatives—the traditional unrenovated nationalism represented by the thatched-cottage nostalgia of Senator Donovan on one hand, and on the other hand the antipathy toward nationalism represented by Tim and Jack and their generation, an antipathy most often voiced by so-called revisionist critics like Edna Longley and Brian McAvera. From a postcolonial perspective *The Communication Cord* astutely recognizes both the artificiality of traditional nationalism's construction of the Irish past and the necessity of that construction. Taken together, *Translations* and *The Communication Cord* also recognize the postcolonial necessity for moving away from traditional nationalism toward a new sense of nation that acknowledges its *inter*national hybridity. As Bhabha says,

> the theoretical recognition of the split-space of enunciation may open the way to conceptualizing an *inter*national culture, based not on the exoticism of multiculturalism or the *diversity* of cultures, but on the inscription and articulation of culture's *hybridity*. To that end we should remember that it is the "inter" — the cutting edge of translation and negotiation, the *in-between* space — that carries the burden of the meaning of culture. It makes it possible to begin envisaging national, anti-nationalist histories of the "people." (1994, 38–39; Bhabha's emphases)

Although nationalism effectively serves the purpose of invoking the impossible purity of a precolonial culture as a means of liberating a people from colonial oppression, once that liberation is achieved, nationalism itself can become the oppressor if it does not transform itself into a responsible sense of nationhood that seeks not only equality for itself among other nations, but equality for everyone within the new nation, whether or not they conform to nationalist identity criteria. For Bhabha this is more likely to occur through a recognition of the hybridity of all cultures rather than through various attempts—such as nationalism, separatism, ethnic cleansing, and multiculturalism—to recognize or acknowledge the putative purity of individual cultures.

Field Day

The issues raised in *Translations* and *The Communication Cord* are not unique to those plays. They open up into the larger arena of Field Day and its various projects. The first of these projects was the production of *Translations,* which premiered in Derry and then toured the country, both north and south of the border. In many ways *Translations,* as a performative enunciation, was an ideal inaugural for Field Day and it remains the group's defining, foundation event. With the production of *Translations* by Field Day, Friel ceased being simply Ireland's leading dramatist and took on an institutional importance that had a substantial impact on Irish literary and political culture over the ensuing decade.

With the founding of Field Day and the production of *Translations,* it appeared as if Friel had finally achieved that goal he had articulated for himself in 1972—to fashion a reasonably consistent perspective in which his art can take root and find sustenance—what he calls, after Sean O'-Faolain, "a faith, a feeling for life, a way of seeing life which is coherent, persistent, inclusive, and forceful enough to give organic form to the totality of my work" (1972b, 19). In his later plays and through his association with Field Day, Friel found that "coherent, persistent, inclusive, and forceful" paradigm in a contemporary view of language that is characterized by a complex awareness of the relation of language to both public and private desire and of the relation of language to politics, culture, and history.

Paradoxically, in 1980 Friel was less interested in giving organic form to the totality of his work than in altering the cultural and political landscape of Ireland. By shifting his focus outward, however, from a more purely formal and literary objective to political and cultural concerns, he found a means of accomplishing the earlier literary objective of coherence at the moment his work opened up to forces that resisted reduction to a single totality. Through Field Day he opened up his own artistic enterprise to others, as increasingly his larger goals could only be achieved collaboratively with others.

Friel resigned from Field Day in 1994, but prior to his resignation the Field Day enterprise had consisted of three major areas of endeavor: an annual theatrical production, a pamphlet series, and an anthology of Irish writing from 500 A.D. to the present. For the purposes of this study, however, the most interesting of the Field Day projects is one that still exists primarily as an imaginative fiction—the compilation of a dictionary of Irish English. Field Day proposes to appropriate the English language for the Irish by identifying and promoting a distinct form of Irish English, distinct in the sense of possessing unique words, syntactical forms, idioms, and spoken rhythms that do not characterize the language in other English-speaking nations. To advance this notion of Irish English, Field Day has proposed the compilation of an Anglo-Irish dictionary.

But even as fiction, the dictionary is one of Field Day's most ambitious and politically charged linguistic projects. Friel points out that even when the British leave Ireland "the residue of their presence will still be with us. . . . and that brings us back to the question of language for this is one of the big inheritances which we have received from the British" (1980b, 60–61). Like Friel, Field Day recognizes profound relations among language, culture, history, and politics. All the Field Day writers, for example, perceive the political crisis in Northern Ireland in terms of language. Friel believes that Ireland's political problem is "going to be solved by language," not just language across the negotiating table, but also "by the recognition of what language means for us on this island" (1982a, 23).

Language has always been used as a political and social weapon. It has been used to oppress a colonized or conquered people and it has been used to police the borders of social class. In Ireland it has been used in both these ways. After the British had consolidated their colonization of Ireland, Gaelic was outlawed and its use stigmatized a class of people who were conquered, oppressed, and impoverished. Before independ-

ence in 1922 Irish-accented English, including degrees of Irish accent, established social hierarchies — the closer to British English, the higher the
class. George Steiner's observation about upper-class British accents applied with particular force in Ireland: "Upper-class English diction, with
its sharpened vowels, elisions, and modish slurs, is both a code for mutual recognition — accent is worn like a coat of arms — and an instrument of ironic exclusion" (1975, 32). Since the late nineteenth century,
however, knowledge of the old Gaelic has been turned into an offensive
political weapon and a badge of Irish nationalist affiliation; and today the
status of the Anglo-Irish language, that is, English as spoken by the Irish,
has become a major concern for Friel and Field Day.

The language problem in Ireland has been brought into focus for
many writers and critics by a passage in Joyce's *Portrait* where Stephen
Dedalus ponders the feel of English on his tongue. Stephen's misgivings
form his response to the English dean of studies, who is somewhat as-
tonished to discover that Dubliners call a funnel a tundish. The priest's
surprise offends Stephen, who thinks, " — The language in which we are
speaking is his before it is mine. How different are the words *home*,
Christ, *ale*, *master*, on his lips and on mine! I cannot speak or write these
words without unrest of spirit. His language, so familiar and so foreign,
will always be for me an acquired speech. I have not made or accepted its
words. My voice holds them at bay. My soul frets in the shadow of his
language" (1976b, 189).

Writing in *TLS* in 1972, Denis Donoghue extrapolates Stephen's un-
ease to Irish writers today: "I believe that many Irish writers who write in
English have a bad conscience in doing so, even though they have spent
their entire lives among English words. . . . In Ireland language is a political fact. Those who do not speak Irish speak English with the intonation
of guilt; they cannot be completely at ease with their acquired speech"
(1972, 291). Seamus Deane explains how this situation arose from Ireland's colonial circumstances: "We've got essentially a colonial heritage
that's had some very deep effects on the language. We write English, but
we write it haunted by the ghost of a lost language. When you write in
English or in Irish, you are, in fact, involving yourself in some kind of
political statement. The linkage between language and politics is more

incestuously close in such a situation than it is in a more settled society" (1987, 29–30).

Friel also feels as uncomfortable as Stephen Dedalus does with English. He notes that all his grandparents were native Gaelic speakers and that two of them were illiterate: "To be so close to illiteracy and to a different language is a curious experience," he says. He claims that, although the Irish "flirt with the English language," they have not comfortably assimilated it, and that "the whole issue of language" remains "very problematic" for the Irish (1982a, 21). Friel has said that the English and the Irish are two cultures "which are ostensibly speaking the same language but which in fact aren't," and that "the whole cultural burden that every word in the English language carries is slightly different to our burden" (1982a, 21, 23). Friel's solution, however, is not to return to Gaelic, but to continue with a process begun by Synge and Joyce, a process of appropriating the English language for the Irish. "We must make English identifiably our own language," he insists; English words must become "distinctive and unique to us" (1980b, 60–61). For Friel, Irish drama, except for Synge, has failed to create a form of English that feels at home on the Irish tongue (1980b, 60). Friel says,

> It's a problem dramatists here never really faced up to: the problem of writing in the language of another country. We're a very recent breed. . . . We've only existed since Synge and Yeats. There was no such thing as an indigenous Irish drama until 1904.
> Dramatists from Ireland before that always had to write for the English stage: to pitch their voice in an English way. . . . The whole Irish drama tradition from Farquaur [sic] to Behan is pitted with writers doing that. Ultimately they were maimed. (1980a)

Historically, one way colonial or postcolonial societies have asserted their national identities and cultural differences from a present or past hegemonic power has been to compile their own dictionary of the colonizer's language. Dictionaries exist, for example, for American, Australian, Canadian, Jamaican, Scottish, and South African versions of English. In the first of Field Day's pamphlet manifestos, entitled "A New Look at the Language Question," Tom Paulin explores the need for such a dictionary in Ireland. According to Paulin, the Anglo-Irish language or

Irish English exists only as a spoken language, and, with its numerous regional and local dialects, it is "in a state of near anarchy." Because there
is no dictionary of Irish English, Paulin says,

> many words are literally homeless. They live in the careless richness of
> speech, but they rarely appear in print. When they do, many readers are
> unable to understand them and have no dictionary where they can dis-
> cover their meaning. The language therefore lives freely and sponta-
> neously as speech, but it lacks any institutional existence and so is
> impoverished as a literary medium. It is a language without a lexicon, a
> language without form. Like some strange creature of the open air, it
> exists simply as *Geist* or spirit. (1986, 11)

A dictionary of Irish English, Paulin claims, would redeem many words
from the obscurity of local dialects and release them "into the shaped
flow of a new public language" (1986, 15).

Richard Wall (1977 and 1986) has demonstrated the dangers of ignoring dialectical peculiarities when reading Joyce. Wall shows how critics
have misread Joyce because they have been unaware of local meanings of
slang and normal English words, unaware of English words obsolete
outside Ireland (like *tundish*), or unaware of words derived from Gaelic
and Danish. He also uncovers misreadings, especially of passages in
Finnegans Wake, based on ignorance of pronunciation that is peculiar to
a region or derived (as in many Anglo-Irish dialects) from eighteenth-
century English.

Paulin, however, is not merely concerned with the lexical value of an
Anglo-Irish dictionary; he is also concerned with its political impact.
Paulin rejects the notion of a politically neutral language. For Paulin
"the language question is a question about nationhood and government" (1986, 7). He notes, for example, how "attempts to refine and ascertain the language almost instinctively relate it to the houses of
parliament, to those institutions where speech exercises power. In his
Dictionary of Modern English Usage H. W. Fowler frequently draws examples from parliamentary debates" (1986, 6). He says that this is why standard British English "must always be impossible for any Irish writer . . .
because the platonic standard has an actual location—it isn't simply free
and transcendental—and that location is the British House of Com-
mons" (1986, 16). Paulin might have added BBC as another abode of the
Platonic standard.

Most of Paulin's essay is devoted to examining the political baggage of several famous dictionary projects—Samuel Johnson's, Noah Webster's, and the *O.E.D.* He argues that Johnson's principles were governed by his own "English patriotism" and "anarchistic conservatism" (1986, 5), whereas Webster's dictionary project was motivated by a desire to throw off British "imperial hegemony." Paulin says, "Webster had to challenge the dominating force of Johnson's dictionary and personality" by creating a uniform American language that would achieve "linguistic and cultural independence" for America. "Webster argues for linguistic self-respect, but he does so as a separatist, not an integrationist," says Paulin (1986, 8–9).

As Webster had to overcome Johnson, so the compilers of the *New English Dictionary* (later the *O.E.D.*) "worked in the shadow" of Noah Webster (1986, 8). But unlike Webster's impulse to overthrow an imperial hegemony, their goal was to consolidate one. According to Paulin, James Murray, editor in chief of the *New English Dictionary,* was motivated by his "identification with Victorian Britain and his sense of the importance of the Scottish scholarly tradition to that cultural hegemony" (1986, 8). As "the chief lexicon" of British English, Paulin says that the *O.E.D.* became "both book and sacred natural object, one of the guardians of the nation's soul . . . one of the cornerstones of the culture which created it." Consequently it "possesses a quasi-divine authority" (1986, 7–8).

Paulin advocates a dictionary for Ireland that would become the repository of its linguistic soul. This dictionary would be based on "a concept of Irish English" governed by an "all-Ireland context." In other words, it would be a form of modern English that draws from Irish, Ulster Scots, Elizabethan English, Hiberno-English, British English, and American English. So conceived, Irish English would become, in Paulin's words, "the flexible written instrument of a complete cultural idea" (1986, 15). The complete cultural idea, of course, is the politically loaded ideal of a united Ireland.

Paulin, however, is not naïvely optimistic about the possibility of achieving such an ideal in what he calls "the present climate of confused opinions and violent politics" (1986, 17). For him neither the North nor the Republic presently fosters an ecumenical view of the Anglo-Irish language: "state education in Northern Ireland is based upon a pragmatic view of the English language and a short-sighted assumption of colonial status, while education in the Irish Republic is based on an idealistic view of Irish which aims to conserve the language and assert the cultural difference of the country" (1986, 11).

Unfortunately this dictionary project is beyond the scope of Field Day's resources and remains an idea only; but as a defining idea it has exerted its force on Field Day's other projects. Obviously related to the dictionary project proposed in Paulin's essay are the Field Day productions of classic plays in Irish idiom, such as Friel's translation of Chekhov's *Three Sisters*, which became Field Day's second annual production in 1981. Friel, who considers translations into a neutral language to be "neutered translation" (1991, 56), says he made the translation because he felt that "the translations which we have received and inherited in some way have not much to do with the language which we speak in Ireland": "I think that the versions of *Three Sisters* which we see and read in this country always seem to be redolent of either Edwardian England or the Bloomsbury set. Somehow the rhythms of these versions do not match with the rhythms of our own speech patterns, and I think that they ought to, in some way. Even the most recent English translation again carries, of necessity, very strong English cadences and rhythms" (1980b, 59).

Although Friel wrote his version of *Three Sisters* as an "act of love" well before the founding of Field Day (Riddel 1981), its production became one of the group's first efforts to identify and promote a uniquely Irish brand of English. In his version Friel replaced restrained British phrasing such as, "They've gone in to lunch already. . . . I'm late. . . . You've got such a lot of visitors. . . . I feel quite shy. . . . How do you do, Baron?" (quoted in Dantanus 1988, 185), with characteristically more animated Irish rhythm and phrasing such as, "Sweet mother of God, I'm late—they're at the dinner already! . . . And look at the crowd of guests! Goodness gracious I could never face in there! Baron, how d'you do" (Friel 1981a, 33). Friel also had Irish actors in mind, who must perform most translated classics in American or British English. "What has always happened up to this," he says, "is that Irish actors have to assume English accents so you end up with being an Irishman pretending you're an Englishman, pretending you're a Russian!" (O'Donnell 1981). Friel wanted a translation of *Three Sisters* that would flow easily over the tongues of Irish actors. "It's all a question of music," he says; "the audience will hear a different music to anything they've heard in Chekhov before" (1981b, 6).

Like Yeats and the earlier Irish revival, Field Day's emphasis on the Anglo-Irish language promotes Irish writing for Irish audiences. Plays are not written for "Broadway or the West End" (Friel 1980a) but to tour Ireland north and south. Moreover, as with Yeats and his movement, the result has been far from parochial; the voices of Irish writers writing for Irish audiences are being heard all over the English-speaking world and in parts of the non-English-speaking world. The Irish may be writing for themselves now, but as Friel points out, not "in any insular or parochial sense" (1980a). In saying this Friel is not necessarily claiming some kind of universality for Irish writing today. It may be that the struggle for identity through language is crucial at this point in history, not only for colonial and postcolonial people but for anyone's sense of orientation and positioning in a radically decentered and pluralistic global environment.

Field Day's conception of an Anglo-Irish language, which informs its proposal for an Anglo-Irish dictionary, its translations of classic texts, and its productions of original texts like *Translations,* constitutes nothing less than an aggressive attempt to appropriate a tongue that was originally forced upon the Irish. As Seamus Deane has said, "The recovery from the lost Irish language has taken the form of an almost vengeful virtuosity in the English language, an attempt to make Irish English a language in its own right rather than an adjunct to English itself" (1990, 10). This appropriation will help remove the discomfort in speaking English that Stephen Dedalus articulates for Irish writers. In this effort Friel and Field Day are calling for a culture and a language in which the Irish, after centuries of billeting an alien other, feel at home with themselves.

9

Making History

U P TO THIS POINT IN HIS CAREER Friel's views on the relations between language and illusion evolved from his early stories and
plays, where it was applied primarily to individual memory and experience (as illustrated, for example, by his memory about his childhood
fishing trip with his father) through the mature plays, such as *The Freedom of the City, Aristocrats, Faith Healer* and *Translations,* which focused
more on the social functions of our linguistic fictions. In his next play,
Making History, Friel extends his Heideggerian views more comprehensively than in earlier plays to his attitudes toward history. *Making History*
premiered in Derry in 1988. It was Friel's fourth Field Day production
and his first new play since *The Communication Cord.* The play focuses on
Hugh O'Neill, the last of the great Gaelic chieftains, who fled to the
continent in 1607. O'Neill's flight, along with Rory O'Donnell and others, known as "the flight of the earls," has come to represent the end of
the old Gaelic order in Ireland. After O'Neill's defeat at Kinsale in 1601,
the English, for the first time since they arrived in Ireland in the twelfth
century, effectively controlled the entire country. O'Neill's defeat at Kinsale marked the end of significant Irish resistance to English rule until
the United Irishmen Uprising of 1798. In his biography of O'Neill Sean
O'Faolain calls Kinsale "one of the decisive moments in the history of
Ireland, incomparably more important than the Battle of the Boyne, or
any other battle in the whole course of her history. . . . Kinsale was to
mean to Ireland, for ever, a parting of the ways, a scission with everything that had gone before, an ending as absolute as death" (1970, 260).

What fascinates Friel about The Great O'Neill, however, is not his
mythic role as Gaelic hero, but his profound ambivalence toward his na-

tive culture in relation to English culture. Although Hugh O'Neill was born into Gaelic culture and, as the O'Neill, became one of Ulster's most powerful leaders, between the ages of nine and seventeen he was educated in England at the houses of some of the most prominent men of Queen Elizabeth's court, including Sidney and Leicester. At Penshurst, country seat of the Sidneys eulogized in Ben Jonson's poem as representing the quintessence of genteel Elizabethan cultivation, he was the playmate of young Philip Sidney, four years his junior. Upon his return to Ireland in 1567 Hugh served his queen loyally for fifteen years, even helping the queen's troops to put down the Desmond rebellion in Munster. He was duly rewarded in 1585 by being made the second Earl of Tyrone at age thirty-five. In 1591 he married Mabel Bagenal, the sister of the queen's marshall, Sir Henry Bagenal. It was not until 1595 with his attack on the fort at Blackwater that O'Neill broke irrevocably with his English patrons. Later that same year he was declared the O'Neill in the traditional Gaelic ceremony at the Tullyhogue crowning-stone. In 1598 O'Neill defeated Sir Henry Bagenal in the Battle of the Yellow Ford, a victory that galvanized Irish resistance to England throughout the country (O'Faolain 1970, 203). Bagenal himself died in the battle. By 1600, according to O'Faolain, "There was no lord in England or on the Continent as powerful" as O'Neill (1970, 223). At that time the colonial government in Ireland controlled only "a tiny tract twenty miles by eight miles between Dublin and Drogheda" (1970, 224). Throughout his career, however, even in the years leading up to Kinsale, O'Neill made periodic submissions and protestations of loyalty to the queen.

This ambivalent O'Neill vacillating between English and Irish culture departs from the traditional nationalist portrait of him as the last of the Gaelic heroes, a tradition begun before his death by Archbishop Peter Lombard's hagiography of the Ulster chieftain. Friel's portrait of O'Neill follows Sean O'Faolain's revisionist biography *The Great O'Neill*, first published in 1942. O'Faolain's biography had a function similar to the goals of Friel and Field Day—to counter the parochial nationalism of the time. Ireland in the first decades after the formation of the Free State in 1922 was dominated by a narrow Gaelic, Catholic, conservative, isolationist nationalism that O'Faolain vehemently opposed. His O'Neill is great, not because he was the last of the Gaelic heroes, but because he was a great Renaissance intellect, the first modern European intellect Ireland had produced, thanks largely to his exposure to English culture and society. O'Faolain, in fact, despite the title of his biography, refers to O'Neill throughout as Tyrone, that is, by his English title rather than by his Irish name and title. In postcolonial terms, O'Faolain recognized the profound hybridity of O'Neill and consequently dates the hybrid nature of Irish culture much earlier than many nationalists would prefer. Traditional Irish nationalists would prefer to imagine Gaelic culture surviving intact throughout the colonial occupation, whereas native cultures begin the hybridization process with the first arrival of colonial forces. The Statutes of Kilkenny, passed in 1366 and designed to halt the integration of the colonial Normans with the Irish, effectively acknowledge the hybrid nature of Irish culture and society since early Norman times.

With its revisionist view of O'Neill, *Making History* continues preoccupations of Friel and Field Day that had begun with *Translations*. Both plays mark key transitions in Irish history and culture. *Making History* marks the transition from Gaelic political, legal, and social structures to English structures as *Translations*, set more than two centuries later, marks the transition from Gaelic to the English language. Moreover, O'Neill's ambivalence echoes the ambivalence in *Translations* of Hugh O'Donnell toward the supplanting of Gaelic by the English language. Both plays also try to represent the ill-fated marriage of two cultures with a love relationship.

Perhaps the most important parallel between *Making History* and *Translations* is that both plays accept the inevitability of a hybrid Anglicized Ireland. Throughout *Making History* we are constantly reminded that O'Neill lives in two worlds, one Gaelic and the other English. At the opening of the play O'Neill is being encouraged by English authorities to send his son to the newly established Trinity College at the same time he is requested to preside over an Irish harper's festival (*MH*, 2). His speech also speaks his hybridity and his ambivalence. Throughout the play he speaks an "upper-class English accent" (*MH*, 1) except when he becomes emotionally distraught; then he speaks in a distinctly Tyrone accent. His English speech also contrasts sharply with the very Irish idiom of Red Hugh O'Donnell, who is his friend and comrade in arms throughout the play. His marriage to Mabel Bagenal, of course, is the primary expression of his attraction to English culture, as is his concern for her place in Lombard's narrative. According to O'Faolain, O'Neill, left to his own devices, "would have balanced native tradition against the New System" (1970, 238). The same is true of Friel's O'Neill. At one point in the play Friel has O'Neill eloquently articulate the difficulties and contradictions of hybridity in terms of his own dual function in Irish history: he says,

> I have spent my life attempting to do two things. I have attempted to hold together a harassed and a confused people by trying to keep them in touch with the life they knew before they were overrun. It wasn't a life of material ease but it had its assurances and it had its dignity. And I have done that by acknowledging and indeed honouring the rituals and ceremonies and beliefs these people have practised since before history, long before the God of Christianity was ever heard of. And at the same time I have tried to open these people to the strange new ways of Europe, to ease them into the new assessment of things, to nudge them towards changing evaluations and beliefs. Two pursuits that can scarcely be followed simultaneously. Two tasks that are almost self-cancelling. (*MH*, 40)

There are also other reminders of O'Neill straddling two cultures. At one point in the play, as his associates enthusiastically discuss the impending landing of the Spanish at Kinsale, the character of O'Neill, very improbably in these circumstances, waxes nostalgic about English culture as he experienced it at Penshurst. The play ends with alternating snatches from two narratives—the beginning of Lombard's hagiography of O'Neill the Gaelic hero and O'Neill's own recitation of his final submission to Queen Elizabeth. As one reviewer put it, "In the *odi et amo* of Hugh O'Neill we seem to be witnessing the moment when the English became integral to any Irish attempt at self-definition" (Edwards 1988, 43).

Friel's choice of O'Faolain's O'Neill, or perhaps we should say his choice of O'Faolain's Tyrone, as the model for his play situates the politics of Friel and Field Day in relation to the position O'Faolain took at an earlier period of postindependence Ireland. The dominant myth of O'Neill in the 1930s was the Gaelic O'Neill, the warrior hero who united the country and nearly overthrew English rule. Unfortunately his failure merely added him to the long list of Irish martyr-heroes who sacrificed themselves in the cause of Cathleen ni Houlihan. This version of O'Neill aptly suited the isolationist economic policies of the new Free State that tried to promote home industries, particularly the Irish farmer, and the conservative, rural, Catholic, family values that would be needed to endure the economic hardships the isolationist policies would entail. Identifying themselves as Gaelic, Catholic, and agrarian marked the Irish as distinctly different culturally and socially from their former colonial masters, and myths, such as the Gaelic O'Neill, contributed to that identity and to the continuing antagonism of that identity, given the unresolved issue of Northern Ireland, toward England.

O'Faolain saw the dangers and limitations of the ethos of the new Free State and set about to recast the image of O'Neill as Tyrone, a modern Renaissance man with an expansive European outlook that contrasted sharply with the myopic tribalism of his fellow Gaelic chieftains. In his preface to *The Great O'Neill* O'Faolain says, in a comment cited in Field Day's program notes to *Making History*, "The traditional picture of the patriot O'Neill, locked into the Gaelic world, eager to assault England, is not supported by the facts and must be acknowledged a complete fantasy. He was by no means representative of the old Gaelic world and had, at most, only an ambiguous sympathy with what he found himself so ironically obliged to defend with obstinacy" (1970, vi). O'Faolain perceived that old Gaelic world as somewhat analogous to the new Gaelic world the Irish Free State attempted to construct during the first several decades of its existence, that is, as a backward society on the brink of extinction and desperately in need of renovation. A tribal society that pillaged and murdered each other, the Elizabethan Gaels were a people but not a nation. In contrast to their typical leaders—comparatively simple men with "tons of courage and hardly an ounce of brains" (1970, 171, 260)—Tyrone introduced intelligence into the Gaelic world. He "was the first modern man who gave that people a form, by giving it a speech that it could understand and which made it realize itself intelligently" (1970, 15). "An able politician and an able general" (1970, 171), he recognized the necessity to throw over tribalism in favor of confederation (1970, 87); he understood "that he and they were not merely local pashas fighting for local power but part of a world conflict" (1970, 278). Consequently, and here again the Field Day program for *Making History* quotes

O'Faolain, "he was the first step that his people made towards some sort of intellectual self-criticism as to their place and their responsibilities in the European system" (1970, 278). For O'Faolain Tyrone was a cosmopolitan hybrid who "came nearer than almost any other Irishman in history to the cold pragmatism of the Renaissance mind" (1970, 129) and he was "perhaps the first modern Irishman" to experience divided loyalties as a result of "the impact of a complex and sophisticated civilization on the quiet certainties of a simpler way of life" (1970, 43). After O'Neill, it was not until the United Irishmen of the 1790s that anything else "but geography and conquest" linked the Irish with the larger currents of "world-thought" (1970, 278).

In O'Faolain's narrative "Tyrone was broken not by England but by Ireland" (1970, 279). The Irish, to their own detriment, did not recognize "the fructifying worth of the man's intelligence" (1970, 278). Like other Irish heroes, he was destroyed by a narrow nationalism that refused to recognize the necessary hybridity of progress and modernization; he was brought down by Gaeldom's "deep atavism and inbreeding, so characteristic of abortive and arrested cultures in all ages of the world's history" (1970, 279).

One of the more interesting psychological insights offered by O'Faolain's compelling portrait is its analysis of O'Neill's motives as a response to the inevitable tensions of his hybrid identity. According to O'Faolain, O'Neill was motivated less by a Gaelic sense of a manifest destiny than by the typical resentment experienced by the colonized that he could never be accepted on equal terms by a society and a culture that had reared him and allowed him to taste the most refined of its fruits.[1] In this sense, O'Faolain's O'Neill represents a detailed psychological portrait of the process theorized by Benedict Anderson (1991) whereby the colonized who are educated and trained in the colonial metropole return to the colony to lead the rebellion against the power that created clones of themselves that it would not acknowledge as one of themselves, a hybrid clone that Bhabha calls "less than one and doubled." O'Faolain portrays O'Neill as gradually alienated by the English slights and distrust rather

---

1. Memmi 1991 gives an excellent account of this typical psychology of the colonized.

than moved by any burning patriotism for the Gaelic ways (1970, 194). O'Neill eventually came to understand that he "could never be a true earl" (1970, 128) and that at best he could assume "the role of a deputy of a deputy of a deputy, always suspect, always in danger, always on sufferance, trusted only when he brought in heads in sacks" (1970, 88). At one point he complained to the colonial authorities that although he had served the queen loyally for sixteen years, "his reward had been suspicion, humiliation, interference, distrust, 'false accusations and corrupt practice'" (1970, 148). According to O'Faolain, once O'Neill had committed himself to rebellion, one of his chief aims was "to make Elizabeth and her counselors, both in London and Dublin, live to regret the day they drove him beside himself" (1970, 152). Moreover, because of his ties with the English his relations with his own people were also characterized by suspicion and mistrust (1970, 129). At the prospect of a war with England, O'Faolain's Tyrone was furious with everyone — with the English colonists, "with the Queen and her counselors whose stupidity drove him mad with wounded pride and outraged common sense, and above all . . . with his own people who, he well knew, were unfitted for war" (1970, 153). Tyrone trusted his own people so little "that he surrounded himself with Scotch bodyguards and English secretaries" (1970, 153).

O'Faolain's project was to puncture the overinflated myth of an Irish Ireland that was being deployed to shore up the policies of the new Free State. Thus he played down O'Neill's patriotism and the unity of the Irish people. In place of Irish Ireland O'Faolain wanted a hybridized European Ireland. Although O'Faolain had no fondness for the English, he recognized that "most modern European customs and ideas were passed on to [Ireland] by Britain" (1991, 102). In *The Great O'Neill* the European ideas O'Neill brought to his Irish cause derived from the Counter Reformation. In O'Faolain's analysis Elizabethan Ireland was the first time in Irish history that nationalism became linked with religion. Once that link was established, O'Neill exploited it, but eventually it took "possession of him" and it has persisted "down the centuries" (1970, 153, 175–76).

In general, O'Faolain's portrait of O'Neill successfully critiques the ideology of Irish Ireland. O'Faolain's own ideology in *The Great O'Neill*, however, is flimsy and vague. From his editorship of *The Bell* O'Faolain had repeatedly argued for progressive ideas, for the modernization and

Europeanization of Ireland, and against the fantasies of what he called "Celtophilism." He also objected to the bourgeois hijacking of the Irish revolution between 1916 and 1922. He says, "It was not a society that came out of the maelstrom. It was a class," a "middle-class *putsch*" (1991, 105). Ever excoriating the narrow, bourgeois, Catholic conservatism that emerged after 1922 under the guise of a restoration of Gaelic Ireland, O'Faolain laments, "We had looked forward to seeing all classes united, all religions equal, all races welded, all ideas welcome " (1991, 106). Nevertheless, in *The Great O'Neill* O'Faolain's ideological ground is nothing more than a vague notion of development derived from nineteenth-century liberalism, also a middle-class ideology. Lacking any substantial critique of the liberal value of progress, he says rather vaguely, "the dominating, germinating, fecundate and even preserving factor is Development. It was self-evident to O'Neill in his own place, in his own problems, in the affairs of his country" (1970, 278).

O'Faolain's O'Neill suited the purposes of Friel and Field Day very well. Field Day critiques contemporary nationalism as O'Faolain critiqued the nationalism of his day. Also Field Day's critique is informed theoretically by ideas imported from abroad, particularly Europe and the United States. The desire to Europeanize Irish culture is evident in the openness of Field Day writers such as Seamus Deane, Tom Paulin, and Declan Kiberd to intellectual influences like Foucault, Marxism, and postcolonial theory. Friel has been deeply absorbed in Russian writers and Heaney in eastern European writers. The European dimension also shows up in the preference of most of the Field Day writers for Joyce over Yeats (Heaney is the major exception here). They perceive Joyce as an Irishman who, like O'Faolain's O'Neill, Europeanized Irish culture and who Hibernicized international modernist literature. Like O'Faolain, Field Day also has disapproved of the direction the Republic of Ireland has taken since 1922, including its early nationalism and, more recently, its modernization in the direction of consumer capitalism. Field Day even falls into the same contradiction as O'Faolain by critiquing the bourgeois values of the Irish Republic at the same time that its own institutional formation has significant links to a distinctly bourgeois ideology commonly known as new nationalism and represented politically by the constitutional nationalism of John Hume and the SDLP. The chief difference between O'Faolain and the Field Day writers lay in their relation to nationalism. O'Faolain, like many revisionists today, is antinationalist, while Field Day's critique operates from within the Irish nationalist tradition in an effort to modernize it.

O'Faolain's calculating, intellectualized O'Neill first emerges in *Making History* in the second scene as he very clearheadedly articulates his dilemma of divided loyalties in an encounter with Mary Bagenal, his wife's sister. Although the probability of O'Neill discussing such matters with the loyal sister of his colonial antagonist strains credulity and is poorly motivated in the play (O'Neill says that he intends that she will report the conversation to her brother [*MH*, 29]), O'Neill nevertheless wrestles with his dilemma out loud for Mary's benefit. Here O'Neill wonders whether he should fight for his fellow chieftain Maguire of Fermanagh, who refuses to render his submission to the colonial authorities. He says, partly in language right out of O'Faolain's *The Great O'Neill* (1970, 129),

> I try to live at peace with my fellow chieftains, with your people [i.e., the English colonists], with the Old English, with Dublin, with London, because I believe—I know—that the slow, sure tide of history is with me, Mary. All I have to do is . . . just sit—and—wait. And then a situation like this arises and how am I to conduct myself. . . . Do I keep faith with my oldest ally, Maguire, and indeed with the Gaelic civilization that he personifies? Or do I march alongside the forces of Her Majesty? . . . It really is a nicely balanced equation. The old dispensation—the new dispensation. My reckless, charming, laughing friend Maguire—or Our Henry [Bagenal]. Impulse, instinct, capricious genius, brilliant improvisation—or calculation, good order, common sense, the cold pragmatism of the Renaissance mind. Or to use a homely image that might engage you: pasture—husbandry. (*MH*, 27–28)

Although O'Neill's "aristocratic instinct" disdains the new order of colonial "Upstarts" represented by Henry Bagenal, his "intelligence comprehends and indeed grudgingly respects" it (*MH*, 28). And even though he is inclined to think the impetuous Maguire is a fool, his more contemplative self realizes, anticipating his own eventual fate, "Maguire has no choice. Maguire has to rise. History, instinct, his decent passion, the composition of his blood—he has no alternative. So he will fulfil his fate" (*MH*, 30).

O'Faolain's O'Neill also appears in a speech of Mabel's as she, very improbably, discusses political strategy with her husband. She says that risking everything on the Spanish invasion is not Hugh's way:

> Calculation—deliberation—caution. You inch forward—you withdraw. You challenge—you retreat. You defy—you submit. Every important move you have ever made has been pondered for months. . . . That's why you're the most powerful man in Ireland: you're the only Irish chieftain who understands the political method. . . . That's why the Queen is never *quite* sure how to deal with you—you're the antithesis of what she expects a Gaelic chieftain to be. That's your strength. And that's why your instinct now is not to gamble everything on one big throw that is more than risky. (*MH*, 37–38; Friel's emphasis)

Despite Friel's modeling on O'Faolain, his own O'Neill is more two dimensional. In general O'Faolain's *The Great O'Neill* portrays a much more complex, less sentimentalized O'Neill than Friel's *Making History*. O'Faolain's Tyrone is a complex psychological study whose lust for power and wealth is as central to his character as his reluctant defense of Gaelic civilization. Friel's sentimentalized O'Neill pales beside O'Faolain's worldly-wise Tyrone who knew that submissions to the queen and protestations of loyalty were part of a political game: O'Faolain says, "All Tyrone's protestations, therefore, about his dear wish to 'obtain Her Majesty's gracious favour' no more deceived the enemy than their pretended trust deceived him" (1970, 177). Friel's O'Neill is politically capable, but he is also nostalgic, romantic, and takes himself far too seriously. His distance is not the distance of the cold, ironic, Renaissance intellect suggested by O'Faolain, but rather the distance of romantic distraction. Also, the character of Harry Hoveden notwithstanding, Friel's O'Neill is not the Tyrone who distrusted even his own people to the point of surrounding himself with foreigners. In Friel's play Hoveden's role as O'Neill's personal secretary is left unexplained and O'Neill's resentment at the repeated unwillingness of the English to accept him as a peer is reduced to a single remembrance of some anti-Irish prejudice he once experienced as a young man at a Penshurst dinner party with the Sidneys (*MH*, 35). What Friel needed was a more ironically aware O'Neill, not the melodramatic character of *Making History*. Friel is quite capable of staging a theatrical tour de force, such as one of O'Neill's calculating submissions to the queen, rather than simply depicting, as he does in the play, O'Neill composing one of his submissions in an agony of melodramatic divided loyalties. I doubt the historical O'Neill took his submissions as seriously as Friel's O'Neill.

Making History has many more problems than its portrait of O'Neill. As a dramatic performance the play fails. As one reviewer put it, Making History "is a wordy, declamatory play, closer to The Enemy Within of the early 'Sixties than to the flexible, subtle Translations of the 'Eighties" (Brennan 1988, 15). There is very little dramatic tension in the play and there are too many improbabilities for an audience to swallow. The reasons for these shortcomings are not hard to find: the central love story is ineffective, characterization in general is problematic and confusing, and Friel failed to develop adequate dramatic devices and metaphors for the material of the play.

While Friel tries to model O'Neill on O'Faolain's portrait of him as the intelligence of Elizabethan Gaeldom, in Making History Friel's love story overshadows O'Faolain's intellectual Renaissance man. Friel even has Lombard anticipate his dramatized love story. Toward the end of the play, as Lombard resists O'Neill's attempts to promote the importance of his English wife in his biography, Lombard says, "she had her own value, her own importance. And at some future time and in a mode we can't imagine now I have no doubt that story will be told fully and sympathetically. It will be a domestic story, Hugh; a love story; and a very beautiful love story it will be" (MH, 69). Declan Kiberd points out in the Field Day program notes that the love story in Making History, like the love scene in Translations between the Irish peasant girl and the British soldier, is supposed to represent the "impossible but desirable fusion of Gaelic and English tradition." Unlike the love scene in Translations, however, the love story in Making History does not make us feel or understand much and it introduces a number of improbabilities into the narrative. It "tells" us that O'Neill is drawn to English culture, but it does not exhibit the power of that attraction or give us much insight into it. Moreover, O'Neill's marriage to Mabel Bagenal is not the primary vehicle of his divided loyalties in the play. The two horns of O'Neill's dilemma are much more ably represented by Hugh O'Donnell and Mabel's sister Mary. Whereas O'Donnell is the major voice imploring O'Neill to rise up against the colonial authorities, Mary Bagenal is the major defender of English culture who urges him to honor his duty to the queen. Mary, however, appears only once and O'Neill's encounter with her has the tone of an exposition rather than of a highly charged confrontation of divided loyalties. For effective drama Mabel should have assumed the role of defending her own culture against the strangeness of the Gaelic ways, as she did in O'Faolain's version.

Rather than representing the charm and sophistication of English culture, Friel's Mabel becomes the defender of the Gaelic ways of her husband against her sister Mary. She also becomes, very improbably, her husband's political confidante and co-strategist. After the defeat at Kinsale, for example, she urges O'Neill to stay on and pick up the pieces. She advises him to offer his submission to the colonial authorities in order to be restored to his land and people. She says the queen will find him useful in governing the Irish. Friel's Mabel, improbably again, is more of a political tactician than her husband (*MH*, 48, 50).

O'Faolain's Mabel, in contrast, found the Gaelic lifestyle so distasteful that she left O'Neill at one point to return to her brother. O'Faolain's imagined scenario about the mutual disillusionment of O'Neill and his English bride is much more probable, compelling, and convincing than Friel's:

> this inexperienced English girl may finally have seemed to his humiliated eyes nothing but a silly little weakling when he realized that his passion had betrayed his pride into a mesalliance, and he saw the contemptuous looks of his own full-blooded women and heard the sniffs of neighbouring amazons like O'Donnell's Ineen Duv . . . On her side his wife must have been utterly broken when she saw at last, quite clearly, to what a rude life she had surrendered herself, with its lapses into cloaked assassination and plain murder; so that when she refused to countenance his mistresses any longer, acknowledged to herself that she hated him, fled from him to her brother and laid public complaint against him before the Council, the humiliation was bitter and mutual. (1970, 121)

In the one eyewitness account reported by O'Faolain, we see a very different relationship between O'Neill and Mabel than the one Friel constructs. One time when O'Neill's role in the assassination of a troublesome kinsman upset her, O'Neill "silenced her hysteria with some vehement speech" (1970, 121–22). This is not Friel's uxorious O'Neill.

My argument here is not that Friel should necessarily be bound to any received historical tradition in constructing his characters. Little enough is known about the marriage of Mabel and O'Neill to give him a very free hand on that account anyway. Rather the problem is that Friel's Mabel is not convincing. She does not adequately represent the allure of English culture for O'Neill nor does she play a role that seems appropriate for a Renaissance lady or appropriate for this play. In short, the love story in this play simply does not work.

Because the love story fails to represent adequately O'Neill's complex divided loyalties, Friel had to rely on two devices he invented for the play to convey O'Neill's dilemma. Neither device is anywhere near as successful as devices he invented for many of his other plays. One way Friel tries to capture O'Neill's historical vacillation between rebellion and submission to the queen is through several slurs he makes in Mabel's presence against the English which he immediately retracts. At one point, for example, he refers to her as an Upstart, a derogatory term the Irish used for the English colonists, but then he immediately apologizes (*MH*, 39). This device expresses in turn his instinctive disdain and his intellectual respect for the invading colonists, but it has little dramatic or emotional power.

Another device Friel uses to suggest O'Neill's torn sympathies is the technique of parallel conversations in which O'Neill is distracted and self-absorbed in a virtual monologue. This technique works reasonably well at the closing of the play with Lombard's patriotic narrative of O'Neill alternating with O'Neill's recitation of his final submission to Queen Elizabeth. This alternation is moving and captures the central thematic conflict in the play. Other instances of the technique are not effective, however. At the opening of the play, for example, O'Neill is preoccupied with flowers arranged for his new bride and cannot focus on the business at hand his personal secretary Harry Hoveden tries to urge upon him. There are other times when he cannot focus on business brought to him by Harry, O'Donnell, or Lombard because he is distracted by his romantic interests. Then when they bring the news of the Spanish landing at Kinsale to him, he very improbably retreats into a nostalgic revery over his days in England as a boy.

Another problem of characterization is the portrait of Hugh O'Donnell. Friel's Red Hugh is a one-dimensional buffoon, a stage Irishman. He
is obviously intended to represent, in contrast to O'Neill, the relatively
more simple-minded chieftains whose instincts and parochial perspectives impelled them to resist the English at any cost, a parallel to traditional nationalism. But Friel draws him too broadly. In *The Great O'Neill*
O'Donnell is one of those impetuous, capricious, improvisational Irish
geniuses, but he also has some substance to him. While "intellectually
and politically Red Hugh was a babe in arms" beside O'Faolain's Tyrone,
he also "represented Gaelic resistance at its most obstinate and inspiring,
fired the imagination of the clansmen as a soldier, and gave the people
what the more cold and aloof Tyrone could never give them—the image
of a popular hero as rooted in their own traditional life as some flashing
figure out of the sagas" (1970, 124). O'Faolain's O'Donnell was "resolute
and haughty" in comparison to the "courteous and diplomatic" Tyrone
(1970, 179), but Friel's O'Donnell is a fatuous, impetuous youth, who at
the prospect of the Spanish landing at Kinsale exudes inappropriate adolescent enthusiasm: "Wherever Kinsale is. This is it, Mabel darling! This
is it! Yipeeeeee!" (*MH*, 42). He reminds one more of a slightly more
highly charged version of his namesake Gar O'Donnell from *Philadelphia, Here I Come!* than of O'Faolain's "resolute and haughty" Irish chieftain. As a chieftain, second only to O'Neill in his time, he is not
believable.

Friel may have taken his cue for depicting O'Donnell from one passage in *The Great O'Neill* where O'Faolain describes Red Hugh and the
other chieftains as "blithe in their irresponsibility" in comparison to
O'Neill's "tragic sense of the drama forced upon him." O'Faolain says
that this distinction was particularly evident in the 1592 ceremony of submission at Dundalk, where O'Donnell, "with his loyalty on his sleeve,
was patently buffooning; only by buffooning could so young and inexpe-
rienced a man have gone through an otherwise profoundly humiliating
performance. For Tyrone the thing was a matter of life and death" (1970,
129). Nevertheless, aside from this particular instance of buffooning, O'-
Faolain gives us a credible O'Donnell whereas Friel does not.

In addition to providing Friel with an Anglicized O'Neill, O'Faolain's
The Great O'Neill probably provided the initial inspiration for *Making His-*

tory and its overriding historiographic theme. In his preface to *The Great O'Neill* O'Faolain issues a challenge to some future Irish playwright: "Indeed, in those last years in Rome the myth was already beginning to emerge, and a talented dramatist might write an informative, entertaining, ironical play on the theme of the living man helplessly watching his translation into a star in the face of all the facts that had reduced him to poverty, exile, and defeat" (1970, vi). What tension there is in *Making History* exists between O'Neill and Lombard over how O'Neill is going to be remembered in Lombard's biography of him. O'Neill, who suspects that Lombard's biography of him will be more of a hagiography and "embalm" him "in a florid lie," urges him to tell the truth, to tell the "whole" story about himself—to include "the schemer, the leader, the liar, the statesman, the lecher, the patriot, the drunk, the soured, bitter émigré — put it *all* in," O'Neill insists, "Record the *whole* life" (*MH*, 63; Friel's emphases). He also is concerned that the centrality of Mabel's role in his life be properly acknowledged in Lombard's narrative. O'Neill says that he is going to make this struggle with Lombard over his biography his "last battle" (*MH*, 62). We know from history, of course, that O'Neill lost this battle, at least until O'Faolain's biography attempted to tell the "whole" story. But even O'Faolain did not give Mabel a central role in his narrative. That remained for Friel to accomplish in *Making History*.

This conflict between O'Neill and Lombard becomes the vehicle for the historiographic concerns of the play, concerns that are important to understanding Friel's career and to understanding the whole Field Day enterprise. Although Hayden White and Foucault's sociopolitical histories provide useful reference points for Friel's historiographic consciousness in *Making History*, George Steiner and Kevin Barry bring that historiography closer to Friel for us. As we saw in chapter 2 Steiner's Heideggerian linguistic theories see history both as an act of translation and, more pertinently for *Making History*, as an act of creative lying. Friel probably took his title for the play from Steiner, who makes the observation that historians *make* history rather than simply record it. Moreover, in making history historians, like literary writers, rely on "*axiomatic fictions*" (1975, 138). In addition to the title, Steiner offers a number of observations about history that are pertinent to Friel's play. He says, for instance,

By far the greatest mass of the past as we experience it is a verbal construct. History is a speech-act, a selective use of the past tense. Even substantive remains such as buildings and historical sites must be 'read,' i.e., located in a context of verbal recognition and placement, before they assume real presence. . . . We have no total history, no history which could be defined as objectively real because it contained the literal sum of past life. . . . We remember culturally, as we do individually, by conventions of emphasis, foreshortening, and omission. The landscape composed by the past tense, the semantic organization of remembrance, is stylized and differently coded by different cultures. . . . The Augustan paradigm of Rome was, like that of Ben Jonson and the Elizabethan Senecans, an active fiction, a 'reading into life.' But the two models were very different. . . . each reading, each translation differs, each is undertaken from a distinctive angle of vision. . . . As every generation retranslates the classics, out of a vital compulsion for immediacy and precise echo, so every generation uses language to build its own resonant past. . . . Without the true fiction of history, without the unbroken animation of a chosen past, we become flat shadows. (1975, 29–30)

As Helen Lojek points out in her essay on Steiner's influence on Friel, *Making History* "both discusses and illustrates the extent to which to write history is indeed to *translate* the past, to *make* a story" (1994, 95; Lojek's emphases). In postcolonial terms, Steiner's "axiomatic fictions" of history correspond to what Bhabha calls insurgent acts of cultural translation that selectively re-member and restage the past as an intervention in the present that opens up the possibility of rewriting the future.

In an unusual essay entitled "*Translations* and *A Paper Landscape*," Kevin Barry provides perhaps the most pertinent apologia for Friel's historiography. Although this essay deals with some of the historical sources for *Translations*, it is even more apt for *Making History*. In this essay Barry provides an enlightening theoretical excursus for an exchange between Friel and John Andrews, author of *A Paper Landscape*, one of Friel's sources for *Translations* on the history of the British ordnance survey. Barry puts Friel's view in perspective by differentiating the traditional positivist notion of history from the poststructuralist view. On the one hand, the traditional view of history, according to Barry, constitutes itself as a discourse and distinguishes itself from other discourses by virtue of its "claim to objectivity." It deploys various terms that suggest the authority of reliable testimony, such as "research," "evidence," "registers," "correspondence," and "documents," and it purports to "discover a writing which exists before interpretation, a writing which only history can repeat." From this perspective facts and events precede the language in which historians record them. This sense of history "projects itself not as a plurality of written histories, but as a chapter of History itself, of one total human narrative," and it "appears to stand in contrast to fiction, although each shadows the other" (1983, 118–19).

On the other hand, poststructuralist history, like fiction, is aware of its status as writing and its intertextuality. This history is "always already written: first, because the past of society is never an unstructured or unimagined memory; second, because history, more than any other discourse except perhaps that of law, depends upon what has been written, upon the surviving documents which are the past's versions of itself" (Barry 1983, 118). From Barry's poststructuralist perspective the positivist history of fact and event existing prior to language can only be that history "which has not been written . . . mere event and place, the overwhelming and silenced past which disappears to elude any recording of itself" (1983, 118). In contrast, poststructuralist history is not the recording of facts but the construction of convincing readings, translations, and fictions that organize and interpret information of various kinds; and not all readings, translations, and fictions are consistent with one another. History, in other words, "becomes a set of histories, conflicting versions of the past each of which pretends to authorise one differentiation of events" (1983, 118). For Barry both history and literature "enable the entry of what has been lost into a society's understanding of its present" by becoming "functions of narrative": "As forms of discourse both emphasise memory, loss, compositions of character and event, human action, plots that go awry . . . [and] both history and fiction imagine and structure a past which neither could make known without sharing the images and structures of narrative" (1983, 119).

A poststructuralist perspective, however, does not simply conflate history and literature, and both Barry and Friel understand this. Barry says, "either discourse understands its own authority quite differently. History cannot pretend to project itself as an unreality. Fiction cannot project itself as unrhetorical" (1983, 119). Friel agrees:

the imperatives of fiction are as exacting as the imperatives of cartography and historiography.

Writing an historical play may bestow certain advantages but it also imposes particular responsibilities. The apparent advantages are the established historical facts or at least the received historical ideas in which the work is rooted and which gives it its apparent familiarity and accessibility. The concomitant responsibility is to acknowledge those facts or ideas but not to defer to them. Drama is first a fiction, with the authority of fiction. You don't go to *Macbeth* for history. (Barry 1983, 123–24)

In this passage Friel is careful not to commit himself to any positivist notion of "historical facts." In other words, in a historical play his responsibility is not to a solid world of fact and event to which language merely refers but to a tradition of "received historical ideas," that is, to the already written.

Improbably and anachronistically enough, in *Making History* the spokesman for this poststructural historiography is Archbishop Lombard, a Renaissance Catholic primate deeply involved in Counter Reformation strategies. In the face of O'Neill's concern that his biography tell the "whole" truth about his life, Lombard, with consummately evasive urbaneness, assures O'Neill that he will make any changes he insists on, but at the same time he instructs him on poststructural historiography. "But are truth and falsity the proper criteria?" Lombard asks disingenuously. He says that most people think they go to history for facts and empirical truth when "what they really want is a story" (*MH*, 66). "Isn't that what history is, a kind of story-telling? . . . Imposing a pattern on events that were mostly casual and haphazard and shaping them into a [satisfying] narrative that is logical and interesting" (*MH*, 8). Lombard assures O'Neill that his story will be "as accurate as possible" (*MH*, 8), "as true and as objective as [he] can make it" (*MH*, 67), but then he also says that his "responsibility will be to tell the best possible narrative" (*MH*, 8) and that "imagination will be as important as information" (*MH*, 9). A historical relativist like Steiner, Lombard explains that no "period of history . . . contains within it one 'true' interpretation just waiting to be mined" but rather "several possible narratives." "The life of Hugh O'Neill," he adds, "can be told in many different ways. And those ways are determined by the needs and the demands and the expectations of different people and different eras" (*MH*, 15–16). When O'Neill pleads with him to tell the whole story Lombard replies, "This isn't the time for a critical assessment of your 'ploys' and your 'disgraces' and your 'betrayal'—that's the stuff of another history for another time. Now is the time for a hero. Now is the time for a heroic literature. So I am offering Gaelic Ireland two things. I'm offering them this narrative that has the elements of myth. And I'm offering them Hugh O'Neill as a national hero. A hero and the story of a hero" (*MH*, 67). When Lombard outlines the key events in O'Neill's life he emphasizes only his Gaelic loyalties and his opposition to English misrule. He describes Kinsale in terms of "the most magnificent Gaelic army ever assembled" and he interprets the Flight of the Earls as the "tragic but magnificent exodus of the Gaelic aristocracy" (*MH*, 65). All this notwithstanding O'Neill's protests that he submitted to Queen Elizabeth a month after being proclaimed the O'Neill at Tullyhogue, that Kinsale was a disgraceful rout, and that he was stoned by his own people as he boarded ship into exile (*MH*, 64–66).

Historically the revisionist critique of Lombard has been severe. O'-Faolain is a good example. He says that Lombard's hagiography of O'Neill is "one of the most dismaying falsifications of history." He also claims that Lombard's portrait of O'Neill as "pious patriot," with "motives so pure that only angels could have been stirred by them," deprived European history of a figure of major intellectual stature who understood the "large nature of the conflict in which he took part." Lombard's biography, in other words, relegated O'Neill to "merely local piety" (1970, 276–77).

This revisionist view of Lombard, however, is somewhat complicated and confused in *Making History*. It is true that Friel's Lombard is clearly in the process of constructing his portrait of O'Neill as local hero while the play itself, like O'Faolain's biography, tries to assert "the whole story" that the character O'Neill desires. Moreover, the Field Day program for *Making History* cites O'Faolain's historical judgment of Lombard and includes an essay by Declan Kiberd that says in Lombard "the Irish historian comes to seem an enemy as deadly as the English coloniser, since both would imprison the subject in their own chosen fictions." Nevertheless, by making Lombard the spokesman for his own views of history, Friel creates confusion with the role. Friel even included a statement of his own in the program about his views of history and that statement contains some of the same language he gives to Lombard's historiographical utterances in the play:

> *Making History* is a dramatic fiction that uses some actual and some imagined events in the life of Hugh O'Neill to make a story. I have tried to be objective and faithful—after my artistic fashion—to the empirical method. But when there was tension between historical 'fact' and the imperative of the fiction, I'm glad to say I kept faith with the narrative. For example, even though Mabel, Hugh's wife, died in 1591,[2] it suited my story to keep her alive for another ten years. Part of me regrets taking these occasional liberties. But then I remind myself that history and fiction are related and comparable forms of discourse and that an historical text is a kind of literary artifact. And then I am grateful that these regrets were never inhibiting. (Field Day 1988)

The connection between Friel's views and Lombard's clearly confused one reviewer who noted that Friel's comment in the program note on the liberties he took with history was "precisely the argument of Archbishop Lombard" in the play. He goes on to argue, "Friel has presented us with a sort of dramatic Uncertainty Principal [*sic*]—the very act of observing and recording will alter the nature of the event or character so that the 'reality' is lost forever," and that "By embracing the belief that an 'historical text is a kind of literary artifact,' Friel is repeating indeed celebrating the very process which poor old Hugh O'Neill deplores within the play. And this lovely existential joke will be repeated with every performance of the play" (Brennan 1988, 15). Although the reviewer is clearly troubled by the premises of poststructural historiography, that is not the primary difficulty with his response from an aesthetic point of view. By giving Lombard the urbane, sophisticated European perspective, Friel does the same thing O'Faolain accuses Lombard's hagiography of doing—he denies O'Neill the stature of European intellectual. Friel also credits Lombard with linking religion and nationalism (*MH*, 33), a grafting that for O'Faolain symbolized O'Neill's European dimension. Irish Catholicism, however, no longer symbolizes European sophistication for Friel and his audience. In the play Lombard's religious

2. O'Faolain sets the marriage of O'Neill and Mabel in August 1591 and her death in December 1595 (1970, 118–22).

interests, rather than enhancing his stature, make his nationalism suspect. Hoveden and O'Donnell, in particular, suspect that in the end Lombard will be willing to sacrifice his nationalist interests to the concerns of
his church. When O'Donnell hears that Lombard went to London the
morning after Kinsale "to sweeten the authorities there—in case there'd
be a backlash against the Catholics in England," he remarks, "They don't
miss a beat, those boys, do they?" (*MH*, 52). But if Irish Catholicism no
longer symbolizes European sophistication, poststructural historiography does, and in *Making History* Lombard, not O'Neill, becomes the representative of the sophisticated European intellect. "Poor old Hugh
O'Neill," in contrast, appears as a distracted romantic who agonizes over
his divided loyalties more like a brooding adolescent rather than as a
hard-bitten, ironic Renaissance man of the world.

In the end, Friel portrays O'Neill as Lombard did, as a symbol of Irish
culture in his day. The chief difference is that for Lombard O'Neill represented Gaelic culture whereas for Friel he represents a hybrid Anglicized
Irish culture. In contrast, O'Faolain's O'Neill represented a Europeanized Gaelic culture. Friel's *Making History*, in other words, seems to
have moved O'Neill only part way toward the Europeanized Ireland
Field Day imagines as its destiny and that Tom Paulin (1984, 98, 146)
found in Joyce's *Ulysses*.

Perhaps the most significant failure of the historiographic materials in
Making History lies in its dramatic handling. In many ways the play is a
staged treatise on poststructural history. In this sense it is like *The Communication Cord*, which dramatizes a linguistic thesis, but *Making History*
is much less successful as a dramatization of an abstraction than *The
Communication Cord* because Friel never devised effective dramatic
metaphors for his abstract arguments. Friel's metaphoric powers, so evident in plays like *Translations* and *The Communication Cord*, where he
brought abstract ideas to life, seem to have deserted him in *Making History*. Almost all of the important ideas in the play are conveyed in various
speeches rather than in dramatic action or metaphoric structure. There
is nothing like the map-making metaphor of *Translations* or that play's
device that indicates when characters are speaking Irish. O'Neill's divergent biographies obviously had great intellectual appeal to Friel, but
they did not activate his dramatic imagination.

The play's failure is unfortunate because it had all the ingredients to become the kind of successful fusion of intellectual, historical, and cultural concerns that *Translations* was. It had a ready-made, highly developed, complex protagonist, an important transitional moment in Irish history, and an innovative, contemporary historiographic consciousness. But Friel dissipated the potential energy that could have been released from the fusion of these concerns with some unfortunate aesthetic choices.

Nevertheless, despite its failure as theater, *Making History* is still an important work in Friel's canon, particularly from the perspective of this book, because it places him squarely within an Irish intellectual tradition by virtue of its views on history as a fictional construct. Friel's own awareness of his place in this tradition is indicated by another citation in the program for the play (on the same page as his own statement on history), this one from Oscar Wilde's "The Critic as Artist": "To give an accurate description of what has never happened is not merely the proper occupation of the historian, but the inalienable privilege of any man of arts and culture" (Field Day 1988).

Making History also reverberates with the postcolonial context of this view of history as lie. The play exhibits an intimate awareness of the vested interests in colonial constructions of history and in the inevitably hybrid nature of those constructions. In this sense the historiography of *Making History* is distinctly postcolonial. Not only does it recognize the function served in colonial situations by histories like Lombard's hagiography, which preserves a selective re-membering and re-staging of the past as a means of negotiating a future that has not yet come to be, but it also recognizes the necessity of rewriting those hagiographies once they have served their purpose. *Making History* is also aware of itself as a hybrid enunciation that selectively evokes the past as an intervention in the present, as what Bhabha calls an "insurgent act of cultural translation" (1994, 7) that produces the lie of the future, "an interstitial future, that emerges *in-between* the claims of the past and the needs of the present" (1994, 219; Bhabha's emphasis).

The nature of this intervention can be gauged by observing how *Making History* served some of Field Day's purposes, particularly those related to the critique of current myths of Irish identity. The historical moment represented by O'Neill served the Field Day agenda very well. As O'Faolain points out, O'Neill and O'Donnell "stood for the rights of something that began to look like an emergent Irish nation. And that was a thing that had not been seen in Ireland since the ancient days of the High Kings at Tara" (1970, 196). He also says that after the collapse of Essex in 1599 O'Neill made demands that "speak out the full pride and dignity of an emergent nation—a new nation, coherent, self-aware, forward looking, intelligent and intelligible, where there had been before an incoherent dynasticism" (1970, 222). Field Day's reading of contemporary Ireland envisions a similar watershed in Irish history as part of the aftermath of the recent troubles in Northern Ireland that began with the civil rights movement in 1968. Northern Ireland, their hope runs, will lead to the traditional nationalist dream of a united Ireland, but one that is considerably different from the existing political entities north and south. Such a resolution would mark the first time since that brief period between the collapse of Essex and the defeat at Kinsale when all of Ireland would be united under its own leader. O'Neill's divided loyalties also mark Field Day's recognition that the traditional nationalist dream of a Gaelic Ireland devoid of British influence is an impossibility at this point in Irish history when the country, for better or worse, has been thoroughly Anglicized. Like *Translations* and the Field Day proposal for a dictionary of Irish English, *Making History* accepts the hybrid heritage of Anglicized Ireland but rewrites that heritage from the perspective of the colonized.

The success of *Making History* in promoting Field Day's agenda is evident from some of the reviews of the play. One Irish reviewer points out how "Friel has created an effective metaphor for the ongoing identity crisis of the Northern Irish in his English-educated Irish chieftain" (Coyle 1988). Another says that Friel's O'Neill reflects "our own need for Anglo-Irish understanding" (Wardle 1988). Another finds *Making History* "utterly contemporary in its implications." He says the dying advice of Sir Nicholas Bagenal to his children—"Never depend totally on London because they don't really understand the difficult job we're doing over here"—"is a sentiment not far removed from elements of present-day Unionism." He also notes that Mabel Bagenal's description of "England and its Queen as 'a nation state that is united and determined and powerful and led by a very resolute woman'" clearly echoes England under Margaret Thatcher (McKeone 1988, 8).

Another sign that *Making History* served Field Day's promotion of Anglo-Irish and Euro-Irish understanding was its appearance on the shortlist for the Ewart-Biggs Memorial Prize. This prize, a memorial to Christopher Ewart-Biggs, the British Ambassador to the Republic of Ireland killed in 1976 by an IRA bomb shortly after he assumed his post, honors "any writer, historian, novelist, playwright or journalist whose work is considered to most strongly promote and encourage peace and understanding in Ireland, strengthen the links between the peoples of Ireland and Britain or closer co-operation between the partners of the European Community" (*Belfast Telegraph*, 22 Feb. 1989). *Translations* had won this prize several years earlier. That *Making History* came close without winning suggests both its limitations and the merit of what it attempted.

10

Dionysus in Ballybeg

Dancing at Lughnasa

IT HAD BECOME A COMMONPLACE MYTH of the Irish revival that beneath the superficial veneer of Catholicism the Irish soul was fundamentally pagan. The survival into the twentieth century of Celtic folk beliefs, fairy lore, and superstitions provided the evidence for the myth. This myth, of course, suited the needs primarily of Protestant writers of the revival, such as Synge and Yeats, who wished to identify with Celtic, peasant Ireland without identifying with its Catholic religion. In both *Dancing at Lughnasa* and *Wonderful Tennessee* Friel subscribes to this myth but also modifies and updates it. As with Joyce, however, Friel's Catholicism eliminated the necessity to minimize the religious veneer. In *Dancing at Lughnasa* in particular, the Catholicism is as prominent as the paganism. Friel also avoids essentializing Celtic paganism, as, say, Matthew Arnold (1962) did in "On the Study of Celtic Literature." Even though in both plays the pagan elements have Celtic or Gaelic identities, as Yeats's "The Celtic Element in Literature" (1961, 173–88) modified Arnold's argument by generalizing Celtic paganism to all ancient religions, so for Friel the paganism in these two plays is sufficiently generalized to suggest that beneath the veneer of civilization we are all Dionysiacs. Nietzsche and Freud, especially the former, are as relevant to these plays as Celtic gods and rituals.

Dancing at Lughnasa, which won awards for best play of the season in both London and New York,[1] is set in 1936 and focuses on a family of five unmarried sisters who live in Friel's favorite fictional town of Ballybeg in

1. *Lughnasa* garnered a number of awards. In London it won the Evening Standard, Writers Guild, Plays and Players, and Olivier awards for best play of the

County Donegal. The sisters were all based on Friel's maternal aunts and his mother and he retained their actual Christian names (1991, 30). Kate Mundy is the eldest sister and the breadwinner in the family. Maggie is mainly in charge of housekeeping, while Agnes and Rose, who is described as "simple," knit at home to bring in extra money. Chris, the youngest, is an unwed mother with a seven-year-old son, Michael. Father Jack, elder brother to these sisters, has been a missionary to Africa, but he has been returned to Ballybeg recently because he had "gone native," so to speak, at his mission in the small leper colony of Ryanga in Uganda.

For its material *Dancing at Lughnasa* returns to unfinished business Friel had not resolved satisfactorily for himself in the stories. The play particularly draws on "A Man's World" and "Aunt Maggie, the Strong One." Rose appears in the former story and Maggie in the latter with the same names and essentially the same personalities as in the play. The boy Michael also carries over from the stories. He is like Bernard in "Aunt Maggie, the Strong One," whose "crystal clear, sharp, alert" brain recorded everything "for some future time when it would play it all back to him" (*SL*, 128). The narrator of *Dancing at Lughnasa* is an older Bernard playing back the "knowledge of all he had witnessed." In the story we are told that this knowledge "could no longer be contained in the intellect alone but was dissolving already and overflowing into the emotions" (*SL*, 131). After finishing *Dancing at Lughnasa*, which is dedicated to the "memory of those five brave Glenties women," Friel said, "The play provides me with an acceptable fiction for them now" (1991, 60).

In *Dancing at Lughnasa*, much to Kate's distress, the Dionysian keeps erupting in various forms into the Apollonian world of rational order. The title of the play refers to the annual Celtic harvest festival of Lughnasa, which in some areas of Ireland has survived until recently. As Michael tells the audience at the opening of the play, Lugh was the ancient Celtic god of the harvest whose feast day was celebrated August 1

1990–91 season. In New York it won a Tony and the New York Drama Critics Circle award for best new play of the 1991–92 season. It also won Tony awards for best director (Patrick Mason) and best featured actress (Bríd Brennan for her portrayal of Agnes). In addition Rosaleen Linehan and Dearbhla Molloy were nominated for Tony awards for best actress for their portrayals of Kate and Maggie respectively. The play also received Tony nominations for choreography, and for set and costume design.

and was then followed by weeks of harvest known as the Festival of Lughnasa. As is often the case with Friel plays, the program notes for the production also provide important information on Lughnasa. Lughnasa was so important to the Gaels that Christianity had to allow it to coexist with Christian rites. Typically Lughnasa was celebrated on mountain tops or beside wells, river banks, or lakes. In ancient times animals were sacrificed and there was always a ritual offering of the first cutting of the grain harvest to Lugh by the head of the family or tribal chieftain. Two Lughnasa customs—bilberry picking and dancing—are particularly germane to Friel's play. In return for their offerings, Lugh gave the people wild bilberries, and bilberry (or blackberry, as in the play) picking and eating has been one of the most lasting traditions associated with Lughnasa. Dancing competitions were also held at a number of Lughnasa festivals.[2]

Lughnasa, however, is only one manifestation of the pagan that intrudes upon this most Christian family of spinster sisters. One of the most effective dramatic devices of the play is the unpredictably temperamental wireless set the sisters bought that summer. Battery problems and overheating cause the set to start and stop apparently of its own volition. Maggie wanted to name the radio set Lugh, but Kate objected strenuously: she said, "it would be sinful to christen an inanimate object with any kind of name, not to talk of a pagan god" (*DL,* 1). So instead they named it Marconi, the name that appeared on the set. Nevertheless, despite Kate's reservations, as the primary purveyor of music in the Mundy household, the wireless came to represent a sort of periodic Dionysian intervention in their lives. As a Dionysus or Pan figure for the five sisters, Marconi enchants them with music and whips them up into a frenzy of dance. Christina calls Marconi "possessed" (*DL,* 69). Awed by "the sheer magic of that radio," Michael says, "I had witnessed Marconi's voodoo derange those kind, sensible women and transform them into shrieking strangers" (*DL,* 2). Typically repressed Kate says Marconi has "killed all Christian conversation in this country" (*DL,* 66). Nevertheless, the Mundy sisters went through batteries for the Marconi "quicker than anyone in Ballybeg" (*DL,* 16).

2. Program notes for the Abbey production of *Dancing at Lughnasa* came mostly from MacNeill 1982.

Dance is another irruption of the pagan world into Christian Ballybeg. Agnes, Rose, and Chris all want to go to the harvest dance. Agnes says, "I don't care how young they are, how drunk and dirty and sweaty they are. I want to dance, Kate. It's the Festival of Lughnasa. I'm only thirty-five. I want to dance." But Kate overrules them: "That's for young people with no duties and no responsibilities and nothing in their heads but pleasure. . . . Do you want the whole country side to be laughing at us?—women of our years? . . . And this is Father Jack's home—we must never forget that—ever. No, no, we're going to no harvest dance" (*DL*, 13).

With the harvest dance interdicted, the Dionysian energies of the sisters find an outlet through Marconi. With Irish dance music playing on Marconi in the kitchen, Maggie smears her face with flour and launches into a wild dance. Soon all the other sisters join her, even Kate. This spontaneous, passionate outburst is choreographed in detail in the stage directions, where Friel tells us, "Throughout the dance Rose, Agnes, Maggie and Chris shout—call—sing to each other. . . . With this too loud music, this pounding beat, this shouting—calling—singing, this parodic reel, there is a sense of order being consciously subverted, of the women consciously and crudely caricaturing themselves, indeed of near hysteria being induced" (*DL*, 22). Brief as it is, this dance galvanizes the first act, where it appears approximately midway. Unfortunately the rest of the play never matches the power and intensity of this moment, even though it continues to explore the same thematic material.

Another irruption of the Dionysian into the routine of the Mundy sisters is the return of Father Jack from his leper colony mission in Africa. Having a missionary priest for a brother had helped the sisters maintain their dignity in their small parish after Christina had given birth to Michael out of wedlock. But when Father Jack returned in disgrace, keeping the wolves from the door would soon prove impossible. At first it was not clear why he had returned, but the reason gradually emerges as he talks about ancestral spirits, medicine men, animal sacrifices, and other indications that he had "gone native" in Ryanga. He also refers to Michael as a "love-child" and recounts how love-children were desired by Ryangan households (*DL*, 39–41). When he describes life in the leper colony, he dwells not on his Christian mission but on his houseboy Okawa, whom he characterizes as "my friend—my mentor—my counsellor" (*DL*, 47). He also describes the ritual ceremonies he participated in that involved animal sacrifices, wine, music, and dance. He admires how the Ryangan religious ceremonies shade into their secular celebrations and how "there is no distinction between the religious and the secular in their culture" (*DL*, 48). With their openness and sense of fun, Father Jack finds the Ryangans much like the Irish. Kate is appalled by these revelations and looks forward to the time when Father Jack will be saying Mass again.

In Michael's mind Father Jack and the Marconi are inextricably linked. Father Jack returned from Africa a few weeks after the sisters bought the wireless, and in Michael's retrospective vision together they presaged the disintegration of the family of Mundy sisters:

> And when I cast my mind back to that summer of 1936, these two memories — of our first wireless and of Father Jack's return — are always linked. So that when I recall my first shock at Jack's appearance, shrunken and jaundiced with malaria, at the same time I remember my first delight, indeed my awe, at the sheer magic of that radio. And when I remember the kitchen throbbing with the beat of Irish dance music beamed to us all the way from Dublin, and my mother and her sisters suddenly catching hands and dancing a spontaneous step-dance and laughing — screaming! — like excited schoolgirls, at the same time I see that forlorn figure of Father Jack shuffling from room to room as if he were searching for something but couldn't remember what. And even though I was only a child of seven at the time I know I had a sense of unease, some awareness of a widening breach between what seemed to be and what was, of things changing too quickly before my eyes, of becoming what they ought not to be. (*DL*, 2)

At the same time the Marconi provides a means of entry for the Dionysian into the lives of the sisters, it also foreshadows the modernization of Irish culture, a modernization whose Dionysian forces destroy as well as exhilarate and intoxicate.[3] Jack's career has been destroyed by the

3. Friel's Marconi is somewhat analogous to Henry Adams's dynamo in "The Dynamo and the Virgin" chapter of *The Education of Henry Adams*. Adams even mentions Marconi as another of the modern inventors of unseen "ultimate energy," which, like that of the dynamo and the atom, Adams perceives as "occult, supersensual, irrational . . . a revelation of mysterious energy like that of the Cross," a revelation of some "divine substance" (1946, 622–25).

Dionysian forces of his African congregation. Yet, this play does not cel-ebrate the Apollonian virtues of Kate and Christianity as an antidote to the Dionysian. On the contrary, the regenerative power of the Dionysian is somehow dependent on its destructiveness: the harvest is secured only by means of a sacrificial offering; death and dismemberment are a ritual prelude to renewal. Part of the emotional appeal of this play is the nos-talgia and sadness over what must pass in order for life to go on—the recognition of vitality destined for demise, Father Jack's mutilated lepers dancing to appease the Great Goddess Obi.

The opposition between an Apollonian impulse for order and ration-ality and a Dionysian impulse for chaos and the irrational can be traced back to the nineteenth century, where it was a common paradigm. The deployment of this opposition had Irish antecedents in Joyce and Yeats, and behind them stood Freud, Pater, and Nietzsche. The Nietzsche of *The Birth of Tragedy* in particular would have approved of the treatment of the Dionysian in *Dancing at Lughnasa*. There are no Apollonian pallia-tives or Christian consolations for the Dionysian terrors in this play. The fear is not explained away. The Dionysian is both its own reward and its own destruction. The older culture must die that the new may be re-born. *Dancing at Lughnasa* is a ceremonial mourning of the passing of the small-town family life figured in the Mundy sisters and energized by Marconi, the symbol simultaneously of its vitality and its impending de-mise at the hands of the instruments of mass culture.

In *Dancing at Lughnasa* the Dionysian has many more manifestations than Marconi, dance, and Father Jack. Each sister has her own particular Dionysian outlet. Rose is being courted by Danny Bradley, whose wife has recently left him. He calls Rose his Rosebud and has invited Rose to accompany him up into the hills during Lughnasa. In the second act, while picking berries with Agnes, Rose does slip away for a picnic with Danny in the hills, where he shows her the Lughnasa fires and the house of young Sweeney, who had burned his legs badly leaping through one of those fires. After she returns she smears berries on her face and dress and refuses to tell Kate and the others any more details of her outing. Toward the end of the play she brings in the bloodied carcass of her pet rooster, killed by the fox. The rooster obviously represents the animal sacrifice associated with ancient Lughnasa rites.

Maggie's Dionysian side reveals itself in several ways: in her reminiscences about a Lughnasa dancing contest she once participated in, in her love of jokes and laughter, in her constant singing of verses from popular songs, and in her addiction to Wild Woodbine cigarettes. "Wonderful Wild Woodbine," she rhapsodizes, "Next best thing to a wonderful, wild man" (*DL*, 23). At one point she admits that she would be happy to substitute even a fat widower for her Wild Woodbines (*DL*, 62).

Agnes is described as the most sensuous and graceful of the sisters when she dances and she has a crush on Gerry Evans, Michael's father, who visits them every year or so. Gerry, another Dionysus figure in the play, returns the affection.

Christina, of course, has her love-child Michael and her continuing susceptibility to his father's charms. Michael too displays his Dionysian side in the images he draws on his kites. These images are alluded to throughout the play by the characters (Kate, for instance, asks if they are ghosts or devils), but when they are finally revealed to the audience by Gerry at the end of the play they suggest images of primitive passion: "On each kite is painted a crude, cruel, grinning face, primitively drawn, garishly painted" (*DL*, 70).

Even Kate has her Dionysian moments. Although she does not shout and sing, she does participate in the wild dance. The stage directions tell us, "Kate dances alone, totally concentrated, totally private; a movement that is simultaneously controlled and frantic . . . a pattern of action that is out of character and at the same time ominous of some deep and true emotion" (*DL*, 22). Also Kate apparently has a crush on Austin Morgan, a local businessman (*DL*, 10). He marries someone else, but after losing her teaching job Kate tutors his children.

Kate's Dionysian proclivities, however, are held severely in check by her conventional Catholic morals, her desire for conventional respectability, and her constitutional need for routine and rational order. In *Dancing at Lughnasa* Kate and her conventional morality serve as the conscience that represses the libido of the five sisters. She nixes attending the Lughnasa dance, she refers to the burned Sweeney boy and his back-hills ilk as pagan savages, and she is constantly admonishing Maggie about her singing—"If you knew your prayers as well as you know the words of those aul pagan songs" (*DL*, 35). After their wild dance the sisters exhibit the pricks of Christian conscience Kate represents: the stage directions tell us, "They look at each other obliquely; avoid looking at each other; half smile in embarrassment; feel and look slightly ashamed and slightly defiant" (DL, 22). Sensing she is losing ground against re-pressed paganism, Kate says, "You work hard at your job. You try to keep the home together. You perform your duties as best you can—because you believe in responsibilities and obligations and good order. And then suddenly, suddenly you realize that hair cracks are appearing every-where; that control is slipping away; that the whole thing is so fragile it can't be held together much longer. It's all about to collapse" (DL, 35). She is right. The forces of Dionysus do swamp her—Lughnasa festivals, Marconi, Father Jack, Gerry Evans and Christina's love-child, Danny Bradley and Rose. Contemplating it all, she exclaims, "What has hap-pened to this house? Mother of God, will we ever be able to lift our heads again . . . ?" (DL, 59). She herself is tarred with Dionysian suspicion when she loses her job on account of Father Jack.

The most Dionysian character in the play is Michael's father, Gerry Evans. He is Welsh, and so also of Celtic ancestry, but he speaks with an English accent. Gerry exudes superficial charm and enthusiasm. Flattery seems to be his stock-in-trade. He is also a garrulous drifter and a dreamer full of broken promises. Kate calls him a loafer and a wastrel. He appears to have held various jobs, but his most recent have been re-lated to his Dionysian role—dance and music. He gave dancing lessons for a while and now he sells Minerva gramophones. By the end of the play he has enlisted to fight for the republicans in Spain. "Give Evans a Big Cause and he won't let you down. It's only everyday stuff he's not so successful at," is how he characterizes himself (DL, 31). The Mundy sis-ters have no illusions about Gerry; nevertheless they cannot entirely re-sist his charms. Chris, Maggie, and Agnes give themselves over to his charm, but even Kate has conflicting emotions about him. Only Rose seems to dislike him entirely.

Gerry's arrival sets the sisters' Dionysian instincts in conflict with the Apollonian, the pagan in conflict with the Christian. Once they see him coming up the lane, they all rush to make their home and themselves presentable to him. Maggie searches for shoelaces and her Woodbines as she laments they have nothing to set a proper tea for him. Rose looks for her Sunday shoes before she decides that she hates him. Agnes focuses "with excessive concentration" on her knitting. Chris is catatonic. Kate begins by exclaiming, "How dare Mr Evans show his face here," but as Chris is about to cry, she consents to inviting him in for tea and to spend the night, albeit alone in the loft (*DL*, 24–26).

Chris is radiant when Gerry is around. He makes her laugh all the time and, Kate says, "Her whole face alters when she's happy" (*DL*, 33). Gerry's chief charm is his dancing ability. During his visits he and Chris often dance in the yard. Even Kate has to admit, "They dance so well together. They're such a beautiful couple" (*DL*, 33). Michael describes one scene when they danced without music, as was sometimes the custom at Lughnasa: he says,

> it was a dance without music; just there, in ritual circles round and round that square and then down the lane and back up again; slowly, formally, with easy deliberation. My mother with her head thrown back, her eyes closed, her mouth slightly open. My father holding her just that little distance away from him so that he could regard her up-turned face. No singing, no melody, no words. Only the swish and whisper of their feet across the grass. . . . they were only conscious of themselves and of their dancing. (*DL*, 42)

Chris is totally enchanted by her delicate, lyrical Dionysian swing across the lawn and down the lane. Yet despite her momentary enchantment, Chris has no illusions about Gerry. When he proposes again, as he usually does on these occasions, she refuses because she knows he will leave her again. "You wouldn't intend to," she says, "but that's what would happen because that's your nature and you can't help yourself" (*DL*, 33).

Like most Dionysian irruptions into ordered existences, Gerry's visits are not without their risks. Dionysian impulses cannot be contained, channeled, or limited to innocent pleasures. Gerry is attracted to Agnes, and she is aware of it. He says to Chris: "Of all your sisters Agnes was the one that seemed to object least to me" (*DL*, 32), and through Chris he sends to Agnes his special love, roses, and a kiss (*DL*, 37). On one of his visits he dances with Agnes while singing a risqué song and pays her dancing the same compliments he pays to Chris's (*DL*, 64–65). Gerry then dances with Maggie, at which point jealous Chris angrily turns off the Marconi. At one point Agnes lashes out at Kate and calls her a "damned righteous bitch" for berating Gerry and refusing to use his Christian name. Kate's response—"You see, that's what a creature like Mr. Evans does: appears out of nowhere and suddenly poisons the atmosphere in the whole house" (*DL*, 34)—suggests the potential for disaster Gerry introduces into their household.

As part of their Dionysian impulses all the sisters yearn for some man: Maggie for some fat widower if she cannot have Brian McGuinness, who took her friend Bernie to a Lughnasa dance; Rose for Danny Bradley; Kate for Austin Morgan; Chris and Agnes for Gerry. At one point Father Jack suggests a Ryangan solution—one husband for them all. Ironically the Ryangan arrangement Father Jack describes mirrors the way they are actually living with Father Jack as titular husband, or Gerry when he visits and dances with them. Kate's scandalized indignation and Chris's jealousy quickly suppress this suggestion, but it nevertheless establishes the link between Father Jack's Irish and Ryangan households.

The impending disintegration of the Mundy household is forecast in the play by omens and hints in the dialogue but especially by Michael's narratives. Well before the end of the play we learn the eventual fate of all the characters. We learn that the Mundy household will break up. Kate will lose her job, mainly because of Father Jack. Rose and Agnes will lose their income to the new knitting factory in Donegal town and they will leave to die destitute in London years later. Father Jack will die of a heart attack within the year and Kate will reconcile herself with "his own distinctive spiritual search." Chris will work the rest of her life in the knitting factory and hate it. Gerry will fall off his motor bike in Barcelona and the injury will end his dancing days. Eventually he stops visiting. When he dies, Michael hears from another Michael Evans, a half-brother his own age as it turns out, who tells him that his father died peacefully in Wales surrounded by his wife and three grown children.

Like many of Friel's plays, *Dancing at Lughnasa* is a memory play, both biographically and in its formal construction as Michael remembering. The premise is established by opening and closing the play with tableaux accompanied by the narration of Michael as a young man looking back on his memories of August 1936. Michael never appears as the seven-year-old. An imaginary child whose lines are spoken by the older Michael interacts with the other characters. As with most of Friel's other

inventive dramatic devices, the convention works flawlessly and unob-
trusively. At the end of the play Michael's concluding remarks echo the
structure of Friel's childhood memory of the fishing trip with his father
that he writes about in "Self-Portrait" where fact and fiction combine to
produce the effects of memory. Michael says,

> what fascinates me about that memory [of Lughnasa in 1936] is that it
> owes nothing to fact. In that memory atmosphere is more real than in-
> cident and everything is simultaneously actual and illusory. . . . the air is
> nostalgic with the music of the thirties . . . a dream music that is both
> heard and imagined; . . . a sound so alluring and so mesmeric that the af-
> ternoon is bewitched, maybe haunted, by it. . . . everybody seems to be
> floating on those sweet sounds, moving rhythmically, languorously, in
> complete isolation; responding more to the mood of the music than to
> its beat. (DL, 71)

This atmosphere is also reminiscent of *Aristocrats,* where Casimir's very
flawed memory and the piano music of Chopin nostalgically recreate the
aristocratic myth of Ballybeg Hall as that myth disintegrated before our
eyes on stage.

As in *Aristocrats,* the nostalgia in *Dancing at Lughnasa* is bittersweet
and juxtaposed with its own subversion. Michael says of his Lughnasa
memories, "When I remember it, I think of it as dancing. Dancing with
eyes half closed because to open them would break the spell" (DL, 71).
The image, of course, refers to his mother Chris dancing with his father
Gerry with her eyes closed. She is well aware that maintaining the genuine enchantment of the moment depends on closing her eyes to
Gerry's glaring deficiencies as a husband and father. The nostalgia in
the play is for those Augusts Friel spent with his aunts, but it is also for
a generation that contained a quaint and unstable mix of Apollonian
and Dionysian impulses that, like the Lughnasa festival, was about to
disappear.

Like Yeats, Friel saw the Dionysian about to overwhelm the Apollonian and he captures this insight in the image of the wireless. The Marconi, however, has a dual function. It both induces the nostalgia with its
music and, because it is also associated with the process of modernization represented by the knitting factory that costs Agnes and Rose their
income, announces the end of the era for which the nostalgia is pro-

duced. Thus it represents simultaneously the Dionysian subversion of conventional values and the nostalgia for the era of those values with all their contradictions. After all, that is the structure of nostalgia; it arises for something that has already slipped away except in memory.

As with Friel's drama in general, *Dancing at Lughnasa* is suffused with postcolonial undercurrents, undercurrents that enunciate a political unconscious for the play. In most colonial situations the Dionysian is associated with the premodern culture of the colonized, as in the essays by Arnold and Yeats on the Celtic temperament. In *Dancing at Lughnasa* Friel's postcolonial turn reverses the stereotype, as it does in *Translations*, and transforms its stigmatized features of the irrational into signs of modernization and progress. These signs are both destructive and transformative; they destroy one phase of a culture as it transforms into another. In this instance the phase destroyed, figured in Kate's hopeless attempts to preserve rationality and order, mimics the values associated with the colonial metropole in the Celtic stereotyping of Arnold. In a sense the play suggests that Ireland of the 1930s, in its attempt to establish the frugal independence of a rural, Gaelic, Catholic society that clearly distinguished it from the urban, Saxon, Protestant society of its former colonizer, actually mimicked the values esteemed by the colonizer for itself in the stereotype it constructed for the Irish. In other words, like the British, the Irish in the first decades of independence sought to suppress the irrational, the chaotic, the Dionysian in its culture, those values with which they were skewered by British stereotypes in colonized times before independence. The association of the Dionysian with Father Jack's African experiences reinforces the colonial syndrome out of which the stereotypical Apollonian/Dionysian opposition emerges. *Dancing at Lughnasa*, however, moves beyond mere stereotypes by suggesting that all cultures both admit and repress the Dionysian at their peril.

In another postcolonial gesture, *Dancing at Lughnasa* also makes selective use of the past toward envisioning a hybrid future. Like modernism and nationalism in Eagleton's analysis, it "unites the archaic and the avant-garde, inflecting what is in fact a modernizing project in the rhetoric of ancient rights and pieties" (1995, 285). As with *Translations* and *Making History*, the play recognizes, with appropriate nostalgia, the necessary passing of an older form of culture and the necessary hybridity of an emergent culture. Kate's Apollonian aspirations are undermined by a Dionysian impulse that is both a return of the premodern past, figured in Father Jack's African experiences, and an incursion, like Henry Adams's dynamo, of a Dionysian modernity of the present, figured in the Marconi wireless and the arrival of the knitting factory. The present in *Dancing at Lughnasa* becomes what Eagleton characterizes as Benjamin's "mere empty passageway" suspended between a past that cannot be relinquished and a transfigured future that has not yet arrived (1995, 280).

This passageway figured in Friel's Glenties aunts is related to his persistent preoccupation with the official myth of rural Ireland in the first decades after independence, a myth that extolled conservative Catholic family values and the frugal routine of an uncomplicated, simple existence. Provincial Donegal in 1936 should have been a likely place to find people embracing this myth, and despite their unconventional circumstances, the Mundy sisters try to live by it. Kate in particular tries to suppress anything that conflicts with it. The myth, however, masks a contradiction and it cannot adequately resist the forces that threaten to subvert it. The denial and demonizing of Dionysian impulses typical of Irish Catholicism, represented by Kate, only disable her and leave her vulnerable. The Dionysian forces of industrialism and mass culture represented by the new knitting factory and the Marconi presage the revolution in Irish society that began to manifest itself more obviously in the 1960s. As George Eliot's *Middlemarch* recreated a rural English society that had already disappeared before she recorded it in her novel, so Friel's play records a moment that already has passed irrevocably into history. In some ways *Dancing at Lughnasa* is a gentler version of *The Gentle Island*; that is, it is a play that explores the undercurrents and contradictions of conventional social mores and their sustaining myths during the first few decades after independence.

One final issue raised by this play is the relation of memory and nostalgia to language. Michael says that when he remembers his mother and sisters dancing at Lughnasa, it was "as if language had surrendered to movement—as if this ritual, this wordless ceremony was now the way to speak, to whisper private and sacred things, to be in touch with some otherness. . . . Dancing as if language no longer existed because words were no longer necessary" (*DL*, 71). There is no doubt the play tries to move beyond merely verbal theater to exploit other modes of articulation, particularly music and dance. As one reviewer says, Friel "has called upon the resources of theatre in a more comprehensive manner than he has ever done before—particularly through visual images, tableaux, light, sound and movement" (West 1990, 11). In the play the music itself draws from popular songs and dance tunes of the 1930s, traditional Irish dance music, and African rhythms. The play is hardly wordless, however, and this realm of articulation beyond language is not, as Elmer Andrews suggests (1995, 212), the ultimate destination toward which Friel's career systematically moved. The language of *Dancing at Lughnasa* is intensely lyrical, particularly the narrative sections by Michael. Those narrative sections themselves suggest a hesitation on Friel's part to trust entirely to visual and musical effects, to the gesture of dance and the mood of music. Michael's narrations, in the act of verbally affirming the self-sufficient efficacy of music and dance, actually deny their nonverbal self-sufficiency, their ability to speak for themselves. Fintan O'Toole captures the right balance between the verbal and nonverbal in this play when he says, "Never before in Friel have visual elements been so central . . . but never at the expense of the lyrical power which Friel can summon with words. . . . The reaching beyond language is not a disavowal of language, but an immense enrichment of it" (1990).

11

Blindsight
Molly Sweeney

FRIEL'S NEXT THREE PLAYS after *Dancing at Lughnasa*, *Wonderful Tennessee*, *Molly Sweeney*, and *Give Me your Answer, Do!*, premiered in 1993, 1994, and 1997, respectively. None of these plays match the popular or artistic success of Friel's best plays. *Wonderful Tennessee* and *Give Me your Answer, Do!*, both of which critique modern, materialistic, and rationalistic Irish society, form part of Friel's continuing critique of the bourgeois consumerism and materialism of the Irish Republic that have emerged as the dominant values of contemporary, postliberation Ireland. Paradoxically *Wonderful Tennessee* was packaged and cast to capitalize on the commercial success of *Dancing at Lughnasa*, but critics found characterization and plot overwhelmed by theme, ritual, and myth (Rich 1993; Taylor 1993). More damaging is the obviousness with which Friel works with theme, ritual, and myth in the play. In *Wonderful Tennessee*, which Friel says is about "the necessity for mystery" as "*Dancing at Lughnasa* is about the necessity for paganism" (1991, 61), a mad revel on Ballybeg pier masks the emptiness, pain, and disappointment in the characters' lives, but at the same time it suggests the power of the irrational and the mysterious to give a higher meaning to the mundane materiality of their middle-class existences. *Give Me your Answer, Do!* is a theme play too—about the necessity for uncertainty in life—but whereas the characterization is improved over *Wonderful Tennessee*, plot, theme, and characterization in this recent play are not well integrated. A number of possibilities are raised but most are left hanging and the tendentious speech toward the end about the necessity of uncertainty in life falls flat and fails to provide any resonance for the plot—which is centered around the question "Will a wealthy Texas university purchase the manuscript archive of a faltering writer?" — or for the three pairs of characters, all of whom live in the uncertainty of some unanswered question. As with *Wonderful Tennessee,* in *Give Me your Answer, Do!* Friel fails to make us care about either the issues or the characters. More important for our purposes here, neither *Wonderful Tennessee* nor *Give Me your Answer, Do!* advances our understanding of Friel's exploration of language and illusion.

Molly Sweeney, in contrast, is another major articulation of language, illusion, and their ability to constitute the reality of experience we inhabit, and if it does not match the artistic merit of Friel's best plays, it is substantially better than either *Wonderful Tennessee* or *Give Me your Answer, Do!* and, like *The Loves of Cass McGuire,* it has the fascination of a minor masterpiece. In the concluding lines of the play the title character, who had her sight restored and then reverted to blindness again says,

> I think I see nothing at all now. But I'm not absolutely sure of that. Anyhow my borderline country is where I live now. I'm at home there. Well . . . at ease there. It certainly doesn't worry me anymore that what I think I see may be fantasy or indeed what I take to be imagined may very well be real — what's Frank's term? — external reality. Real — imagined — fact — fiction — fantasy — reality — there it seems to be. And it seems to be alright. And why should I question any of it anymore? (*MS,* 67)

This statement appears to conclude Friel's exploration of language and illusion with a whimper rather than a bang. Molly's simple acceptance of the blurred realms of her borderline country between seeing and blindness, however, belies a much more complex metaphorical excursion into a devastating and tragic collision of divergent language worlds.

Molly Sweeney is the story of a woman in her early forties who has been blind since early childhood. A perpetual but inept do-gooder named Frank marries her as his latest cause and brings her to Dr. Rice, a world famous ophthalmologist gone to seed and now practicing in a regional hospital in Ballybeg. Rice sees Molly as an opportunity to restore his career and recapture his illustrious reputation. He operates and restores her sight. At first Molly is ebullient, but as the difficulties of adapting to a sighted world mount, she regresses toward the blind world where she once operated comfortably, confidently, and competently. By the end she has lost her moorings entirely and she winds up in the same mental institution that once housed her mother. Such is the plot of *Molly Sweeney*. Its surface simplicity, however, is densely layered and textured with psychological, neurological, and epistemological subtleties.

In form, theme, and emotional power *Molly Sweeney* resembles *Faith Healer*, although it does not quite match the achievement of the earlier play. Like *Faith Healer, Molly Sweeney* consists of separate monologues by three characters. Only unlike the four lengthy monologues of *Faith Healer*, the monologues in *Molly Sweeney* are much shorter, they are inter-leaved with one another throughout the play, and all three of the charac-ters remain on stage throughout the play. The characters never interact with one another, however. Instead "each character inhabits his/her own special acting area" (*MS*, 13). Their separation on stage as they narrate a series of events they shared suggests the radically divergent needs and perspectives each brought to those events and the divergent narratives they have to tell about them. *Faith Healer* also dealt with divergent narra-tives, but in those narratives the objects of desire were the other people and the tragedy resulted from the lack of reciprocal desire between any two of the three characters. In *Molly Sweeney* Molly's investment in Dr. Rice and Frank as individuals and their investment in her as an individual do not match the personal investments of the characters of *Faith Healer* in one another. Consequently in *Molly Sweeney* the tension between the characters is much less and so the emotional impact is attenuated. Both Dr. Rice and Frank are devoted primarily to their own ego gratification, and Molly's blindness provides them with an opportunity. Neither male character has the tortured complexity of Frank Hardy, and Molly does not have the emotional charge of Grace. We feel sadness for the fate of an admirable, well-adjusted, trusting soul like Molly, but her characteri-zation does not have the complex intrigue of Grace's.

Thematically, however, both *Faith Healer* and *Molly Sweeney* explore some profound implications about how we create the narrative scenarios we live by out of images and illusions spawned by our most pressing needs. These plays also explore the relations of language, narrative, and illusion to the formation of individual identity and they demonstrate how radically different needs or conditions produce narratives that struc-ture experience in radically different ways. In both plays incompatible narratives and identities collide with tragic consequences. In *Faith Healer*, however, the narratives and identities are more deeply entangled with one another; the different strands, so to speak, are more tightly twisted and more tautly stretched than in *Molly Sweeney*.

Molly's particular situation of having her sight restored as an adult after being blind from early childhood is crucial to its metaphoric function in the play. Clinically, Molly was not completely blind and had not always been blind. When she was ten months old she developed cataracts and suffered some damage to her retinas, but she could still detect light and shadows and she could tell when a hand passed before her face. When Rice examined her he found old scar tissue, but no active disease present. Rice called her functionally blind, which meant there was some possibility of restoring her sight, whereas for the clinically blind there is no possibility.

Friel's fascination for Molly's condition is not without historical precedent. Some twenty cases of people recovering from blindness since early childhood have been recorded over the past thousand years and the fascination with this type of blindness has a distinguished intellectual pedigree ranging from the Bible to Oliver Sacks. Molly herself, in a dismissive but nevertheless suggestive remark, links her condition with profound mystical questions (*MS*, 64). For Friel the most germane of these precedents are the Irish philosopher George Berkeley and Sacks.

Through Frank, who researched Molly's condition in his distinctly chaotic and random fashion, Friel introduces Berkeley's *An Essay Towards a New Theory of Vision*, published in 1709. This essay provides a foundation for Berkeley's classic of empirical philosophy *A Treatise Concerning the Principles of Human Knowledge*, published the following year. Frank cites the question proposed by another Irish philosopher, William Molyneux, to his friend John Locke as to whether a blind man who could distinguish a cube and a sphere by touch would be able to distinguish them by sight alone if his vision were restored. In his *An Essay Concerning Human Understanding* (1689) Locke answers this in the negative. Berkeley agreed with Locke, although he disagreed profoundly with the rationales of both Molyneux and Locke.

Berkeley's *Essay Towards a New Theory of Vision* refutes previous theories of vision from Descartes to Locke that were founded on rational appeals to geometry or mechanistic appeals to anatomy and physics. Berkeley wanted to ground vision in experience and, ultimately, in theology: *"vision,"* he says, *"is the language of the Author of Nature"* (1975, 241; Berkeley's emphasis). Refuting Locke's distinction between primary and secondary qualities in sense perception, Berkeley argued that the senses of sight and touch are wholly distinct from each other. Locke had claimed that primary qualities — solidity, extension, figure, motion, and number — inhered in the object of perception and the perception itself "resembled" the quality in the object. Qualities that did not inhere in the object itself but have the power "to produce various sensations in us by their primary qualities" Locke calls secondary qualities. These would include sensations such as color, sound, taste, and smell (Locke 1975, bk. 2, chap. 8, secs. 8–26). Primary qualities are perceived only through the senses of sight and touch, whereas secondary qualities can be perceived by all five senses. Even though Locke agreed that a blind man whose sight was restored would not recognize objects by sight alone, he nevertheless claimed that the ideas of extension, figure, and motion produced by sight were identical to the ideas of extension, figure, and motion produced by touch.

Berkeley, in contrast, claimed that visible qualities like distance and magnitude existed not in the objects or in any space external to the mind but in the mind itself, like secondary qualities. Moreover, distance and magnitude were not products of immediate perception but rather of the repeated experience of various perceptions through various senses. For Berkeley vision perceived only light and color, and other qualities were learned by vision through experience in conjunction with other senses. Since light and color were peculiar to vision, the ideas derived from them could not be identical to those perceived by touch.

Berkeley's favorite illustration of his thesis on vision is a person blind from birth who at some point later in life has sight restored. Such a person, Berkeley claims, initially would not be able to make any sense whatsoever out of the visual world:

> From what hath been premised it is a manifest consequence that a man born blind, being made to see, would, at first, have no idea of distance by sight; the sun and stars, the remotest objects as well as the nearer, would all seem to be in his eye, or rather in his mind. The objects intromitted by sight would seem to him (as in truth they are) no other than a

new set of thoughts or sensations, each whereof is as near to him as the perceptions of pain or pleasure, or the most inward passions of his soul. For our judging objects perceived by sight to be at any distance, or without the mind, is entirely the effect of experience, which one in those circumstances could not yet have attained to. (1975, 19)

Nor would the newly sighted be able to make any connections between the visible and tactile worlds: "a man born blind would not at first reception of his sight think the things he saw were of the same nature with the objects of touch, or had anything in common with them; but that they were a new set of ideas, perceived in a new manner, and entirely different from all he had ever perceived before: so that he would not call them by the same name, nor repute them to be of the same sort with anything he had hitherto known" (1975, 46). At the time Berkeley offered his analysis, he had no empirical evidence to support it. Within twenty years, however, Berkeley had his verification. In 1728 an English surgeon named Cheselden removed cataracts from a thirteen-year-old boy who had been born blind (Sacks 1995, 110). In "The Theory of Vision Vindicated and Explained" (1733) Berkeley cites an account of the boy's newly sighted experience that appeared in *Philosophical Transactions* (No. 42):

When he first saw, he was so far from making any judgment about distances that he thought all objects whatever touched his eyes (as he expressed it) as what he felt did his skin; and thought no objects so agreeable as those which were smooth and regular, though he could form no judgment of their shape, or guess what it was in any object that was pleasing to him. He knew not the shape of anything, nor any one thing from another, however different in shape or magnitude: but upon being told what things were, whose form he before knew from feeling, he would carefully observe that he might know them again: but having too many objects to learn at once, he forgot many of them: and (as he said) at first he learned to know, and again forgot, a thousand things in a day. Several weeks after he was couched, being deceived by pictures, he asked which was the lying sense, feeling or seeing? He was never able to imagine any lines beyond the bounds he saw. The room he was in, he said, he knew to be but part of the house, yet he could not conceive that the whole house could look bigger. He said every new object was a new delight, and the pleasure was so great that he wanted ways to express it. (1975, 250)

In *Molly Sweeney* Friel is much less interested in how Berkeley differs from Molyneux and Locke than in how they agree on the separation of two entirely different ways of organizing experience—sight and touch. Frank mentions the Molyneux, Locke, Berkeley discussion, but he refers mainly to Berkeley's claim "that there was no necessary connection *at all* between the tactile world—the world of touch—and the world of sight; and that any connection between the two could be established only by living, only by experience, only by learning the connection" (*MS*, 21; Friel's emphasis). Frank also cites Rice's Berkeleyan remarks to the effect that we literally make the world we perceive with our various senses "through our experience": "most of us are born with all five senses; and with all the information they give us, we build up a sight world from the day we are born—a world of objects and ideas and meanings. We aren't given that world, he [Rice] said. We make it ourselves—through our experience, by our memory, by making categories, by interconnections" (*MS*, 21–22). What this means for Molly, according to Rice, is that if she regained her sight, "everything would have to be learned anew: she would have to *learn* to see. She would have to build up a whole repertory of visual engrams and then, then she would have to establish connections between these new imprints and the tactile engrams she already possessed. Put it another way: she would have to create a whole new world of her own" (*MS*, 22; Friel's emphasis).

In a sense Friel is using the empiricist Berkeley in a post-Heideggerian manner. The themes of this play are very much related to the more obviously Heideggerian plays, such as *Aristocrats, Faith Healer, Translations, The Communication Cord,* or even *The Freedom of the City,* where various language worlds or worlds of discourse collide, always with destructive results. If we read Molly Sweeney's dilemma not simply as a conflict between two different ways of experiencing *the* world (an empiricist perspective) but rather (as I think Friel encourages us to read it) as a conflict between two different worlds, each with its own distinct vocabulary and syntax, its own principles of organization, selection, and orientation, its own biases, reference points, and master narratives, then we are in much more of a post-Heideggerian world of competing discursive practices than an empirical world. A conflict between incompatibly constructed discourses also has obvious relevance to postcolonial experience where the historical narratives of the colonized inevitably and tragically collide with the master narratives of the colonizers.

Even more central to *Molly Sweeney* than Berkeley is the story of another case of restored sight by Oliver Sacks, neurologist and would-be anthropologist whose popularized case studies explore the shadowlands and borderlands of anomalous worlds that people with various types of neurological abnormalities construct and inhabit. Sacks's story "To See and Not See" originally appeared in *The New Yorker* in May of 1993, where Friel must have seen it. Sacks later included this story as part of the collection *An Anthropologist on Mars: Seven Paradoxical Tales*. Not since George Steiner's *After Babel* has a single text been woven so pervasively through Friel's writing. Not only did Sacks provide Friel with the case history and clinical details on which *Molly Sweeney* is based, but he also provided many of the incidental details, the general intellectual framework, and a brief discussion of its philosophical pedigree in Molyneux, Locke, and Berkeley. Like Steiner's book, Sacks's story resonated with concerns Friel had been pondering throughout his writing career and provided him with a metaphor that at last may have brought those concerns to some sort of resolution.

Sacks's story tells of Virgil, a fifty-year-old man functionally blind since early childhood. By age six he had thick cataracts and his retinas were scarred and damaged, but there was no active disease. He went to a school for the blind and afterward trained as a massage therapist and worked at a YMCA. He was good at his job and highly esteemed, which gave him real pleasure and pride in his work. Despite his disability, he made a good life for himself. He had a steady job, was self-supporting, had friends, read Braille papers and books, and had a passion for sports, particularly baseball.

Virgil's fiancee Amy worked at another Y as a swimming coach. She saw Virgil as stuck in a repetitive and limited routine and resolved to restore his sight. She said there was nothing to lose and perhaps much to gain. Amy brought Virgil to a new ophthalmologist who determined that since he "could still see light and dark, the direction from which light came, and the shadow of a hand moving in front of his eyes," the destruction of his retinas was not total (Sacks 1995, 108). Virgil was very passive about the project: "he showed no preference in the matter; he seemed happy to go along with whatever they decided" (Sacks 1995, 113). The operation successfully restored much of his sight and on the first day after the bandages were removed there was euphoria all around. Problems soon arose, however, and Vigil's initial successes were eventually overwhelmed by the difficulties of reorganizing his understanding of the world according to a whole new sensory apparatus. After an illness that resulted in respiratory failure, Virgil reverted to near total blindness.

Like Sacks's patient Virgil, Molly Sweeney had coped quite well with being blind. At age forty-one she is described by Rice as having lived a "full life" without feeling "at all deprived" (MS, 16). He says she was calm and independent with "no self-pity, no hint of resignation" (MS, 16). Working as a massage therapist in a local health club, she was self-supporting and she enjoyed a wide range of activities, especially swimming. Molly herself says, "I knew only my own world. I didn't think of it as a deprived world. Disadvantaged in some ways; of course it was. But at that stage I never thought of it as deprived" (MS, 24). Molly actually felt privileged in some ways. Without sight, the blind often experience considerably heightened sensitivity with the other senses. That heightened sensitivity often is a matter of survival, since the blind must organize and negotiate their worlds of experience exclusively through the other four senses. This lack of any sense of being deprived especially characterizes those who have been blind since early childhood and who never had any significant visual experience to refer to. Molly was no exception to this privileged sense of heightened awareness: she says,

> And how could I have told those other doctors how much pleasure my world offered me? From my work, from the radio, from walking, from music, from cycling. But especially from swimming. . . . I really did believe I got more pleasure, more delight, from swimming than sighted people can ever get. . . . every pore open and eager for that world of pure sensation, of sensation alone—sensation that could not have been enhanced by sight—experience that existed only by touch and feel . . . I used to think that other people in the pool with me, the sighted people, that in some way their pleasure was actually diminished because they could see, because seeing in some way qualified the sensation; and that if they only knew how full, how total my pleasure was, I used to tell myself that they must, they really must envy me. (MS, 24)

Molly's coping skills and self-esteem as a blind person were fostered in her childhood largely through the efforts of her father. Every evening after work he would teach her how to orient herself and to identify objects with her remaining senses. She particularly remembered the hours spent learning to identify flowers by smell and touch, and how her father identified her with nemophila. When they came to them in the garden, he always said the same thing to her: "Nemophila are sometimes called Baby Blue Eyes. I know you can't see them but they have beautiful blue eyes. Just like you. You're my nemophila" (MS, 14). The efforts of Molly's father also taught her to trust, and he helped to reassure her that she was not deprived at all. He would say, "I promise you, my darling, you aren't missing a lot; not a lot at all. Trust me" (MS, 15).

Molly's sense of trust sustained her as a blind person; but tragically, it also betrayed her in the end. It was her sense of trust, in both Dr. Rice and her husband Frank, that induced her to submit to the operations, despite her own reservations. She never suspected that both Frank and Rice were motivated by self-interest and did not have her best interests at heart. Molly herself was quite passive about having her sight restored. She agreed to the operations mainly to please Frank and Rice: she said that she hoped neither of them would "be too disappointed because it had all become so important for them" (MS, 41).

When asked by Rice whether the possibility of seeing excited her or frightened her, she said it excited Frank but she could not see why it would be frightening (MS, 24). Molly, however, did have dim intimations that having her sight restored might not be the unmitigated blessing that Frank in particular imagined. She realized that even if the operation was successful, she would only have partial sight restored and that entering the sighted world might entail the loss of the blind world she had so comfortably accommodated herself to. At one point during the party for her the night before her first operation Molly suddenly felt "utterly desolate." Among the reasons for this feeling she suspected,

> maybe it was because I was afraid that if things turned out as Frank and Mr Rice hoped, I was afraid that I would never again know these people as I knew them now, with my own special knowledge of each of them, the distinctive sense each of them exuded for me . . . I wondered would I ever be as close to them as I was now.
>
> And then with as sudden anger I thought: Why am I going for this operation? None of this is my choosing. Then why is this happening to

me? I am being used. Of course I trust Frank. Of course I trust Mr Rice.
But how can they know what they are taking away from me? . . . And
have I anything to gain? Anything? Anything?

And then I knew, suddenly I knew why I was so desolate. It was the
dread of exile, of being sent away. It was the desolation of homesick-
ness. (*MS*, 31)

Enraged by this desolate feeling, she danced through the rooms of her
home "mad and wild and frenzied" but with complete adroitness, without bumping a thing, with complete confidence and assurance (*MS*,
31–32). One other moment in the play that indicates Molly had some
sense that she was definitely about to lose something by regaining her
sight occurs just before the bandages are removed after the first operation. At this point she wanted to take one last walk through the hospital
in her "own world" (*MS*, 40).

Despite her reservations, on the morning of her first operation Rice
observed Molly walk up to the hospital "briskly with her usual confidence; her head high; her face alert and eager" (*MS*, 38). At one point
Molly admitted that she wanted to see, but only temporarily to devour
everything there was to devour visually and then, she says, "return home
to my own world with all that rare understanding within me forever."
On second thought, however, she called this hope a "stupid fantasy" (*MS*,
41), an insight that turned out to be prophetic. For most people in
Molly's situation the transition to a sighted world is so traumatic that
they never wholly make it; but at the same time they also can never "return home" to a comfortable and confident blind world they were accustomed to.

People like Molly and Virgil who have their sight restored after virtually a lifetime of blindness typically experience a process of both psychological and neurological decline that passes through several states or
conditions: euphoria, gnosis, temporary blindness, blindsight, and finally
total psychic blindness. Both alternation and progression characterize
this process: that is, the newly sighted alternate among the various states
while they follow a general progression from euphoria to total psychic
blindness.

Initially there is euphoria, excitement, and exhilaration as a fascinating new world of color, shapes, and movement opens up to them. For

the first few weeks after the operation Molly found the world exciting, "a world of wonder and surprise and delight": "Oh, yes; wonderful, surprising, delightful. And joy—such joy, small unexpected joys that came in such profusion and passed so quickly that there was never enough time to savour them. . . . Every colour dazzled. Every light blazed. Every shape an apparition, a spectre that appeared suddenly from nowhere and challenged you" (*MS*, 49–50). But along with the euphoria, and eventually overtaking it, there were some profoundly disturbing feelings. As Molly entered the world of sight, while she found it fascinating and exhilarating, she also found it to be foreign, disquieting, and "even alarming": "And all that movement—nothing ever still—everything in motion all the time; and every movement unexpected, somehow threatening. Even the sudden sparrows in the garden, they seemed aggressive, dangerous" (*MS*, 50).

Molly's description of what she saw after the bandages were removed, a scene taken directly from Sacks (1995, 114), indicates the nature of the problems that followed. At first Molly saw "Nothing. Nothing at all. Then out of the void a blur; a haze; a body of mist; a confusion of light, colour, movement. It had no meaning." Only when Dr. Rice spoke did she recognize the blur in front of her as a face. When he held his hand up before her, all she saw was a "reddish blob . . . rotating; liquefying; pulsating" (*MS*, 42). What was happening here was that her eyes were seeing but her mind was not comprehending what she saw. Only when another sense gave her a clue did she recognize what she was looking at. The sound of Dr. Rice's voice told her that she was looking at a face. Frank brought her flowers, but in order to identify them she had to smell and feel them. This condition of "seeing but not seeing" neurologists call gnosis and patients who experience that condition are called agnosic or agnostic (*MS*, 22, 54; Sacks 1995, 115, 117, 135, 151). As Rice explains it, after her operations "from the medical point of view" Molly could see, but psychologically she was still blind because she had not yet learned to see (*MS*, 51).

This agnosic condition goes to the heart of Berkeley's insight. Following Berkeley, Sacks explains how normally sighted people spend a lifetime learning to see. In lines virtually quoted by Friel, Sacks says, "We are not given the world: we make our world through incessant experience, categorization, memory, reconnection" (Sacks 1995, 115; cf. *MS*, 21–22). Sacks says that with the newly sighted who have been blind since early childhood there are "no visual memories to support a perception," no "world of experience and meaning" to draw upon. What the newly sighted see has no coherence. The retinas and optic nerves transmit impulses, but the brain cannot make any sense out of them. The newly sighted can see colors and movement, but they cannot identify shapes and objects (Sacks 1995, 115). Thus they see without recognizing *what* they see.

This condition of gnosis makes the adjustment from blindness to sightedness extremely traumatic. Friel does not elaborate much on the clinical symptoms of this condition, but Sacks gives many details of what his patient Virgil experienced. Including a few more of these symptoms might have given Friel's play even more emotional impact than it has and it would have given the audience a better understanding of what Molly was up against. Initially after the bandages were removed from Virgil's eyes, the sighted world was an undifferentiated chaos of shape, color, and motion; Virgil said "Everything ran together" (Sacks 1995, 119). Because nothing he saw had any meaning for him, "it was almost impossible for the eye to fixate on targets; it kept losing them, making random searching movements, finding them, then losing them again" (Sacks 1995, 115). He would not spontaneously attend to things visually, but only if asked or if something was pointed out to him (Sacks 1995, 117). When Virgil did gradually learn to identify discrete shapes visually, he still had no sense of what went together as a complex entity. For example, visually he kept confusing his dog and his cat, who were both black and white. He could identify parts of them—a nose, tail, paw, ear, and so forth—but he could not see either animal as a complex, whole entity. He was perfectly capable of identifying them by touch, however (Sacks 1995, 121–23). One time when visiting a zoo Virgil was asked to describe a gorilla he had just observed. He was only able to give a most elementary description of it as like a large man. Nearby there was a statue of a gorilla, and after Virgil has been requested to examine the statue with his hands, he was able to describe the animal with great confidence and detail, particularly in ways that it differed from a man (Sacks 1995, 132–33).

While Virgil's sense of touch was very assured and highly developed, visually even the most obvious connections had to be learned. So much had to be learned that much more was forgotten than learned on any given day (Sacks 1995, 122). As far as learning to see was concerned, Virgil was like a baby "just learning to see, everything new, exciting, scary, unsure of what seeing means" (Sacks 1995, 109). But Virgil was unlike a baby in that his other senses were very highly developed, and so he had an adult awareness of just how inadequate his visual sense was. He was not able to process visual stimuli as quickly or as successfully as other stimuli, and so he had great difficulty trusting his vision.

As Berkeley had theorized, Virgil had trouble with shapes, distance, size, and perspective. He had trouble with shapes because for him there was no correspondence between visual shapes and tactile shapes (Sacks 1995, 126). Virgil had difficulty connecting the hills that he saw with the hills that he walked up. As Sacks explains, "Sensation itself has no 'markers' for size and distance; these have to be learned on the basis of experience. Thus it has been reported that if people who have lived their entire lives in dense rain forest, with a far point no more than a few feet away, are brought into a wide, empty landscape, they may reach out and try to touch the mountaintops with their hands; they have no concept of how far the mountains are" (Sacks 1995, 119n).

Understandably then, Virgil found walking scary and confusing without his cane because his sense of space and distance was so uncertain (Sacks 1995, 120). He also had trouble navigating through his house on vision alone, whereas when he was blind his movements at home were confident and assured. He took a long time to build up the sense of spatial relationships within a single room (Sacks 1995, 127).

The newly sighted are baffled by the very concept of appearance, which has no analogue in the other senses (Sacks 1995, 128n). Virgil could not pick people or objects out of still pictures and had no understanding of the concept of representation (Sacks 1995, 129). On the TV all he saw were "streaks of light and colors and motions" and "all the rest (what he *seemed* to see) was interpretation, performed swiftly, and perhaps unconsciously, in consonance with the sound," as was evident when the sound was turned off (Sacks 1995, 130; Sacks's emphasis). Sacks mentions the young man who verified Berkeley's theory of vision twenty years after the fact, who when confronted with paintings expected the objects to feel like the things they represented and when they did not asked "which was the lying sense, feeling or seeing?" (Sacks 1995, 130).

Seeing was such a conscious effort for Virgil that "when he got tired he could see less and less, and had more and more difficulty making sense of what he could see" (Sacks 1995, 130). Five weeks after surgery Sacks's patient "felt more disabled than he had felt when he was blind, and he had lost the confidence, the ease of moving, that he had possessed then" (Sacks 1995, 121). This sense of disability creates a special problem for the newly sighted. In order to enter the world of vision the blind must renounce the unsighted world to which their neurological and psychological apparatus have adapted. As Sacks says, "one must die as a blind person to be born again as a seeing person" (Sacks 1995, 141–42). This is an extremely difficult transition. As Sacks explains about Virgil, "how skillful and self-sufficient he had been as a blind man, how naturally and easily he had experienced his world with his hands, and how much we were now, so to speak, pushing him against the grain: demanding that he renounce all that came easily to him, that he sense the world in a way incredibly difficult for him, and alien" (Sacks 1995, 133).

Although Friel does not adequately dramatize the neurological symptoms of newly sighted agnosics, he does narrate some of Molly Sweeney's response to her difficulties, for instance her response to a condition of psychic overload. Sacks explains that, finding themselves in a "chaos of continually shifting, unstable, evanescent appearances" (1995, 128n), the newly sighted discover that their neurological and psychological apparatus are incapable of processing it adequately. They soon arrive at a state of psychic overload. In response to this overload they typically revert from time to time to their former unseeing world. Of her experience of psychic overload Molly says,

> So that after a time the mind could absorb no more sensation. Just one more colour—light—movement—ghostly shape—and suddenly the head imploded and the hands shook and the heart melted with panic. And the only escape—the only way to live—was to sit absolutely still; and shut the eyes tight; and immerse yourself in darkness; and wait. Then when the hands were still and the heart quiet, slowly open the

eyes again. And emerge. And try to find the courage to face it all once more. . . . how *terrifying* it all was. (*MS*, 50; Friel's emphasis)

Periods of "blurriness" also characterized this condition of gnosis. Sometimes the periods lasted hours or even days (Sacks 1995, 135). At one point Molly "began getting spells of dizziness when everything seemed in a thick fog, all external reality became just a haze" (*MS*, 53).

Typically the newly sighted behave neither as sighted people do nor as blind people do. Although Sacks's patient Virgil had his sight restored, "using his eyes, looking . . . was far from natural to him; he still had many of the habits, the behaviors, of a blind man" (Sacks 1995, 117). This limboland where the newly sighted have rejected the old blind world and not yet developed the mechanisms to cope with their bright new world of vision is particularly terrifying. "Not being able to make a visual world, and at the same time being forced to give up his own," Virgil "found himself between two worlds, at home in neither—a torment from which no escape seemed possible" (Sacks 1995, 151–52). Molly Sweeney's experience is similar to Virgil's. Dr. Rice says,

> The dangerous period for Molly came—as it does for all patients— when the first delight and excitement at having vision have died away. The old world with its routines, all the consolations of work and the familiar, is gone forever. A sighted world—a partially sighted world, for that is the best it will ever be—is available. But to compose it, to put it together, demands effort and concentration and patience that are almost superhuman.
>
> So the question she had to ask herself was: How much do I want this world? And am I prepared to make that enormous effort to get it? (*MS*, 53)

Molly's dilemma of being caught between her old world, which is no longer available to her, and her new world, which she cannot quite enter, is illustrated by one scene Frank describes. The scene is modeled on a similar scene with Sacks's Virgil. Molly is sitting in front of a mirror trying to arrange her hair. But she could barely see her reflection, which would have been only a blur to her. After fruitlessly trying to arrange her hair in different ways, she gave up in frustration, switched off the light and "gazed listlessly" into the dark mirror for an hour (*MS*, 53). In the corresponding scene from Sacks, while shaving before a mirror Virgil "would start to peer uncertainly at his face in the mirror, or try to confirm what he half saw by touch. Finally, he would turn away from the mirror, or close his eyes, or turn off the light, and finish the job by feel" (Sacks 1995, 134).

The terror and trauma of inhabiting a limboland often led to behavioral problems for agnosics. Like Virgil, Molly lost all her old confidence, assurance, and ease of relating to the world "with her hands alone" (*MS*, 58), and at one point she insisted on diving off an eighty-foot cliff into the Atlantic (*MS*, 52–53). Eventually Molly began to withdraw. She lost her job and her friends and just sat in her bedroom alone with her eyes shut, sometimes listening to the radio. Frank was unable to entice her out of the house (*MS*, 55–56). In the end she lost touch with the world altogether. Virgil too lost the life he had built up for himself as a blind person: he lost his health, his job, his house, and his independence (Sacks 1995, 151).

The newly sighted often experience this changeover from a blind world to a seeing world in "literally life-and-death terms" because it involves radical shifts in epistemological, psychological, and neurological functioning. It also involves a radical shift in identity, in the sense of self (Sacks 1995, 141).

Epistemologically the blind constitute and appropriate the world in temporal terms exclusively. They live in a sequential world of time and have no experience of space. They "build their worlds from sequences of impressions (tactile, auditory, olfactory) and are not capable, as sighted people are, of a simultaneous visual perception, the making of an instantaneous visual scene" (Sacks 1995, 124). Frank Sweeney noted that "Molly's world isn't perceived instantly, comprehensively. She composes a world from a sequence of impressions; one after the other, in time" (*MS*, 35). The blind, to use Lessing's terms, live exclusively in the realm of *nacheinander* (one after another) and have no experience whatsoever of the *nebeneinander* (one beside another). A cat's body, for instance, is experienced as a series of tactile impressions with no one impression encompassing the whole cat, which is why Virgil could not recognize his cat by just looking at it. Moreover, space for the blind, Sacks asserts, quoting Valvo (1971), "is reduced to one's own body, and the position of the body is known not by what objects have been passed but by how long it has been in motion. Position is thus measured by time" (Sacks 1995, 125). People are also experienced differently by the blind. They are experienced mainly through their voices. If they are not heard, they are not there, as far as the blind are concerned. Like ghosts, they come and go, appear and disappear out of nowhere (Sacks 1995, 125). This temporal world of the blind "then becomes a *different* condition, a different form of being, one with its own sensibilities and coherence and feeling" (Sacks 1995, 142; Sacks's emphasis).

Psychologically, newly sighted agnosics have a great deal to adjust to. For example, as the world of appearances or visual representation has no analogue in the world of touch, neither does color. Initially the blind try to forge analogues to tactile sensations (for example, they think the things they see are actually touching the eye), but these false analogies are of little help and often confuse them. Another problem relates to the function of engrams, the memorized imprints the various senses leave in the brain. Although Sacks uses the term "visual engrams" in passing (1995, 128), Friel seems to have worked up his own elaboration of this term. Frank Sweeney tells us that engram comes "from the Greek word meaning something that is etched, inscribed, on something," and that it is the mechanism that enables us to instantly recognize someone we have not seen for thirty years (*MS,* 20). Over a lifetime a blind person builds up a huge repertory of tactile engrams that enable them to effectively and efficiently negotiate the world of touch. An adult who has been blind since birth or early childhood has no such repertory of visual engrams, and so must begin the arduous and slow process of accumulating them. A baby has years of leisure without pressure to perform adult tasks to assemble a working repertory of visual engrams. A baby also has no other highly developed system of engrams to compare to the immature visual system.

Neurologically, a change as radical as the psychological adjustment is involved. Sacks explains that in normally sighted people half the cerebral cortex is devoted to visual processing (Sacks 1995, 136). He suspects that in a blind person the tactile and auditory portions of the cerebral cortex would be enlarged and that part of the cortex normally dedicated to visual processing may be appropriated for tactile and auditory processing.[1] Without stimulation the remainder of the visual cortex would atrophy. He says, "The cortex of an early blinded adult such as Virgil has already become highly adapted to organizing perceptions in time and not in space" (Sacks 1995, 140). So a newly sighted adult, to behave as a normal sighted adult, would have to reprogram that part of the visual cortex appropriated by other senses, and in addition, try to develop and use, almost immediately, that part of the visual cortex that had atrophied during blindness. It is easy to see why so many newly sighted adults never make the transition.

As the pathology of gnosis in the newly sighted progresses, they often develop a condition called blindsight. Sacks describes this intermediate state between blindness and vision as a state in which the newly sighted act as if they can see (for example, they pick up or walk around objects as a sighted person would), but they are unconscious of seeing anything. As Sacks explains this condition, "Visual signals are perceived and are responded to appropriately, but nothing of this perception reaches consciousness at all." In neurological terms, "the visual centers in the subcortex remain intact" but "the visual parts of the cerebral cortex are knocked out" (Sacks 1995, 146–47). Molly also developed this condition (*MS*, 56).

The unique epistemology, psychology, and neurology of the blind all contribute to a unique sense of identity. Sacks notes that in *Letter on the Blind: For the Use of Those Who Can See* (1749) Diderot suggested that the blind "construct a complete and self-sufficient world, have a complete 'blind identity' and no sense of disability or inadequacy." For Diderot the perception of blindness as a problem to be cured is the perception of the sighted not of the blind (Sacks 1995, 139n). So in addition to renouncing a world in which they have learned to exist competently and comfortably, the blind also must renounce an identity that conformed to their blind condition. Thus Diderot concluded, in a quote Friel uses as an epigraph

---

1. This suspicion has been confirmed recently by Leonardo G. Cohen et al. whose study concluded "that blindness from an early age can cause the visual cortex to be recruited to a role in somato-sensory processing. We propose that this cross-modal plasticity may account in part for the superior tactile perceptual abilities of blind subjects" (1997, 180).

to the play, "Learning to see is not like learning a new language. It's like learning language for the first time" (*MS*, 11; cf. Sacks 1995, 141). No wonder Sacks warns of "the emotional dangers of forcing a new sense on a blind man." He says, "after an initial exhilaration, a devastating (and even lethal) depression can ensue" (Sacks 1995, 138).

The final state for many newly sighted adults who had been blind since childhood is what Sacks calls "total psychic blindness," where "an individual not only becomes blind but ceases to behave as a visual being, offers no report of any change in inner state, is completely oblivious of his own visuality or lack of it" (Sacks 1995, 136). This can happen when the perceptual self, a construct of the perceptual-cognitive processes, collapses along "with the collapse of perceptual systems," thus "altering the orientation and the very identity of the individual" (Sacks 1995, 136). Virgil passed in and out of total psychic blindness before his visual processing system, from retinas to visual cortex, shut down completely. This final blindness, however, is not a return to the world the blind knew before they had their vision restored. Their confidence in negotiating any version of the world has been destroyed and they have no functioning identity as either a blind person or a sighted person. Molly ends in this state. As Rice describes her, "She wasn't in her old blind world—she was exiled from that. And the sighted world, which she had never found hospitable, wasn't available to her anymore. My sense was that she was trying to compose another life that was neither sighted nor unsighted, somewhere she hoped was beyond disappointment; somewhere, she hoped, without expectation" (*MS*, 59).

Molly is not the only person in Friel's play who suffers from blindness. Both her ophthalmologist Dr. Rice and her husband Frank have their own special forms of blindness. Although their blindness is metaphoric, it is no less disabling emotionally and psychologically than Molly's.

Frank's peculiar form of blindness stems from his undisciplined enthusiasms for oddball, usually hopeless, causes. Unlike Molly at the beginning, metaphorically we could say that Frank was clinically and incurably blind. Rice calls him Mr. Autodidact (*MS*, 25) and gives an unflattering but salient description of him: "Yes, an ebullient fellow; full of energy and enquiry and the indiscriminate enthusiasms of the self-taught. . . . He had worked for some charitable organisation in Nigeria.

Kept goats on an island off the Mayo coast and made cheese. Sold storage batteries for those windmill things that produce electricity. Endured three winters in Norway to ensure the well-being of whales. That sort of thing" (*MS*, 16). Molly's blindness was just the latest in a series of causes he devoted his energies to. After wooing and marrying her, Frank plunged into research on sight and blindness, including the views of Berkeley, Locke, and Molyneux. After her operation he took on the task of retraining Molly to see, as her father had taught her to identify things when she was blind (*MS*, 49).

Molly knew that part of Frank's fascination for her was her blindness: she says, "He couldn't resist the different, the strange. I think he believed that some elusive off-beat truth resided in the quirky, the off-beat" (*MS*, 38). Nevertheless she liked his passion, energy, and enthusiasm and the fact that he was very different from her father. However different from her father he was, he assumed the role her father had played as her guide and tutor, and she trusted him as she had trusted her father.

The attachment between Molly and Frank is not well drawn or powerfully developed as is the attachment between Frank Hardy and Grace in *Faith Healer*. Friel does not adequately motivate Molly's attraction to Frank and Frank is incapable of any enduring attachment. Friel calls the depths of Frank's enthusiasms into question with the frequency of how often they shift and the inconsequential nature of their outcomes. Molly is no exception. When he is able to do no more for her, she is virtually obliterated from his mind (he never mentions her in his final monologue) as he heads for Ethiopia to help reform its economy (*MS*, 61). Friel seals his verdict on Frank by having him sell Molly's story to a yellow journalist (*MS*, 57).

Friel also uses Frank to create some interesting and amusing analogues and metaphors for Molly's blindness that help both to characterize Frank and to extend the range and significance of the blindness motif. Central to these analogues and metaphors is the notion of engrams, those mental imprints that enable us to recognize what we have experienced before. The first analogue appears in Frank's story of the Iranian goats he tried to raise to produce cheese on an island off the Mayo coast. The experiment failed, it turned out, because of the goats' temporal engrams. They never adjusted to Irish time. They had perpetual jet lag. So Frank had to feed them at three in the morning and they could not be kept awake for milking after eight in the evening. The second analogue relates to the issue of identity and appears in Frank's meditation on Abyssinia/Ethiopia. He notes how Ethiopians never liked the name Abyssinia, which derives from the word *habesh* which means "mixed—on account of the varied nature of its peoples." But the Ethiopians did not want to think of themselves as mixed and they considered the appellation Abyssinian to be derogatory (*MS*, 33–34). The third analogue is the comic attempt by Frank and his friend Billy Hughes to relocate a badger pair out by nearby Lough Anna. The town had decided to raise the water level of Lough Anna to improve the reliability of their water supply. Frank and Billy had heard about the badgers lodged at the edge of the lake and decided to make them their next philanthropic project by relocating them to an abandoned burrow on higher ground. The badgers, however, refused to accept the new home and frantically tried to return to their old home, which Frank and Billy had destroyed in digging them out. Frank describes how the badgers went berserk, biting and knocking him and Billy down and careening crazily down the mountainside to their old burrow. The parallel to Molly being dispossessed of her blind world and unable to adjust to a new, sighted world is obvious. Frank even notes how badgers are half-blind and how in their mad dash they were "stumbling into bushes and banging into rocks and bumping into each other and sliding and rolling and tumbling all over the place" (*MS*, 60). Frank and Billy laughed themselves silly after the event. Rice was out walking that day and observed the whole fiasco with detached amusement.

What all three of these analogues have in common is the functioning of something like a set of engrams that have programmed the goats, the Ethiopians, and the badgers to one sort of situation, identity, or environment and that makes any change extraordinarily difficult or even impossible. Engrams, of course, were important to Molly's situation because she had no visual engrams to coordinate with her highly developed set of tactile engrams (*MS*, 19–21). In the mad scene over the badgers and particularly in the ultimate lack of real concern on the part of Frank and Billy for the badgers, Rice undoubtedly did not recognize the parallel effort he and Frank made to restore Molly's sight. Because both Rice and

Frank were operating more out of concerns that fed their own egos than out of genuine concern for Molly, when they failed and Molly withdrew from the world, they both walked away with relatively clear consciences.

Rice's blindness results from his egotistical investment in his career. Prior to his self-imposed exile to Ballybeg, he had a distinguished career as one of the top four young ophthalmologists in the world. He traveled the international lecture circuit with the other three—Hans Girder of Berlin, Hiroko Matoba from Kyoto, and Roger Bloomstein of New York. Rice referred to their quartet as the meteors, the four horsemen, the young Turks. Rice's beautiful and charming Swiss wife Maria was the Galatea of their gatherings. When Molly developed blindsight, it reminded Rice of a time when Bloomstein asked him if he knew how beautiful his own wife was. When Rice replied in the affirmative, Bloomstein said he did not act as if he thought she was beautiful, that he behaved like a man with blindsight (*MS*, 56–57). Later, at one of their international meetings in Cairo, Rice's wife left him for Bloomstein. Rice received the news from Bloomstein, who called him from the airport and hoped that Rice would eventually come to understand. Rice's response invokes the trope of gnosis: "The mind was instantly paralysed. All I could think was: He's confusing seeing with understanding. Come on, Bloomstein. What's the matter with you? Seeing isn't understanding" (*MS*, 33). After his wife left, Rice went into a tailspin for more than seven years. At age thirty-two he left the medical profession and disappeared. He resurfaced in Ballybeg, and when Molly came to him as a patient, he recognized in her an opportunity to restore the luster to his career.

As the frequent references to Rice's alcoholic breath suggest, intoxication is a condition he is susceptible to and the possibility of restoring Molly's sight, however imperfectly, and thus performing the twenty-first such restoration "in over a thousand years," triggered in him "a dizzying, exuberant, overmastering, intoxicating" impulse to telephone his former superstar colleagues (*MS*, 27–28). This intoxicating impulse effectively blinded him to fully considering the potential dangers of restoring sight to an adult who had been blind since childhood. Friel makes it clear that Rice was aware of those dangers, but he suppressed and rationalized them: "And if there is a chance, any chance that she might be able to see, we must take it, mustn't we? How can we not take it? She has nothing to lose, has she? What has she to lose?—Nothing! Nothing!" (*MS*, 17). Although Molly herself sensed what she had to lose, she trusted Rice as she trusted her father and her husband; but when she tried to explain to Rice how she felt about leaving a world she had known all her life and felt quite comfortable in, all Rice had to say to her was "I know what you mean" (*MS*, 24). On the day of the operation, as Rice watched Molly walk into the hospital with confidence and poise, he suddenly allowed his reservations to surface: "I suddenly knew that that courageous woman had everything, everything to lose" (*MS*, 39). This realization did not prevent Rice from operating, however.

Rice became just as intoxicated with his success after the operation as he had been with his fantasy of success before it. After the bandages were removed and it was clear Molly had partial sight, Rice was so excited he shook Frank's hand as if he was the one to be congratulated (*MS*, 43). Rice also congratulated himself as if he had been both the surgeon and the patient:

> for seventy-five minutes in the theatre on that blustery October morning, the darkness miraculously lifted, and I performed—I watched myself do it—I performed so assuredly and with such skill, so elegantly, so efficiently, so economically—yes, yes, yes, of course it sounds vain—vanity has nothing to do with it—but suddenly, miraculously all the gifts, all the gifts were mine again, abundantly mine, joyously mine; and on that blustery October morning I had such a feeling of mastery and—how can I put it?—such a sense of playfulness for God's sake that I knew I was restored. (*MS*, 47–48)

He says that he will remember dreary little Ballybeg as the place "Where the terrible darkness lifted. Where the shaft of light glanced off me again" (*MS*, 48). Clearly, in Rice's intoxicated version of how the operation went, the patient has disappeared and the miraculous restoration of light is bestowed on himself and his career.

Notwithstanding this restoration of light, Rice remained willfully blind to the darker possibilities for Molly, as he undoubtedly did with regard to his wife in their marriage. When Molly first came to him she reminded him of his wife, although he could not quite figure out why (*MS*, 16). Like Molly, Rice remained subject to periods of gnosis and blindsight. When he could no longer ignore the deterioration of Molly's condition, Rice disengaged emotionally and was content to clinically describe the pathology of her decline. Later, when he met Hans Girder at Bloomstein's funeral (he was killed in an air crash), Girder, who had read about Molly's case, inquired about both her sight and mental state. When he heard that she was totally blind again and mentally unstable, he said, "No, no. They don't survive. That's the pattern. But they'll all insist on having the operation, won't they? And who's to dissuade them" (MS, 63). Rice responded by heading for the bar to buy another round of drinks.

Just before he left Ballybeg Rice paid Molly a visit in the mental hospital. He found her frail and apparently asleep. (We find out later that she was not asleep.) Seeing her recalled his fantasy of a year earlier about rescuing his career. Although he acknowledged that he failed her, he assuaged his conscience with the thought that for a short time she did see and that "she understood more than any of us what she did see" (MS, 64). When we hear Molly's own version of Rice's last visit, we realize that his vision of things is no more reliable than hers. Molly remembered that while she pretended to sleep Rice came in smelling of whisky, as usual, but she remembered him apologizing, saying "I'm sorry, Molly Sweeney, I'm so sorry," and then walking off (MS, 66).

What Molly saw and understood, of course had little to do with eyesight. In the end she comes to understand her father, her mother, her husband, and Rice, all of whom betrayed her trust. Before Molly had her sight restored she identified more with her father than with her mother. Her mother, who spent much of her time in a mental hospital, was mostly an absent figure in her life. As Molly's psychological problems with her new vision mount, however, she begins to think less about her father and more about her mother. When Molly winds up in her mother's old hospital, she imagines visits from her long dead mother during which the mother "sits uneasily on the edge of my bed, as if she were waiting to be summoned." At this point Molly says, "I think I know her better than I ever knew her and I begin to love her all over again" (MS, 66). She imagines visits from her dead father also and they take "imaginary tours of the walled garden" where he used to teach her how to identify all the flowers and plants. But when she asks why he never sent her to blind school and he says her mother needed her whenever she came home from the hospital for visits, she knows he is lying and realizes that he was too cheap to pay the blind school fees (*MS*, 67).

Of Frank, Molly says that she received a letter from him full of enthusiasm for Ethiopia and saying he had never "felt so committed, so passionate, so fulfilled" (*MS*, 66). He also enclosed a money order for two pounds, a gesture that links him with her miserly father. She sums up Rice with his apology, which he may or may not have actually made, and the smell of whiskey on his breath that Molly found so suffocating that she pretended to be asleep. Molly never condemns any of these people with explicit judgments. Like a playwright or storyteller, she merely describes and narrates what she hears and realizes with apparent naïveté but in a way that, like a Joycean epiphany, reveals the spiritual pathologies and blindnesses of the other characters.

As Molly's blind world differed in so many ways from her sighted world—its unique syntax derived from its exclusively temporal orientation, its reliance on tactile and auditory engrams, its neurological organization, its very sense of identity—so her world generally, blindness aside, also differed substantially from the worlds of experience constructed by Frank and Dr. Rice. Molly's way of relating to other people, her sense of trust, her quiet assurance and self-confidence, her internalized discourses, her master narrative for being in the world, all differ radically from those of Frank and Rice. Frank operated in accordance with what we might call the salvation discourse of liberal causes, which takes the general form of "We need to save X from Y"—to save the whales from extinction, the environment from pollution, the Ethiopians from poverty and hunger, the badgers from flooding, Molly from blindness. In order to find life fulfilling Frank had to devote himself to some cause. He had to feel that he was contributing in some way to the improvement of the world. When he felt he was no longer making a significant impact on a particular problem, he simply moved on to another problem. Even if his failure was due to his own ineptitude, as it often was, he never stopped to examine himself. He felt fulfilled simply to pour his energies into a cause. People were not central to this need and the nature of the cause was not crucial; saving the badgers from flooding had the same status as saving the Ethiopians from hunger or rescuing Molly from blindness. With this master narrative Frank organized his world very differently from the way Molly organized hers, and he directed his energies in different directions. Although their worlds coincided for a time, they were neither commensurable nor compatible.

Likewise, Rice had constructed his world out of a discourse of professional overachievement and a master narrative that included international recognition, association with the best of his profession, and a glamorous wife and lifestyle. When his narrative foundered, he suffered an identity collapse analogous to Molly's. Even after his success with Molly gave him hope of reinscribing his life with his earlier master narrative, his whiskey-besotted breath at his last visit to Molly suggests that the former luster of that narrative will never be wholly recaptured. As with Frank's narrative, Rice's was neither commensurable nor compatible with Molly's. The collision of these three worlds (each constructed on the basis of different discourses, narratives, values, orientations, principles of organization) proved disastrous for Molly. The discourses of Frank and Rice were parasitic on Molly's discourse of trust and self-sufficiency based on a blind identity. In this instance the parasites destroyed the host.

Another difference between Molly, on the one hand, and Frank and Rice, on the other hand, is that Molly understood the unreliability of her vision, that she was not able to distinguish light and dark. Metaphorically, in the end she no longer suffered from blindsight or gnosis; there was no longer a gap between what she understood and what she saw. As Rice suspected, she understood better than they did what she saw, and what she saw was the unreliability of what she saw, the inability to distinguish between reality and illusion, the recognition that the discourses and master narratives through which we negotiate our experience in the world are composed of fact, fiction, reality, and illusion, and that that compound is satisfactory, or at least it is all we have to work with. Unfortunately for Molly, she came to this recognition only after the internalized discourses and master narratives that formed her sense of identity had collapsed. As with Oedipus, she acquired a knowledge that came too late to do her any good. In the end she no longer commanded any means by which she could negotiate a satisfactory relation with the world beyond the self.

In Molly's final monologue, Friel creates a very effective metaphor for her insight into her terminal condition of psychic blindness. Here, as she

recounts the "loads of visitors" she receives (MS, 65), we become aware
that some of these visits are imaginary because earlier in the play we
were told that these people were dead (e.g., her mother, her father, and
Dan McGrew's wife). Also her account of the visit from Rice differs from
his account. Consequently her whole list is suspect. Yet, we cannot dismiss the entire list as fantasy, because we know from Rice that he did
visit and some of the other visitors are plausible. So what we know in the
end is that some of the visits actually occurred, some definitely did not
occur, and some may have occurred. When she tells us that she received
a long letter from Frank, we do not know whether she did. The last time
we heard from Frank he had virtually erased Molly from his thoughts.
Nonetheless, the letter, which talks about importing African bees to Ireland and reading Aristotle, sounds very much like Frank (MS, 66). The
point of all this is it does not matter what actually happened, what did
not happen, or what may have happened. All three categories of events
constitute Molly's condition at this point and she is less blind than the
rest of us because she recognizes that fact.

Molly's final insanity, in other words, represents the human condition
for both the sighted and the blind. In the end Molly acknowledges that
"after all that anxiety and drudgery we went through with engrams and
the need to establish connections between visual and tactile engrams
and synchronising sensations of touch and sight and composing a whole
new world" (MS, 65), she still cannot distinguish between light and dark
and even her sense of touch has atrophied. At the end of this very Beckettian play, she arrives at a very Beckettian insight: "I think I see nothing
at all now. But I'm not absolutely sure of that" (MS, 67). Her response is
also Beckettian: "It certainly doesn't worry me anymore. . . . Real—
imagined—fact—fiction—fantasy—reality—there it seems to be. And it
seems to be alright. And why should I question any of it anymore?" (MS,
67). As with Beckett's Murphy, her mind has become a "closed system,
subject to no principle of change but its own, self-sufficient and imper-
meable to the vicissitudes of the body," and the meaning and etiology of
it all has ceased to matter (S. Beckett 1957, 109).

Thus Friel constructs Molly's final limbo world in terms of his career-
long exploration of the nature and function of illusion. Unable to distinguish between what was actually happening to her from what she

imagined was happening, Molly herself characterizes this state of psychic blindness as "living on a borderline between fantasy and reality" where she no longer trusts her sight (*MS*, 58–59). Her conclusion — "the less it mattered, the more I thought I could see" (*MS*, 59) — suggests, as David Richards (1994, C13) and John Lahr (1994, 107) note, that psychic state of the artist, who, like Tiresias, sees more as a result of blindness because what is imagined is what is seen and what is seen can no longer be distinguished from what is imagined. Perhaps that is what Keats meant by "'Beauty is truth, truth beauty,' — that is all/Ye know on earth, and all ye need to know." In this sense Virgil's and Molly's problem "of seeing but not seeing, not being able to make a visual world" (Sacks 1995, 151) in the sense of an externally perceived world, is not the central problem for Friel's play. What Molly realizes in the end is that making that visual world of external reality is not the primary task of one's psychological and neurological apparatus. This realization has certainly characterized Friel's career as an artist, perhaps as the dominating insight of that career.

Oedipus is not the only relevant precedent for *Molly Sweeney*. Synge's *Well of the Saints* also uses blindness as a metaphor for a special kind of seeing, in this case an artistic vision that creates a more desirable alternative world to the sighted world of ordinary experience. Like Molly Sweeney, Martin and Mary Doul revert to blindness, but unlike Molly, they are able to create new fictions for themselves that enable them to negotiate their world successfully. Their new blindness even improves over their original blind state because they no longer wish to see and to have their new sustaining illusions shattered. When the saint volunteers to restore their sight a second time, Martin insists on their right to their blindness. As far as Martin is concerned, "it's few sees anything but them is blind for a space" (Synge 1960, 151). Synge obviously had no interest in the actual pathology of restored sight. For him blindness was a metaphor for the Romantic imagination that asserted the Wildean aesthetic that life imitates art.

While *Molly Sweeney* reminds us that Friel inherits the tradition of Irish idealism and Romanticism that includes Berkeley, Wilde, Yeats, Synge, and Joyce, it also updates this tradition in Heideggerian fashion by recognizing how the imagination is a function of language, discourse, and narrative. For Friel Molly Sweeney's blindness is not simply a Romantic metaphor for the superiority of the aesthetic imagination over crass realism. The artist's conception of the world may be as different from that of the scientist as Molly's is from that of Dr. Rice, but that is only one example among a potential infinity of different ways the world might be constituted through various discourses and narratives. Metaphorically Molly's blindness represents the potential for any radically different way of seeing and construing things. The phenomenon Molly represents of having sight restored as an adult after being blind since early childhood fascinated Friel as much as it did Berkeley because it highlights just how differently from normally sighted people she processed, organized, and understood her experience in the world. Her acceptance of illusion and her recognition of her inability to distinguish what she actually experienced from what she thought she experienced may ally her with artists, but Friel's treatment of this theme throughout his entire oeuvre suggests that Molly's awareness is also part of the necessary equipment for negotiating ordinary experience. This insight about the role illusion plays in our lives may be what the artist has to offer the rest of us. What Friel found in Molly's blindness, as he did in Frank Hardy's faith-healing mission, is a metaphor for the artist and for the artist-like appeal to illusion in ordinary experience.

Contrary to Fintan O'Toole's judgment that *Molly Sweeney* "never quite attains the metaphorical richness of Faith Healer" (1994, 10), *Molly Sweeney* functions metaphorically in other ways as well. As discussed in chapter 3, critics often have noted how Friel's drama, for better or worse, is closely tied to the storyteller's art. *Molly Sweeney* has been criticized for being "storytelling on a grand scale but theatre on a small one," and that may be true if our sense of theater is limited to the traditional emphasis on "dialogue, song, and dramatic action" (Lahr 1994, 110). But Friel has experimented relentlessly with his dramatic forms, particularly in those borderlands where drama and narrative overlap. Like Molly's experience of the world during her blindness, the audience of *Molly Sweeney* experiences her world almost exclusively in the mode of *nacheinander,* one after the other, sequentially in time, as Virgil experienced his cat. This is also the mode of language and narrative. *Molly Sweeney* has little stage setting. The only experience of the spatial or the *nebeneinander* the audience has is the simultaneous presence of the three characters on stage. But even then, they never interact and the audience experiences them sequentially through their monologues. The logic of the play almost seems to require a dark theater where we hear only the voices of the three characters. Pushing the logic to that extreme, however, might stretch the conventions of the genre to the point where it ceases to be theater at all and becomes something like a radio play performed in a theater. Even Beckett backed away from this extreme in *Not I,* which permitted the audience to see only a mouth and a barely perceptible, ghostly "auditor" figure.

As with other Friel texts, the situation of Northern Ireland lies just beneath the surface of *Molly Sweeney,* structuring the author's perceptions even if it never emerges overtly. O'Toole himself points out how "key concepts of Friel's bigger plays are a constant presence in Molly Sweeney," particularly ideas of exile and borderlands (1994, 10). Molly's borderline existence "between fantasy and reality" suggests Friel's own existence moving back and forth across the border between Northern Ireland and the Republic of Ireland. It also suggests Bhabha's hybrid identities produced by colonization. Equally germane are the colliding narratives of *Molly Sweeney,* which, like many other texts by Friel, remind us of the colliding historical narratives of Northern Ireland. Obvious examples of conflicting historical or political narratives related to the Northern problems would include *The Enemy Within, The Freedom of the City, Volunteers, Translations,* and *Making History;* but less obvious examples that reproduce the structure of colliding narratives without explicit Northern historical or political content would include *The Loves of Cass McGuire, Lovers, Aristocrats, Faith Healer, Dancing at Lughnasa,* and *Molly Sweeney.* The absence of explicit historical or political material does not obviate the possibility that the colliding narratives of Northern Ireland, with their different discourses and master narratives for their joint history together, both consciously and unconsciously help to structure Friel's general sense of how we construct our worlds of experience. Nationalist discourses, for example, emphasize Ireland's Gaelic heritage and its centuries-long resistance to British colonial rule. Unionists, in contrast, emphasize the triumph of Protestantism in the "Glorious Revolution" of 1688–89, the Siege of Derry, and the Battle of the Boyne, as well as the centuries-old links between Ireland and Britain, particularly via Scotland. For nationalists the desire for self-determination governs the value system of their discourse, whereas for unionists loyalty to the British crown is a paramount value. Nationalists read the same historical events radically differently from unionists. For example, nationalists, on the one hand, see the United Irishmen Uprising of 1798 as the first of a series of nationalist uprisings against the injustice of colonial rule. This series culminates with the Easter Uprising of 1916 and the formation of the Irish Free State in 1922. In the nationalist narrative, the blood sacrifice of Easter 1916 has the status of a founding event for the Irish nation, a nation still not whole because of the partition of Northern Ireland. Protestant unionists, on the other hand, emphasize the rational, liberal humanism of 1798, and they typically link it not with other Irish rebellions but with the American Revolution, Constitution, and Bill of Rights. When they cite the role of Catholic nationalists in the 1798 rebellion, they usually mention how they massacred Protestants in Wexford as evidence that they were "unfit for liberty." Although the American revolutionists also rebelled against Britain, one would never know it from unionist accounts, which typically focus on individual liberty and the contributions of Northern Irish immigrants to early American political history. For unionists 1916 conjures up not the Easter Uprising but the Battle of the Somme, where so many of them gave their lives, a blood sacrifice that has come to symbolize unionist loyalty to the British crown. Unionists perceive the Easter Uprising as an act of treason in time of war and contrast it sharply with their ultimate act of loyalty at the Somme. Typically, neither nationalists nor unionists mention the fact that many Catholic nationalists also gave their lives in World War I as soldiers in the British army.

The notion of engrams also applies to Northern Ireland, where certain values, myths, historical narratives, and ways of thinking have been ingrained for centuries in the two opposing communities, and any change would be difficult or perhaps even impossible for either community. This insight may explain, in part at least, the intransigence on both sides. If we allow for a certain degree of Freudian displacement in our interpretation, *Molly Sweeney* could be read as an unconscious defense of maintaining certain nationalist values that, as Desmond Fennell has argued in *The Revision of Irish Nationalism,* have provided the Irish with an orientation, structure of values, myths, historical narratives, and so forth. Without these provisions any sense of Irish identity would be dissolved within Britain, the European Union, and international capitalism. Of course, similar arguments could be made for the unionist identity and its supporting structures. Read this way, *Molly Sweeney* offers a very pessimistic prognosis for the North that suggests that radical shifts in ways of perceiving and understanding often lead to fatal disruptions of identity.

12

Conclusion, Resistances,
and Reconsiderations

THE PRECEDING CHAPTERS demonstrate how Friel's interrogation of the borderlands between reality and illusion, fact and fiction first appeared incipiently in his early stories, evolved and deepened throughout his career, especially in its recognition of the role played by language, discourse, and narrative, and culminated in *Molly Sweeney*. In 1972 Friel explicitly articulated this major preoccupation of his career in the autobiographical essay "Self-Portrait," where he realizes that his memory about a fishing trip with his father combines fact and fiction. At the time he concluded that what mattered was not the factual accuracy of the memory but the function it served in forming a "truth of its own" that had become part of his own identity (1972b, 18). Despite his acknowledgment of this fusion of fact and fiction, his continuing exploration of the problem in almost every original play he wrote since 1972 belies a complacent acceptance of it. As with Beckett's Murphy, accepting the inevitability of a split between mind and matter and ceasing to inquire about the meaning and etiology of it does not necessarily imply a lack of interest in "the manner in which it might be exploited" artistically (S. Beckett 1957, 110). *The Freedom of the City* marks the beginning of Friel's awareness of the function of language and discourse in the negotiations between reality and illusion. In *Faith Healer* he achieves his most powerful and sophisticated realization of the complex negotiations among conflicting narratives driven by desire. And *Translations* is his fullest expression of his preoccupations with language, discourse, myth, and illusion in the public domain of Irish history and politics.

Through this career-long exploration of language and illusion and their relation to social and political experience Friel achieved the goal he outlined for himself in "Self-Portrait": "what I hope is emerging is, in the words of Sean O'Faolain, a faith, a feeling for life, a way of seeing life which is coherent, persistent, inclusive, and forceful enough to give organic form to the totality of my work" (1972a, 19). Although it is no longer fashionable to talk about totalizing coherence and organic form, Friel's inhabiting of the borderlands of fact, fantasy, fiction, myth, history, memory, illusion, and his perception of all these as constructs of language, discourse, and narrative, has persisted in his work. If this habitat cannot legitimately claim coherence and inclusiveness in a poststructuralist world of discontinuity and fragmentation, then at least it can claim to have given Friel's work an identity that serves to signify the geographical, social, and political borderlands he has inhabited all his life. This habitat of borderlands, this hybrid, in-between space, as with Molly Sweeney, is part of the structure of Friel's perceptual-cognitive apparatus, part of his neurological programming, a syntax that organizes his senses of language and narrative. Like Berkeley's theory of vision, this structure is neither an abstract universal nor innate in any Kantian sense, but the product of experience, the product of Friel's particular history as a colonial and postcolonial subject. This perceptual-cognitive structure operates in his texts at both conscious and unconscious levels.[1] For example, this structure along with its (post)colonial origins can be detected in its more obvious forms in plays such as *The Freedom of the City, Translations, The Communication Cord,* and *Making History,* but it also structures the narratives of less obviously political plays, such as *The Loves of Cass McGuire, Faith Healer, Dancing at Lughnasa,* and *Molly Sweeney.* From the perspective of the various borderland and in-between sites Friel has occupied throughout his career, all of his writing to one degree or another rewrites the master narratives he inherited, both the master narratives he inherited from the imperial power, as in *Translations,* and, more frequently, the master narratives of Irish nationalism that he inherited from his native tradition, as in *The Gentle Island, The Mundy Scheme, Volunteers, The Communication Cord,* and *Making History.* In *The Freedom of the City* he rewrites both the native and the imperial master narratives.

---

1. Conscious and unconscious, that is, with respect to the text and not necessarily with respect to the author of those texts.

Postcolonial theory successfully theorizes these in-between spaces occupied by the cultures of formerly colonized peoples, particularly the native populations of former colonies. It accounts very well for the typical
structures and syndromes of nationalist resistance to imperial power.
Moreover, Bhabha's notion of hybridity indicates what lies beyond the
phase of nationalist liberation that initially frees the colonized from imperial power. As Frantz Fanon realized, after liberation nationalism often
mimics the former imperial power by oppressing many of those it liberated. Earlier theorists, however, including Fanon, have not adequately
theorized the nature of this postliberation phase. For Bhabha the dangers of postliberation nationalist oppression are more likely to be
avoided by recognizing the hybridity of all cultures rather than by at-
tempting to assert the putative purity of individual cultures, whether
those attempts be called nationalism, separatism, ethnic cleansing, or
multiculturalism. Bhabha insists, "we should remember that it is the
'inter' — the cutting edge of translation and negotiation, the in-between
space — that carries the burden of the meaning of culture. It makes it
possible to begin envisaging national, anti-nationalist histories of the
'people'" (1994, 38–39).

Friel's importance to Irish culture lies in his rewriting of the master
narratives he inherited, a rewriting situated on the margins between cultures. If the early work of Yeats and the Irish Literary Renaissance is, as
Edward Said has claimed for Yeats, the literature of decolonization that
takes Irish culture to the threshold of liberation (1988, 20–24), then most
of Friel's writing is the literature of that third phase that follows nationalist decolonization and liberation. This third postliberation phase is
only murkily adumbrated by Fanon, who had a much clearer sense of
what he did not want — a bourgeois appropriation of the structures of
colonial imperialism. Postliberation Ireland has been perceived by many
as just such a bourgeois hijacking of the revolution, what Sean O'Faolain
has called "a middle-class *putsch*" (1991, 105). Although Bhabha himself
does not advocate decolonization that simply substitutes bourgeois nationalist oppression for colonial oppression, theoretically his notion of
hybridity can countenance "a middle-class *putsch*" as well as a
Fanonesque national, as opposed to nationalist, culture of the people.
Friel's role has been to critique the master narratives of both postlibera-

tion Ireland and Northern Ireland, which is still stalled in the prelibera-
tion phase of decolonization. Friel's critique, and that of the Field Day
Theatre Group he helped found, is situated within Irish nationalism but
as a rewriting from its margins. Within the context of the Republic of
Ireland this new nationalism is not marginalized in the sense of an oppressed and disenfranchised minority, but in Northern Ireland it is marginalized in that sense. Friel's attitude toward the dominant nationalist
culture within Ireland as a whole is colored, as it is for many Northern-
ers, by his experience of that culture as a minority in the North.

Unlike traditional Irish nationalism, the moderate "new" nationalism
of Friel and his Field Day Theatre Group, which also characterizes the
moderate nationalism of John Hume and the Social Democratic and
Labour Party (SDLP) in Northern Ireland, acknowledges the hybridity of
Irish culture in plays such as *Translations* and *Making History*. As traditional nationalism opened up a future of new possibilities by rewriting
the imperial master narratives, so new nationalism opens up productive
possibilites foreclosed by the master narratives of traditional Irish nationalism. Without rejecting nationalism, new nationalism has tried to
modernize it by opening it up to the transnational translation of Irish
culture, particularly within a broader European as well as an Anglo-Irish
context. This opening up of Irish nationalism does not undo the "middle-class *putsch*" or deliver Fanon's national culture of the people, but in
the case of Friel and Field Day new nationalism does critique the materialistic values of Ireland's middle-class culture and it tries to temper the
excesses and rigidities of traditional nationalism and make it more open
and accepting of otherness. In this sense it is another transition phase to
a national, antinationalist culture and society of the kind theorized by
Bhabha.

This new openness, however, is not without its blind spots and lacunae, but they are blind spots and lacunae that characterize postcolonial
theory as well. Although Bhabha and postcolonial theory effectively theorize Irish nationalist structures and syndromes, there are some significant lacunae both within postcolonial theory and in my own handling of
it here. In writing this book I have been aware that I have been begging
some questions and glossing over some controversial problematics that
should be acknowledged. One of these problematics is the distinction

between using postcolonial theory on one hand as a cultural critique and reading strategy and on the other hand as a cultural politics. In this book I have deployed postcolonial theory primarily as a reading strategy. Ignored here is the realm of cultural politics, for instance in Northern Ireland, where the more extreme versions of republicanism and loyalism resist postcolonial notions of hybridity.[2] For example, the assassination in December of 1997 of Billy Wright in the Maze prison by Irish National Liberation Army (INLA) prisoners and the retaliation hours later by Wright's Loyalist Volunteer Force is only one example of efforts on both sides to wreck the peace talks that led to the 1998 Belfast Agreement, which in effect institutionalizes the hybrid status of Northern Ireland.[3] John Hume of the SDLP was a major architect of the principles underlying the agreement, and the majority of the people of Northern Ireland and the Republic of Ireland voted for it. Within a significant minority of republicans and loyalists, however, even though both communities already and irrevocably are hybrids of Ireland's colonial history, violent identity politics resist the kind of transnational hybridity theorized by Bhabha as a form of agency capable of rewriting the master narratives of Western culture. Die-hard republicans and loyalists much prefer the older colonial as opposed to postcolonial narratives.

The situation of republicans and loyalists, in comparison to more moderate forms of nationalism and unionism, also brings up the issue of class within a colonized people, another complication of postcolonial theory. In Northern Ireland moderate nationalists and unionists tend to be mostly from the middle class, whereas more extreme republicans and loyalists tend to be working class. For most people in Northern Ireland, however, class identity consistently has been subordinated to national identity.

2. For an assessment of Friel from the perspective of cultural politics see S. Richards 1997.

3. All three strands of the 1998 Belfast Agreement acknowledge this hybridity. Strand one focuses on relations between the two dominant communities within the in-between space of Northern Ireland. Strand two focuses on another border realm — the relations between Northern Ireland and the Republic. And strand three focuses on other interrelations — those between Dublin and London within the context of a Council of the Isles that also includes Scotland and Wales.

Another problematic is the notion of Ireland as a postcolonial/third-world culture, a notion resisted by many of the Irish themselves and by many postcolonial critics. As a member of the European Union and as one of the fastest growing economies in Europe, Ireland is clearly part of the first world. Nonetheless, more than eight centuries of colonization has left Ireland, north and south, with a (post)colonial legacy resembling that of many third-world developing countries. That legacy is abundantly evident in virtually all Irish social, political, and cultural institutions. One very recent manifestation is the current debate in the Republic of Ireland over European security arrangements, a debate that treads directly on the Republic's postcolonial sensitivities about infringing on the sovereignty of other nations.

Much of postcolonial theory is predicated on racial difference, and this is another reason many object to perceiving Ireland in postcolonial terms. Although this is a topic for another book, several points can be made briefly on this issue of race in colonial and postcolonial Ireland. Throughout Ireland's colonial history the Irish were deemed an inferior race by the British. Gerald of Wales, one of the earliest Normans to arrive in Ireland in the twelfth century, said that the Irish, though well endowed by nature, lived like beasts and were "so barbarous that they cannot be said to have any culture" (1982, 100–101). More recently, Victorian racial "science" regularly simianized the Irish and, against all visual evidence, lumped them with the swarthier races of the earth (Michie 1996, 585–90). As Fanon (1967) has amply demonstrated, the psychic damage of racial prejudice does not erase easily, and residues of racial oppression as well as a keen sense of that oppression persist in Ireland. During the 1960s the civil rights movement in Northern Ireland consciously modeled itself on the black civil rights movement in the United States. Martin Luther King and Gandhi, particularly the former, served as models for the leaders of the movement. Republican murals in Belfast and Derry invoke Nelson Mandela and the ANC, the PLO, and the American Indian Movement as fellow victims of imperialist oppression. In the Republic of Ireland the lingering residue of centuries of racial oppression can be detected in texts as different as Hugh Leonard's *Da,* with its portrait of Da's servile postcolonial mentality, and Roddy Doyle's *The Commitments,* with its Dublin working-class identification with black America and its music. Irish professionals have experienced discrimination in England, especially during periods of IRA bombing campaigns, whereas they always feel treated as equals in the rest of Europe. "Race" can be defined in more ways than the color of one's skin, and where skin color does not suffice to separate "us" from the "other," other markers of "race" have been employed, such as language, religion, heritage, or breeding. Racially the Irish were often depicted by Victorian Britain as hybrids, as "white chimpanzees" or "Africanoid celts" (Curtis 1997; Michie 1996, 584, 586), and that hybrid legacy has persisted to the present, particularly in Northern Ireland, where nationalists identify with first-world Europeans as well as with Indians, American and South African blacks, and Palestinians.

Although a detailed examination of these problematics is beyond the scope of this conclusion, there are two others I would like to address briefly here—the potential resistances to postcolonial readings offered by texts that focus on Irish women and on unionism or what might be called "settler nationalism." In both cases certain dynamics threaten to disrupt Bhabha's theoretical insights that work so effectively for nationalist texts such as Friel's. A truly comprehensive postcolonial theory, however, should not elide the experiences of major participants in the colonial enterprise, and Bhabha's theory needs to be examined for its ability to account for the experiences of Irish women and unionists.

Gayatri Spivak's "Can the Subaltern Speak?" mounts a substantial feminist challenge to postcolonial theory. Spivak argues that the subaltern woman, caught between a patriarchal traditional culture and a patriarchal imperial culture, cannot speak for herself. It is not even a matter of silence, but of always already being spoken for within one patriarchal power structure or another. For Spivak "there is no space [hybrid or otherwise] from which the sexed subaltern subject can speak" (1994, 103).

Friel's writings contain a number of sympathetic portraits of women, and his plays offer a number of prominent roles for women. None of Friel's female portraits or roles, however, acknowledges the dynamic of double oppression Spivak articulates. While Friel's women often possess and signify particular structures of colonial and postcolonial Ireland, for example Cass McGuire or Molly Sweeney, they do not experience them uniquely as women; rather, the subaltern position of women represents a male or generalized ungendered experience of colonial circumstances. Spivak's structural dynamic of double oppression is evident, however, in a play like Anne Devlin's *Ourselves Alone*. In this play three women are subject to a double colonization, colonization by the British and by a particularly virulent form of internal colonization—patriarchal republicanism. Each of the three women responds differently to her colonized status and each establishes a different relation to her colonizers, but by the end of the play none of these women has been able to find a voice, hybrid or otherwise, that has not already been appropriated or haunted by a patriarchal discourse.

Ourselves Alone provides a grotesquely powerful image of the subaltern woman in Northern Ireland with the figure of Auntie Cora, who is blind, deaf, dumb, and without hands. At the age of eighteen, she was moving ammunition for her IRA brother Malachy when the weeping powder exploded in her face. The explosion "took the skin off her face" and "her hair's never really grown properly since." This accident not only ruined Cora's life but also the lives of her sister Bridget, who remained a maid to take care of her, and her niece Frieda, who, at least up to this point, has taken care of them both. As with her life, the significance of Cora's suffering is appropriated by her brother and the IRA: Frieda tells us, "They stick her out at the front of the parades every so often to show the women of Ireland what their patriotic duty should be" (Devlin 1986, 29). Of course the spectacle of Cora on parade also would have signified the brutality of the colonizer as the ultimate cause of her affliction.[4] When Cora "speaks," she suffers, quite literally in her case, the double effacement of the subaltern female, an effacement that does not obliterate her but violently appropriates and overdetermines her significance. As Spivak says, "the figure of the woman disappears, not into a pristine nothingness, but into a violent shuttling which is the displaced figuration of the 'third-world woman' caught between tradition and modernization" (1994, 102).

Although Spivak's conclusions are very apt for the three republican women in *Ourselves Alone,* in Devlin's *After Easter,* written a decade later, the gendered subaltern voice does begin to articulate itself. In this play

4. Sharpe 1994 has shown how the treatment of women figured in the rationales of British imperialism.

Greta, the protagonist, struggles to be reborn after experiencing a death of her self shortly after she left Ireland and married. Greta had experienced the death of her self when she passively consented to being objectified within the patriarchal structures of family and church. In another double effacement, two fathers, a biological one and a priestly one, conspired to snuff out her subjectivity, a loss depicted by a memory of a priest trying to suffocate her and a scene in which her dead father tries to strangle her. Her English husband continues the patriarchal obliteration of her selfhood begun by church and family. Greta's rebirth is characterized as a recovery of her own voice: "My voice has come back to me. After all these years. From the night it left me in Exmoor and I died. Tonight it came back. Oh I'm so happy. Do you know what this means? . . . It means I'm back. It means that from now on everything I say will be true" (Devlin 1996, 17). Once Greta recovers her own voice, as opposed to mimicking the patriarchal voice of her heritage, she realizes immediately that she must return home to Belfast to deal with her mother and father, the oedipal sources of her voicelessness. The final step of her renewal of selfhood is to exorcize the voice of her father. After she has scattered her father's ashes in both the Bann and the Thames, her renewed subjecthood is figured in the voice of a laughing baby. The play concludes as she tells her baby what Nora McGuinness calls "a mythic story which asserts both the pre-Oedipal experience of the girl's relation to the mother and the feminine power to transform the patriarchy, to establish a new relation between genders." The story takes place after Easter as Greta and her mother were out hunting. They came upon a stag "from the cold north":

> My mother was afraid, but I saw it was only hungry. I took some berries from my bag and fed the stag from the palm of my hand. The stag's face was frozen and I had to be careful because it wanted to kiss me, and if I had let it, I would have died of cold. But gradually as it ate, its face was transformed and it began to take on human features. And then the thaw set in. . . . So I got on the stag's back and flew with it to the top of the world. And he took me to the place where the rivers come from, where you come from . . . and this is my own story. (Devlin 1996, 75)

In this final image of the subaltern woman astride the patriarchal stag, Devlin constructs a hybrid position from which Greta can control her own destiny, subjectivity, and voice. Instead of passively submitting to the stag's kiss, which would result in the death of the self, she mounts it, and from this position of dominance she has the stag take her back to where everything begins; from there she begins to rewrite her narrative of identity, to reconstruct a subjectivity that, while dependent on the patriarchal stag, is no longer dominated by him.

Beyond Devlin's plays and literary culture generally, evidence exists that the gendered subaltern voice has begun to emerge in Northern Ireland. This fledgling emergence is both acknowledged and quantified politically by the one percent of the popular vote received by the Women's Coalition in the election of representatives to the peace talks on the future of Northern Ireland. This vote entitled them to two of the 110 seats at the talks assembly, the same number of seats secured by the Labour Party and two extreme loyalist parties (the Progressive Unionist Party and Ulster Democratic Party). Nevertheless, despite these intimations of an emerging subaltern voice, Northern Ireland has not exactly been fertile ground for feminism. Neither republicanism nor unionism has been particularly hospitable to feminism.

In order to further refine Spivak's insights and for an indication of what may lie in the future for women in Northern Ireland, we need to turn to the Irish Republic. There the subaltern voice of women has been articulating itself from the margins of patriarchal nationalism in more fully developed form than in Northern Ireland, and Bhabha's postcolonial theory ably accounts for it. The recognition, maturity, and impact of the sexed subaltern voice in the Republic can be gauged politically, socially, and culturally by a number of events, including the presidency of Mary Robinson, the successful outcome of the second divorce referendum, and the publication of the LIP series of pamphlets by Attic Press. The controversy over the *Field Day Anthology of Irish Writing* also suggests that the subaltern voice of Irish women can no longer be ignored in the Irish Republic. It is also significant that the most substantial political acknowledgment of the subaltern woman's voice of Northern Ireland has come from the South with the succession of Mary McAleese to the presidency of the Republic. Although McAleese is not perceived to represent feminist concerns to the same degree as Mary Robinson, that she was put forward by Fianna Fail represented a successful appeal to both nationalism and women (if not feminism). The election of McAleese may also suggest the hope, expressed earlier in the Northern Peace Movement and in Stewart Parker's play *Pentecost*,[5] that women might play a prominent role in the national reconciliation of Ireland.

In comparison to the fledgling subaltern voice of women in Northern Ireland, the writing of Eavan Boland, particularly her pamphlet *A Kind of Scar* and her collection of poems *Outside History*, illustrates the more advanced presencing of the female voice at the margins of patriarchal nationalist culture in the Republic of Ireland. Boland's strategy in *Outside History* and *A Kind of Scar* conforms precisely to how Bhabha envisions hybrid enunciations materializing at the margins of the dominant discourse, rewriting the master narratives of that discourse from which women were edited out, and, through this subversive act of agency, reconstituting cultural and historical norms.

As a young woman Boland aspired to be a poet in the Irish national tradition. At the same time Boland felt she could not "do without the idea of a nation" (1989, 19), she also felt that it was a flawed concept and that she "could not as a woman accept the nation formulated for [her] by Irish poetry and its traditions" (1989, 8). As a consequence of aspiring to be an Irish poet, Boland found herself to be an anomaly. As she put it, "I was a woman and a poet in a culture which had the greatest difficulty associating the two ideas" (1989, 11). For Boland the Irish poetic tradition presented two major obstacles: it provided no female predecessors and it portrayed women as passive, decorative icons, particularly "where the nation became a woman and the woman took on the national posture" (1989, 12). Boland could not accept these oversimplified women as representations of actual women's experience in Irish history, and they provided no models for her own poetry. In Boland's view Irish poets were "evading the real women of an actual past: women whose silence their poetry should have broken"; and they "ran the risk of turning a terrible witness into an empty decoration" (1989, 24). In effect, patriarchal na-

5. The pattern of characterization in the play favors women as the potential source for reconciliation in Northern Ireland. Perhaps Parker meant to suggest the Peace People, a movement begun in 1976 by two Catholic women who became fed up with the violence and whose efforts earned them the Nobel Peace Prize for 1977. Although the play is set in 1974, it was written after the Peace People had been in operation for approximately a decade (Parker 1989).

tionalism and its male dominated poetic tradition had edited her own experience as a woman out of Irish history and Irish literature.

If Boland was not to remain permanently outside of her national literary tradition, "cut off from its archive, at a distance from its energy,"
she somehow had to "repossess it" (1989, 8). As a strategy to "relocate
[herself] within the Irish poetic tradition" (1989, 20), Boland decided to
exploit her marginality to subvert that tradition by writing about Irish
women "in such a way that [she] never colluded with the simplified images of women in Irish poetry" (1989, 23). In "Mise Eire" (1990, 78) she insists that she will not go back to

> my nation displaced
> into old dactyls,
>
> . . .
>
> the songs
> that bandage up the history,
> the words
> that make a rhythm of the crime.

By writing about the past "with the complexity with which it was suffered" (1989, 24), Boland would unlock that past's untapped potential
with a subaltern act of subversion.

Boland achieves her subversive objective by invoking American feminist poets like Adrienne Rich, as well as classical precedents, such as Sap-
pho and ancient myths of womanhood, and by grafting these female
models and her own experience onto the male-dominated Irish poetic
tradition she inherited. Boland's graft does not simply preserve the inherited tradition but alters it into a new hybrid entity through critique
and subversion. As an act of agency this rewriting of the Irish past also
constitutes a rewriting of Irish female subjectivity. Boland says that in the
past, like Ralph Ellison's invisible man, woman, "the real woman behind
the image," is invisible in Irish culture, "edited out of our own literature
by conventional tribalisms" (1989, 19–20). But "over a relatively short
time—certainly no more than a generation or so—women have moved
from being the subjects and objects of Irish poems to being the authors
of them" (1989, 6). In the contemporary poetry of Irish women those
simplified icons of the Irish poetic tradition, its fictive queens and national sibyls, "those emblems are no longer silent. They have acquired

voices. They have turned from poems into poets" (1989, 24). "A hundred years ago," Boland says, "I might have been a motif in a poem. Now I could have a complex self within my own poem" (1989, 23). For Boland this transition "changes our idea of the Irish poem; of its composition and authority, of its right to appropriate certain themes and make certain fiats" (1989, 7). One might add also that this transition, as evidenced in Boland's writing, transforms our idea of Irish women and of Irish poets, and it rewrites Irish history in the process from the margins of a patriarchal nationalist tradition. By grafting herself onto that tradition, Boland mounts Devlin's patriarchal stag and rides it to a new beginning.

The evidence of Irish women writers, and of women's situation in Ireland generally, suggests that the validity of Spivak's claims that post-colonial theory does not adequately account for the subaltern woman's voice needs to be qualified and refined. In his critique of Spivak, Bart Moore-Gilbert has pointed out that her "contention that 'If the subaltern can speak then, thank God, the subaltern is not a subaltern any more' does not sufficiently recognize that there may be a number of intermediate positions between 'full' subalternity and hegemony" (1997, 107–8). He also claims, "While Spivak is excellent on 'the itinerary of silencing' endured by the subaltern, particularly historically, there is little attention to the process by which the subaltern's 'coming to voice' might be achieved" (1997, 106).[6] One might further suggest that the validity of Spi-

---

6. Moore-Gilbert acknowledges that in her recent work "Spivak argues in no uncertain terms that the subaltern can indeed speak—and act resistantly" (1997, 108). Nevertheless, he argues, "While one must acknowledge the force of Spivak's argument about the dangers of constructing 'a monolithic collectivity of "women" in the list of the oppressed whose unfractured subjectivity allows them to speak for themselves,' there seem to be equivalent dangers in seeing the contemporary female subaltern, equally monolithically, as *incapable* of coming to the point of voice or self-representation. . . . Spivak often appears to deny the subaltern any possibility of access to the (self-)liberating personal and political trajectories enabled by the growth of the modern women's movement in the West, for instance" (1997, 106; Moore-Gilbert's emphasis). He hastens to add, however, that this critique does not "detract from the force of Spivak's argument that the subaltern is still, characteristically, only heard through the mediation of the non-subaltern, or that while the subaltern can speak, the West may choose not to hear, or that the terms in which the subaltern speaks may be overdetermined, so that no 'pure' form of subaltern consciousness can be retrieved" (1997, 108).

vak's claims about subaltern women is limited to those situations where women remain colonized within patriarchal structures and have not yet achieved a consciousness of being colonized, or at least have not yet begun the process of decolonization. As Frantz Fanon points out, "all decolonization is successful" (1963, 37), and once the process of decolonization begins, the search for a voice to enunciate that process inevitably begins also, and, as *bricolage,* that hybrid voice, the feminized stag, begins to make herself heard from the margins of the patriarchal discourse that once dominated and effaced it.

If postcolonial theory can accommodate the writing of Irish women, what about Northern unionists? One of the areas least theorized by postcolonial studies involves the situations of settler colonies.[7] This lacuna in postcolonial theory leaves an important element of colonial history and postcolonial theory in theoretical limbo.

Like women, settlers are doubly marginalized although the structure of that marginalization differs. Like natives, settlers exist on the margins of two cultures, that of the colonized natives and that of the colonial power, but their relation to these two cultures differs from that of the natives; it is characterized by a double ambivalence — one toward the native culture and one toward the colonial metropole. This double ambivalence makes them doubly hybrid as well. Friel's texts seldom portray Northern unionists and, with the possible exception of Grace in *Faith Healer,* none has a prominent role in his plays. Field Day, in its pamphlet series, in some of its productions, and in its *Anthology of Irish Writing,* has attempted to reach out to the Protestant other, but as an organization its efforts have consisted mainly of attempts to entice unionism under its own nationalist umbrella, a gesture not likely to appeal to many unionists. Nevertheless, one of the plays Field Day produced, *Pentecost,* by the late Stewart Parker, is a trenchant critique of Northern

7. Major exceptions to this lack of attention to theorizing settler colonies would include Albert Memmi's *The Colonizer and the Colonized* (1991), an early study first published in 1957, and *The Empire Writes Back* (1989), by Ashcroft, Griffiths, and Tiffin. *The Empire Writes Back,* however, focuses primarily on long and well-established settler colonies, such as the United States, Canada, Australia, and New Zealand, rather than on the more threatened and tenuous settler colonies like those in Northern Ireland, South Africa, and elsewhere.

Irish unionism by someone who did experience the double ambivalence and hybridity of the settler condition. Parker, who said that critics found his own plays "very Irish in England" and "very British in Ireland" (Bowman 1987), expresses the hybrid ambivalence of Northern Protestants in terms of existing on the margins of several cultures:

> Growing up in Belfast as a working class Protestant, I had access to all sorts but did not feel a part of any of them. You're led to believe you're British, yet the English don't recognise you as such. On the other hand, you're Irish because you're born in Ireland, but the people in the Free State don't recognise you as such. The working class element adds another dimension, because you are alienated from the Unionist establishment. You feel conversant with all of those things, but not obliged to any of them. In a sense you inhabit no-man's land. . . . As an individual it can be very destructive. You have no identity, no ideology, you don't know where you belong, but as a writer that's not a bad way to be. You've got a hell of a lot to explore. (Purcell 1987)

Parker's "no-man's land" is a lot like Bhabha's in-between space, the site of colonial and postcolonial hybridity.

Other characteristics of unionist and other settler cultures also can be illuminated by Bhabha's theory. Settler narratives typically are parasitic on the hegemonic narratives of the colonial power, yet they also undergo the same type of splitting, difference, and deferral as the narratives of native nationalist populations. As with the natives, there is both identification and difference in relation to the colonizer. Settlers typically identify with these hegemonic narratives and the colonial enterprises they support and adapt them to fit their own particular situations. In Northern Ireland, for instance, the religious wars of the seventeenth century and the "glorious revolution" of 1688 are memorialized in the Siege of Londonderry and the Battle of the Boyne, but unionist accounts tend to localize the significance of this phase of Irish history in terms of saving Ireland from popery rather than in terms of the Reformation and its larger European or even British context. So while unionists identify with Britain's "glorious revolution," they re-member, restage, and refigure it in its specifically Irish context. Thus, like the anticolonial Catholic nationalist narrative, the parasitic version of the unionists estranges itself from the colonizer's master narrative to the extent that the British barely recognize it as part of their own history. In effect, unionist history reduces the complicated history of the Reformation and Counter Reformation to the consolidation of Protestant ascendancy in Ireland.

From a postcolonial perspective unionist narratives have much in common with nationalist narratives. As with the nationalists, unionists, in Bhabha's terms, "negotiate and translate their cultural identities in a discontinuous intertextual temporality of cultural difference" (1994, 38). Likewise, the unionist narrative is "constructed from two incommensurable temporalities of meaning that threaten its coherence" (1994, 158); that is, it is split between the pedagogic and the performative, between an eternal history and an enunciative present. As with the nationalist narrative, in relation to the British master narrative the unionist mimicry of British history is "less than one and doubled," estranged, displaced temporally as well as spatially, metonymic rather than mimetic, a performative enunciation from the margins of empire. Unlike nationalist narratives, however, the unionist rewriting of the grand narratives of British history serves not to pose the future as an open question, an open space in which the marginalized may narrate their own way to liberation, but rather, like the apprentice boys of Londonderry, it serves to slam shut the gates of history so that unionists may continue to enjoy the privileges of the colonial past.

Recognizing settler nationalism as a legitimate part of postcolonial studies opens up the possibility of exploiting the in-betweenness of settler cultures. Emphasizing this in-betweenness, and thus its structural similarities with native nationalism, suggests that settlers are more likely to find common cause with the natives they see themselves in opposition to rather than with the colonizers they identify with, as has often been the case in the history of colonialism, including Irish colonialism, as in 1798. Nationalism, historically and by a certain logic or necessity, is the inevitable product of colonialism. The only alternatives to nationalism are assimilation or subjection. Few cultures have chosen these alternatives. Thus nationalism has been the necessary route out of colonialism. Historically settler nationalism as well as native nationalism often has led to liberation from the colonial power, although the liberation of settler nations has not necessarily liberated the natives of those nations. Both settler nationalism and native nationalism, however, can only be temporary phases of liberation if nations are to achieve stability through means other than a police state. Both forms of nationalism must metamorphose into something else, and Bhabha's notion of in-betweenness or hybridity suggests what that something else might be. If nationalism is the necessary transition phase in overcoming colonial power, once liberation is achieved nationalism must shed its archaic cloak of impossible purity and embrace its own inevitable hybridity as well as hybrid others within its national boundaries, for it is at this site, this in-between space on the margins of cultures, that new national and inter-national antinationalist cultures will emerge.

The historical and cultural significance of Friel's texts lies in their recognition and exploitation of the hybridity of Irish culture, a hybridity built into the linguistic and narrative structures of those texts. This hybridity is less a product of Friel's individual artistic genius than of his particular historical circumstances, of the in-between spaces on the margins of two cultures that he has occupied as both a British citizen of Northern Ireland and as a citizen of the Irish Republic. Although various problems and resistances, particularly the subaltern voices of women and settlers, suggest the necessity for caution, the yield of postcolonial theory in relation to Friel's texts indicates that continued effort as well as revision is warranted in applying that theory to Ireland's experience.

Texts Cited

Adams, Henry. 1946. *The Education of Henry Adams*. Boston: Houghton Mifflin.

Anderson, Benedict. 1991. *Imagined Communities: Reflections on the Origin and Spread of Nationalism*. 2nd ed. London: Verso.

———. 1994. "Exodus." *Critical Inquiry* 20 (winter): 314–27.

Andrews, Elmer. 1995. *The Art of Brian Friel: Neither Dreams nor Reality*. New York: St. Martins Press.

Andrews, J[ohn] H. 1975. *A Paper Landscape: The Ordnance Survey in Nineteenth-Century Ireland*. Oxford: Clarendon Press.

Arnold, Matthew. 1962. "On the Study of Celtic Literature." In *Lectures and Essays in Criticism*, edited by R. H. Super, 291–395. Ann Arbor: Univ. of Michigan Press.

Ashcroft, Bill, Gareth Griffiths, and Helen Tiffin. 1989. *The Empire Writes Back: Theory and Practice in Post-Colonial Literatures*. London and New York: Routledge.

Bakhtin, M. M. 1981. *The Dialogic Imagination: Four Essays*. Ed. Michael Holquist. Trans. Caryl Emerson and Michael Holquist. Austin, Tex.: Univ. of Texas Press.

Barry, Kevin. 1983. With John Andrews and Brian Friel. "*Translations* and *A Paper Landscape*: Between Fiction and History." *Crane Bag*, 7, no. 2: 118–24.

Beckett, J. C. 1966. *The Making of Modern Ireland 1603–1923*. London: Faber and Faber.

Beckett, Samuel. 1957. *Murphy*. New York: Grove.

Bell, Sam Hanna. 1972. *The Theatre in Ulster*. Totowa, N.J.: Rowman and Littlefield.

Berkeley, George. 1975. *Philosophical Works*. Ed. M. R. Ayers. London: Dent.

Bhabha, Homi. 1994. *The Location of Culture*. London: Routledge.

Boland, Eavan. 1970. "The Northern Writer's Crisis of Conscience." *Irish Times*, 12, 13, 14 Aug.

———. 1973. "Brian Friel: Derry's Playwright." *Hibernia* (16 Feb.): 18.

———. 1989. *A Kind of Scar: The Woman Poet in a National Tradition.* Dublin: Attic Press.

———. 1990. *Outside History: Selected Poems 1980–1990.* New York: W. W. Norton.

Bowman, Jonathan Philbin. 1987. "Party Piece." *In Dublin,* 30 Sept.

Brennan, Brian. 1988. "The Reinvention of Hugh O'Neill." *Sunday Independent,* 25 Sept.: 15.

Brown, Terence. 1985. *Ireland: A Social and Cultural History, 1922 to the Present.* Ithaca: Cornell Univ. Press.

———. 1993. "'Have We a Context'?: Transition, Self and Society in the Theatre of Brian Friel." In *The Achievement of Brian Friel,* edited by Alan Peacock, 190–201. Gerrards Cross, Buckinghamshire: Colin Smythe.

Canby, Vincent. 1994. "On an Endless Journey to One's Better Half." *New York Times,* Sunday, 18 Sept.: H5.

Cohen, Leonardo G., Pablo Celnik, Alvaro Pascual-Leone, Brian Corwell, Lala Faiz, James Dambrosia, Manabu Honda, Norihiro Sadato, Christian Gerloff, M. Dolores Catalá, and Mark Hallett. 1997. "Functional Relevance of Cross-Modal Plasticity in Blind Humans." *Nature* 389 (1 Sept.): 180–83.

Connolly, Sean. 1987. "Dreaming History: Brian Friel's *Translations.*" *Theatre Ireland* 13 (Nov.): 4–44.

———. 1993. "Translating History: Brian Friel and the Irish Past." In *The Achievement of Brian Friel,* edited by Alan Peacock, 149–63. Gerrards Cross, Buckinghamshire: Colin Smythe.

Coyle, Jane. 1988. "Friel Play's Touch of First Night Nerves." *Sunday Press,* 25 Sept.

Curtis, L. Perry Jr. 1997. *Apes and Angels: The Irishman in Victorian Caricature.* Washington and London: Smithsonian Institution Press.

Dantanus, Ulf. 1985. *Brian Friel: The Growth of an Irish Dramatist.* Gothenburg Studies in English Series 59. Göteborg, Sweden: Universitatis Gothoburgensis.

———. 1988. *Brian Friel: A Study.* London: Faber and Faber.

Deane, Seamus. 1974. "The Writer and the Troubles." *Threshold* 25: 13–17.

———. 1979. Introduction to *Selected Stories,* by Brian Friel. Ed. Peter Fallon. Dublin: Gallery Press.

———. 1981. "Brian Friel." *Ireland Today* 978: 7–10.

———. 1986a. *Heroic Styles: The Tradition of an Idea.* Field Day Pamphlet 4. Derry: Field Day Theatre Company, 1984. Reprinted as "Heroic Styles: The Tradition of an Idea." In *Ireland's Field Day,* 43–58. Notre Dame, Ind.: Univ. of Notre Dame Press.

———. 1986b. Introduction to *Selected Plays,* by Brian Friel. Washington, D.C.: Catholic Univ. of America Press.

————. 1987. "Field Day Tours America." Interview by Geoffrey Stokes. *An Gael* (summer): 29–30.

————. 1990. Introduction to *Nationalism, Colonialism, and Literature,* by Terry Eagleton, Fredric Jameson, and Edward Said. Minneapolis: Univ. of Minnesota Press.

————, ed. 1991. *The Field Day Anthology of Irish Writing.* 3 vols. Derry: Field Day Publications.

————. 1993. "Brian Friel: The Name of the Game." In *The Achievement of Brian Friel,* edited by Alan Peacock, 103–12. Gerrards Cross, Buckinghamshire: Colin Smythe.

Devlin, Anne. 1986. *Ourselves Alone.* London: Faber and Faber.

————. 1996. *After Easter.* London: Faber and Faber.

Dewey, John. 1981. *The Philosophy of John Dewey.* Ed. John J. McDermott. Chicago: Univ. of Chicago Press.

Donoghue, Denis. 1972. "The Problems of Being Irish." *Times Literary Supplement,* 17 Mar., 291–92.

Eagleton, Terry. 1988. *Nationalism, Colonialism and Literature: Nationalism: Irony and Commitment.* Field Day Pamphlet 13. Derry: Field Day Theatre Company.

————. 1995. *Heathcliff and the Great Hunger: Studies in Irish Culture.* London: Verso.

Edwards, Christopher. 1988. "Man of Action." *Spectator,* 10 Dec., 43.

Ellmann, Richard. 1967. *Eminent Domain.* New York: Oxford Univ. Press.

Euripides. 1958. *Three Great Plays of Euripides.* Trans. Rex Warner. New York: New American Library.

Fallis, Richard. 1977. *The Irish Renaissance.* Syracuse: Syracuse Univ. Press.

Fanon, Frantz. 1963. *The Wretched of the Earth.* New York: Grove.

————. 1967. *Black Skin, White Masks.* New York: Grove.

Field Day Theatre Company. 1980. Program for *Translations.* Derry: Field Day.

————. 1986. *Ireland's Field Day.* Notre Dame, Ind.: Univ. of Notre Dame Press.

————. 1988. Program for *Making History.* Derry: Field Day.

Foster, John Wilson. 1974. *Forces and Themes in Ulster Fiction.* Totowa, N.J.: Rowman and Littlefield.

Friel, Brian. n.d. "Extracts from a Sporadic Diary." In *Ireland and the Arts,* edited by Tim Pat Coogan, 56–61. London: Namara House.

————. 1957. "For Export Only." *Commonweal* 65 (15 Feb.): 509–10.

————. 1962. *The Saucer of Larks.* Garden City, N.Y.: Doubleday.

————. 1965. "An Ulster Writer: Brian Friel." Interview by Graham Morison. *Acorn* (Londonderry) 8: 4–15.

————. 1967. "The Theatre of Hope and Despair." *Critic* 26: 13–18.

————. 1968. *Lovers* (1967). New York: Farrar, Straus and Giroux.

————. 1970a. "The Future of Irish Drama." Interview by Fergus Linehan. *Irish Times*, 12 Feb., 14.

————. 1970b. *Two Plays: Crystal and Fox and The Mundy Scheme.* New York: Farrar Straus.

————. 1972a. "Plays Peasant and Unpeasant." *Times Literary Supplement*, 17 Mar., 305–6.

————. 1972b. "Self-Portrait." *Aquarius* 5: 17–22.

————. 1973. *The Gentle Island* (1971). Oldcastle: Gallery Press.

————. 1979a. *The Enemy Within* (1962). Introd. Tom Kilroy. Oldcastle: Gallery Press.

————. 1979b. *Selected Stories.* Oldcastle: Gallery Press.

————. 1980a. "Finding Voice in a Language Not Our Own." Interview by Ciaran Carty. *Sunday Independent*, 5 Oct.

————. 1980b. "Talking to Ourselves." Interview by Paddy Agnew. *Magill*, Dec., 59–61.

————. 1981a. *Anton Chekhov's "Three Sisters": A Translation.* Dublin: Gallery Press.

————. 1981b. "Brian Friel." Interview by Elgy Gillespie. *Irish Times*, 5 Sept., 6.

————. 1982a. "The Man from God Knows Where." Interview by Fintan O'Toole. *In Dublin*, 28 Oct., 20–23.

————. 1982b. "Rehearsing Friel's New Farce." Interview by Ray Comiskey. *Irish Times*, 14 Sept., 8.

————. 1983. *The Communication Cord* (1982). London: Faber and Faber; Oldcastle: Gallery Press.

————. 1984a. *Crystal and Fox.* Oldcastle: Gallery Press; London: Faber and Faber.

————. 1984b. *The Loves of Cass McGuire* (1966). Oldcastle: Gallery Press; London: Faber and Faber.

————. 1986. *Selected Plays.* London: Faber and Faber, 1984; Washington: Catholic Univ. of America Press. (Includes *Philadelphia, Here I Come!, The Freedom of the City, Living Quarters, Aristocrats, Faith Healer,* and *Translations.*)

————. 1989a. *Making History* (1988). London: Faber and Faber; Oldcastle: Gallery Press.

————. 1989b. *Volunteers* (1975). Oldcastle: Gallery Press.

————. 1990. *Dancing at Lughnasa* (1990). London: Faber and Faber; Winchester, Mass.: Faber Inc.; Oldcastle: Gallery Press.

————. 1991. "From Ballybeg to Broadway." Interview by Mel Gussow. *New York Times Magazine*, 29 Sept., 30, 55–61.

————. 1993. *Wonderful Tennessee* (1993). London: Faber and Faber.

————. 1994. *Molly Sweeney* (1994). New York: Penguin; Oldcastle: Gallery Press.

————. 1997. *Give Me Your Answer, Do!* Oldcastle: Gallery Press.

Gerald of Wales. 1982. *The History and Topography of Ireland.* Trans. John J. O'Meara. London: Penguin.

Gibbons, Luke. 1992. "Identity Without a Center: Irish Nationalism in a Colonial Frame." *Cultural Studies* 6, no. 3: 358–76.

Harrington, John, ed. 1991. *Modern Irish Drama.* New York: W. W. Norton.

Heaney, Seamus. 1975. "Digging Deeper." *Times Literary Supplement,* 21 Mar., 806.

————. 1980. Review of *Translations,* by Brian Friel. *Times Literary Supplement,* 24 Oct., 1199.

————. 1990. *Selected Poems 1966–1987.* New York: Farrar, Straus and Giroux.

Henderson, Lynda. 1986. "A Dangerous Translation." *Fortnight,* 10 Mar.

Jameson, Fredric. 1988. *Nationalism, Colonialism and Literature: Modernism and Imperialism.* Field Day Pamphlet 14. Derry: Field Day Theatre Company.

Jent, William. 1994. "Supranational Civics: Poverty and the Politics of Representation in Brian Friel's *The Freedom of the City." Modern Drama* 37: 568–87.

Joyce, James. 1961. *Ulysses.* New York: Random House.

————. 1976a. *Dubliners.* New York: Penguin.

————. 1976b. *A Portrait of the Artist as a Young Man.* New York: Penguin.

Kauffmann, Stanley. 1966. "*Philadelphia, Here I Come!* Arrives." *New York Times,* 17 Feb., 28.

Kearney, Richard. 1983. "Language Play: Brian Friel and Ireland's Verbal Theatre." *Studies: An Irish Quarterly Review* 72, no. 285: 20–56. Reprinted as "The Language Plays of Brian Friel." In *Transitions: Narratives in Modern Irish Culture,* 123–60. Manchester: Manchester Univ. Press, 1988.

————. 1987. "Friel and the Politics of Language Play." *Massachusetts Review: A Quarterly of Literature, the Arts and Public Affairs* 28, no. 3: 510–515.

Kerwin, William, ed. 1997. *Brian Friel: A Casebook.* New York: Garland.

Kiberd, Declan. 1984. "Inventing Irelands." *Crane Bag* 8, no. 1: 11–23.

————. 1985. "Brian Friel's *Faith Healer.*" In *Irish Writers and Society at Large,* edited by Masaru Sekine, 106–21. Irish Literary Studies 22. Gerrards Cross, Buckinghamshire: Colin Smythe.

————. 1986. *Anglo-Irish Attitudes.* Field Day Pamphlet 6. Derry: Field Day Theatre Company, 1984. Reprinted as "Anglo-Irish Attitudes." In *Ireland's Field Day,* 81–105. Notre Dame, Ind.: Univ. of Notre Dame Press.

————. 1995. *Inventing Ireland: The Literature of the Modern Nation.* Cambridge: Harvard Univ. Press.

Kiely, Niall. 1981. "An Irishman's Diary." *Irish Times,* 17 Sept.

Kilroy, Tom. 1979. Introduction to *The Enemy Within.* Dublin: Gallery Press.

———. 1993. "Theatrical Text and Literary Text." In *The Achievement of Brian Friel,* edited by Alan Peacock, 91–102. Gerrards Cross, Buckinghamshire: Colin Smythe.

Lahr, John. 1994. "Brian Friel's Blind Faith." *New Yorker,* 17 Oct., 107–10.

Leary, Daniel. 1983. "The Romanticism of Brian Friel." In *Contemporary Irish Writing,* edited by James D. Brophy and Raymond J. Porter, 127–41. Library of Irish Studies 2. Boston: Twayne for Iona College Press.

Levin, Milton. 1972. "Brian Friel: An Introduction." *Eire-Ireland: A Journal of Irish Studies* 7, no. 2: 132–36.

Lewis, Oscar. 1966. *La Vida: A Puerto Rican Family in the Culture of Poverty— San Juan and New York.* New York: Random House.

Linehan, Fergus. 1967. "The Art of Brian Friel." *Hibernia,* Sept., 26.

Lloyd, David. 1987. *Nationalism and Minor Literature: James Clarence Mangan and the Emergence of Irish Cultural Nationalism.* Berkeley and Los Angeles: Univ. of California Press.

———. 1993. *Anomalous States: Irish Writing and the Post-Colonial Moment.* Dublin: Lilliput.

Locke, John. 1975. *An Essay Concerning Human Understanding.* 1689. Ed. Peter H. Nidditch. Oxford: Oxford Univ. Press.

Lojek, Helen. 1994. "Brian Friel's Plays and George Steiner's Linguistics: Translating the Irish." *Contemporary Literature* 35, no. 1: 83–99.

Longley, Edna. 1985. "Poetry and Politics in Northern Ireland." *Crane Bag* 9, no. 1: 26–40.

———. 1990. *From Cathleen to Anorexia.* LIP Pamphlet. Dublin: Attic Press.

MacNeill, Máire. 1982. *The Festival of Lughnasa.* Dublin: Comhairle Bhéaloideas Eireann, Univ. College Dublin.

Maxwell, D.E.S. 1973. *Brian Friel.* Irish Writers Series. Lewisburg, Penn.: Bucknell Univ. Press.

McAvera, Brian. 1985. "Brian Friel: Attuned to the Catholic Experience." *Fortnight Magazine* 215 (Mar.): 19–20.

McGowan, Moray. 1980. "Truth, Politics and the Individual: Brian Friel's *The Freedom of the City* and the Northern Ireland Conflict." *Literatur in Wissenschaft und Unterricht* 12: 287–303.

McGrath, F. C. 1989. "Irish Babel: Brian Friel's *Translations* and George Steiner's *After Babel.*" *Comparative Drama* 23, no. 1: 31–49.

McGuinness, Nora A. 1997. "Proactive Feminism and the Voice of Woman in Anne Devlin's *After Easter.*" Paper delivered at the session on New Perspectives on Irish Drama. Modern Language Association Annual Convention. Toronto, December.

McKeone, Gary. 1988. "Fact and Faction." *Theatre Ireland* 17: 7–8.

Memmi, Albert. 1991. *The Colonizer and the Colonized.* Boston: Beacon.

Michie, Elsie. 1996. "White Chimpanzees and Oriental Despots: Racial Stereotyping and Edward Rochester." In *Jane Eyre*, edited by Beth Newman, 584–98. Case Studies in Contemporary Criticism. Boston: Bedford.

Moore-Gilbert, Bart. 1997. *Postcolonial Theory: Contexts, Practices, Politics*. London: Verso.

Murray, Christopher. 1982. "Recent Irish Drama." In *Studies in Anglo-Irish Literature*, edited by Heinz Kosok, 439–46. Bonn: Bouvier Verlag Herbert Grundmann.

Niel, Ruth. 1987. "Non-Realistic Techniques in the Plays of Brian Friel: The Debt to International Drama." In *Literary Interrelations: Ireland, England and the World*. 3 vols. Edited by Wolfgang Zach and Heinz Kosok, 2: 349–59. Studies in English and Comparative Literature. Tübingen: Gunter Narr.

O'Brien, George. 1989. *Brian Friel*. Dublin: Gill and Macmillan.

O'Connor, Ulick. 1989. *Brian Friel: Crisis and Commitment, The Writer and Northern Ireland*. Dublin: Elo Publications.

O'Day, Alan, and John Stevenson, eds. 1992. *Irish Historical Documents since 1800*. Savage, Md.: Barnes and Noble.

O'Donnell, Donal. 1981. "Friel and a Tale of Three Sisters." *Sunday Press*, 30 Aug.

O'Faolain, Sean. 1970. *The Great O'Neill*. Dublin: Mercier Press. Originally published by Longmans, Green and Company in 1942.

———. 1991. "The Stuffed-Shirts." In *The Field Day Anthology of Irish Writing*. 3 vols. Edited by Seamus Deane, 3: 101–7. Derry: Field Day Publications. Originally published as an editorial in *The Bell* June 1943.

Ormsby, Frank. 1970. "The Plays of Brian Friel." *Honest Ulsterman* 23: 27–31.

O'Toole, Fintan. 1990. "Beyond Language." *Irish Times*, 28 Apr.

———. 1994. "Small Is Beautiful." *Irish Times*, 27 Sept., 10.

Owens, Cóilín, and Joan Radner, eds. 1990. *Irish Drama 1900–1980*. Washington, D.C.: Catholic Univ. of America Press.

Parker, Stewart. 1989. *Pentecost*. In *Three Plays for Ireland by Stewart Parker*, 145–208. Birmingham: Oberon.

Paulin, Tom. 1984. *Ireland and the English Crisis*. Newcastle upon Tyne: Bloodaxe Books.

———. 1986. *A New Look at the Language Question*. Field Day Pamphlet 1. Derry: Field Day Theatre Company, 1983. Reprinted as "A New Look at the Language Question." In *Ireland's Field Day*, 3–18. Notre Dame, Ind.: Univ. of Notre Dame Press.

Peacock, Alan. 1993. "Translating the Past: Friel, Greece and Rome." In *The Achievement of Brian Friel*, edited by Alan Peacock, 113–33. Gerrards Cross, Buckinghamshire: Colin Smythe.

Pine, Richard. 1990. *Brian Friel and Ireland's Drama*. London: Routledge.

Pirandello, Luigi. 1952. *Naked Masks*. New York: Dutton.

Purcell, Deirdre. 1987. "The Illusionist." *Sunday Tribune*, 27 Sept.

Rich, Frank. 1993. "Critic's Notebook: After and Beyond *Lughnasa*." *New York Times*, 17 July, sec. 1, 9.

Richards, David. 1994. "Now Starring in Dublin: A Poetic Friel Heroine." *New York Times*, 7 Sept., C13.

Richards, Shaun. 1997. "Placed Identities for Placeless Times: Brian Friel and Post-Colonial Criticism." *Irish University Review* 27, no. 1: 55–68.

Riddel, Lynne. 1981. "Three Russian Sisters Go Irish—and Take a Bow in Derry." *Belfast Telegraph*, 2 Sept.

Rix, Walter R. 1980. "Reflexionen des Nordirlandskonflikts: Das Irishe Drama als Forum des Zeitgeschehens" (Reflections on Irish drama as a forum for the Northern Ireland conflict). In *Das Moderne Drama in Englischunterricht der Sekundarstufe*. 2 vols. Edited by H. Groene and B. Schik, 2: 77–98. Königstein/Taunus: Scriptor.

Roche, Anthony. 1994. *Contemporary Irish Drama*. Dublin: Gil and Macmillan.

Rolston, Bill. 1992. *Drawing Support: Murals in the North of Ireland*. Belfast: Beyond the Pale.

Sacks, Oliver. 1995. "To See and Not See." *An Anthropologist on Mars: Seven Paradoxical Tales*, 108–52. New York: Knopf. Originally published in *The New Yorker*, 10 May 1993, 59–73.

Said, Edward. 1988. *Nationalism, Colonialism and Literature: Yeats and Decolonization*. Field Day Pamphlet 15. Derry: Field Day Theatre Company.

Sharpe, Jenny. 1994. "The Unspeakable Limits of Rape: Colonial Violence and Counter-Insurgency." In *Colonial Discourse and Post-Colonial Theory: A Reader*, edited by Patrick Williams and Laura Chrisman, 221–43. New York: Columbia Univ. Press. First published in *Genders* 10 (spring 1991): 25–46.

Smith, Robert. 1991. "The Hermeneutic Motion in Brian Friel's *Translations*." *Modern Drama* 34, no. 3: 392–409.

Spivak, Gayatri Chakravorty. 1994. "Can the Subaltern Speak?" In *Colonial Discourse and Post-Colonial Theory: A Reader*, edited by Patrick Williams and Laura Chrisman, 66–111. New York: Columbia Univ. Press. First published in *Marxism and the Interpretation of Culture*, edited by C. Nelson and L. Grossberg, 271–313. Basingstoke: Macmillan Education, 1988.

Steiner, George. 1975. *After Babel: Aspects of Language and Translation*. New York: Oxford Univ. Press.

Synge, John M. 1960. *The Complete Plays*. New York: Random House.

Taylor, Paul. 1993. "Absolute Beginners: Paul Taylor Reports from Dublin on the Premiere of Brian Friel's New Play." *Independent*, 5 July, 12.

Valvo, Alberto, M. D. 1971. *Sight Restoration after Long-Term Blindness: The Problems and Behavior Patterns of Visual Rehabilitation.* New York: American Foundation for the Blind.

Verstraete, Ginette. 1988. "Brian Friel's Drama and the Limits of Language." In *History and Violence in Anglo-Irish Literature,* edited by Joris Duytschaever and Geert Lernout, 85–96. Amsterdam: Rodopi.

Wall, Richard. 1977. "Joyce's Use of the Anglo-Irish Dialect of English." In *Place, Personality and the Irish Writer,* edited by Andrew Carpenter, 121–35. Gerrards Cross, Buckinghamshire: Colin Smythe.

———. 1986. *An Anglo-Irish Dialect Glossary for Joyce's Works.* Syracuse: Syracuse Univ. Press.

Wardle, Irving. 1988. "Language a Key to Life." (London) *Times,* 6 Dec.

West, Derek. 1990. With Richard Pine and David Grant. "Dancing at Lughnasa." *Theatre Ireland* 22 (spring): 7–11.

Widgery, The Rt. Hon. Lord, O.B.E., T.D. 1972. *Report of the Tribunal Appointed to Inquire into the Events on Sunday, 30th January 1972, Which Led to Loss of Life in Connection with the Procession in Londonderry on That Day.* London: Her Majesty's Stationery Office.

Wilde, Oscar. 1965.*The Picture of Dorian Gray.* Ed. Jerry Allen. New York: Harper and Row.

———. 1973. "The Decay of Lying." *De Profundis and Other Writings.* Ed. Hesketh Pearson. Harmondsworth: Penguin.

Wiley, Catherine A. 1987. "Recreating Ballybeg: Two Translations by Brian Friel." *Journal of Dramatic Theory & Criticism* 1, no. 2: 51–61.

Winkler, Elizabeth Hale. 1981. "Brian Friel's *The Freedom of the City:* Historical Actuality and Dramatic Imagination." *Canadian Journal of Irish Studies* 7, no. 1: 12–31.

———. 1982. "Reflections of Derry's Bloody Sunday in Literature." In *Studies in Anglo-Irish Literature,* edited by Heinz Kosok, 411–21. Bonn: Bouvier Verlag Herbert Grundmann.

Yeats, W. B. 1961. *Essays and Introductions.* New York: Macmillan.

———. 1983. *The Poems of W. B. Yeats.* Ed. Richard J. Finneran. New York: Macmillan.

Index